4 Symbols

REFERENCE MAPS

Relief and physical features

▲ 8848	Spot height (metres)
⊃⊂	Pass
▭	Permanent ice cap

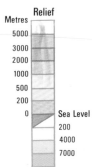

Relief

Metres
- 5000
- 3000
- 2000
- 1000
- 500
- 200
- 0 — Sea Level
- 200
- 4000
- 7000

Relief and physical names   *ALPS*   *Zaïre Basin*   *Nicobar Islands*   *Mt. Cook*

Water features

	Submarine contour
. 11034	Ocean depth (metres)
	Reef
	River
	Intermittent river
	Falls/Dam
	Gorge
	Canal
	Lake/Reservoir
	Intermittent lake
	Marsh/Swamp

Water names   *PACIFIC OCEAN*   *Red Sea*   *Lake Erie*   *Amazon*

Communications

——Tunnel——	Railway
——Tunnel——	Road
– – – – – –	Proposed road/desert track
⊕	Main airport

Administration

———	International boundary
– – –	Undefined or disputed boundary
–·–·–	Internal boundary
▨ ◉ ◎ ⊙	National capitals

Country name   **CHILE**   Internal division   **IOWA**   Territorial admin.   *(Fr.)*

Settlement

- ▨ **Dhākā**
- ◉ **Khulna**
- ◎ **Imphal**
- ⊙ Thimbu

City and town symbols in order of size.

MAP SYMBOLS

Symbols are used on a map to show the location of features such as roads, rivers and towns. The meaning of each symbol used on the map is explained in the key.

Map symbols often look like the features they represent. The colour of a symbol may also provide a clue to its meaning. The importance of a feature might be shown by the size of the symbol, the size of the printing or the thickness of the line.

Many maps in this atlas use the same symbols: the meanings of these symbols are shown on this page. Where different colours or symbols are used, their meaning is explained in a key next to the map.

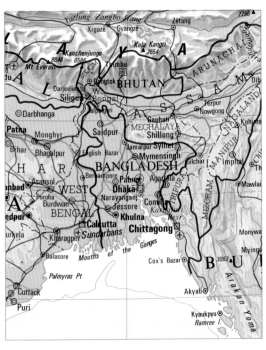

To draw a map of the world, or of a part of the world, the real area has to be reduced in size, or scaled down, to fit onto the map sheet or atlas page. The **scale** of any map therefore tells us precisely how much the real area has been reduced in size.

To use a map to work out the size of areas or distances on the real ground, we need to refer to the scale of that particular map. Map scales can be shown in several ways:

As a **linear scale** — a horizontal line is marked off in units which show how the real ground distances are represented on the map, as in the example below.

As a **statement of scale** — the linear scale above would be written as *1 cm to 1 km*. This means that 1 cm on the map represents 1 km on the real ground.

As a **representative fraction** — for example the scale shown above would be *1:100 000*. This means that every 1 unit of measurement on the map represents 100 000 units on the real ground.

As the scale becomes smaller the amount of real ground that can be fitted onto the map becomes larger. But in making the scale smaller, the accuracy of the map, and the detail it can show, have to be reduced.

The four examples on this page show what happens when the map scale is made smaller. As the scale decreases from the top to the bottom of the page, the details shown on the maps become less precise and more generalised.

On Map A, at a scale of *1:1 000 000,* the Isle of Wight is shown as a county of England, and detail of roads, the location of towns and relief is clearly shown. It is possible to distinguish bays and inlets around the coast.

On Map B, at a scale of *1:4 000 000,* a larger area of the south of England is shown. Thus the coastline of the Isle of Wight has been generalised, and there are few details about the island other than its name.

On Map C, at a scale of *1:16 000 000,* it is possible to show the whole of England and part of the mainland of Europe. The coastline of the Isle of Wight is very generalised, and the island is no longer named.

On Map D, at a scale of *1:85 000 000,* all of Europe can be shown, but the Isle of Wight is represented only by a small dot. At this small scale it is impossible to show any detail of the actual shape of the island, but its location is marked.

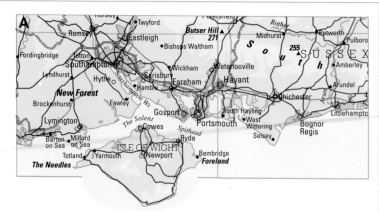

The scale of this map is 1:1 000 000 or 1cm represents 10 km

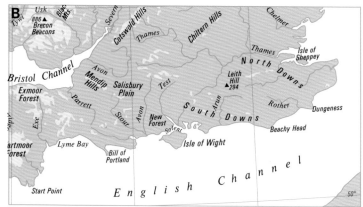

The scale of this map is 1:4 000 000 or 1cm represents 40 km

The scale of this map is 1:16 000 000 or 1cm represents 160 km

The scale of this map is 1:85 000 000 or 1cm represents 850 km

Lines of latitude and longitude are imaginary lines drawn around a globe or on maps of the whole, or part of the world. Like the grid lines on Ordnance Survey maps they can be used to locate a place accurately.

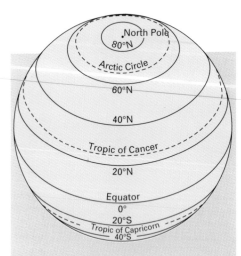

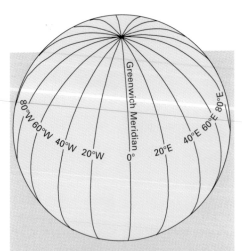

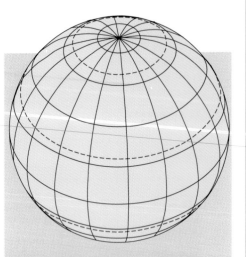

LATITUDE

Lines of **latitude** (or *parallels*) are drawn parallel to the Equator. They are numbered in **degrees** either *north* or *south* of the Equator.
The Equator is numbered 0°, the North Pole 90°N and the South Pole 90°S.

Other important lines of latitude are the Tropic of Cancer (23$1/2$°N) and the Tropic of Capricorn (23$1/2$°S), the Arctic Circle (66$1/2$°N) and the Antarctic Circle (66$1/2$°S).

LONGITUDE

Lines of **longitude** (or *meridians*) are drawn from the North Pole to the South Pole. The prime meridian, numbered 0°, runs through the Greenwich Observatory in London and is called the Greenwich Meridian. Lines of longitude are numbered in **degrees** either *east* or *west* of the Greenwich Meridian. The 180° line of longitude, exactly opposite the Greenwich Meridian on the other side of the globe, is the International Date Line.

THE EARTH'S GRID SYSTEM

When lines of latitude and longitude are drawn on a globe or map they form a grid. By using a combination of a place's latitude and longitude that place can be accurately located on the globe or map.

To be really accurate each degree of latitude and longitude can be divided into smaller units called **minutes**. There are 60 minutes in one degree. For example the location of Moscow is 55° 45' north of the Equator, and 37° 42' east of the Greenwich Meridian – this latitude and longitude reference is usually shortened to 55 45N 37 42E.

THE HEMISPHERES

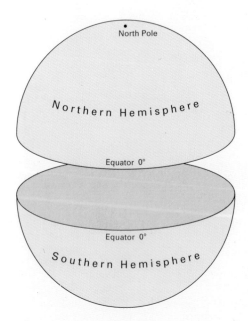

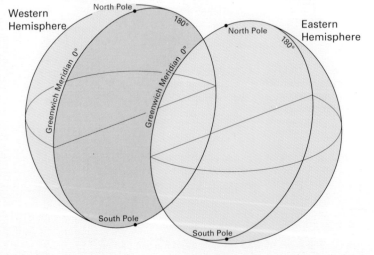

By splitting the globe along the line of the Equator the earth can be divided into two halves, called the Northern and Southern **hemispheres**. If the globe is divided into two from the North Pole to the South Pole, along the 0° and 180° lines of longitude, the halves are called the Eastern Hemisphere and the Western Hemisphere.

An atlas map of the world shows the whole world on the flat surface of the page. Yet in reality the earth is actually a sphere. This means that a system has to be used to turn the round surface of the earth into a flat map of the world, or part of the world. This cannot be done without some distortion – on a map some parts of the world have been stretched, other parts have been compressed. A system for turning the globe into a flat map is called a **projection**.

There are many different projections, each of which distorts different things to achieve a flat map. Correct area, correct shape, correct distances or correct directions can be achieved by a projection; but, by achieving any of these things the others have to be distorted. When choosing the projection to use for a particular map it is important to think which of these things it is most important to have correct.

The maps below illustrate four types of world projections, including some of those used in this atlas.

WORLD MAP PROJECTIONS

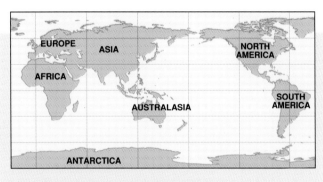

Plate Carrée projection – Pacific-centred

The Plate Carrée projection is used for many of the world maps in this atlas. The version shown here is 'Pacific-centred'. In other words the flat map has been drawn with the Pacific Ocean at its centre. For people living in countries around the Pacific, such as Australia and Japan , this is a more useful way of mapping the world.

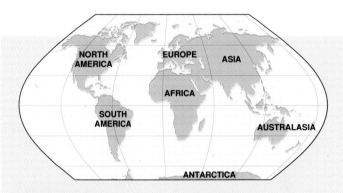

Winkel projection

The Winkel projection is an equal-area projection. Equal-area projections are useful for world maps where it is important to show the correct relative sizes of continental areas. The Winkel projection has curved meridians (lines of longitude), which help to suggest the spherical nature of the earth.

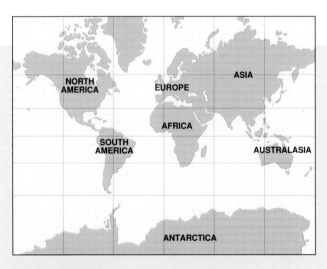

Mercator projection

The Mercator projection was once one of the most commonly used. Its advantage is that it avoids distorting land shapes. To do this, however, it has to show areas near the poles larger than they should be. For example, the island of Greenland near the North Pole seems larger than Australia, when in fact the opposite is true. The projection is useful for navigation as directions can be plotted as straight lines.

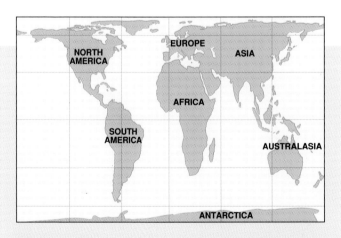

Peters projection

The aim of Peters projection is to show the correct size of the continents in relation to each other. To achieve this the projection has to distort the shapes of the continents. Compared with other world maps the land near the equator may appear to have been stretched in a north/south direction. One reason for showing the world like this has been to emphasise the size of the countries of the poorer, developing world.

ORKNEY ISLANDS

SHETLAND ISLANDS

Scale 1:4 000 000

0   50   100   150 km

Conic Projection

© Collins ◇ Longman Atlases

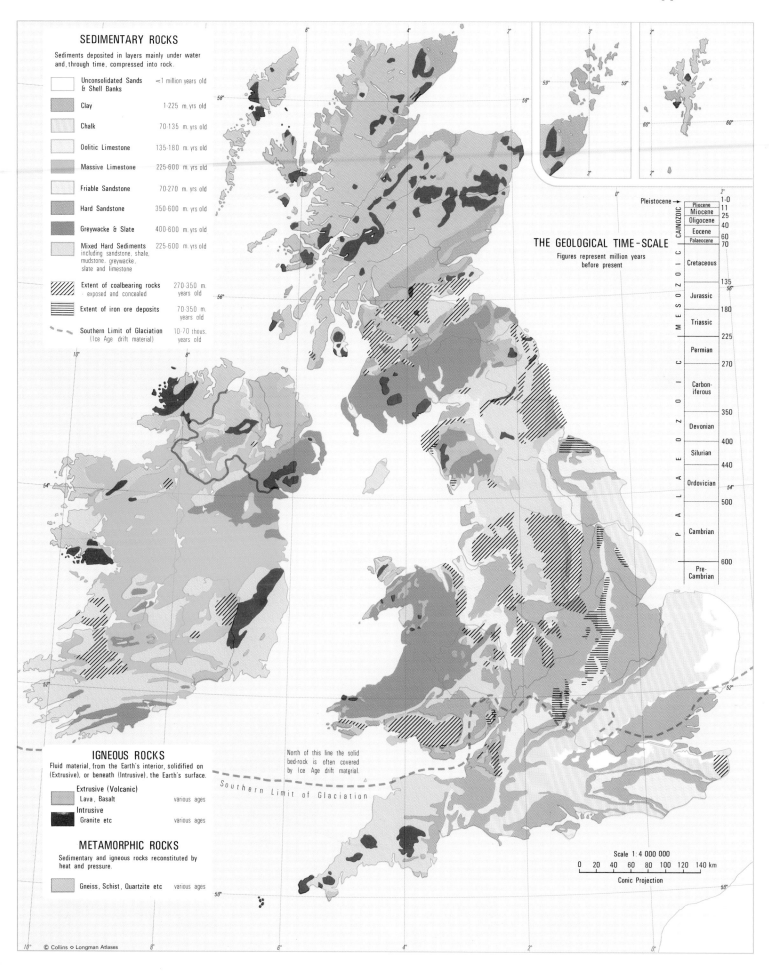

SEDIMENTARY ROCKS

Sediments deposited in layers mainly under water and, through time, compressed into rock.

	Unconsolidated Sands & Shell Banks	<1 million years old
	Clay	1-225 m. yrs old
	Chalk	70-135 m. yrs old
	Oolitic Limestone	135-180 m. yrs old
	Massive Limestone	225-600 m. yrs old
	Friable Sandstone	70-270 m. yrs old
	Hard Sandstone	350-600 m. yrs old
	Greywacke & Slate	400-600 m. yrs old
	Mixed Hard Sediments including sandstone, shale, mudstone, greywacke, slate and limestone	225-600 m. yrs old
	Extent of coalbearing rocks - exposed and concealed	270-350 m. years old
	Extent of iron ore deposits	70-350 m. years old
	Southern Limit of Glaciation (Ice Age drift material)	10-70 thous. years old

IGNEOUS ROCKS

Fluid material, from the Earth's interior, solidified on (Extrusive), or beneath (Intrusive), the Earth's surface.

	Extrusive (Volcanic) Lava, Basalt	various ages
	Intrusive Granite etc	various ages

METAMORPHIC ROCKS

Sedimentary and igneous rocks reconstituted by heat and pressure.

	Gneiss, Schist, Quartzite etc	various ages

THE GEOLOGICAL TIME-SCALE

Figures represent million years before present

Pleistocene →

CAINOZOIC		1·0
	Pliocene	11
	Miocene	25
	Oligocene	40
	Eocene	60
	Palaeocene	70
MESOZOIC	Cretaceous	
		135
	Jurassic	
		180
	Triassic	
		225
PALAEOZOIC	Permian	270
	Carbon-iferous	
		350
	Devonian	
		400
	Silurian	440
	Ordovician	
		500
	Cambrian	
		600
	Pre-Cambrian	

North of this line the solid bed-rock is often covered by Ice Age drift material.

Southern Limit of Glaciation

Scale 1: 4 000 000

0 20 40 60 80 100 120 140 km

Conic Projection

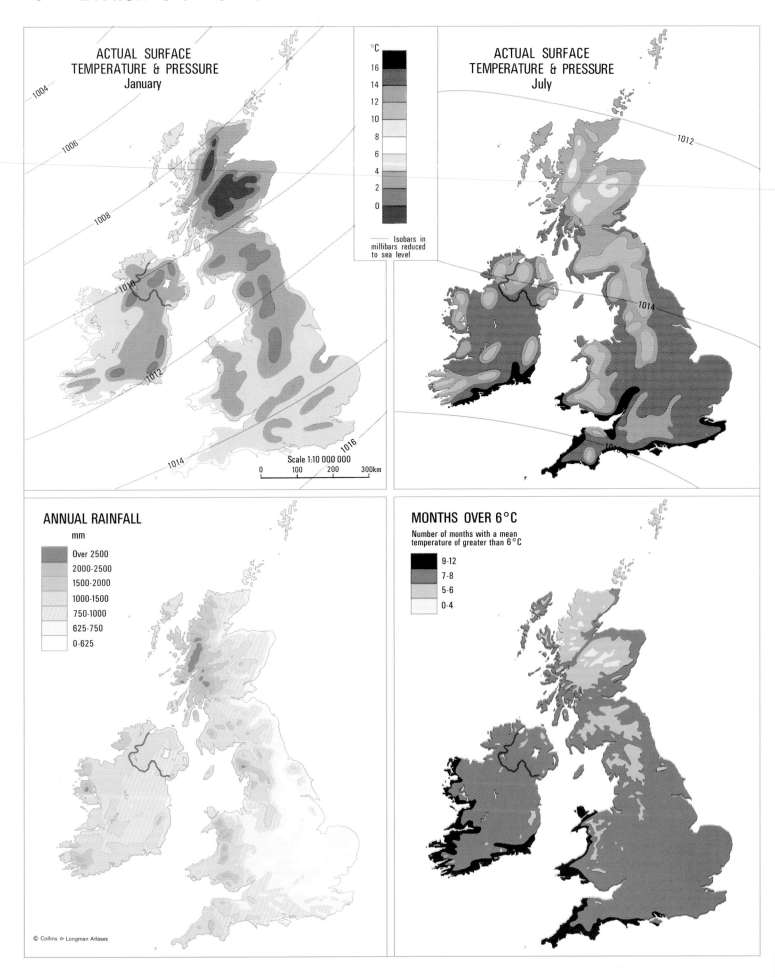

ACTUAL SURFACE
TEMPERATURE & PRESSURE
January

ACTUAL SURFACE
TEMPERATURE & PRESSURE
July

°C
16
14
12
10
8
6
4
2
0

Isobars in
millibars reduced
to sea level

1004
1006
1008
1010
1012
1014
1016

1012
1014
1016

Scale 1:10 000 000
0   100   200   300km

ANNUAL RAINFALL

mm

Over 2500
2000-2500
1500-2000
1000-1500
750-1000
625-750
0-625

MONTHS OVER 6°C

Number of months with a mean
temperature of greater than 6°C

9-12
7-8
5-6
0-4

© Collins ◇ Longman Atlases

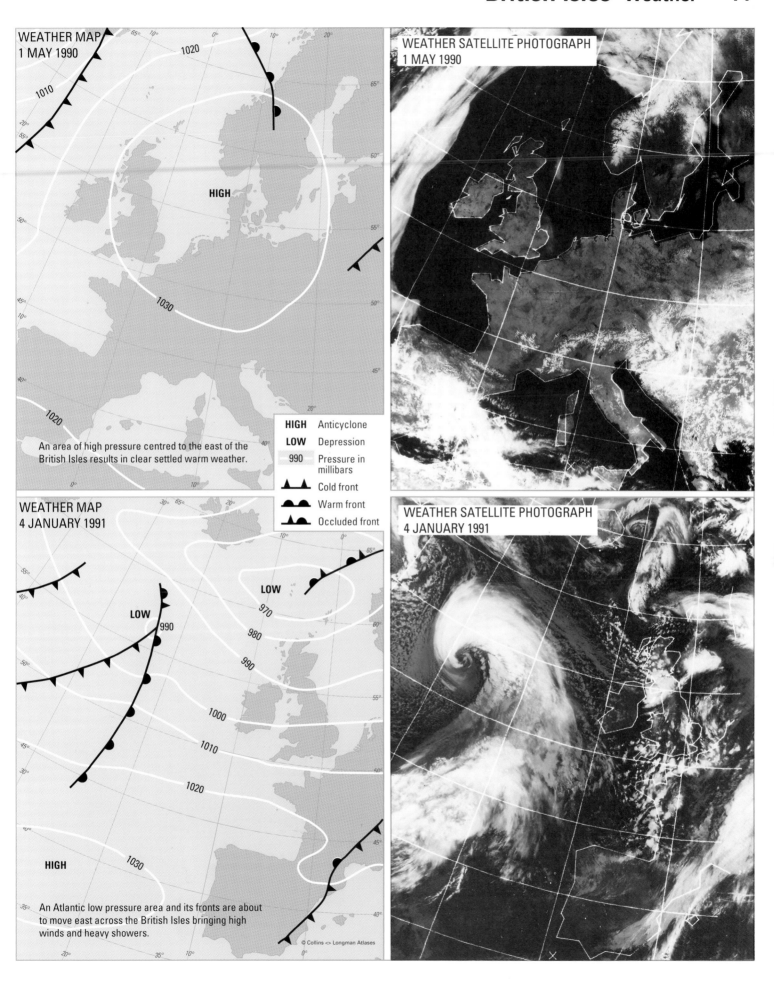

WEATHER MAP
1 MAY 1990

1020

1010

HIGH

1030

1020

An area of high pressure centred to the east of the British Isles results in clear settled warm weather.

HIGH	Anticyclone
LOW	Depression
990	Pressure in millibars
▲▲	Cold front
●●	Warm front
▲●▲●	Occluded front

WEATHER SATELLITE PHOTOGRAPH
1 MAY 1990

WEATHER MAP
4 JANUARY 1991

LOW

LOW

990

970

980

990

1000

1010

1020

HIGH

1030

An Atlantic low pressure area and its fronts are about to move east across the British Isles bringing high winds and heavy showers.

© Collins <> Longman Atlases

WEATHER SATELLITE PHOTOGRAPH
4 JANUARY 1991

CLIMATE GRAPHS

POPULATION 1961 - 89

	1961	1971	1981	1989
TOTAL	3 712 000	4 111 800	4 381 300	4 652 400
MALES	1 796 000	1 989 900	2 117 200	2 247 000
FEMALES	1 916 000	2 121 900	2 264 100	2 405 400
LIVE BIRTHS	60 500	61 700	50 400	58 300
DEATHS	46 200	50 700	54 400	56 300
NATURAL INCREASE	14 300	11 000	-4 000	2 000

EMPLOYMENT 1989

Agriculture, forestry & fishing

Energy

Manufacturing

Construction, transport & communications

Other services

Total employed: 1 754 100
Males employed: 920 300
Females employed: 833 800

ETHNIC GROUPS 1987-89

All Ethnic Groups

Ethnic minority population

White

Ethnic Minority Population

Indian, Pakistani & Bangladeshi

West Indian & African

Other

MIGRATION 1989

Inflow

Origin / Destination of migrants

Old Commonwealth

New Commonwealth

European Community

USA

Rest of the World

Total Inflow: 10 500

Outflow

Total Outflow: 16 500

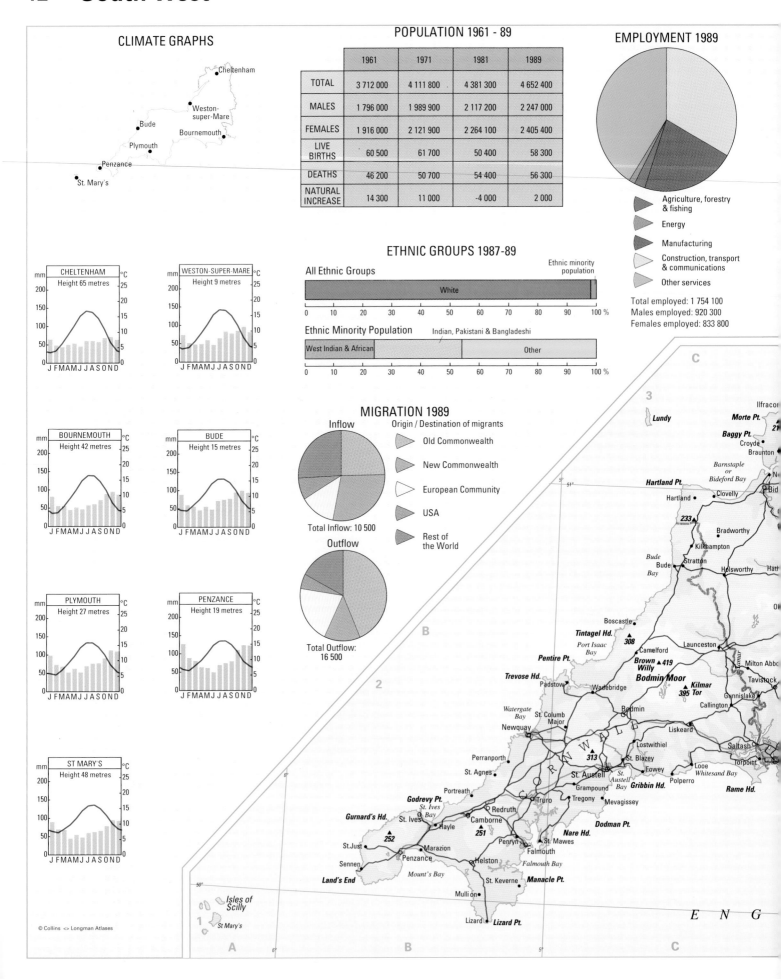

© Collins <> Longman Atlases

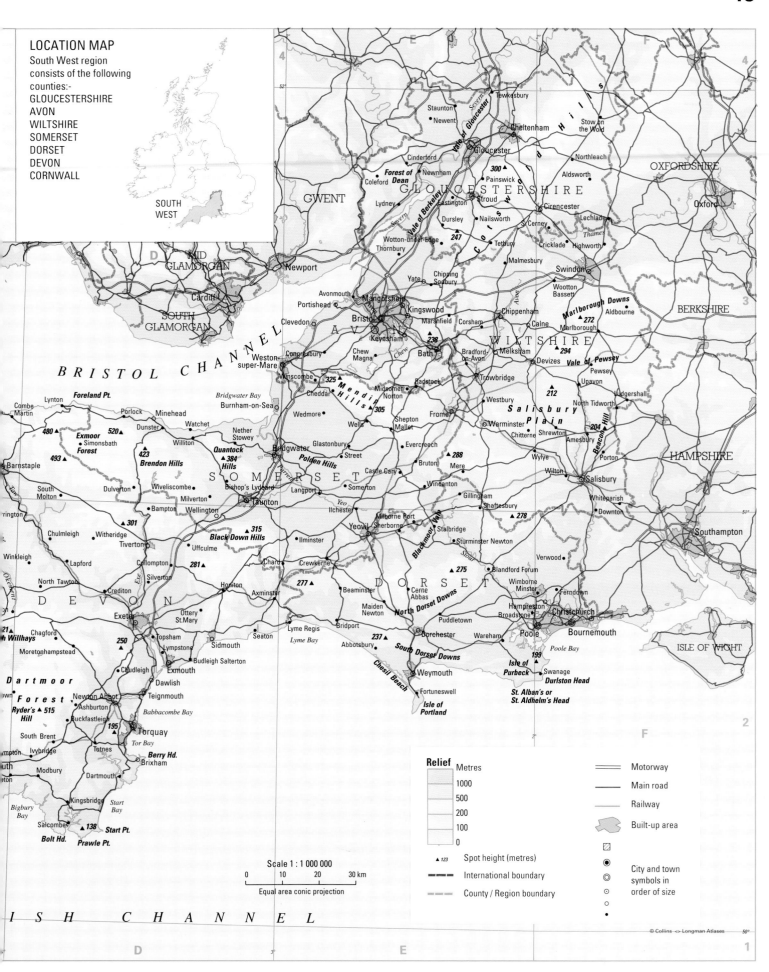

CLIMATE GRAPHS

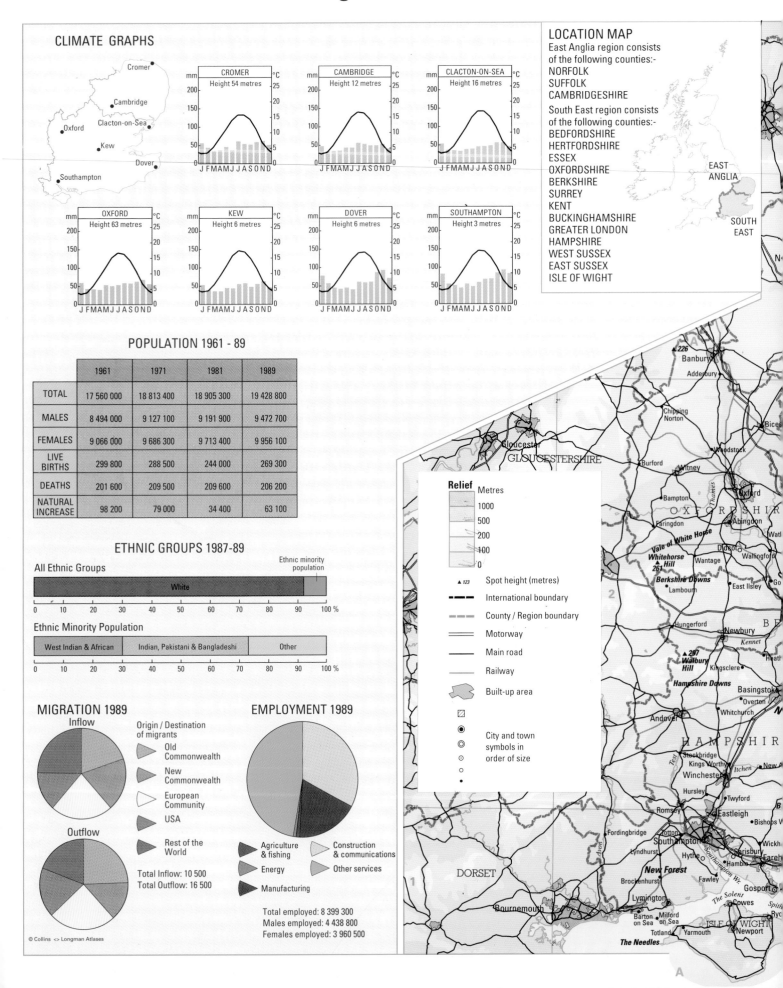

Cromer
Cambridge
Oxford
Clacton-on-Sea
Kew
Dover
Southampton

CROMER — Height 54 metres
CAMBRIDGE — Height 12 metres
CLACTON-ON-SEA — Height 16 metres
OXFORD — Height 63 metres
KEW — Height 6 metres
DOVER — Height 6 metres
SOUTHAMPTON — Height 3 metres

LOCATION MAP

East Anglia region consists of the following counties:-
NORFOLK
SUFFOLK
CAMBRIDGESHIRE

South East region consists of the following counties:-
BEDFORDSHIRE
HERTFORDSHIRE
ESSEX
OXFORDSHIRE
BERKSHIRE
SURREY
KENT
BUCKINGHAMSHIRE
GREATER LONDON
HAMPSHIRE
WEST SUSSEX
EAST SUSSEX
ISLE OF WIGHT

EAST ANGLIA
SOUTH EAST

POPULATION 1961 - 89

	1961	1971	1981	1989
TOTAL	17 560 000	18 813 400	18 905 300	19 428 800
MALES	8 494 000	9 127 100	9 191 900	9 472 700
FEMALES	9 066 000	9 686 300	9 713 400	9 956 100
LIVE BIRTHS	299 800	288 500	244 000	269 300
DEATHS	201 600	209 500	209 600	206 200
NATURAL INCREASE	98 200	79 000	34 400	63 100

ETHNIC GROUPS 1987-89

All Ethnic Groups
White
Ethnic minority population
0 10 20 30 40 50 60 70 80 90 100 %

Ethnic Minority Population
West Indian & African | Indian, Pakistani & Bangladeshi | Other
0 10 20 30 40 50 60 70 80 90 100 %

MIGRATION 1989

Inflow

Origin / Destination of migrants
Old Commonwealth
New Commonwealth
European Community
USA
Rest of the World

Outflow

Total Inflow: 10 500
Total Outflow: 16 500

EMPLOYMENT 1989

Agriculture & fishing
Energy
Manufacturing
Construction & communications
Other services

Total employed: 8 399 300
Males employed: 4 438 800
Females employed: 3 960 500

© Collins <> Longman Atlases

Relief
Metres
1000
500
200
100
0

▲ 123   Spot height (metres)
International boundary
County / Region boundary
Motorway
Main road
Railway
Built-up area

● City and town symbols in order of size

Banbury
Adderbury
Chipping Norton
Bicester
Gloucester
GLOUCESTERSHIRE
Burford
Witney
Woodstock
Oxford
OXFORDSHIRE
Bampton
Faringdon
Abingdon
Vale of White Horse
Whitehorse Hill
Wantage
Didcot
Wallingford
Watl
Berkshire Downs
Lambourn
East Ilsley
Go
Hungerford
Newbury
Kennet
Walbury Hill
Kingsclere
Heath
Hampshire Downs
Basingstoke
Overton
Andover
Whitchurch
HAMPSHIRE
Stockbridge
Kings Worthy
New
Winchester
Itchen
Hursley
Twyford
Romsey
Eastleigh
Bishops W
Fordingbridge
Totton
Southampton
Wickh
Salisbury
Fareh
DORSET
Avon
Lyndhurst
Hythe
Southampton Wr
New Forest
Fawley
Gosport
Lymington
The Solent
Cowes
Bournemouth
Barton on Sea
Milford on Sea
ISLE OF WIGHT
Yarmouth
Newport
Totland
The Needles

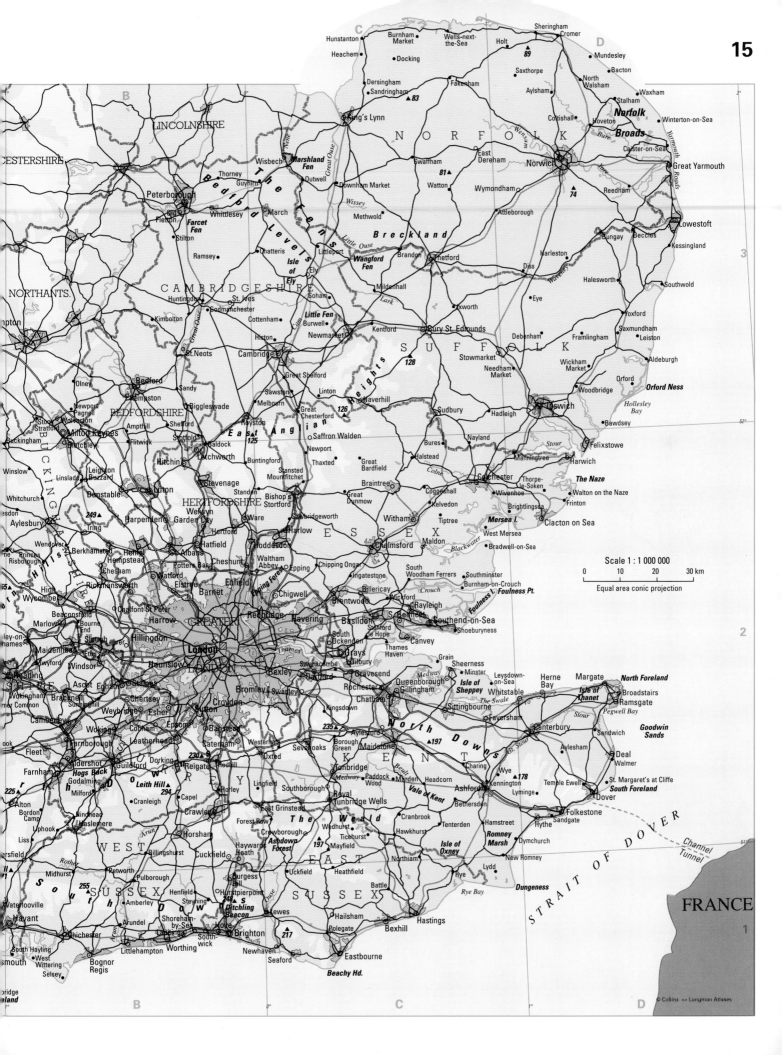

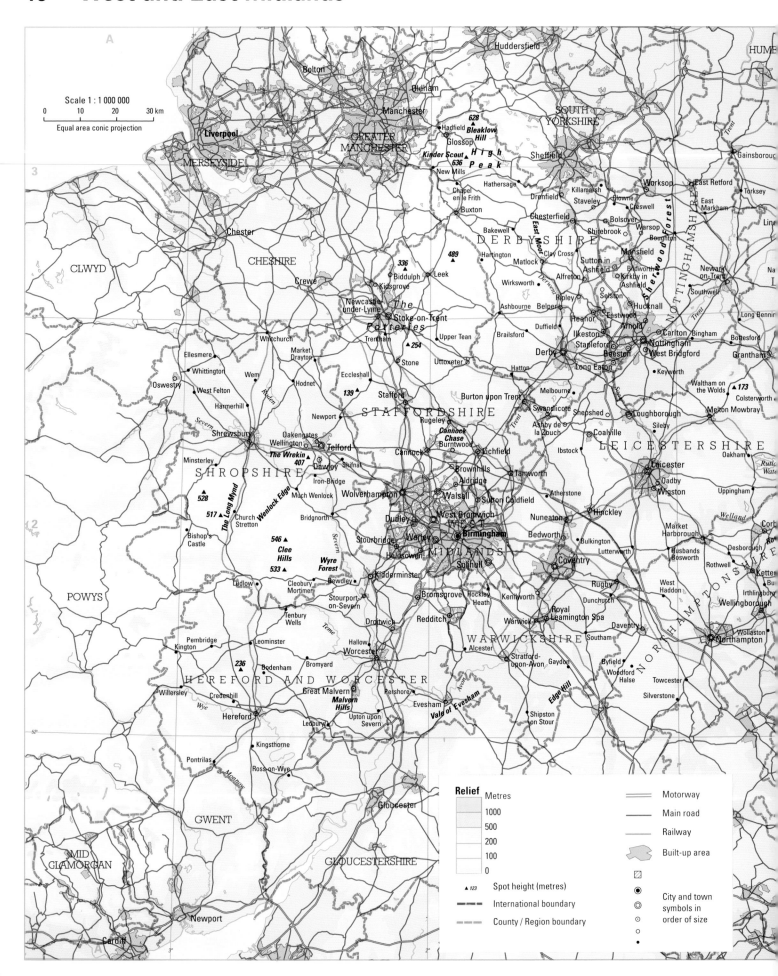

Scale 1 : 1 000 000

0   10   20   30 km

Equal area conic projection

Relief

Metres

1000
500
200
100
0

▲ 123 Spot height (metres)

— — — International boundary

— — — County / Region boundary

═══ Motorway

─── Main road

········ Railway

Built-up area

◉ City and town symbols in order of size
◎
○
•

A

HUDDERSFIELD

HUME

Bolton

Oldham

Manchester

SOUTH YORKSHIRE

Liverpool

GREATER MANCHESTER

628 Bleaklow Hill

Hadfield

Glossop

Kinder Scout
636

High Peak

New Mills

Gainsborough

MERSEYSIDE

Sheffield

Chester

Chapel en le Frith

Buxton

Hathersage

Dronfield

Killamarsh

Glowne

Worksop

East Retford

Torksey

East Markham

CLWYD

CHESHIRE

336

489

Biddulph

Leek

Bakewell

DERBYSHIRE

Staveley

Chesterfield

Bolsover

Creswell

Warsop

Boughton

Lin

Na

Crewe

Kidsgrove

Hartington

Matlock

Clay Cross

Sutton in Ashfield

Bidworth

Mansfield

Kirkby in Ashfield

Newark-on-Trent

East Moor

Sherwood Forest

Newcastle-under-Lyme

The Potteries

Stoke-on-Trent

Wirksworth

Ashbourne

Belper

Ripley

Selston

Eastwood

Hucknall

Southwell

Whitchurch

Trentham

254

Upper Tean

Uttoxeter

Brailsford

Heanor

Ilkeston

Arnold

Carlton

Bingham

Long Bennin

Ellesmere

Market Drayton

Eccleshall

Stone

Hatton

Stapleford

Nottingham

West Bridgford

Grantham

Whittington

Wem

Hodnet

139

Stafford

Burton upon Trent

Melbourne

Duffield

Derby

Long Eaton

Beeston

Keyworth

Waltham on the Wolds

173

Colsterworth

Oswestry

West Felton

Harmerhill

Ryton

Newport

STAFFORDSHIRE

Swadlincote

Shepshed

Loughborough

Sileby

Melton Mowbray

Shrewsbury

Severn

Oakengates

Wellington

Telford

Rugeley

Cannock Chase

Burntwood

Ashby de la Zouch

Coalville

Ibstock

Coalville

LEICESTERSHIRE

Oakham

Rutland Water

Minsterley

The Wrekin
407

Dawley

Shifnal

Cannock

Lichfield

Atherstone

Leicester

Oadby

Wigston

Uppingham

SHROPSHIRE

Iron-Bridge

Brownhills

Tamworth

Welland

528

The Long Mynd

Wenlock Edge

Much Wenlock

Wolverhampton

Walsall

Sutton Coldfield

Nuneaton

Hinckley

Market Harborough

Desborough

Corb

517

Church Stretton

Bridgnorth

Dudley

West Bromwich

WEST

Birmingham

Bedworth

Bulkington

Lutterworth

Husbands Bosworth

Rothwell

Kette

Bishop's Castle

546

Clee Hills

533

Severn

Wyre Forest

Stourbridge

Warley

MIDLANDS

Halesowen

Solihull

Coventry

Rugby

Dunchurch

West Haddon

NORTHAMPTONSHIRE

Irthlingborough

Wellingborough

Bu

POWYS

Ludlow

Cleobury Mortimer

Bewdley

Kidderminster

Bromsgrove

Hockley Heath

Kenilworth

Wollaston

Northampton

Stourport-on-Severn

Redditch

Royal Leamington Spa

Daventry

Tenbury Wells

Tene

Droitwich

Warwick

Southam

Byfield

Woodford Halse

Towcester

Pembridge

Kington

Leominster

Bromyard

Hallow

Worcester

WARWICKSHIRE

Alcester

Stratford-upon-Avon

Gaydon

Silverstone

HEREFORD AND WORCESTER

236

Bodenham

Great Malvern

Malvern Hills

Pershore

Evesham

Vale of Evesham

Edge Hill

Shipston on Stour

Willersley

Credenhill

Wye

Upton upon Severn

Avon

Hereford

Ledbury

Kingsthorne

Pontrilas

Ross-on-Wye

Monnow

GWENT

Gloucester

MID GLAMORGAN

GLOUCESTERSHIRE

Newport

Cardiff

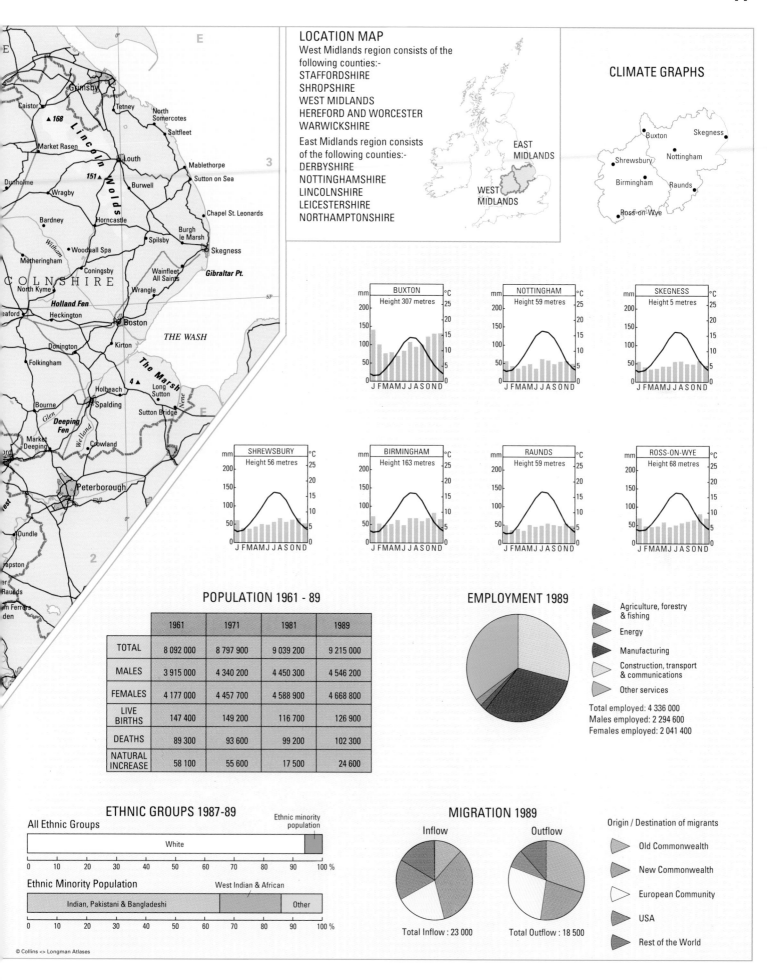

LOCATION MAP

West Midlands region consists of the following counties:-

STAFFORDSHIRE
SHROPSHIRE
WEST MIDLANDS
HEREFORD AND WORCESTER
WARWICKSHIRE

East Midlands region consists of the following counties:-

DERBYSHIRE
NOTTINGHAMSHIRE
LINCOLNSHIRE
LEICESTERSHIRE
NORTHAMPTONSHIRE

EAST MIDLANDS

WEST MIDLANDS

CLIMATE GRAPHS

Buxton · Skegness · Nottingham · Shrewsbury · Birmingham · Raunds · Ross-on-Wye

Climate Graphs

BUXTON — Height 307 metres	NOTTINGHAM — Height 59 metres	SKEGNESS — Height 5 metres
SHREWSBURY — Height 56 metres	BIRMINGHAM — Height 163 metres	RAUNDS — Height 59 metres
ROSS-ON-WYE — Height 68 metres		

POPULATION 1961 - 89

	1961	1971	1981	1989
TOTAL	8 092 000	8 797 900	9 039 200	9 215 000
MALES	3 915 000	4 340 200	4 450 300	4 546 200
FEMALES	4 177 000	4 457 700	4 588 900	4 668 800
LIVE BIRTHS	147 400	149 200	116 700	126 900
DEATHS	89 300	93 600	99 200	102 300
NATURAL INCREASE	58 100	55 600	17 500	24 600

EMPLOYMENT 1989

- Agriculture, forestry & fishing
- Energy
- Manufacturing
- Construction, transport & communications
- Other services

Total employed: 4 336 000
Males employed: 2 294 600
Females employed: 2 041 400

ETHNIC GROUPS 1987-89

All Ethnic Groups

White — Ethnic minority population

0 10 20 30 40 50 60 70 80 90 100 %

Ethnic Minority Population

Indian, Pakistani & Bangladeshi — West Indian & African — Other

0 10 20 30 40 50 60 70 80 90 100 %

MIGRATION 1989

Inflow

Outflow

Origin / Destination of migrants

- Old Commonwealth
- New Commonwealth
- European Community
- USA
- Rest of the World

Total Inflow : 23 000

Total Outflow : 18 500

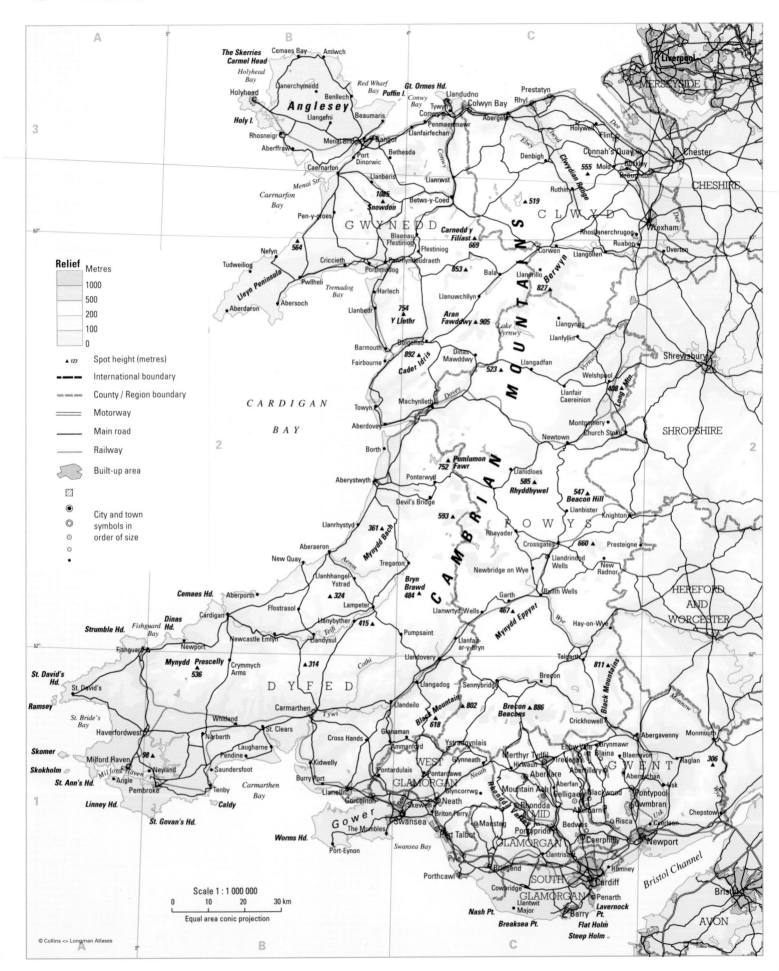

Relief

Metres
- 1000
- 500
- 200
- 100
- 0

▲ 123   Spot height (metres)

Scale 1 : 1 000 000

0   10   20   30 km

Equal area conic projection

© Collins <> Longman Atlases

LOCATION MAP

Wales consists of the
following counties:-
GWYNEDD
CLWYD
DYFED
POWYS
WEST GLAMORGAN
MID GLAMORGAN
SOUTH GLAMORGAN
GWENT

WALES

CLIMATE GRAPHS

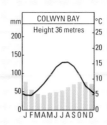

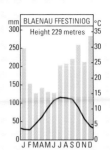

COLWYN BAY
Height 36 metres

BLAENAU FFESTINIOG
Height 229 metres

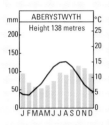

ABERYSTWYTH
Height 138 metres

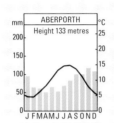

ABERPORTH
Height 133 metres

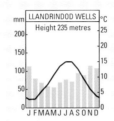

LLANDRINDOD WELLS
Height 235 metres

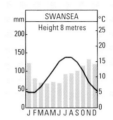

SWANSEA
Height 8 metres

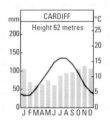

CARDIFF
Height 62 metres

POPULATION 1961 - 89

	1961	1971	1981	1989
TOTAL	2 635 000	2 740 300	2 813 400	2 873 100
MALES	1 275 000	1 328 500	1 365 000	1 393 500
FEMALES	1 360 000	1 411 800	1 448 400	1 479 600
LIVE BIRTHS	44 900	43 100	35 800	38 000
DEATHS	33 700	34 800	35 000	35 100
NATURAL INCREASE	11 200	8 300	800	2 900

ETHNIC GROUPS 1987-89

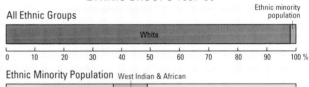

All Ethnic Groups — White — Ethnic minority population

Ethnic Minority Population — West Indian & African — Indian, Pakistani & Bangladeshi — Other

MIGRATION 1989

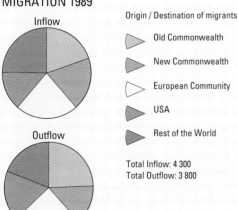

Inflow

Outflow

Origin / Destination of migrants
Old Commonwealth
New Commonwealth
European Community
USA
Rest of the World

Total Inflow: 4 300
Total Outflow: 3 800

EMPLOYMENT 1989

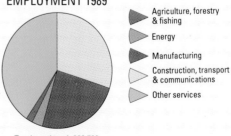

Agriculture, forestry & fishing
Energy
Manufacturing
Construction, transport & communications
Other services

Total employed: 986 700
Males employed: 521 700
Females employed: 465 000

© Collins <> Longman Atlases

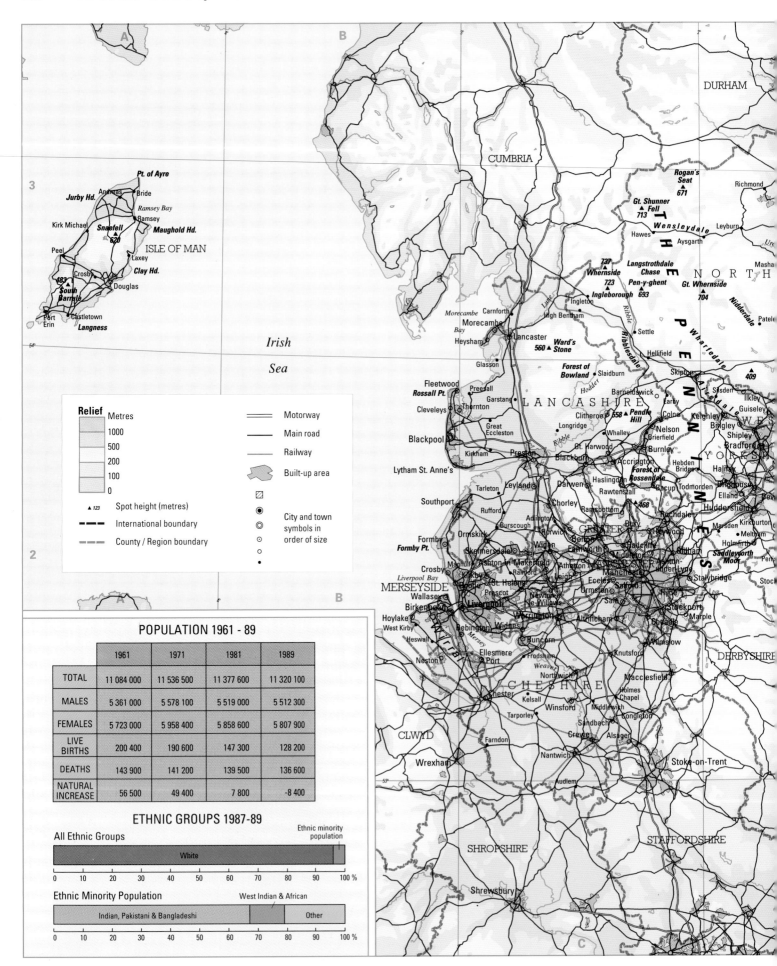

Relief

	Metres
	1000
	500
	200
	100
	0

▲ 123 Spot height (metres)

– – – International boundary

– – – County / Region boundary

══ Motorway

── Main road

── Railway

Built-up area

◉ ⊚ ⊙ ○ · City and town symbols in order of size

ISLE OF MAN

Pt. of Ayre
Jurby Hd.
Andreas
Bride
Kirk Michael
Ramsey Bay
Ramsey
Snaefell ▲ 620
Maughold Hd.
Peel
Laxey
Clay Hd.
Crosby
483 ▲
South Barrule
Douglas
Port Erin
Castletown
Langness

Irish
Sea

POPULATION 1961 - 89

	1961	1971	1981	1989
TOTAL	11 084 000	11 536 500	11 377 600	11 320 100
MALES	5 361 000	5 578 100	5 519 000	5 512 300
FEMALES	5 723 000	5 958 400	5 858 600	5 807 900
LIVE BIRTHS	200 400	190 600	147 300	128 200
DEATHS	143 900	141 200	139 500	136 600
NATURAL INCREASE	56 500	49 400	7 800	-8 400

ETHNIC GROUPS 1987-89

All Ethnic Groups

Ethnic minority population

| White |

0 10 20 30 40 50 60 70 80 90 100 %

Ethnic Minority Population

West Indian & African

| Indian, Pakistani & Bangladeshi | | Other |

0 10 20 30 40 50 60 70 80 90 100 %

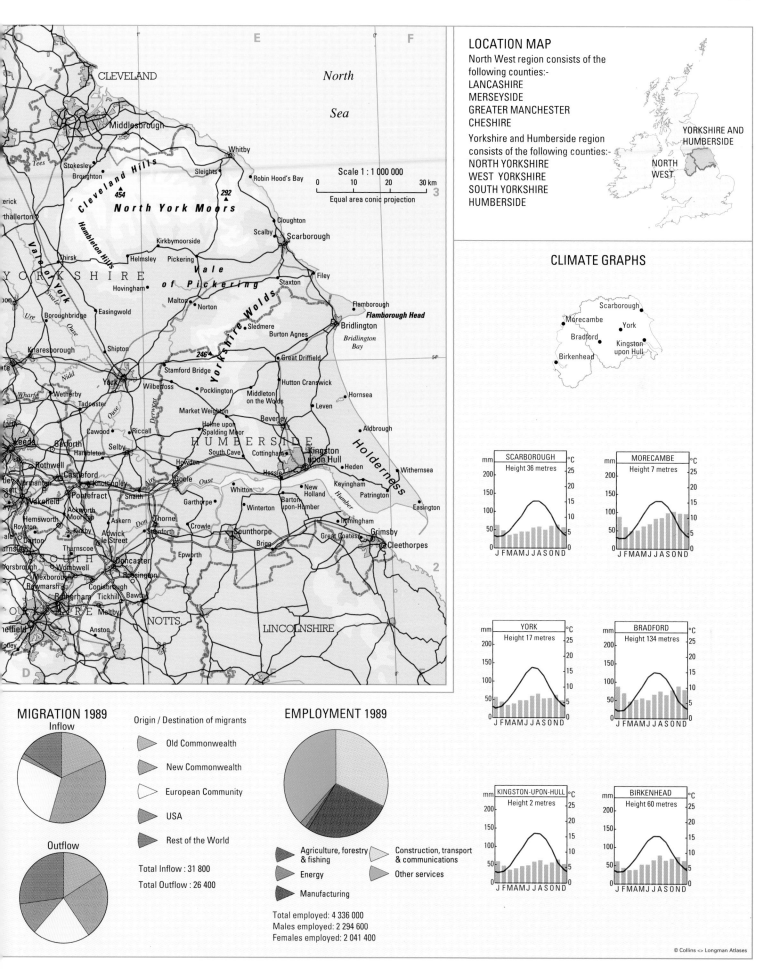

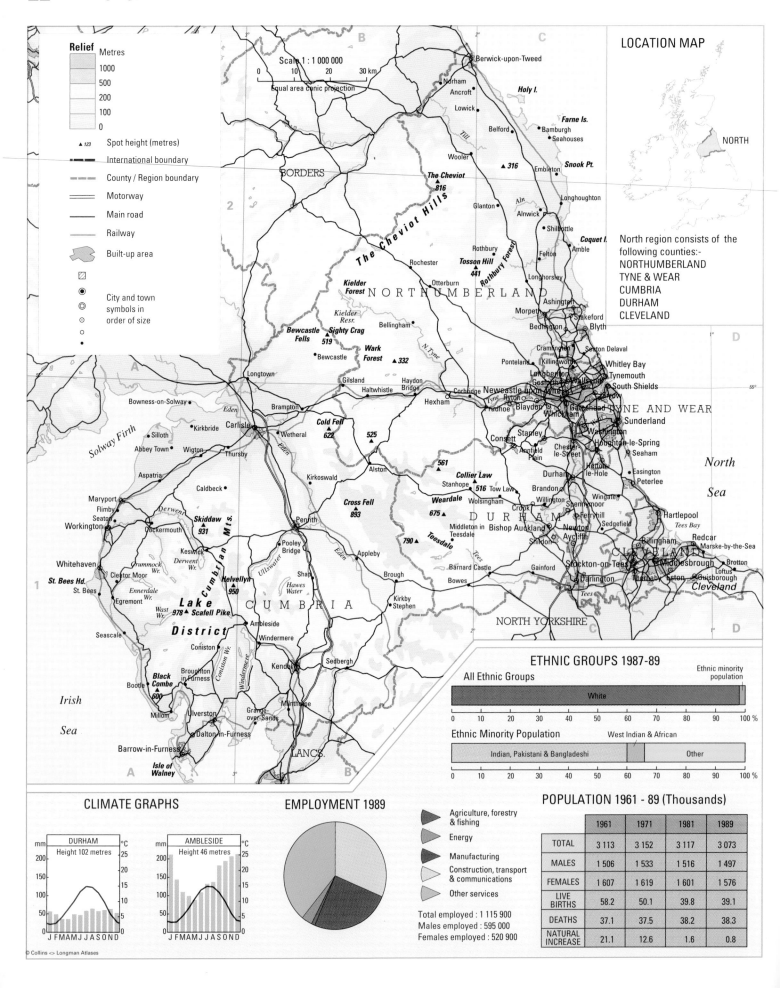

LOCATION MAP

NORTH

North region consists of the following counties:-
NORTHUMBERLAND
TYNE & WEAR
CUMBRIA
DURHAM
CLEVELAND

Relief

Metres
1000
500
200
100
0

▲ 123 Spot height (metres)

International boundary

County / Region boundary

Motorway

Main road

Railway

Built-up area

City and town symbols in order of size

Scale 1 : 1 000 000

0   10   20   30 km

Equal area conic projection

ETHNIC GROUPS 1987-89

All Ethnic Groups — Ethnic minority population

White

0 10 20 30 40 50 60 70 80 90 100 %

Ethnic Minority Population — West Indian & African

Indian, Pakistani & Bangladeshi | Other

0 10 20 30 40 50 60 70 80 90 100 %

CLIMATE GRAPHS

DURHAM
Height 102 metres

mm / °C

J F M A M J J A S O N D

AMBLESIDE
Height 46 metres

mm / °C

J F M A M J J A S O N D

EMPLOYMENT 1989

- Agriculture, forestry & fishing
- Energy
- Manufacturing
- Construction, transport & communications
- Other services

Total employed : 1 115 900
Males employed : 595 000
Females employed : 520 900

POPULATION 1961 - 89 (Thousands)

	1961	1971	1981	1989
TOTAL	3 113	3 152	3 117	3 073
MALES	1 506	1 533	1 516	1 497
FEMALES	1 607	1 619	1 601	1 576
LIVE BIRTHS	58.2	50.1	39.8	39.1
DEATHS	37.1	37.5	38.2	38.3
NATURAL INCREASE	21.1	12.6	1.6	0.8

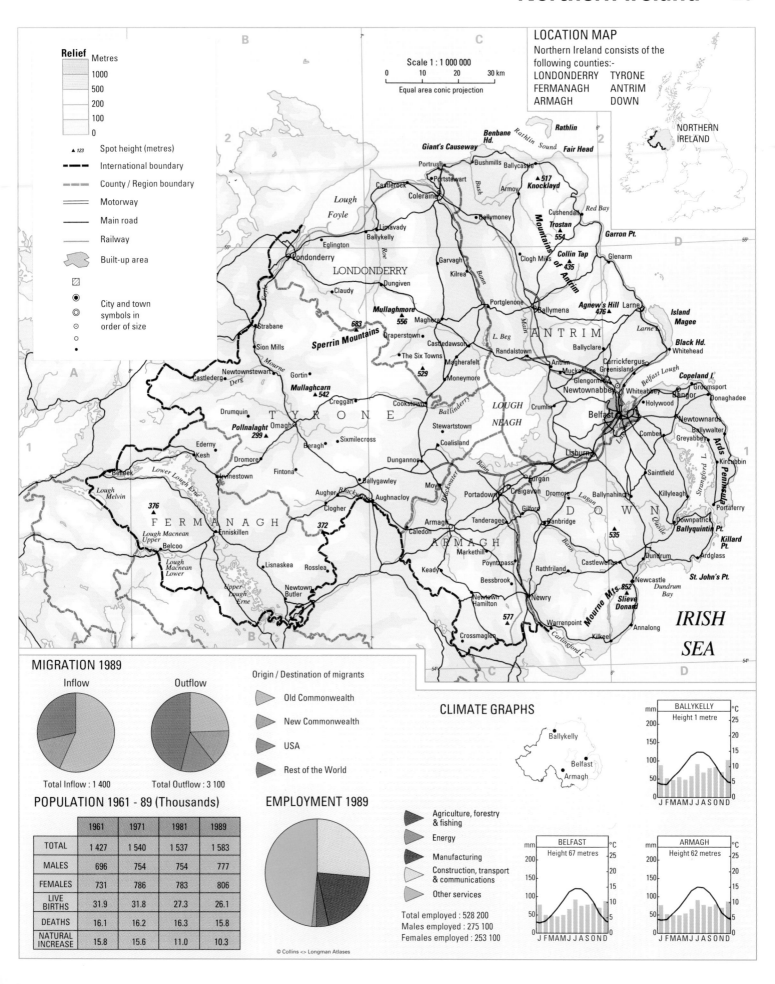

Relief
Metres
1000
500
200
100
0

▲ 123   Spot height (metres)

- - -   International boundary

- - -   County / Region boundary

═══   Motorway

───   Main road

·····   Railway

Built-up area

City and town symbols in order of size

LOCATION MAP
Northern Ireland consists of the following counties:-
LONDONDERRY   TYRONE
FERMANAGH   ANTRIM
ARMAGH   DOWN

NORTHERN IRELAND

Scale 1 : 1 000 000
0   10   20   30 km
Equal area conic projection

MIGRATION 1989

Inflow   Outflow

Total Inflow : 1 400   Total Outflow : 3 100

Origin / Destination of migrants
- Old Commonwealth
- New Commonwealth
- USA
- Rest of the World

POPULATION 1961 - 89 (Thousands)

	1961	1971	1981	1989
TOTAL	1 427	1 540	1 537	1 583
MALES	696	754	754	777
FEMALES	731	786	783	806
LIVE BIRTHS	31.9	31.8	27.3	26.1
DEATHS	16.1	16.2	16.3	15.8
NATURAL INCREASE	15.8	15.6	11.0	10.3

EMPLOYMENT 1989

- Agriculture, forestry & fishing
- Energy
- Manufacturing
- Construction, transport & communications
- Other services

Total employed : 528 200
Males employed : 275 100
Females employed : 253 100

CLIMATE GRAPHS

Ballykelly
Belfast
Armagh

BALLYKELLY
Height 1 metre
mm   °C
J F M A M J J A S O N D

BELFAST
Height 67 metres
mm   °C
J F M A M J J A S O N D

ARMAGH
Height 62 metres
mm   °C
J F M A M J J A S O N D

© Collins <> Longman Atlases

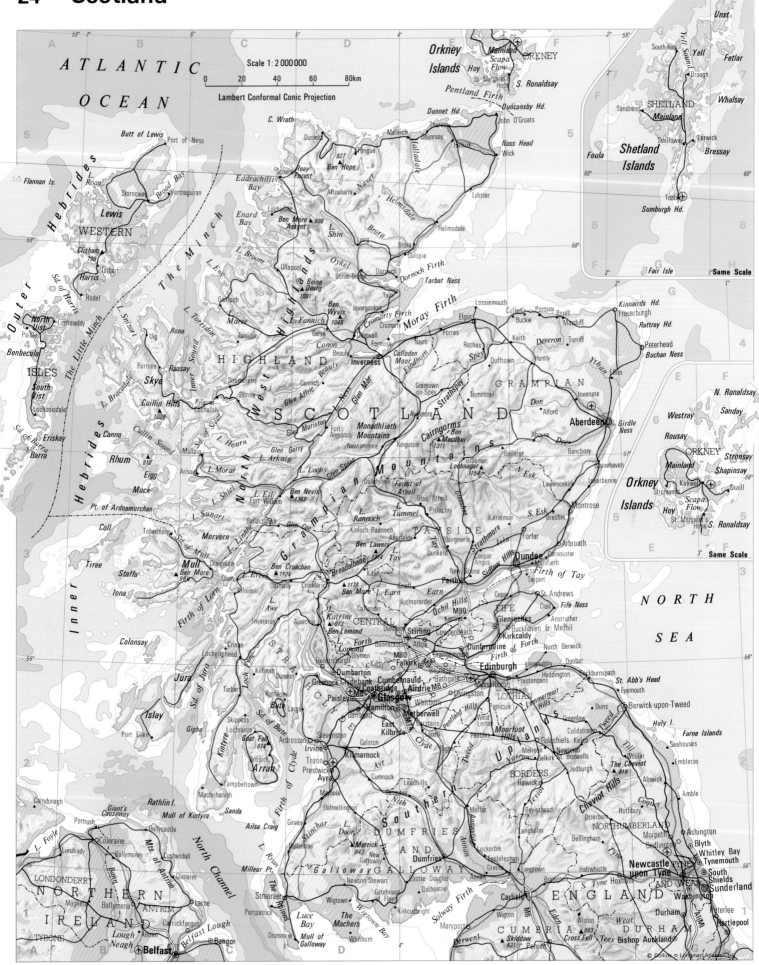

Scale 1:2 000 000

0   20   40   60   80km

Lambert Conformal Conic Projection

LOCATION MAP

Scotland consists of the
following regions:-
SHETLAND ISLANDS
ORKNEY ISLANDS
WESTERN ISLES
HIGHLAND
GRAMPIAN
TAYSIDE
CENTRAL
FIFE
STRATHCLYDE
LOTHIAN
BORDERS
DUMFRIES & GALLOWAY

CLIMATE GRAPHS

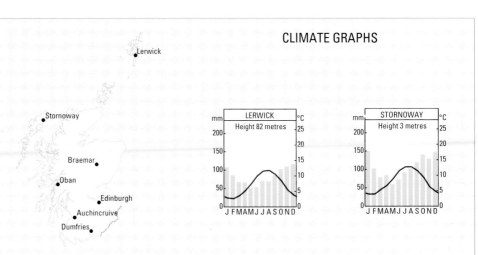

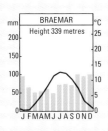
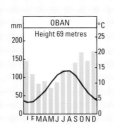
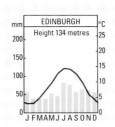
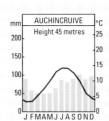
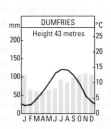

POPULATION 1961 - 89

	1961	1971	1981	1989
TOTAL	5 184 000	5 235 600	5 180 200	5 090 700
MALES	2 485 000	2 515 700	2 494 900	2 460 400
FEMALES	2 699 000	2 719 900	2 685 300	2 630 300
LIVE BIRTHS	101 200	86 700	69 100	63 500
DEATHS	63 900	61 600	63 800	65 000
NATURAL INCREASE	37 300	25 100	5300	-1 500

ETHNIC GROUPS 1987-89

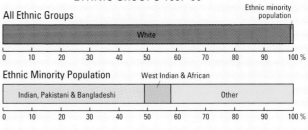

MIGRATION 1989

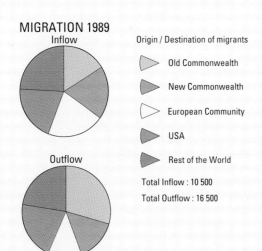

Origin / Destination of migrants
- Old Commonwealth
- New Commonwealth
- European Community
- USA
- Rest of the World

Total Inflow : 10 500

Total Outflow : 16 500

EMPLOYMENT 1989

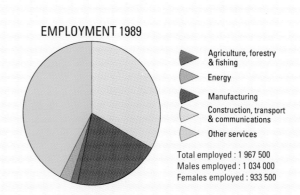

- Agriculture, forestry & fishing
- Energy
- Manufacturing
- Construction, transport & communications
- Other services

Total employed : 1 967 500
Males employed : 1 034 000
Females employed : 933 500

Atlantic

Ocean

Relief Metres
1000
500
200
100
0

▲ 123 Spot height (metres)
– – – International boundary
– – – County / Region boundary
═══ Motorway
─── Main road
····· Railway

Built-up area

◉ City and town
◎ symbols in
⊙ order of size
○
•

© Collins <> Longman Atlases

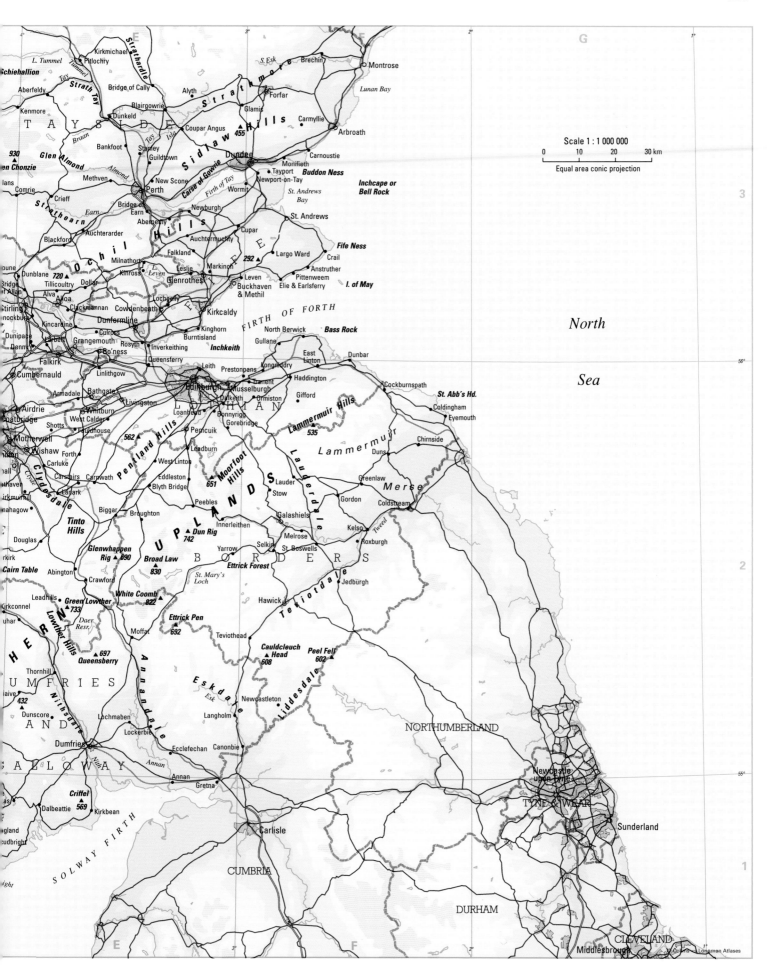

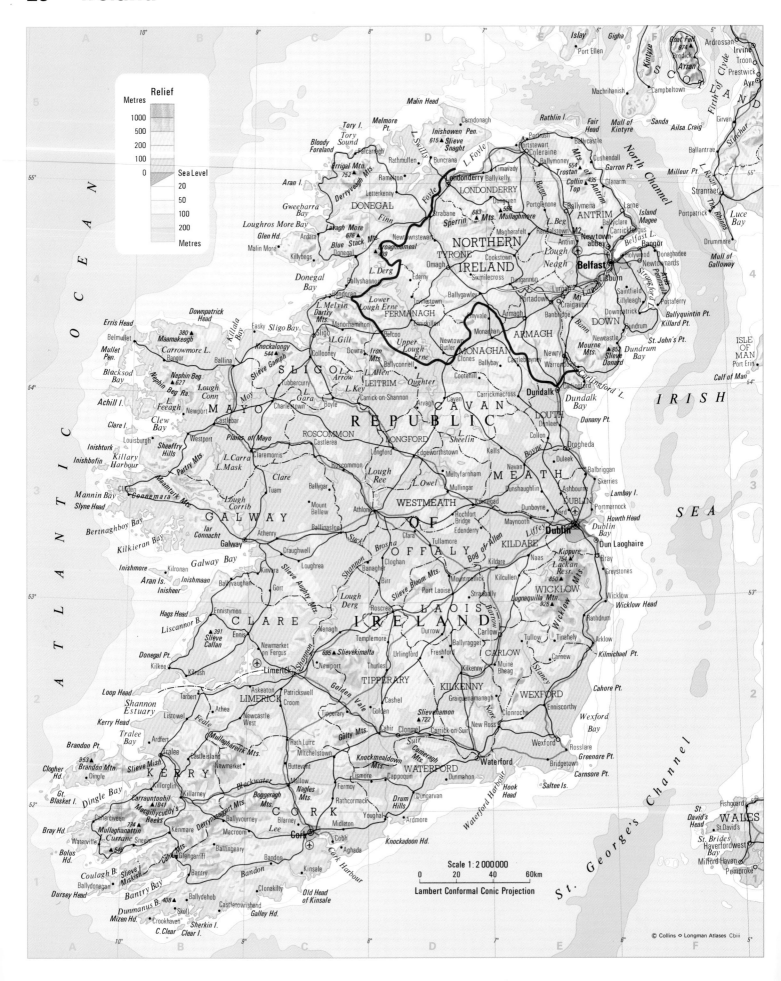

Relief

Metres
1000
500
200
100
0
Sea Level
20
50
100
200
Metres

Scale 1 : 2 000 000

0   20   40   60km

Lambert Conformal Conic Projection

© Collins ○ Longman Atlases Cbiii

ORKNEY

Kirkwall

SHETLAND

Lerwick

Legend:

- ━━━ International boundary
- ─── National boundary
- ─── County or region boundary
- ----- Historic counties in Northern Ireland
- Former metropolitan county
- Greater London
- Administrative headquarters (those underlined contain the offices of more than one county)

The local government boundaries for England & Wales shown on this map were officially approved by an Act of Parliament in October 1972, and those for Scotland and Northern Ireland in October 1973. The sub-division of Counties and Regions is not shown.

In 1986 the executive powers of the Metropolitan Counties were taken over by joint boards and agencies made up of representatives from the Metropolitan Districts and central government.

NORTHERN IRELAND
1 Region
26 Districts

SCOTLAND
9 Regions
3 Island Authorities
53 Districts

ENGLAND
39 Counties
6 Former Metropolitan Counties
Greater London
36 Metropolitan Districts
296 Non-Metropolitan Districts

WALES
8 Counties
37 Districts

REPUBLIC OF IRELAND
26 Counties

G.M.   GREATER MANCHESTER
S.G.   SOUTH GLAMORGAN
W.M.   WEST MIDLANDS

Scale 1:4 000 000

0   50   100   150km

Conic Projection

© Collins ◇ Longman Atlases

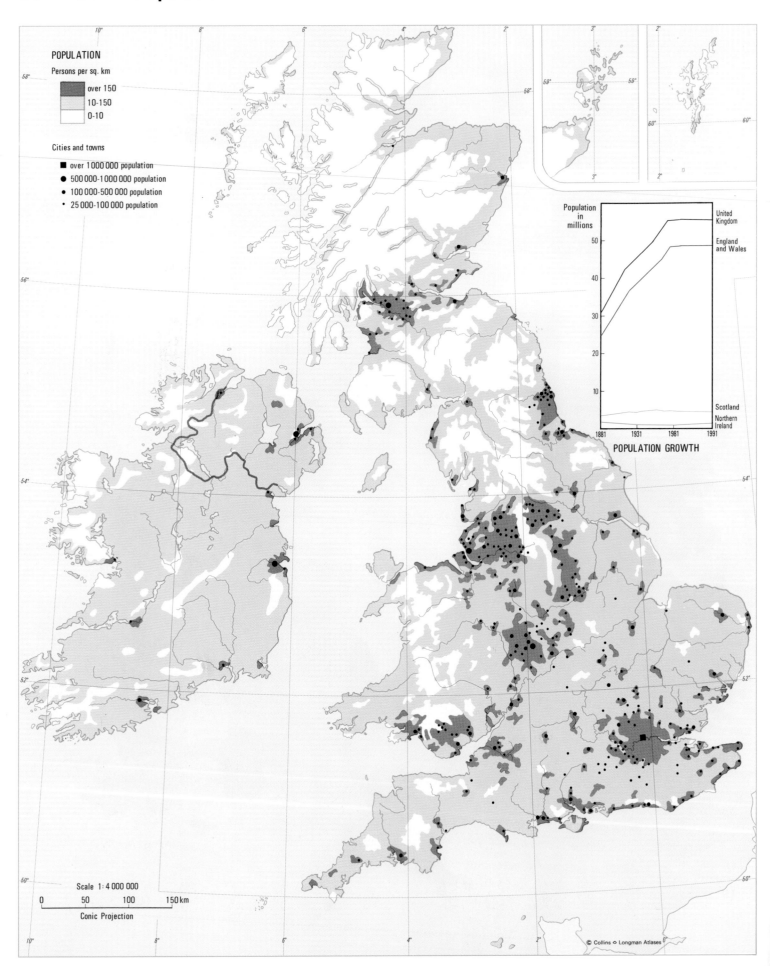

POPULATION

Persons per sq. km

over 150
10-150
0-10

Cities and towns

■ over 1 000 000 population
● 500 000-1 000 000 population
● 100 000-500 000 population
· 25 000-100 000 population

Population in millions

United Kingdom

England and Wales

Scotland
Northern Ireland

1881 1931 1981 1991

POPULATION GROWTH

Scale 1:4 000 000

0   50   100   150 km

Conic Projection

© Collins ◇ Longman Atlases

**POPULATION OVER
PENSION AGE, 1989**
(Women aged 60 and over,
men aged 65 and over.)

21% and over
20.1 - 21%
19.1 - 20%
18.1 - 19%
17.1 - 18%
16.1 - 17%
14.0 - 16%

UK average 18%

Scale 1 : 10 000 000
0   100   200   300 km

**UNEMPLOYMENT RATE,
JANUARY 1991**

12% and over
10 - 11.9%
7 - 9.9%
4 - 6.9%
0 - 3.9%

UK average 6.9%

Scale 1 : 10 000 000
0   100   200   300 km

AGE STRUCTURE, UK AND SELECTED REGIONS - 1966, 1978, 1989

NORTHERN IRELAND

AGE GROUP
65 and over
45-64
15-44
5-14
0-4

Male Female 1966   Male 1978 Female   Male 1989 Female

NORTH ENGLAND

AGE GROUP
65 and over
45-64
15-44
5-14
0-4

Male 1966 Female   Male 1978 Female   Male 1989 Female

SOUTH WEST ENGLAND

AGE GROUP
65 and over
45-64
15-44
5-14
0-4

Male 1966 Female   Male 1978 Female   Male 1989 Female

UNITED KINGDOM

AGE GROUP
65 and over
45-64
15-44
5-14
0-4

Male 1966 Female   Male 1978 Female   Male 1989 Female

% of total

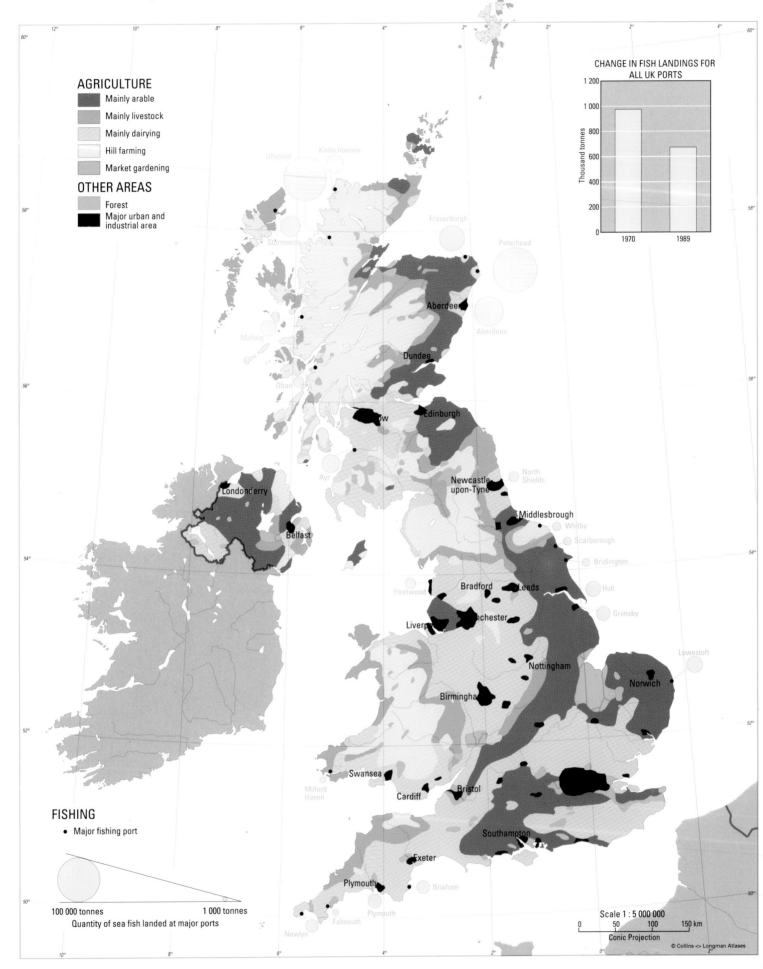

AGRICULTURE

- Mainly arable
- Mainly livestock
- Mainly dairying
- Hill farming
- Market gardening

OTHER AREAS

- Forest
- Major urban and industrial area

FISHING

- Major fishing port

100 000 tonnes   1 000 tonnes
Quantity of sea fish landed at major ports

CHANGE IN FISH LANDINGS FOR ALL UK PORTS

Thousand tonnes

1970   1989

Scale 1 : 5 000 000

0   50   100   150 km

Conic Projection

© Collins ◇ Longman Atlases

Ullapool, Kinlochbervie, Stornoway, Mallaig, Oban, Fraserburgh, Peterhead, Aberdeen, Dundee, Glasgow, Edinburgh, Ayr, Newcastle upon-Tyne, North Shields, Middlesbrough, Whitby, Scarborough, Bridlington, Hull, Grimsby, Fleetwood, Londonderry, Belfast, Bradford, Leeds, Manchester, Liverpool, Nottingham, Birmingham, Norwich, Lowestoft, Swansea, Cardiff, Milford Haven, Bristol, Southampton, Exeter, Plymouth, Brixham, Newlyn, Falmouth

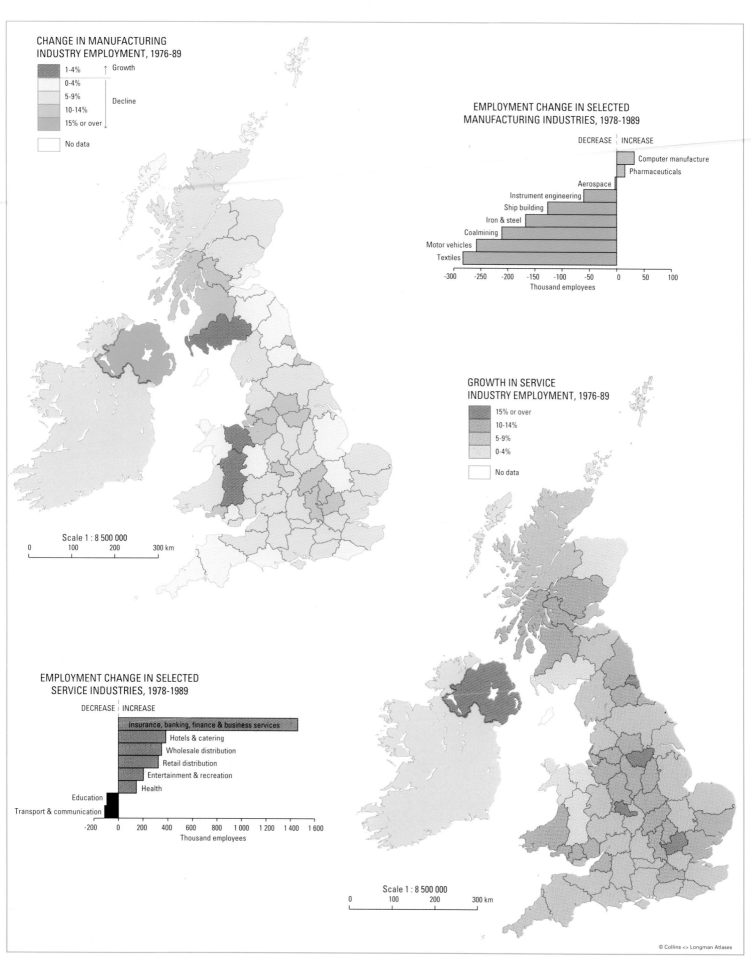

CHANGE IN MANUFACTURING
INDUSTRY EMPLOYMENT, 1976-89

1-4%   ↑ Growth
0-4%
5-9%   Decline
10-14%
15% or over ↓

No data

EMPLOYMENT CHANGE IN SELECTED
MANUFACTURING INDUSTRIES, 1978-1989

DECREASE | INCREASE

Computer manufacture
Pharmaceuticals
Aerospace
Instrument engineering
Ship building
Iron & steel
Coalmining
Motor vehicles
Textiles

-300 -250 -200 -150 -100 -50   0   50   100
Thousand employees

GROWTH IN SERVICE
INDUSTRY EMPLOYMENT, 1976-89

15% or over
10-14%
5-9%
0-4%

No data

Scale 1 : 8 500 000
0   100   200   300 km

EMPLOYMENT CHANGE IN SELECTED
SERVICE INDUSTRIES, 1978-1989

DECREASE | INCREASE

Insurance, banking, finance & business services
Hotels & catering
Wholesale distribution
Retail distribution
Entertainment & recreation
Health
Education
Transport & communication

-200   0   200 400 600 800 1 000 1 200 1 400 1 600
Thousand employees

Scale 1 : 8 500 000
0   100   200   300 km

© Collins <> Longman Atlases

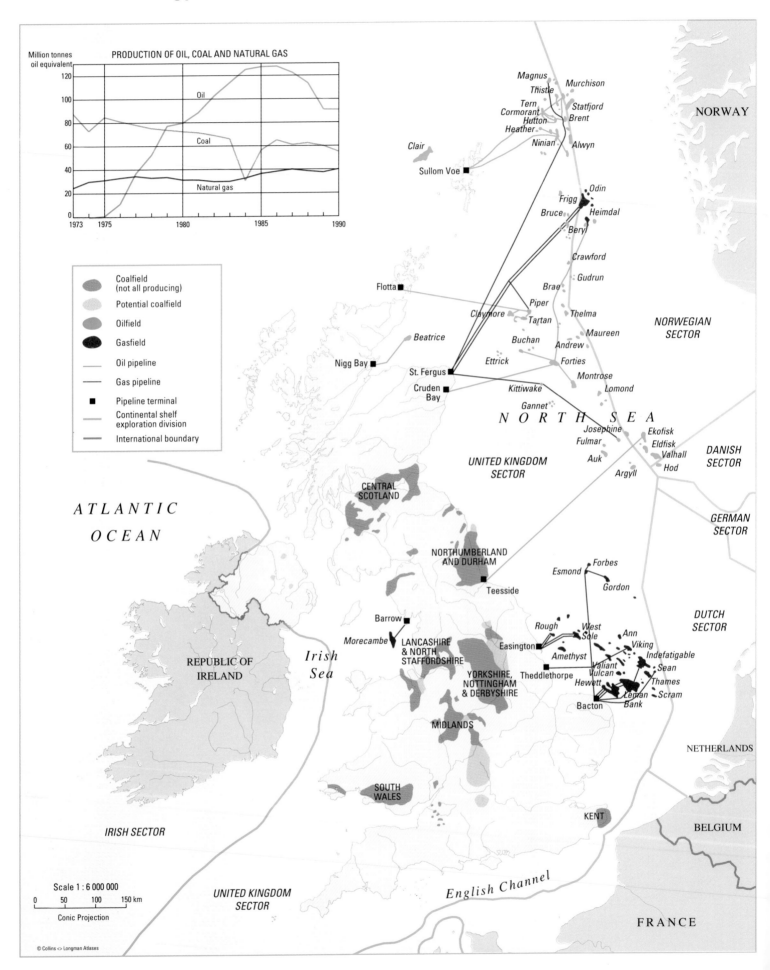

Million tonnes oil equivalent

PRODUCTION OF OIL, COAL AND NATURAL GAS

Oil

Coal

Natural gas

1973 1975 1980 1985 1990

Legend:

- Coalfield (not all producing)
- Potential coalfield
- Oilfield
- Gasfield
- Oil pipeline
- Gas pipeline
- ■ Pipeline terminal
- Continental shelf exploration division
- International boundary

NORWAY

Magnus
Murchison
Thistle
Tern
Statfjord
Cormorant
Brent
Hutton
Heather
Clair
Ninian
Alwyn

Sullom Voe

Odin
Frigg
Bruce
Heimdal
Beryl

Crawford
Gudrun

Flotta
Brae

Piper
Claymore
Tartan
Thelma

NORWEGIAN SECTOR

Beatrice
Maureen
Buchan
Andrew
Nigg Bay
Ettrick
Forties

St. Fergus
Montrose
Cruden Bay
Kittiwake
Lomond

Gannet

N O R T H   S E A

Josephine
Ekofisk
Fulmar
Eldfisk
Auk
Valhall
Argyll
Hod

UNITED KINGDOM SECTOR

DANISH SECTOR

GERMAN SECTOR

A T L A N T I C

O C E A N

CENTRAL SCOTLAND

NORTHUMBERLAND AND DURHAM

Teesside

Forbes

Esmond
Gordon

DUTCH SECTOR

REPUBLIC OF IRELAND

Irish Sea

Barrow

Morecambe
LANCASHIRE & NORTH STAFFORDSHIRE

Rough
West Sole
Ann
Viking
Indefatigable

Easington
Amethyst
Sean

YORKSHIRE, NOTTINGHAM & DERBYSHIRE

Theddlethorpe
Valiant
Vulcan
Thames

Hewett
Scram

Bacton
Leman Bank

MIDLANDS

NETHERLANDS

SOUTH WALES

KENT

BELGIUM

IRISH SECTOR

UNITED KINGDOM SECTOR

English Channel

Scale 1 : 6 000 000

0   50   100   150 km

Conic Projection

FRANCE

© Collins ◇ Longman Atlases

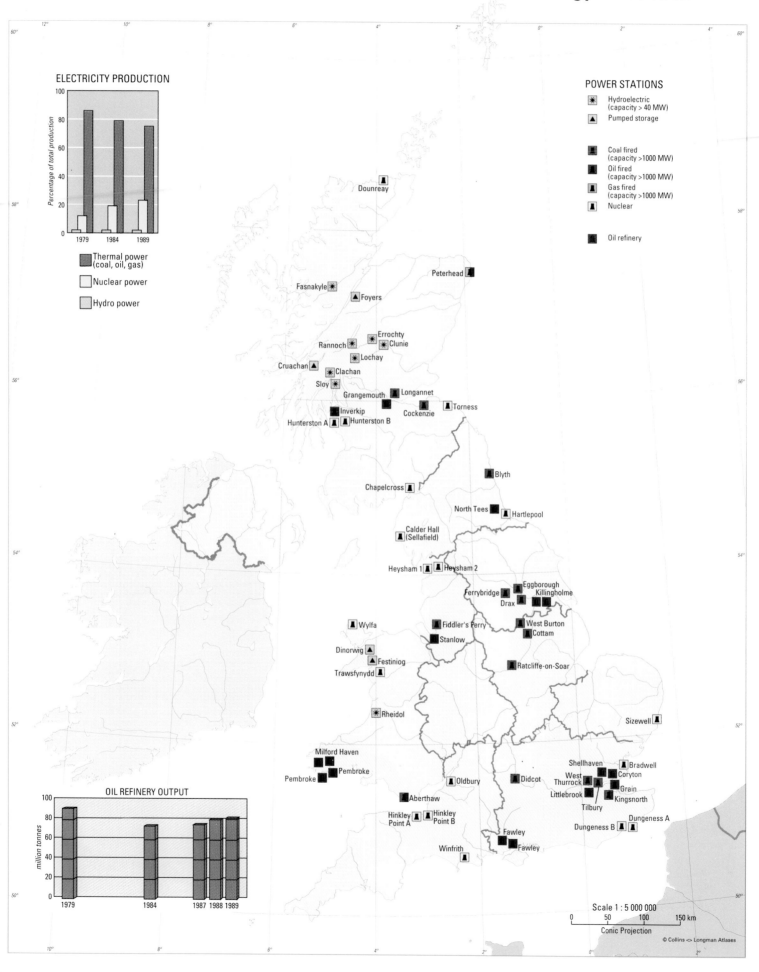

ELECTRICITY PRODUCTION

Percentage of total production

100
80
60
40
20
0

1979   1984   1989

■ Thermal power
(coal, oil, gas)

☐ Nuclear power

☐ Hydro power

POWER STATIONS

☀ Hydroelectric
(capacity > 40 MW)

▲ Pumped storage

■ Coal fired
(capacity >1000 MW)

■ Oil fired
(capacity >1000 MW)

■ Gas fired
(capacity >1000 MW)

▮ Nuclear

▦ Oil refinery

Dounreay

Peterhead

Fasnakyle
Foyers

Errochty
Rannoch   Clunie
Lochay
Cruachan
Clachan
Sloy
Grangemouth   Longannet
Inverkip   Cockenzie   Torness
Hunterston A   Hunterston B

Blyth

Chapelcross

North Tees   Hartlepool

Calder Hall
(Sellafield)

Heysham 1   Heysham 2

Ferrybridge   Eggborough
Killingholme
Drax
Wylfa   Fiddler's Ferry   West Burton
Stanlow   Cottam
Dinorwig
Festiniog
Trawsfynydd   Ratcliffe-on-Soar

Rheidol

Sizewell

Milford Haven
Pembroke
Pembroke

Shellhaven   Bradwell
West   Coryton
Thurrock
Oldbury   Didcot   Grain
Littlebrook   Kingsnorth
Aberthaw   Tilbury
Dungeness A
Hinkley   Hinkley   Dungeness B
Point A   Point B
Fawley
Winfrith   Fawley

OIL REFINERY OUTPUT

million tonnes

100
80
60
40
20
0

1979   1984   1987 1988 1989

Scale 1 : 5 000 000

0   50   100   150 km

Conic Projection

© Collins <> Longman Atlases

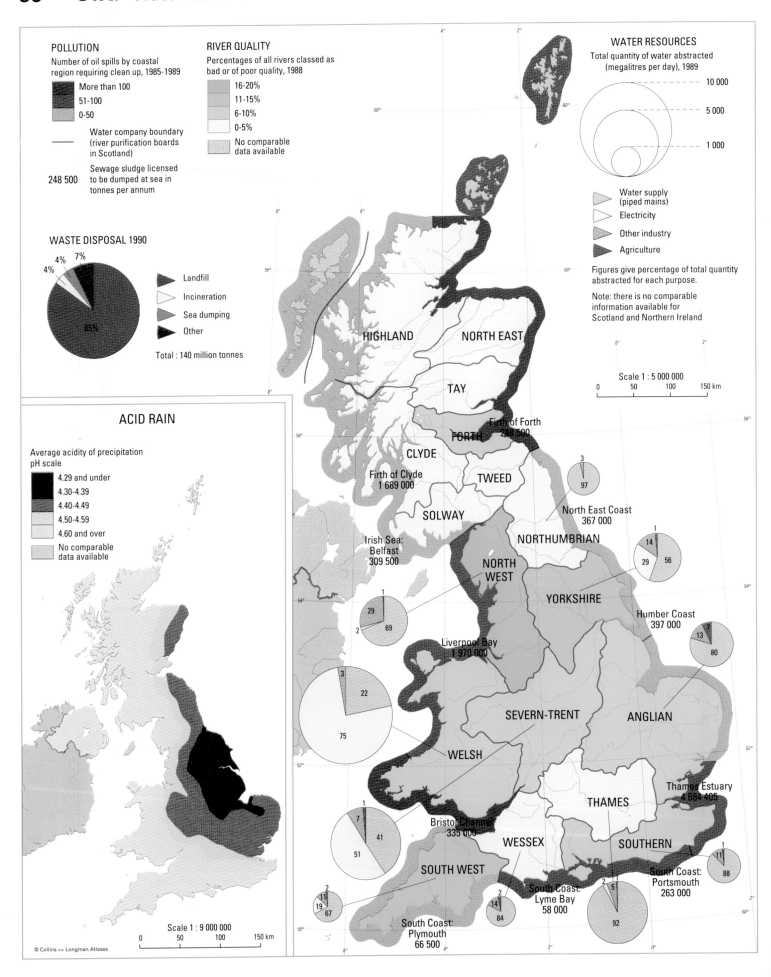

POLLUTION

Number of oil spills by coastal region requiring clean up, 1985-1989

- More than 100
- 51-100
- 0-50

——— Water company boundary (river purification boards in Scotland)

248 500   Sewage sludge licensed to be dumped at sea in tonnes per annum

RIVER QUALITY

Percentages of all rivers classed as bad or of poor quality, 1988

- 16-20%
- 11-15%
- 6-10%
- 0-5%
- No comparable data available

WATER RESOURCES

Total quantity of water abstracted (megalitres per day), 1989

- 10 000
- 5 000
- 1 000

- Water supply (piped mains)
- Electricity
- Other industry
- Agriculture

Figures give percentage of total quantity abstracted for each purpose.

Note: there is no comparable information available for Scotland and Northern Ireland

Scale 1 : 5 000 000
0   50   100   150 km

WASTE DISPOSAL 1990

- Landfill
- Incineration
- Sea dumping
- Other

7%
4%
4%
85%

Total : 140 million tonnes

ACID RAIN

Average acidity of precipitation
pH scale

- 4.29 and under
- 4.30-4.39
- 4.40-4.49
- 4.50-4.59
- 4.60 and over
- No comparable data available

Scale 1 : 9 000 000
0   50   100   150 km

© Collins <> Longman Atlases

HIGHLAND

NORTH EAST

TAY

FORTH   Firth of Forth
248 500

CLYDE

Firth of Clyde
1 689 000

TWEED

SOLWAY

North East Coast
367 000

3
97

NORTHUMBRIAN

Irish Sea:
Belfast
309 500

NORTH
WEST

1
14
29   56

YORKSHIRE

Humber Coast
397 000

1
29
2   69

Liverpool Bay
1 970 000

7
13
80

3
22
75

SEVERN-TRENT

ANGLIAN

WELSH

Thames Estuary
4 684 405

1
7
41
51

Bristol Channel
335 000

THAMES

SOUTHERN

WESSEX

2
5
92

SOUTH WEST

South Coast:
Lyme Bay
58 000

South Coast:
Portsmouth
263 000

1
11
88

2
11
19   67

2
14   84

South Coast:
Plymouth
66 500

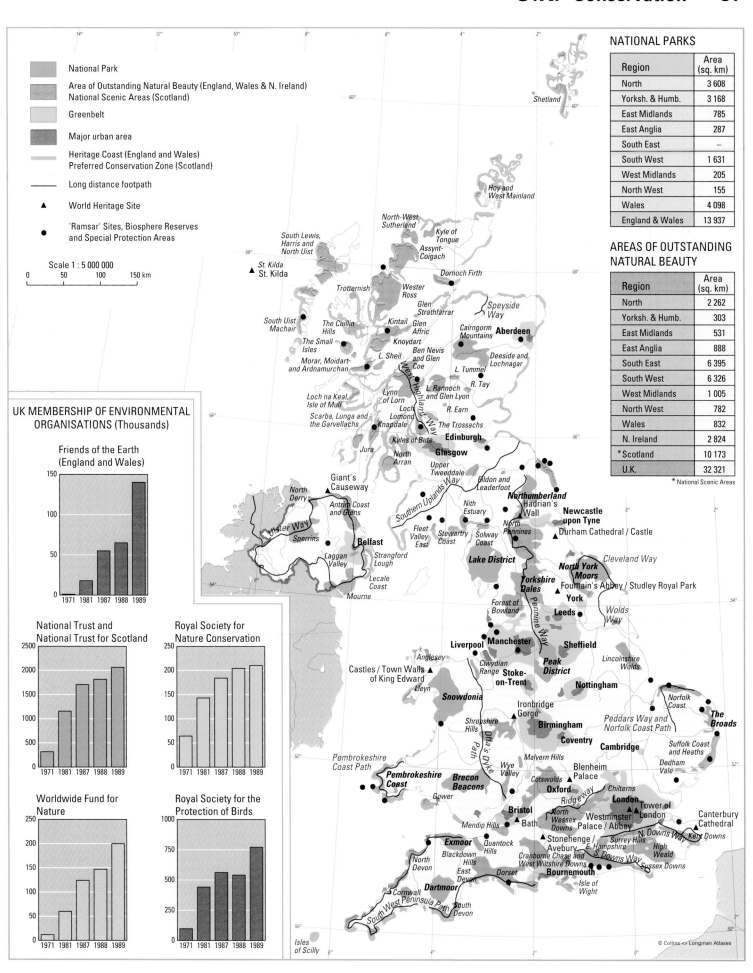

Legend

- National Park
- Area of Outstanding Natural Beauty (England, Wales & N. Ireland) National Scenic Areas (Scotland)
- Greenbelt
- Major urban area
- Heritage Coast (England and Wales) Preferred Conservation Zone (Scotland)
- Long distance footpath
- ▲ World Heritage Site
- ● 'Ramsar' Sites, Biosphere Reserves and Special Protection Areas

Scale 1 : 5 000 000

0   50   100   150 km

NATIONAL PARKS

Region	Area (sq. km)
North	3 608
Yorksh. & Humb.	3 168
East Midlands	785
East Anglia	287
South East	–
South West	1 631
West Midlands	205
North West	155
Wales	4 098
England & Wales	13 937

AREAS OF OUTSTANDING NATURAL BEAUTY

Region	Area (sq. km)
North	2 262
Yorksh. & Humb.	303
East Midlands	531
East Anglia	888
South East	6 395
South West	6 326
West Midlands	1 005
North West	782
Wales	832
N. Ireland	2 824
*Scotland	10 173
U.K.	32 321

* National Scenic Areas

UK MEMBERSHIP OF ENVIRONMENTAL ORGANISATIONS (Thousands)

Friends of the Earth (England and Wales)

150, 100, 50, 0 — 1971 1981 1987 1988 1989

National Trust and National Trust for Scotland

2500, 2000, 1500, 1000, 500, 0 — 1971 1981 1987 1988 1989

Royal Society for Nature Conservation

250, 200, 150, 100, 50, 0 — 1971 1981 1987 1988 1989

Worldwide Fund for Nature

250, 200, 150, 100, 50, 0 — 1971 1981 1987 1988 1989

Royal Society for the Protection of Birds

1000, 750, 500, 250, 0 — 1971 1981 1987 1988 1989

© Collins ◇ Longman Atlases

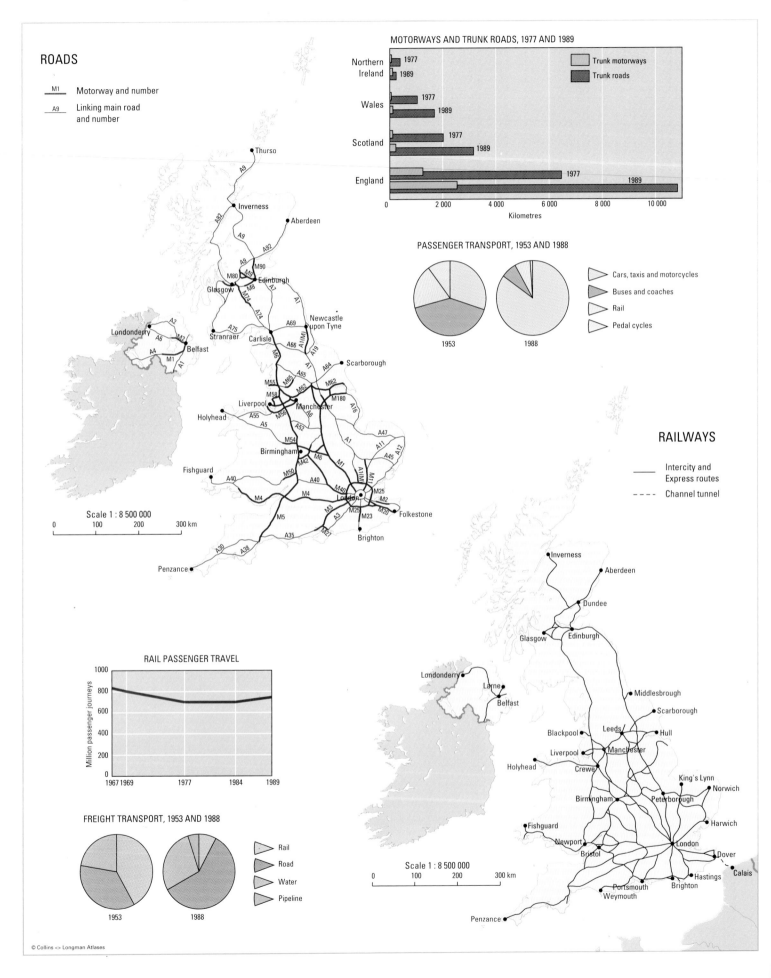

ROADS

M1 — Motorway and number

A9 — Linking main road and number

MOTORWAYS AND TRUNK ROADS, 1977 AND 1989

Trunk motorways
Trunk roads

Northern Ireland — 1977, 1989
Wales — 1977, 1989
Scotland — 1977, 1989
England — 1977, 1989

Kilometres
0   2 000   4 000   6 000   8 000   10 000

PASSENGER TRANSPORT, 1953 AND 1988

1953   1988

Cars, taxis and motorcycles
Buses and coaches
Rail
Pedal cycles

RAILWAYS

Intercity and Express routes
Channel tunnel

Scale 1 : 8 500 000
0   100   200   300 km

RAIL PASSENGER TRAVEL

Million passenger journeys

1000
800
600
400
200
0

1967 1969   1977   1984   1989

FREIGHT TRANSPORT, 1953 AND 1988

1953   1988

Rail
Road
Water
Pipeline

Scale 1 : 8 500 000
0   100   200   300 km

AIRPORTS

PASSENGERS HANDLED PER YEAR ('000)

✈ Over 10 000
✈ 2 000 - 10 000
✈ 1 000 - 2 000
✈ 200 - 1 000
● Other airports

MAIN INTERNATIONAL DESTINATIONS FROM UK AIRPORTS

Far East
Portugal
Switzerland
Netherlands
Ireland
Canary Islands
Italy
Greece
France
Germany
USA
Spain

0   2   4   6   8   10   12
Million passengers

AIR PASSENGER TRAFFIC, UK AIRPORTS, 1988

Domestic
International

Unst
Scatsta
Lerwick
Kirkwall
Wick
Stornoway
Benbecula
Inverness
Aberdeen
Tiree
Dundee
Islay
Glasgow
Edinburgh
Prestwick
Newcastle
Londonderry
Carlisle
Belfast
Teesside
Belfast Harbour
Isle of Man
Leeds/Bradford
Blackpool
Humberside
Liverpool
Manchester
Hawarden
Norwich
Birmingham
East Midlands
Gloucester/Cheltenham
Luton
Stansted
Swansea
Cardiff
Heathrow
Bristol
Southend
London City
Southampton
Gatwick
Lydd
Shoreham
Exeter
Bournemouth
Penzance
Plymouth
Isles of Scilly
Sullom Voe

Scale 1 : 10 000 000
0   100   200   300 km

PORTS

● Port handling more than 1 million tonnes of cargo, 1990

Kirkwall
Cromarty Firth
Peterhead
Aberdeen
Dundee
Clyde
Forth
Ayr
Blyth
Larne
Stranraer
Tyne
Belfast
Sunderland
Tees/Hartlepool
Warrenpoint
Heysham
Fleetwood
Hull/Humber
Manchester
Goole
Hull
Holyhead
Liverpool
Grimsby/Immingham
Boston
King's Lynn
Great Yarmouth
Ipswich
Felixstowe
Milford Haven
Harwich
Cardiff
Swansea
Newport
Medway
Port Talbot
Barry
Bristol
Ramsgate
Southampton
Dover
Poole
Shoreham
Fowey
Portsmouth
Newhaven
Plymouth

Scale 1 : 10 000 000
0   100   200   300 km

FERRY PORTS AND ROUTES

■ Ferry port
- - - Main ferry route

Lerwick
Stromness
Kirkwall
Scrabster
Burwick
Gills Bay
Stornoway
Tarbert
Ullapool
Lochmaddy
Uig
Kyle of Lochalsh
Lochboisdale
Kyleakin
Aberdeen
Castlebay
Armadale
Mallaig
Arinagour
Lochaline
Scarinish
Craignure
Oban
Rothesay
Scalasaig
Dunoon
Port Askaig
Gourock
Kennacraig
Wemys Bay
Ardrossan
Brodick
Cairnryan
Stranraer
Larne
Tynemouth
Belfast
Douglas
Heysham
Hull
Esbjerg
Stavanger
Bergen
Göteborg
Rotterdam
Zeebrugge
Liverpool
Holyhead
Dublin
Rosslare
Göteborg
Esbjerg
Hamburg
Hook of Holland
Zeebrugge
Vlissingen
Dunkirk
Östende
Calais
Boulogne
Fishguard
Felixstowe
Pembroke
Harwich
Cork
Swansea
Sheerness
Ramsgate
Dover
Southampton
Newhaven
Poole
Portsmouth
Cowes
Plymouth
Penzance
Caen
Le Havre
Cherbourg
Dieppe
St Mary's
Channel Islands
St Malo
Santander
Roscoff

Scale 1 : 10 000 000
0   100   200   300 km

TRAFFIC THROUGH PRINCIPAL UK PORTS

■ 1989 □ 1985 □ 1975

million tonnes

60
50
40
30
20
10
0

London
Sullom Voe
Tees and Hartlepool
Grimsby and Immingham
Milford Haven
Southampton
Forth
Liverpool
Felixstowe
Medway
Dover

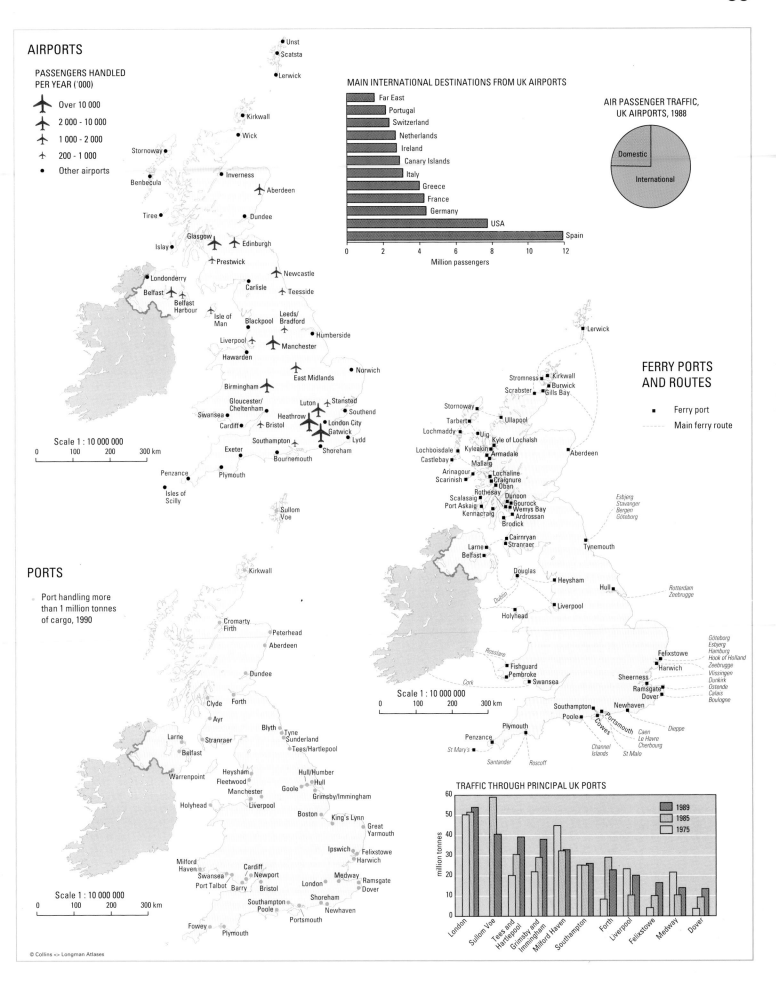

© Collins <> Longman Atlases

ARCTIC

North Cape

NORWEGIAN SEA

Arctic Circle

ATLANTIC OCEAN

Straumnes
Snaefell 1833
Surtsey
Vatnajökull
Mt. Hekla 1491

Faroe Is.

Shetland Is.

Hebrides
Orkney Is.
Moray Firth
Ben Nevis 1343
Grampian Mountains
Malin Head
Firth of Forth
Southern Uplands
Galway Bay
Clyde
Wicklow Mts.
Shannon
Irish Sea
Snowdon 1085
The Pennines
Cape Clear
Cambrian Mts.
Trent
Celtic Sea
Severn
The Wash
St. George's Channel
The Fens
Land's End
Thames
Isles of Scilly
English Channel
Channel Is.
Str. of Dover

NORTH SEA

Vesterålen
Lofoten
Vestfjorden
Kebnekaise ▲2123
LAPLAND
Torne
Muonio
Inari
Kemi
Storavan
Lule
Skellefte
Frohavet
Ume
Storsjön
Indals
Gulf of Bothnia
Oulujärvi
Dovrefjell
Glittertind ▲2470
Jotunheimen
Sognefjorden
Giama
Ljusnan
Näsijärvi
Hardangerfjorden
Mjösa
Lågen
Vänern
Åland Is.
Gulf of Finland
Otra
Oslofjorden
Göta
Vättern
L. Peipus
Lindesnes
Skagerrak
Mälaren
Gotland
Saaremaa
Gulf of Riga
Limfjorden
Kattegat
Lagan
Öland
Jutland
Lagan
BALTIC SEA
Neman
Funen
Zealand
Bornholm
Kiel Canal
Frisian Is.
IJsselmeer
Elbe
Oder
Warta
Vistula
Bug
Neman

Bay of Biscay

Brittany

Scale 1:16 000 000
0   200   400   600   800 km
Conic Projection

Maas
Rhine
Ardennes
Mosel
Taunus
Weser
Harz Mts.
Spree
Ore Mts.
Elbe
Sudeten Mts.
Silesian Plateau
Vistula
NORTH EUROPEAN
Gerlachovka ▲2663
Carpathian
Seine
Marne
Vosges
Rhine
Black Forest
Danube
Bohemian Forest
Inn
Morava
Seine
Saône
Jura Mts.
L. Constance
Brenner Pass
Gross Glockner ▲3798
Dra va
Tisza
Hungarian Plain
Loire
Vienne
Allier
L. Geneva
Rhône
Mt. Blanc ▲4807
Mt. Rosa ▲4634
ALPS
Dolomites
Mures
Gironde
Mont Dore ▲1886
Massif Central
Rhône
Adige
Po
Drava
Danube
Transylvanian
Iron Gate
Garonne
Dordogne
Cevennes
Durance
G. of Genoa
Ligurian Sea
Arno
APENNINES
Sava
Dinaric Alps
Dring
Morava
Danube
Balkan

C. Finisterre
Cantabrian Mts.
Douro
Iberian Mts.
Ebro
Pyrénées
Pico de Aneto ▲3404
Gulf of Lions
C. Creus
Tiber
2914 ▲Mt. Corno
ADRIATIC SEA
2522 ▲Durmitor
L. Shkoder
Rhodope
Struma
Musala ▲2925

C. Roca
Douro
Iberian Peninsula
Tagus
Gulf of Gascony
Ebro Delta
Balearic Is.
Minorca
Corsica
Str. of Bonifacio
1277 ▲Vesuvius
Axios
Guadiana
Majorca
Ibiza
Sardinia
Mt. Olympus ▲2911
Mt. Athos ▲203

C. St. Vincent
Sierra Morena
Guadalquivir
Mulhacén 3482
Sierra Nevada
C. de la Nao
C. Palos
Tyrrhenian Sea
G. of Taranto
Str. of Otranto
Corfu
Ionian Islands
Pindus Mts.
Euboea

Str. of Gibraltar
Gulf of Cadiz
Stromboli 926 ▲
Sicily
MEDITERRANEAN
Ionian Sea
Killini ▲2376
Aeg

Rif Mts.
Sebou
Cheliff
Tell Atlas
Mejerda
Mt. Etna ▲3340
C. Spartivento
C. Matapan
Cre

Oum er Rbia
Toubkal 4165 ▲
High Atlas
Chott ech Chergui
Saharan Atlas
C. Bon
C. Passero

Relief
Metres
5000
3000
2000
1000
500
200
0   Sea Level
Land Dep.
200
4000
7000
Metres

© Collins ○ Longman Atlases

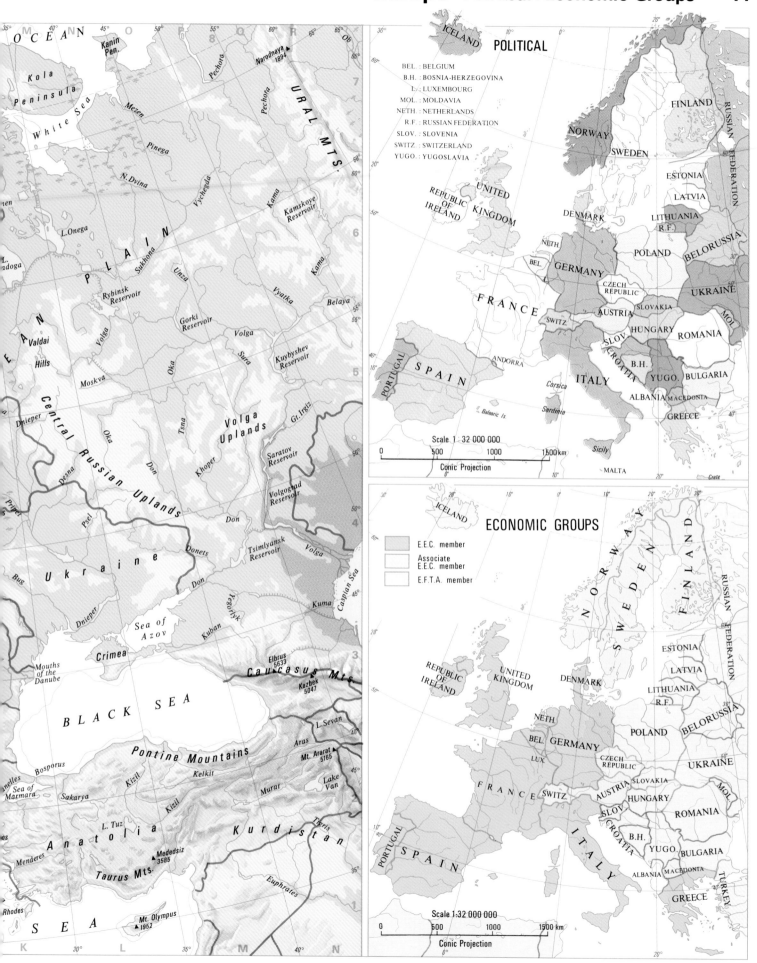

POLITICAL

BEL. : BELGIUM
B.H. : BOSNIA-HERZEGOVINA
L. : LUXEMBOURG
MOL. : MOLDAVIA
NETH. : NETHERLANDS
R.F. : RUSSIAN FEDERATION
SLOV. : SLOVENIA
SWITZ. : SWITZERLAND
YUGO. : YUGOSLAVIA

ICELAND

NORWAY SWEDEN FINLAND RUSSIAN FEDERATION

UNITED KINGDOM

REPUBLIC OF IRELAND

DENMARK ESTONIA LATVIA LITHUANIA R.F.

NETH. POLAND BELORUSSIA

BEL. GERMANY UKRAINE

FRANCE CZECH REPUBLIC SLOVAKIA MOL.

SWITZ. AUSTRIA HUNGARY ROMANIA

PORTUGAL SPAIN SLOV. CROATIA B.H. YUGO. BULGARIA

ANDORRA ITALY ALBANIA MACEDONIA

Corsica GREECE

Balearic Is. Sardinia

Scale 1 : 32 000 000

0   500   1000   1500 km

Conic Projection

Sicily   MALTA   Crete

ECONOMIC GROUPS

E.E.C. member

Associate E.E.C. member

E.F.T.A. member

ICELAND

NORWAY SWEDEN FINLAND RUSSIAN FEDERATION

UNITED KINGDOM

REPUBLIC OF IRELAND

DENMARK ESTONIA LATVIA LITHUANIA R.F.

NETH. POLAND BELORUSSIA

BEL. GERMANY UKRAINE

LUX. CZECH REPUBLIC

FRANCE SWITZ. AUSTRIA SLOVAKIA MOL.

HUNGARY ROMANIA

PORTUGAL SPAIN SLOV. CROATIA B.H. YUGO. BULGARIA

ITALY ALBANIA MACEDONIA

TURKEY

GREECE

Scale 1:32 000 000

0   500   1000   1500 km

Conic Projection

OCEAN

Kola Peninsula

Kanin Pen.

White Sea

Narodnaya 1894

URAL MTS.

Pechora

Mezen

Pinega

N. Dvina

Vychegda

Kama

Kamskoye Reservoir

L.Onega

EAN PLAIN

Sukhona

Unza

Kama

Rybinsk Reservoir

Vyatka

Belaya

Valdai Hills

Volga

Gorki Reservoir

Volga

Kuybyshev Reservoir

L.adoga

Moskva

Oka

Sura

Central Russian Uplands

Dnieper

Desna

Don

Tsna

Khoper

Volga Uplands

Gt. Irgiz

Saratov Reservoir

Pripet

Psel

Donets

Don

Volgograd Reservoir

Bug

Ukraine

Donets

Tsimlyansk Reservoir

Volga

Dnieper

Don

Yegorlyk

Kuma

Caspian Sea

Sea of Azov

Kuban

Crimea

Mouths of the Danube

Elbrus 5633

Caucasus Mts.

Kazbek 5047

BLACK SEA

L.Sevan

Pontine Mountains

Aras

Mt. Ararat 5165

Bosporus

Kizil

Kelkit

Murat

Lake Van

nelles

Sea of Marmara

Sakarya

Kizil

Kizil

Tigris

Kurdistan

Menderes

Anatolia

L. Tuz

Mededsiz 3585

Euphrates

Taurus Mts.

Rhodes

SEA

Mt. Olympus 1952

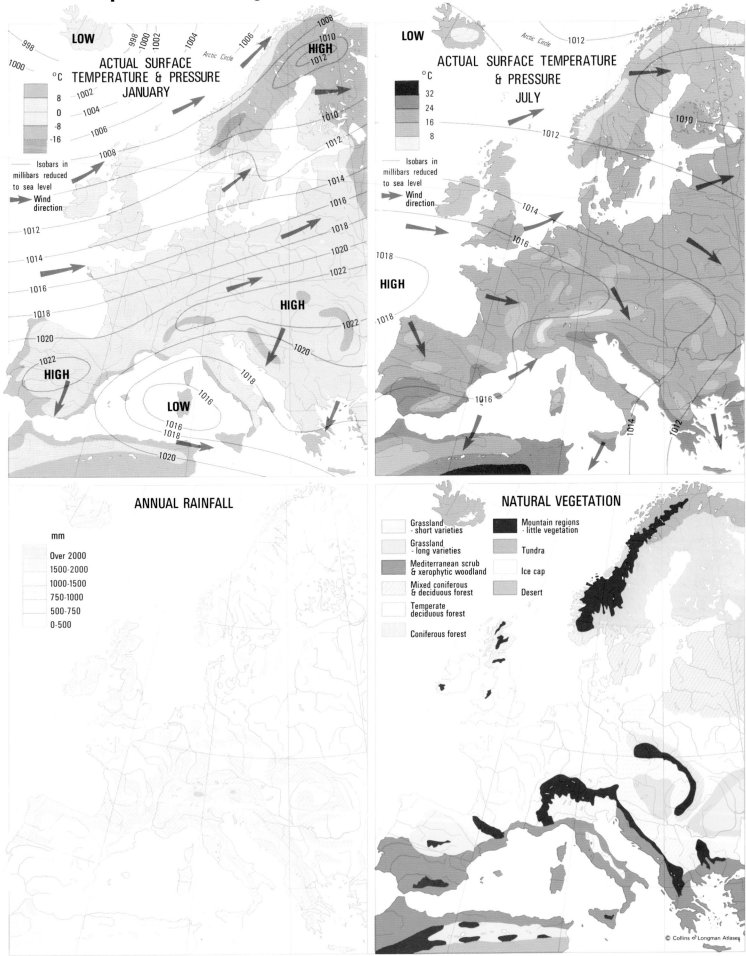

ACTUAL SURFACE TEMPERATURE & PRESSURE JANUARY

°C
8
0
-8
-16

Isobars in millibars reduced to sea level

Wind direction

LOW
998
1000
1002
1004
1006
Arctic Circle
1008
1010
1012
HIGH
1014
1016
1018
1020
1022
HIGH
LOW
1016
1018
1020

ACTUAL SURFACE TEMPERATURE & PRESSURE JULY

°C
32
24
16
8

Isobars in millibars reduced to sea level

Wind direction

LOW
Arctic Circle
1012
1010
1014
1016
HIGH
1018
1016
1014
1012

ANNUAL RAINFALL

mm
Over 2000
1500-2000
1000-1500
750-1000
500-750
0-500

NATURAL VEGETATION

Grassland - short varieties

Grassland - long varieties

Mediterranean scrub & xerophytic woodland

Mixed coniferous & deciduous forest

Temperate deciduous forest

Coniferous forest

Mountain regions - little vegetation

Tundra

Ice cap

Desert

© Collins & Longman Atlases

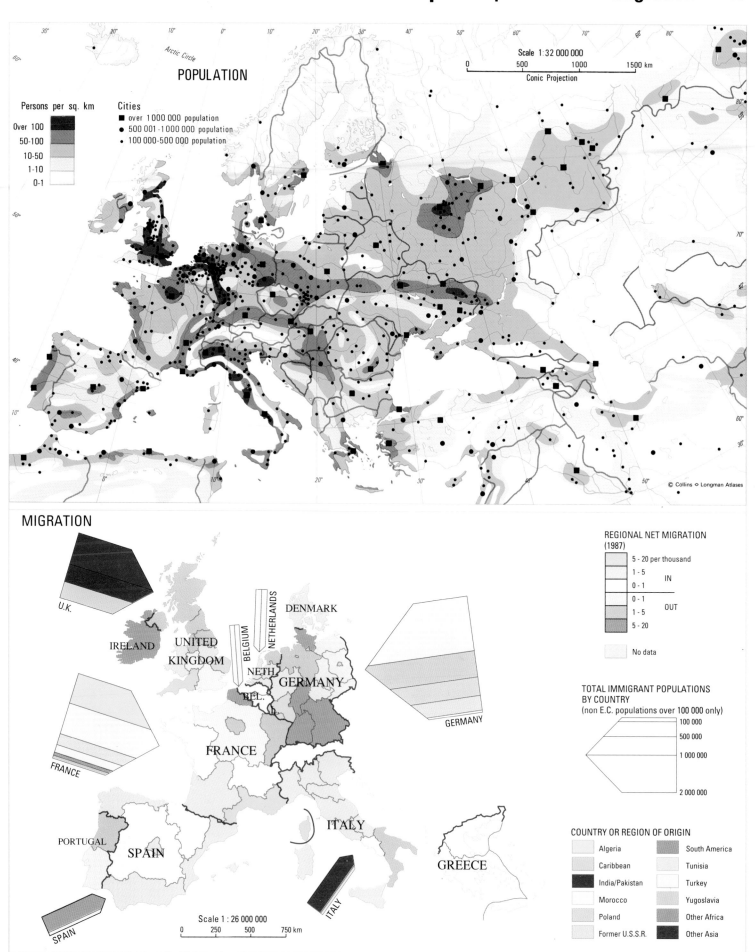

POPULATION

Persons per sq. km

- Over 100
- 50-100
- 10-50
- 1-10
- 0-1

Cities

- ■ over 1 000 000 population
- ● 500 001 - 1 000 000 population
- • 100 000 - 500 000 population

Scale 1:32 000 000

0   500   1000   1500 km

Conic Projection

© Collins ◇ Longman Atlases

MIGRATION

U.K.

DENMARK

NETHERLANDS

BELGIUM

IRELAND

UNITED KINGDOM

NETH.

GERMANY

BEL.

GERMANY

FRANCE

FRANCE

ITALY

PORTUGAL

SPAIN

ITALY

GREECE

SPAIN

Scale 1 : 26 000 000

0   250   500   750 km

REGIONAL NET MIGRATION (1987)

- 5 - 20 per thousand
- 1 - 5
- 0 - 1   IN
- 0 - 1   OUT
- 1 - 5
- 5 - 20

No data

TOTAL IMMIGRANT POPULATIONS BY COUNTRY
(non E.C. populations over 100 000 only)

- 100 000
- 500 000
- 1 000 000
- 2 000 000

COUNTRY OR REGION OF ORIGIN

- Algeria
- Caribbean
- India/Pakistan
- Morocco
- Poland
- Former U.S.S.R.
- South America
- Tunisia
- Turkey
- Yugoslavia
- Other Africa
- Other Asia

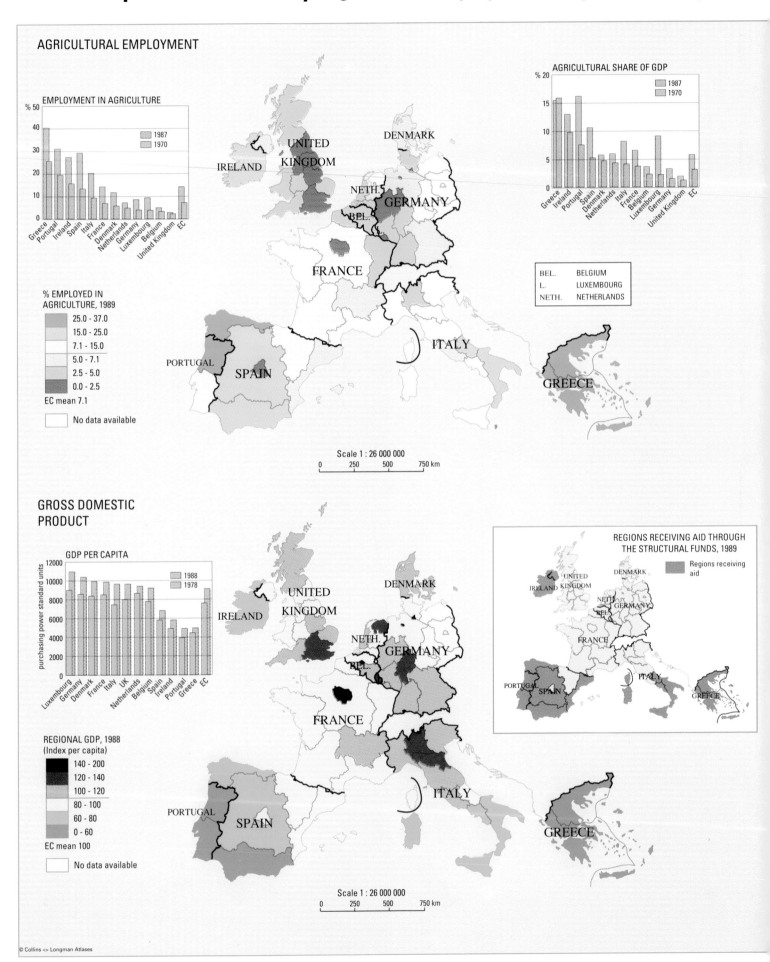

AGRICULTURAL EMPLOYMENT

EMPLOYMENT IN AGRICULTURE
% 50
40
30
20
10
0
1987
1970

Greece, Portugal, Ireland, Spain, Italy, France, Denmark, Netherlands, Germany, Luxembourg, Belgium, United Kingdom, EC

AGRICULTURAL SHARE OF GDP
% 20
15
10
5
0
1987
1970

Greece, Ireland, Portugal, Spain, Denmark, Netherlands, Italy, France, Belgium, Luxembourg, Germany, United Kingdom, EC

% EMPLOYED IN AGRICULTURE, 1989
- 25.0 - 37.0
- 15.0 - 25.0
- 7.1 - 15.0
- 5.0 - 7.1
- 2.5 - 5.0
- 0.0 - 2.5

EC mean 7.1

No data available

BEL.	BELGIUM
L.	LUXEMBOURG
NETH.	NETHERLANDS

DENMARK
UNITED KINGDOM
IRELAND
NETH.
BEL.
GERMANY
FRANCE
ITALY
PORTUGAL
SPAIN
GREECE

Scale 1 : 26 000 000
0 250 500 750 km

GROSS DOMESTIC PRODUCT

GDP PER CAPITA
12000
10000
8000
6000
4000
2000
0
purchasing power standard units
1988
1978

Luxembourg, Germany, Denmark, France, Italy, UK, Netherlands, Belgium, Spain, Ireland, Portugal, Greece, EC

REGIONAL GDP, 1988 (Index per capita)
- 140 - 200
- 120 - 140
- 100 - 120
- 80 - 100
- 60 - 80
- 0 - 60

EC mean 100

No data available

DENMARK
UNITED KINGDOM
IRELAND
NETH.
BEL.
GERMANY
FRANCE
ITALY
PORTUGAL
SPAIN
GREECE

Scale 1 : 26 000 000
0 250 500 750 km

REGIONS RECEIVING AID THROUGH THE STRUCTURAL FUNDS, 1989
Regions receiving aid

UNITED KINGDOM
IRELAND
DENMARK
NETH.
BEL.
GERMANY
FRANCE
ITALY
PORTUGAL
SPAIN
GREECE

UNEMPLOYMENT

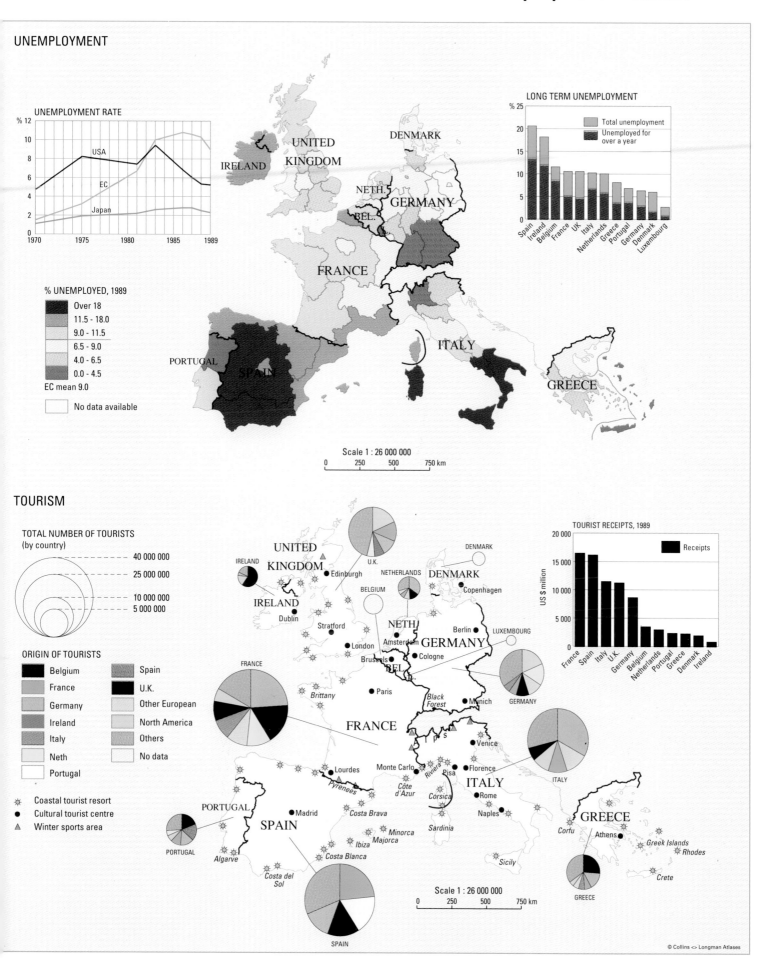

UNEMPLOYMENT RATE

% 12
10
8
6
4
2
0

USA
EC
Japan

1970   1975   1980   1985   1989

% UNEMPLOYED, 1989

Over 18
11.5 - 18.0
9.0 - 11.5
6.5 - 9.0
4.0 - 6.5
0.0 - 4.5

EC mean 9.0

No data available

LONG TERM UNEMPLOYMENT

% 25
20
15
10
5

Total unemployment
Unemployed for over a year

Spain, Ireland, Belgium, France, UK, Italy, Netherlands, Greece, Portugal, Germany, Denmark, Luxembourg

Scale 1 : 26 000 000
0   250   500   750 km

TOURISM

TOTAL NUMBER OF TOURISTS
(by country)

40 000 000
25 000 000
10 000 000
5 000 000

ORIGIN OF TOURISTS

Belgium
France
Germany
Ireland
Italy
Neth
Portugal

Spain
U.K.
Other European
North America
Others
No data

☼ Coastal tourist resort
● Cultural tourist centre
▲ Winter sports area

TOURIST RECEIPTS, 1989

20 000
15 000
10 000
5 000
0

US $ million

Receipts

France, Spain, Italy, U.K., Germany, Belgium, Netherlands, Portugal, Greece, Denmark, Ireland

Scale 1 : 26 000 000
0   250   500   750 km

© Collins <> Longman Atlases

AGRICULTURE & SOILS

Heath and dune - poorest sandy soils.

Dairying on fertile alluvial soils.

Extensive livestock farming with fodder crops on poor sandy soils.

Livestock farming with cereals on fertile clay soils.

Intensive dairying and pig farming with cereals and sugar beet on fertile clay soils.

Scale 1:2 000 000

0   20   40   60   80 km

Conic Projection

NORWAY Kristiansand
Mandal

Skagerrak

Orust
Mollösund
Tjörn

Tannis Bugt
Grenen
Skagen
Ålbaek

Hirtshals

Kattegat

Hjörring Sindal Frederikshavn
Lökken Saeby
NORD-
JYLLANDS

Jammer Bugt
Brönderslev
136
Dronninglund

Roshage
Bulbjerg 47
Hanstholm Brovst
Nörresundby
Ålborg

Laesö

Thisted Lögstör Nibe Svenstrup
Mors Års Stövring Dokkedal
Nyköbing Åsted Farsö Binderup
Ydby Harre Ålestrup Hadsund

Ålborg
Bugt

Thyborön
Nissum
Bredning VIBORG Hobro Mariager Udbyhöj

Anholt

Lemvig Skive Skals
Struer Viborg
Torsminde Vinderup Bjerringbro Randers Allingåbro Örum
Nissum Storå Holstebro Langå AARHUS Grenå
Fjord Karup Kjellerup Hadsten Rönde
RINGKÖBING Hammel
Herning Silkeborg Vejlby Ebeltoft
Ringköbing Ikast 147 Braband Århus
Arnborg Skjern Mosso Skanderborg
Skjern Brande 173 Odder
Tarm Åstrup
Holmsland Hoven VEJLE Törring Horsens
Klit Ölgod Jelling

Fornaes

Samsö

Samsö Baelt

NORTH

64

SEA

Oksby Varde Grindsted 137
Vejen Vejle Juelsminde
Esbjerg Bramming Fredericia Bogense
Fanö Kolding Middelfart Otterup
Gredstedbro 113 Kerteminde
Ribe Christiansfeld Arup Odense Langeskov
Gram 131 Ringe Nyborg
Skaerbaek Haderslev FYNS Hårby
Römö Vojens Assens Svendborg
SÖNDERJYLLANDS Fåborg
Lögumkloster Åbenrå Als
Sylt Nordborg Varnaes
Westerland Tönder Tinglev Gråsten Tasinge
Als Sönderborg
Niebüll Padborg Aerö
North Hörup Marstal
Förh Sande Flensburg
Amrum Wanderup
Frisian Bredstedt Kappeln
Islands Nordstrand Husum Schleswig Eckernförde

Kolby

Ulstrup

Store Baelt

Lille Baelt

Treene

Schlei

Flensburg Fjord

DENMARK

RIBE

Langeland

Spodsbjerg

Zealands
Odde

Skälderviken
Arild Angelholm
Gilleleje Helsingör Höganäs Klippan Hässleholm
Hundested Helsinge Hilleröd Halsingborg
Nyköbing FREDERIKSBORG Landskrona SWEDEN
Ise- Frederikssund Farum Ringsjön
fjord Höör
Hagested Roskilde Copenhagen Eslöv Hörby
Holbaek COPENHAGEN Lund
Kalundborg Tåstrup Amager Bjärret
Helsinge Zealand Malmö
VESTJAELLANDS Köge Svedala
Slagelse Ringsted ROSKILDE Köge Skurup
Korsör Bugt Skanör Genarp
Skaelskör Haslev Sjöbö
123 Naestved Vellinge
Menstrup Rödvig Trelleborg Ystad
Fakse
Praestö Bugt

Örum

Öre Sund

Ringsjön

BALTIC
SEA

Smålands-
farvandet STORSTROMS Vordingborg Mön 143
Nakskov Saksköbing Stubbeköbing
Maribo Falster Wittow Sassnitz
Lolland Nyköbing Rügen
Rödby Zingst Bergen
Gedser Darss Barth

Femer Baelt

Kiel
Bay Puttgarden
Fehmarn
Heiligenhafen

Mecklenburg
Bay

Karnin
Stralsund
Reinberg

Laboe Oldenburg Warnemünde Ribnitz-Damgarten Grimmen
Holtenau Dahme
Friedrichstadt Rendsburg Kiel Lütjenburg Bad Rostock Gnoien
Sankt Peter Erfde Preetz Plön Doberan Bad Sülze Greifswald
Tönning Heide Bordesholm Sprenge Eutin Neustadt Lübeck Laage Peene
Wesselburen Meldorf Plöner Bay Bad Neukalen
Büsum Eider See Doberan
Kiel Canal Neumünster Demmin

Heligoland
Bay

GERMANY

Marne Itzehoe Bad Dassow Grevesmühlen Wismar Bützow
Brunsbüttel Bramstedt Bad Schwartau Lübeck
Cuxhaven Elbe Bad Segeberg

Lübeck
Bay

© Collins © Longman Atlases

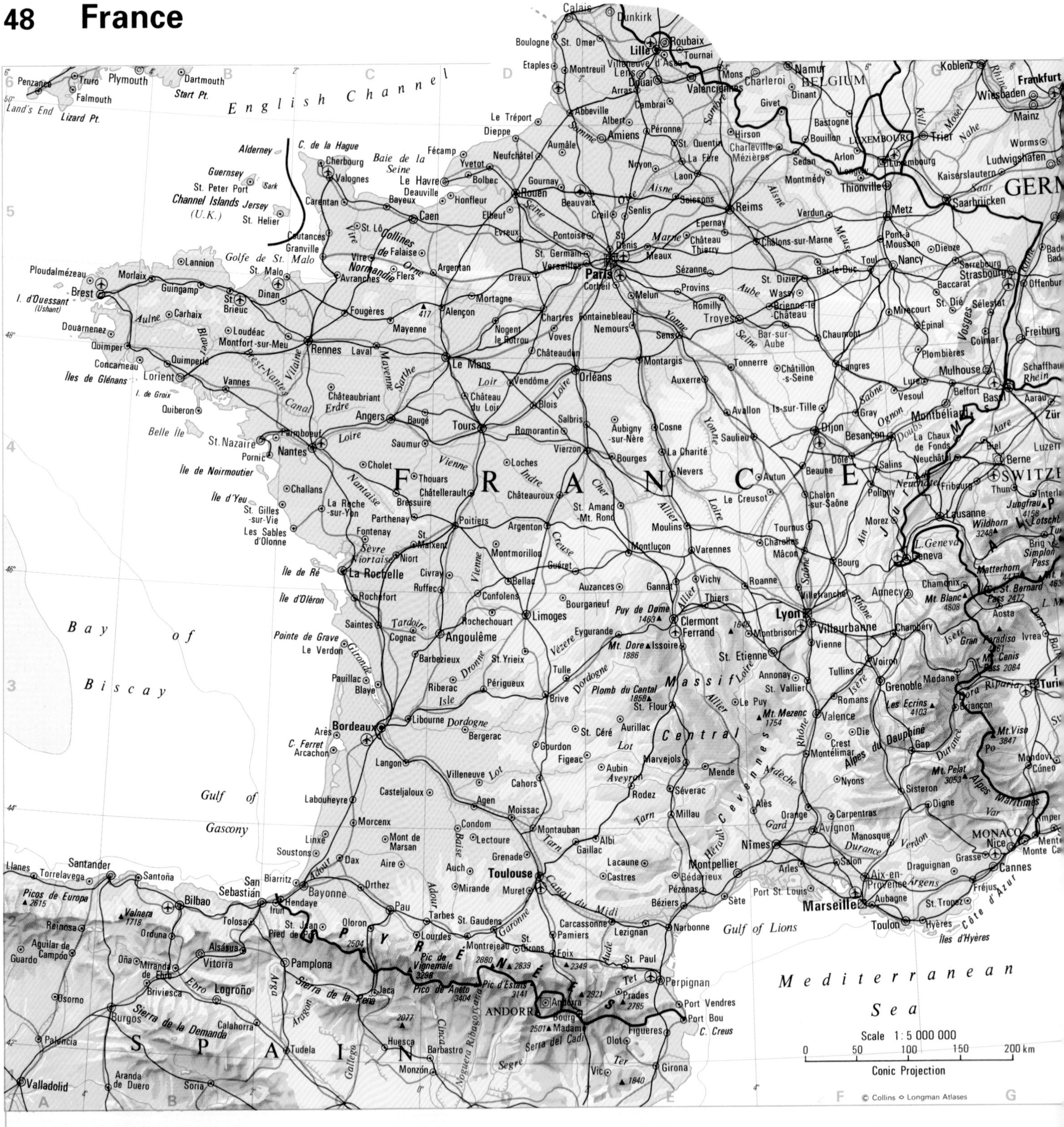

English Channel

CLIMATE GRAPHS

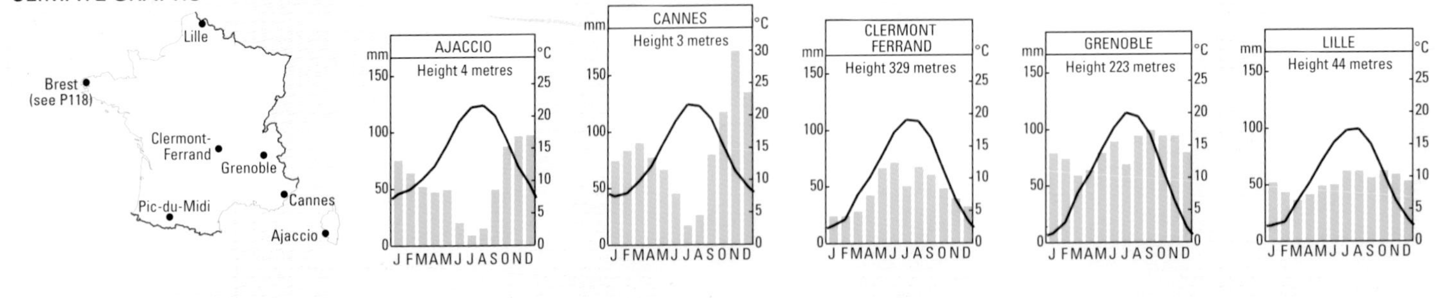

AJACCIO Height 4 metres

CANNES Height 3 metres

CLERMONT FERRAND Height 329 metres

GRENOBLE Height 223 metres

LILLE Height 44 metres

Brest (see P118)

Clermont-Ferrand

Grenoble

Pic-du-Midi

Cannes

Ajaccio

Lille

Scale 1 : 5 000 000

Conic Projection

© Collins ◊ Longman Atlases

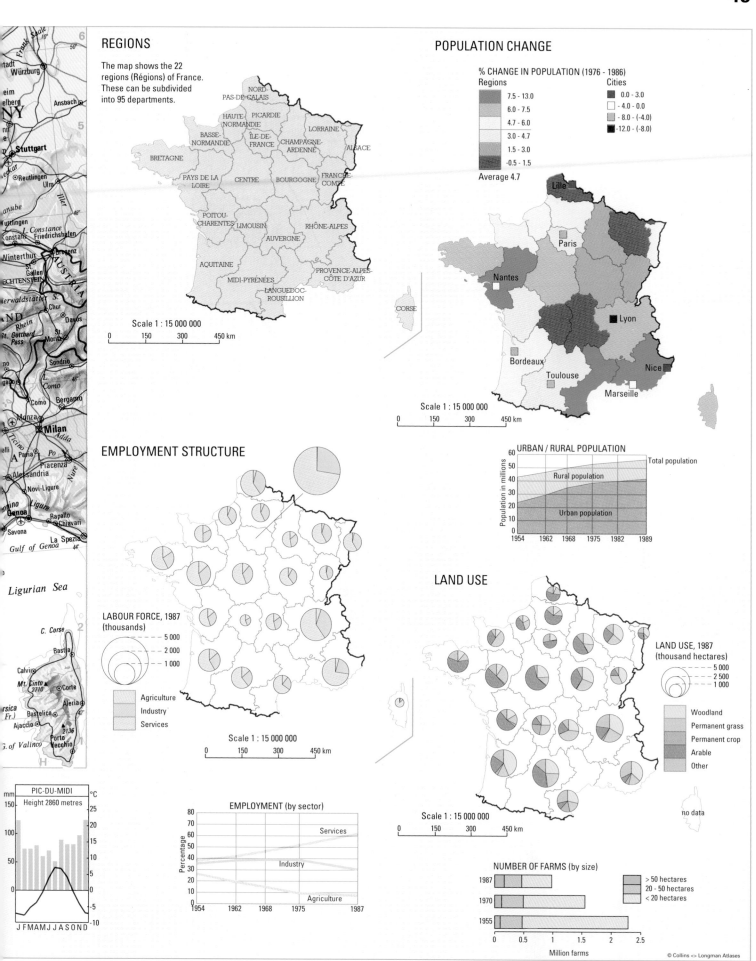

REGIONS

The map shows the 22 regions (Régions) of France. These can be subdivided into 95 departments.

NORD-PAS-DE-CALAIS
HAUTE-NORMANDIE
PICARDIE
LORRAINE
BASSE-NORMANDIE
ÎLE-DE-FRANCE
CHAMPAGNE-ARDENNE
ALSACE
BRETAGNE
PAYS DE LA LOIRE
CENTRE
BOURGOGNE
FRANCHE-COMTÉ
POITOU-CHARENTES
LIMOUSIN
RHÔNE-ALPES
AUVERGNE
AQUITAINE
MIDI-PYRÉNÉES
LANGUEDOC-ROUSILLION
PROVENCE-ALPES-CÔTE D'AZUR
CORSE

Scale 1 : 15 000 000
0   150   300   450 km

POPULATION CHANGE

% CHANGE IN POPULATION (1976 - 1986)

Regions
- 7.5 - 13.0
- 6.0 - 7.5
- 4.7 - 6.0
- 3.0 - 4.7
- 1.5 - 3.0
- -0.5 - 1.5

Average 4.7

Cities
- 0.0 - 3.0
- -4.0 - 0.0
- -8.0 - (-4.0)
- -12.0 - (-8.0)

Lille
Paris
Nantes
Lyon
Bordeaux
Toulouse
Nice
Marseille
CORSE

Scale 1 : 15 000 000
0   150   300   450 km

EMPLOYMENT STRUCTURE

LABOUR FORCE, 1987 (thousands)
- 5 000
- 2 000
- 1 000

- Agriculture
- Industry
- Services

Scale 1 : 15 000 000
0   150   300   450 km

URBAN / RURAL POPULATION

Total population
Rural population
Urban population

Population in millions
60, 50, 40, 30, 20, 10, 0
1954 1962 1968 1975 1982 1989

LAND USE

LAND USE, 1987 (thousand hectares)
- 5 000
- 2 500
- 1 000

- Woodland
- Permanent grass
- Permanent crop
- Arable
- Other

no data

Scale 1 : 15 000 000
0   150   300   450 km

PIC-DU-MIDI
Height 2860 metres

mm
150
100
50

°C
20
15
10
5
0
-5
-10

J F M A M J J A S O N D

EMPLOYMENT (by sector)

Percentage
80, 70, 60, 50, 40, 30, 20, 10

Services
Industry
Agriculture

1954 1962 1968 1975 1987

NUMBER OF FARMS (by size)

1987
1970
1955

- > 50 hectares
- 20 - 50 hectares
- < 20 hectares

0   0.5   1   1.5   2   2.5
Million farms

© Collins <> Longman Atlases

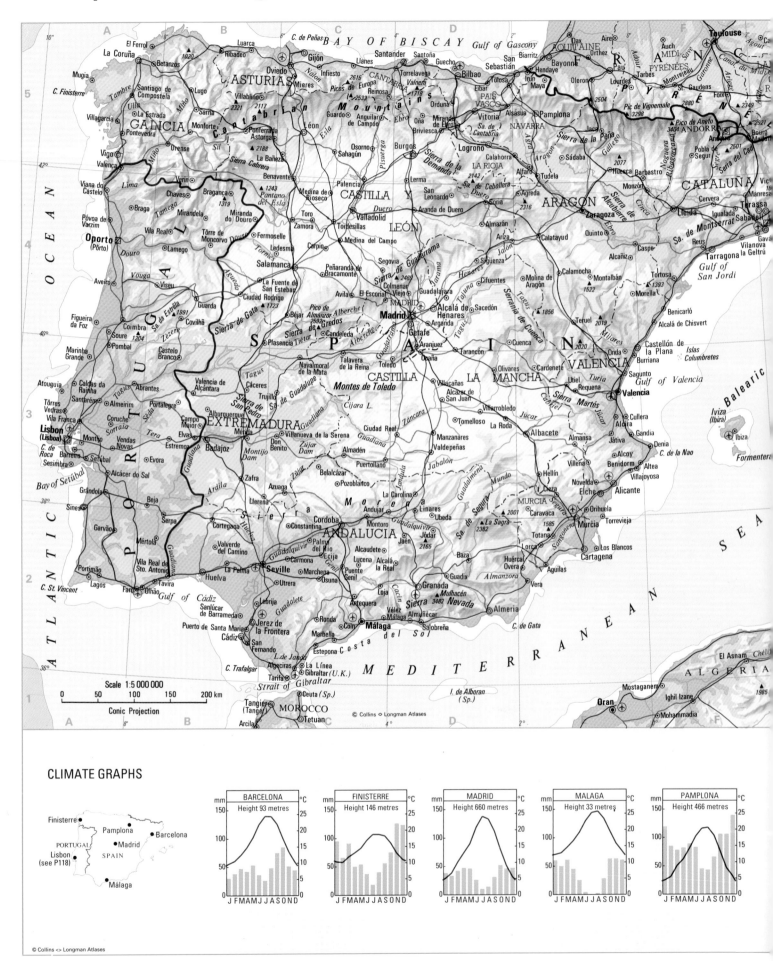

CLIMATE GRAPHS

BARCELONA Height 93 metres

FINISTERRE Height 146 metres

MADRID Height 660 metres

MALAGA Height 33 metres

PAMPLONA Height 466 metres

© Collins ◇ Longman Atlases

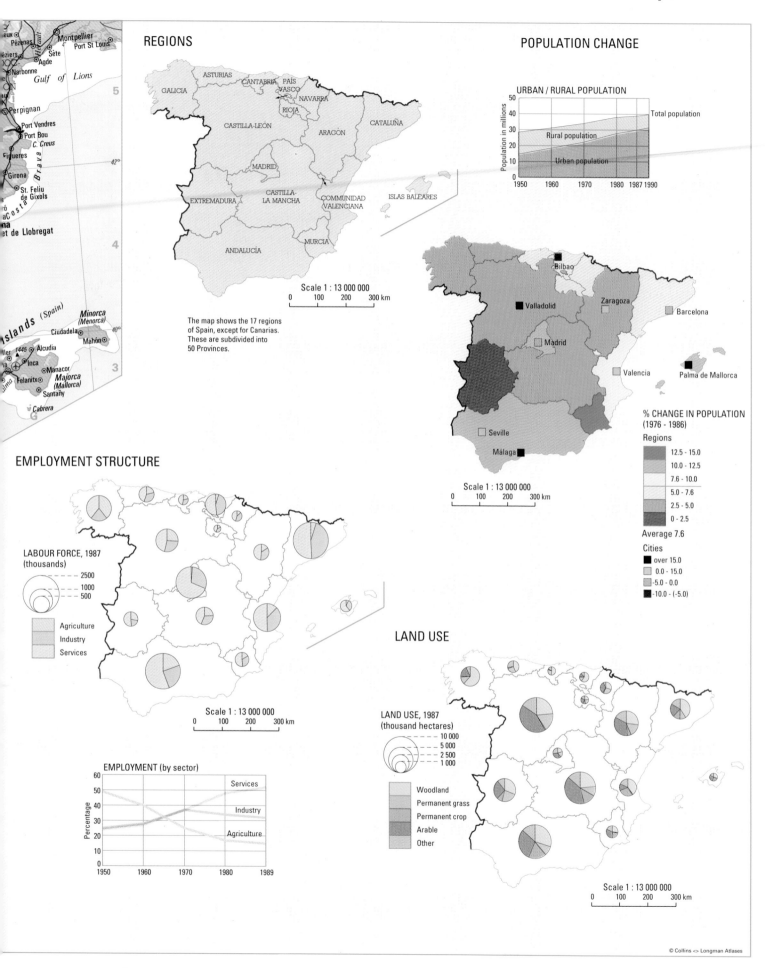

REGIONS

GALICIA · ASTURIAS · CANTABRIA · PAÍS VASCO · NAVARRA · RIOJA · CASTILLA-LEÓN · ARAGÓN · CATALUÑA · MADRID · EXTREMADURA · CASTILLA-LA MANCHA · COMUNIDAD VALENCIANA · ISLAS BALEARES · ANDALUCÍA · MURCIA

Scale 1 : 13 000 000
0   100   200   300 km

The map shows the 17 regions of Spain, except for Canarias. These are subdivided into 50 Provinces.

POPULATION CHANGE

URBAN / RURAL POPULATION

Total population
Rural population
Urban population

Population in millions
1950 1960 1970 1980 1987 1990

Bilbao · Valladolid · Zaragoza · Barcelona · Madrid · Valencia · Palma de Mallorca · Seville · Málaga

Scale 1 : 13 000 000
0   100   200   300 km

% CHANGE IN POPULATION (1976 - 1986)
Regions
- 12.5 - 15.0
- 10.0 - 12.5
- 7.6 - 10.0
- 5.0 - 7.6
- 2.5 - 5.0
- 0 - 2.5

Average 7.6

Cities
- over 15.0
- 0.0 - 15.0
- -5.0 - 0.0
- -10.0 - (-5.0)

EMPLOYMENT STRUCTURE

LABOUR FORCE, 1987 (thousands)
- 2500
- 1000
- 500

- Agriculture
- Industry
- Services

Scale 1 : 13 000 000
0   100   200   300 km

EMPLOYMENT (by sector)

Services
Industry
Agriculture

Percentage
1950 1960 1970 1980 1989

LAND USE

LAND USE, 1987 (thousand hectares)
- 10 000
- 5 000
- 2 500
- 1 000

- Woodland
- Permanent grass
- Permanent crop
- Arable
- Other

Scale 1 : 13 000 000
0   100   200   300 km

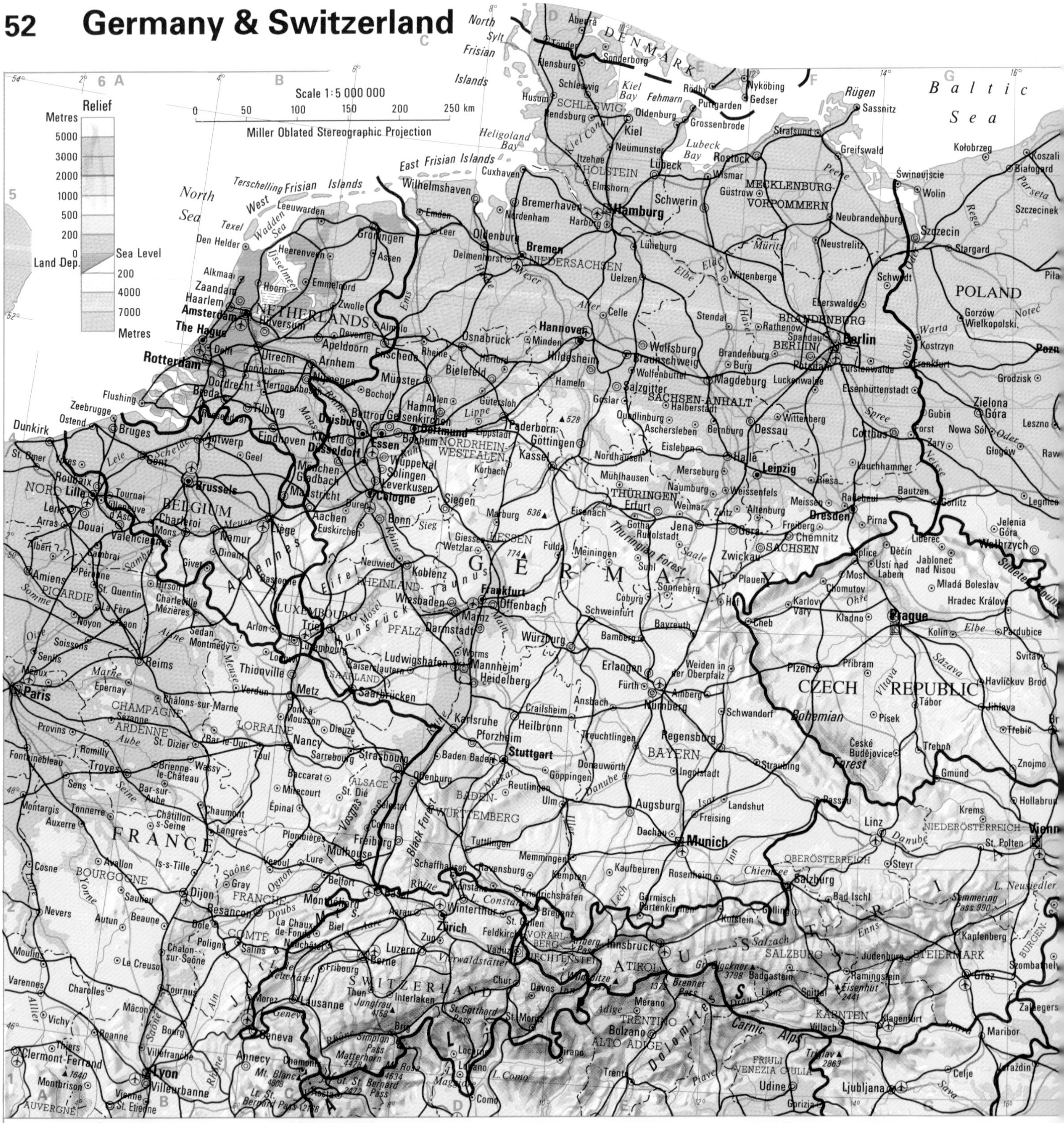

Relief

Metres	
5000	
3000	
2000	
1000	
500	
200	
0	Sea Level
	Land Dep.
200	
4000	
7000	
Metres	

Scale 1:5 000 000

0 50 100 150 200 250 km

Miller Oblated Stereographic Projection

North Sea · Frisian Islands · East Frisian Islands · West Frisian Islands · Heligoland Bay · Wadden Sea · Baltic Sea

NETHERLANDS · BELGIUM · LUXEMBOURG · FRANCE · GERMANY · SWITZERLAND · CZECH REPUBLIC · POLAND · DENMARK

Amsterdam · The Hague · Rotterdam · Brussels · Paris · Hamburg · Bremen · Hannover · Berlin · Cologne · Frankfurt · Stuttgart · Munich · Zürich · Prague · Wien

CLIMATE GRAPHS

Kiel · Berlin (see P118) · Cologne · Coburg · Freiburg · Munich

COBURG Height 336 metres
J F M A M J J A S O N D

COLOGNE Height 45 metres
J F M A M J J A S O N D

FREIBURG Height 259 metres
J F M A M J J A S O N D

KIEL Height 3 metres
J F M A M J J A S O N D

MUNICH Height 524 metres
J F M A M J J A S O N D

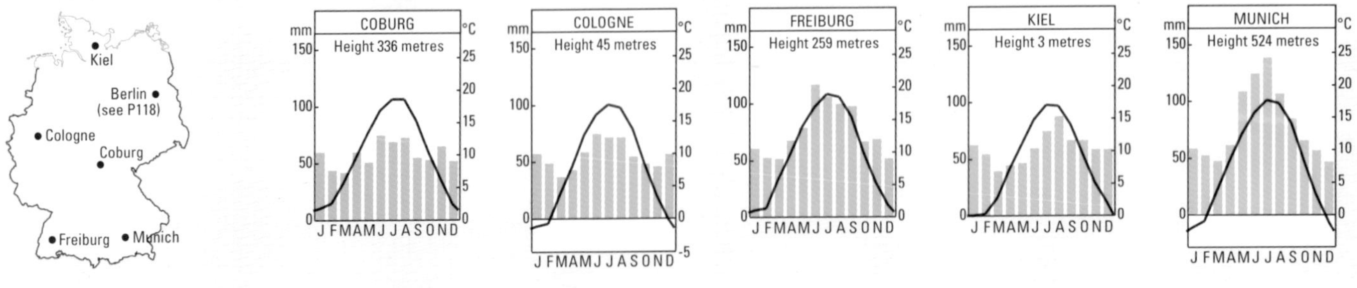

© Collins <> Longman Atlases

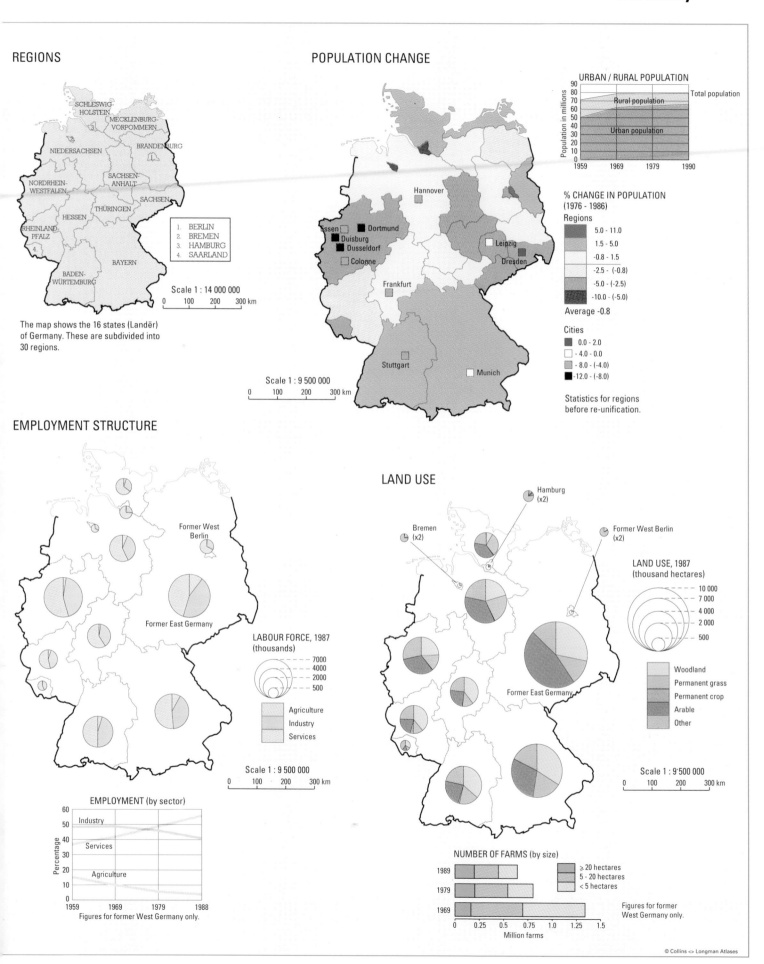

REGIONS

SCHLESWIG-HOLSTEIN

MECKLENBURG-VORPOMMERN

NIEDERSACHSEN

BRANDENBURG

NORDRHEIN-WESTFALEN

SACHSEN-ANHALT

SACHSEN

HESSEN

THÜRINGEN

RHEINLAND-PFALZ

BAYERN

BADEN-WÜRTEMBURG

1. BERLIN
2. BREMEN
3. HAMBURG
4. SAARLAND

Scale 1 : 14 000 000

0   100   200   300 km

The map shows the 16 states (Landër)
of Germany. These are subdivided into
30 regions.

POPULATION CHANGE

Hannover

Essen   Dortmund
Duisburg
Dusseldorf
Cologne

Leipzig

Dresden

Frankfurt

Stuttgart

Munich

Scale 1 : 9 500 000

0   100   200   300 km

URBAN / RURAL POPULATION

Total population

Rural population

Urban population

1959   1969   1979   1990

% CHANGE IN POPULATION
(1976 - 1986)

Regions

- 5.0 - 11.0
- 1.5 - 5.0
- -0.8 - 1.5
- -2.5 - (-0.8)
- -5.0 - (-2.5)
- -10.0 - (-5.0)

Average -0.8

Cities

- 0.0 - 2.0
- -4.0 - 0.0
- -8.0 - (-4.0)
- -12.0 - (-8.0)

Statistics for regions
before re-unification.

EMPLOYMENT STRUCTURE

Former West Berlin

Former East Germany

LABOUR FORCE, 1987
(thousands)

- 7000
- 4000
- 2000
- 500

Agriculture

Industry

Services

Scale 1 : 9 500 000

0   100   200   300 km

EMPLOYMENT (by sector)

Industry

Services

Agriculture

1959   1969   1979   1988

Figures for former West Germany only.

LAND USE

Hamburg
(x2)

Bremen
(x2)

Former West Berlin
(x2)

Former East Germany

LAND USE, 1987
(thousand hectares)

- 10 000
- 7 000
- 4 000
- 2 000
- 500

- Woodland
- Permanent grass
- Permanent crop
- Arable
- Other

Scale 1 : 9 500 000

0   100   200   300 km

NUMBER OF FARMS (by size)

1989

1979

1969

- ≥ 20 hectares
- 5 - 20 hectares
- < 5 hectares

0   0.25   0.5   0.75   1.0   1.25   1.5
Million farms

Figures for former
West Germany only.

POPULATION CHANGE

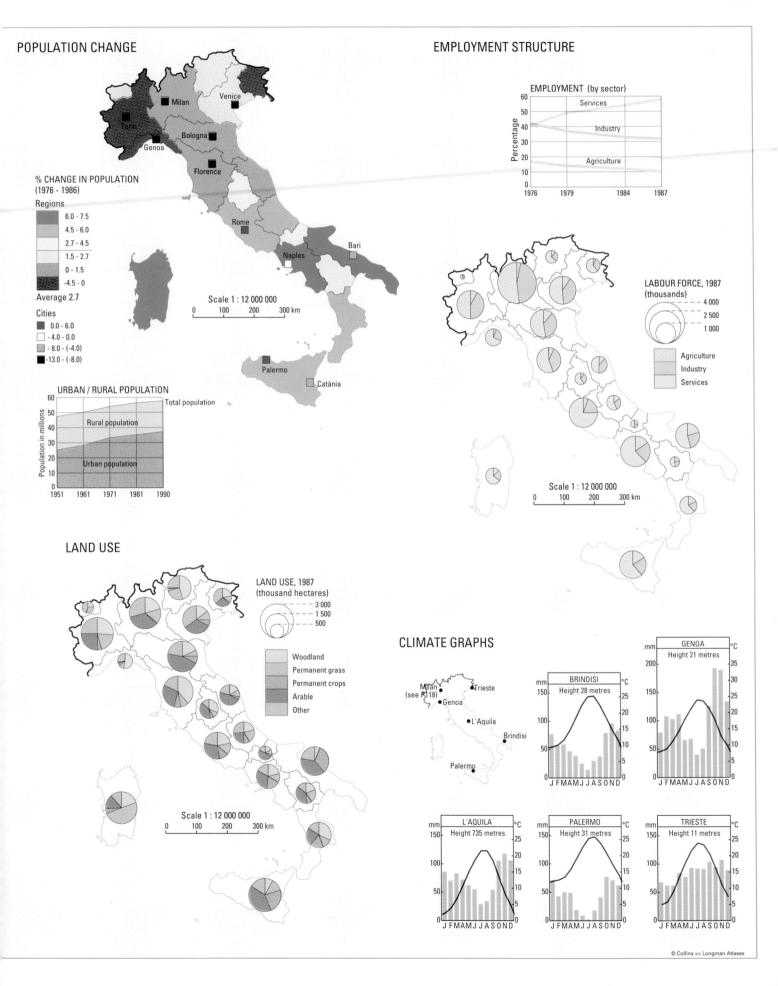

% CHANGE IN POPULATION
(1976 - 1986)
Regions

- 6.0 - 7.5
- 4.5 - 6.0
- 2.7 - 4.5
- 1.5 - 2.7
- 0 - 1.5
- -4.5 - 0

Average 2.7

Cities

- 0.0 - 6.0
- -4.0 - 0.0
- -8.0 - (-4.0)
- -13.0 - (-8.0)

Scale 1 : 12 000 000
0   100   200   300 km

URBAN / RURAL POPULATION

Population in millions

Total population
Rural population
Urban population

1951   1961   1971   1981   1990

LAND USE

LAND USE, 1987
(thousand hectares)

- 3 000
- 1 500
- 500

- Woodland
- Permanent grass
- Permanent crops
- Arable
- Other

Scale 1 : 12 000 000
0   100   200   300 km

EMPLOYMENT STRUCTURE

EMPLOYMENT (by sector)

Percentage

Services
Industry
Agriculture

1976   1979   1984   1987

LABOUR FORCE, 1987
(thousands)

- 4 000
- 2 500
- 1 000

- Agriculture
- Industry
- Services

Scale 1 : 12 000 000
0   100   200   300 km

CLIMATE GRAPHS

Milan (see P.118)
Trieste
Genoa
L'Aquila
Brindisi
Palermo

BRINDISI
Height 28 metres
mm   °C
J F M A M J J A S O N D

GENOA
Height 21 metres
mm   °C
J F M A M J J A S O N D

L'AQUILA
Height 735 metres
mm   °C
J F M A M J J A S O N D

PALERMO
Height 31 metres
mm   °C
J F M A M J J A S O N D

TRIESTE
Height 11 metres
mm   °C
J F M A M J J A S O N D

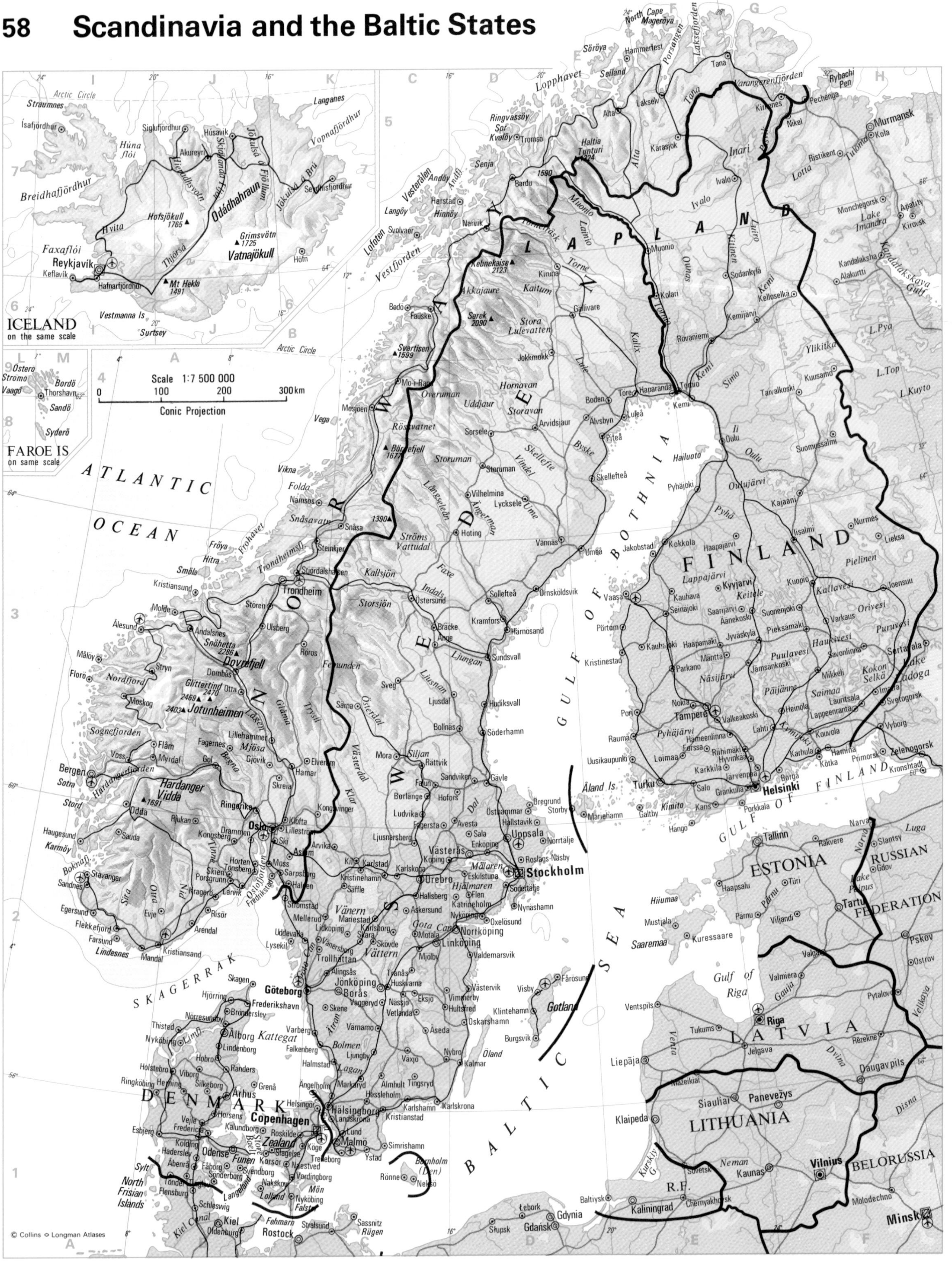
ICELAND
on the same scale
FAROE IS
on same scale
Scale 1:7 500 000
0 100 200 300 km
Conic Projection
Arctic Circle
ATLANTIC
OCEAN
NORWAY
SWEDEN
FINLAND
LAPLAND
ESTONIA
LATVIA
LITHUANIA
BELORUSSIA
RUSSIAN FEDERATION
DENMARK
R.F.
GULF OF BOTHNIA
GULF OF FINLAND
BALTIC SEA
SKAGERRAK
Kattegat
Gulf of Riga
Reykjavík
Keflavík
Hafnarfjördur
Akureyri
Húsavík
Siglufjördur
Ísafjördur
Seydisfjördur
Höfn
Vatnajökull
Hofsjökull 1765
Grimsvötn 1725
Mt Hekla 1491
Ódádhahraun
Faxaflói
Breidhafjördhur
Húna flói
Vopnafjördhur
Langanes
Straumnes
Vestmanna Is
Surtsey
Thorshavn
Oslo
Stockholm
Helsinki
Copenhagen
Tallinn
Riga
Vilnius
Minsk
Bergen
Trondheim
Stavanger
Kristiansand
Göteborg
Malmö
Tampere
Turku
Oulu
Tromsø
Narvik
Kiruna
Murmansk
Kaliningrad
Gdańsk
Gdynia
Kiel
Rostock
Klaipeda
Kaunas
Tartu
Daugavpils
Ålborg
Århus
Odense
Gotland
Öland
Bornholm (Den)
Åland Is.
Hiiumaa
Saaremaa
Zealand
Funen
Lolland
Falster
Sylt
North Frisian Islands
Lofoten
Vesterålen
Kebnekaise 2123
Sarek 2090
Svartisen 1599
Börgefjell 1677
Snöhetta 2286
Dovrefjell
Glittertind 2470
Jotunheimen
Hardanger Vidda
Sognefjorden
Vänern
Vättern
Mälaren
Siljan
Lake Ladoga
Saimaa
Päijänne
Inari
Lake Imandra
North Cape
Magerøya
Varangerfjorden
Rybachi Pen
© Collins ○ Longman Atlases

Relief

Metres
5000
3000
2000
1000
500
200
0
Sea Level
Land Dep.
200
4000
7000

I C N Severnaya Zemlya
Komsomolets
October Revolution
Bolshevik
C. Chelyuskin

Taymyr Peninsula
Byrranga Mts.
Pyasina
Upper
Taymyr
L.Taymyr
Khatangskiy G.
Olenekskiy Gulf
Nordvik
Khatanga
Anabar
Ust Olenek
Olenek
Bulun
Lena
Tiksi
Kazachye

L A P T E V   S E A

New Siberian Is
Kotelnyy
Bolshoi Lyakhovskiy
Novaya Siberia

E A S T   S I B E R I A N   S E A

Ambarchik
Arctic Circle
Anadyr
180°

G. of Tona
Yana
Verkhoyansk
Indigirka
Srednе Kolymskaya
Kolyma
Omolon
Anadyr

Cherskogo Range
Mt Chen 2682
Mt Pobeda 3147
Oymyakon

Koryak Range
Gizhiga
Penzhina
Kamenskoye
Palana

B E R I N G   S E A

Norilsk
Kamen 2037
Putoran Mts
Tura

Central Siberian Plateau

Lower Tunguska
Stony Tunguska
Markha
Olenek
Vilyuysk
Vilyuy
Yakutsk
Aldan
Amga
Ust'Maya
Okhotsk

Kamchatka Peninsula
Ust Kamchatsk
Klyuchevskaya
Petropavlovsk-Kamchatskiy

R U S S I A N   F E D E R A T I O N

Yeniseysk
Angara
Chuna
Ust Kut
Kirensk
Olekminsk
Lena
Aldan
Aldan
Olekma
Mt Topko 1906
Dzhugdzhur Range
Ayan
Shantar Is

S E A   O F   O K H O T S K

Kansk
Tayshet
Bratsk
Bratsk Resr
Nizhneudinsk
Tulun
Cheremkhovo
Usolye Sibirskoye
Angarsk
Irkutsk
Skalinnyy 2482
Stanovoy Range
Skovorodino
Zeya
Svobodnyy
Komsomolsk-na-Amur
Nikolayevsk-na-Amur
Amgun
Aleksandrovsk Sakhalinskiy
Poronaysk
Sakhalin

Krasnoyarsk
Eastern Sayan
Munku Sardyk 3492
Khöbsögöl Dalai
Kyzyl
u Ola Ra
Ubsa Nur
L. Baikal
Ulan-Ude
Petrovsk
Zabaykal'skiy
Yablonovy Range
Chita
Vitim
Shilka
Blagoveshchensk
Amur
Birobidzhan
Zeya
Khabarovsk
Sovetskaya Gavan
Uglegorsk
Gulf of Tartary
Yuzhno-Sakhalinsk

Kuril Islands

La Perouse Str.
Wakkanai
Hokkaido
Asahi daki 2290
Sapporo
Hakodate

Ulan Bator
Undur Khan

M O N G O L I A
Gobi
Altai

INNER MONGOLIA (NEI MONGGOL)
MONGOLIA (MONGGOL)

Da Hinggan Ling

C H I N A

Sikhote-Alin Range
L.Khanka
Ussuriysk
Olga
Vladivostok
Nakhodka

Harbin
Mudanjiang
Songhua Jiang
Nen Jiang

Jilin
Changchun
Fushun
Shenyang
Anshan
Liaodong Bay

J A P A N

Honshu
Niigata
Tokyo
Yokohama
Fujiyama 3775
Kyoto
Nagoya
Kobe
Osaka

S E A   O F   J A P A N

NORTH KOREA
Pyongyang
Korea Bay

SOUTH KOREA
Seoul

Baotou
Hohhot
Zhangjiakou
Beijing
Korea Str.

Bering Str.
De Long Str.
Wrangel I.
Chuckchee Pen
Gulf of Anadyr

Armenia, Azerbaijan, Belorussia, Georgia, Kazakhstan, Kirghizia, Moldavia, Russian Fed., Tajikistan, Turkmenistan, Ukraine, Uzbekistan

ETHNIC GROUPS

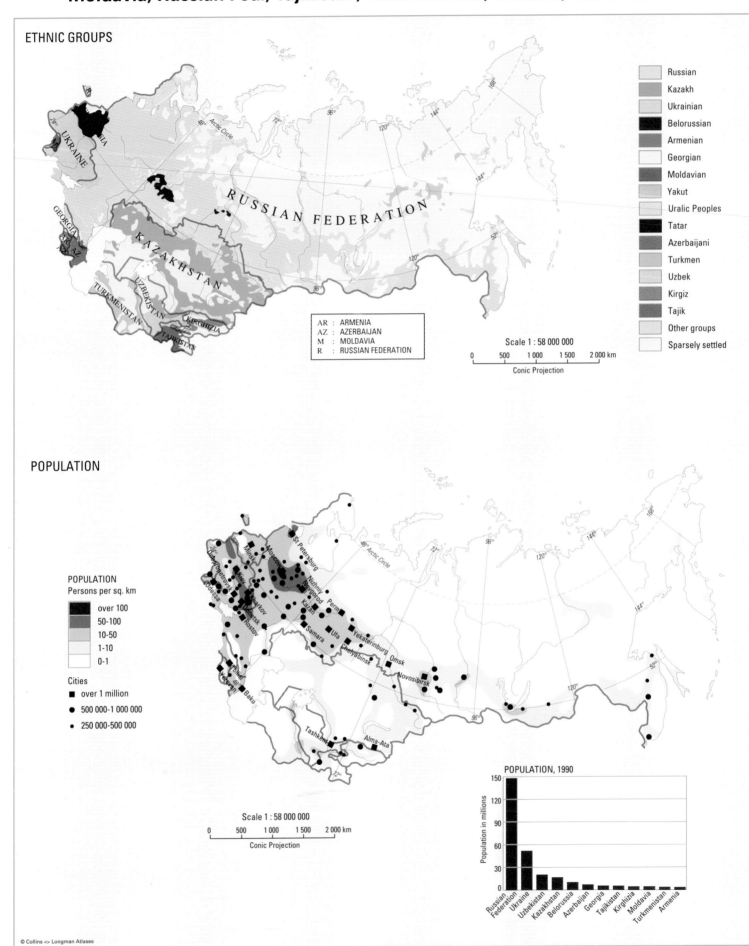

Russian
Kazakh
Ukrainian
Belorussian
Armenian
Georgian
Moldavian
Yakut
Uralic Peoples
Tatar
Azerbaijani
Turkmen
Uzbek
Kirgiz
Tajik
Other groups
Sparsely settled

AR : ARMENIA
AZ : AZERBAIJAN
M : MOLDAVIA
R : RUSSIAN FEDERATION

Scale 1 : 58 000 000

0   500   1 000   1 500   2 000 km

Conic Projection

POPULATION

POPULATION
Persons per sq. km

over 100
50-100
10-50
1-10
0-1

Cities

over 1 million
500 000-1 000 000
250 000-500 000

Scale 1 : 58 000 000

0   500   1 000   1 500   2 000 km

Conic Projection

POPULATION, 1990

Population in millions

Russian Federation
Ukraine
Uzbekistan
Kazakhstan
Belorussia
Azerbaijan
Georgia
Tajikistan
Kirghizia
Moldavia
Turkmenistan
Armenia

RESOURCES AND INDUSTRY

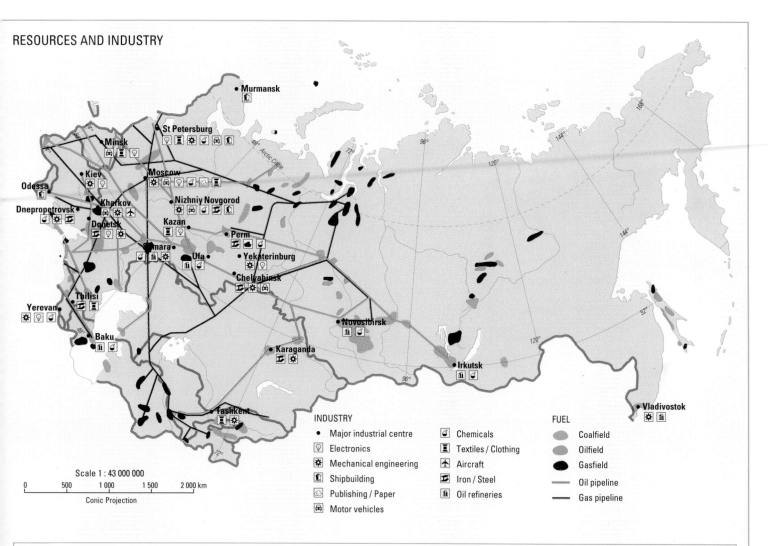

INDUSTRY

- • Major industrial centre
- Electronics
- Mechanical engineering
- Shipbuilding
- Publishing / Paper
- Motor vehicles
- Chemicals
- Textiles / Clothing
- Aircraft
- Iron / Steel
- Oil refineries

FUEL

- Coalfield
- Oilfield
- Gasfield
- Oil pipeline
- Gas pipeline

Scale 1 : 43 000 000

0   500   1 000   1 500   2 000 km

Conic Projection

FACTfile

COUNTRY	POPULATION (millions)	AREA (sq. km)	CAPITAL CITY	MAJOR AGRICULTURAL PRODUCTS (1000 tonnes)	MAJOR MINERAL RESOURCES
ARMENIA	3.3	30 000	Yerevan	Vegetables, 567; Grain, 375; Fruit, 241; Grapes, 205	Copper, zinc, aluminium, molybdenum, granite, marble
AZERBAIJAN	7.1	87 000	Baku	Grain, 1 417; Cotton, 616; Grapes, 1 247; Vegetables, 880	Oil, iron, aluminium, copper, lead, zinc, precious metals
BELORUSSIA	10.3	208 000	Minsk	Grain, 6 922; Meat, 1169; Milk, 7 501; Potatoes, 7 708	Peat, rock salt
GEORGIA	5.5	70 000	Tbilisi	Grain, 714; Tea, 458; Citrus fruit, 439; Potatoes, 326; Other vegetables, 641	Manganese, oil, marble, cement
KAZAKHSTAN	16.7	2 717 000	Alma-Ata	Grain, 22 600; Potatoes, 2 300; Milk, 5 300; Vegetables, 1 400	Coal, tungsten, copper, lead, zinc, oil, manganese
KIRGHIZIA	4.4	199 000	Bishkek	Grain, 1 758; Vegetables, 548; Meat, 220; Milk, 1 063	Figures not available
MOLDAVIA	4.4	34 000	Kishinev	Grain, 3 052; Sugar beet, 2 272; Grapes, 1 120; Vegetables, 1 281	Lignite, phosphorites, gypsum
RUSSIAN FED.	148.0	17 075 000	Moscow	Figures not available	Iron ore, coal, oil, gold, platinum, copper, zinc, lead, tin
TAJIKISTAN	5.3	143 000	Dushanbe	Cotton, 963; Vegetables, 556; Fruit, 208; Grapes, 178	Coal, lead, zinc, oil, uranium, radium
TURKMENISTAN	3.6	488 000	Ashkhabad	Cotton, 1 341; Grain, 435; Vegetables, 373; Grapes, 164	Oil, coal, sulphur, salt
UKRAINE	51.8	604 000	Kiev	Grain, 47 400; Sugar beet, 48 100; Milk, 24 000; Potatoes, 13 500	Coal, iron ore, salt, oil
UZBEKISTAN	20.3	447 000	Tashkent	Cotton, 5 365; Vegetables, 2 760; Grain, 2 199; Grapes, 640	Oil, coal, copper

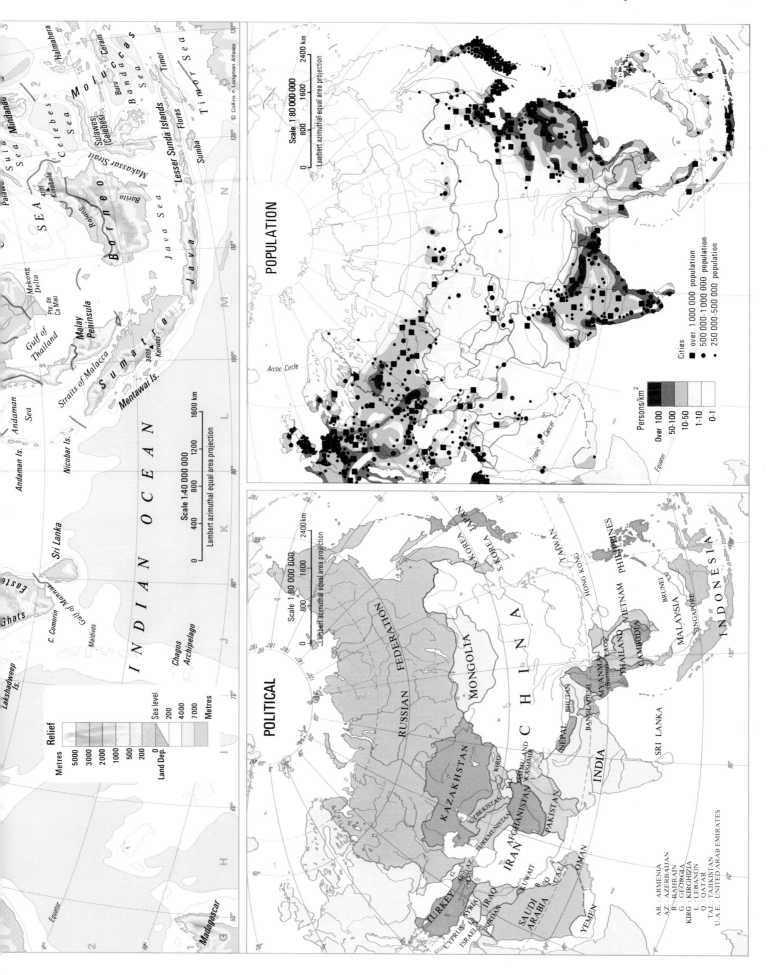

POPULATION

Cities
- ■ over 1 000 000 population
- ● 500 000-1 000 000 population
- • 250 000-500 000 population

Persons/km²
Over 100
50-100
10-50
1-10
0-1

Arctic Circle

Tropic of Cancer

Equator

Scale 1:80 000 000

0 800 1600 2400 km

Lambert azimuthal equal area projection

POLITICAL

RUSSIAN FEDERATION

MONGOLIA

CHINA

KAZAKHSTAN

UZBEKISTAN

TURKMENISTAN

AFGHANISTAN

PAKISTAN

IRAN

INDIA

NEPAL

BHUTAN

BANGLADESH

MYANMAR (Burma)

THAILAND

LAOS

VIETNAM

CAMBODIA

SRI LANKA

MALAYSIA

BRUNEI

SINGAPORE

INDONESIA

PHILIPPINES

TAIWAN

HONG KONG

N.KOREA

S. KOREA

JAPAN

TURKEY

CYPRUS

SYRIA

IRAQ

LEBANON

ISRAEL

JORDAN

SAUDI ARABIA

KUWAIT

BAHRAIN

QATAR

U.A.E.

OMAN

YEMEN

JAMMU and KASHMIR

KIRG.

AR. : ARMENIA
AZ. : AZERBAIJAN
B. : BAHRAIN
G. : GEORGIA
KIRG. : KIRGHIZIA
L. : LEBANON
Q. : QATAR
TAJ. : TAJIKISTAN
U.A.E. : UNITED ARAB EMIRATES

Scale 1:80 000 000

0 800 1600 2400 km

Lambert azimuthal equal area projection

SOUTH CHINA SEA

Palawan

Halmahera

Ceram

Buru

Timor

Sula

Mindanao

Celebes Sea

Moluccas

Banda Sea

Timor Sea

Sulawesi (Celebes)

Lesser Sunda Islands

Flores

Sumba

Java Sea

Makassar Strait

Rantuk

Borito

Kinabalu 4101

Borneo

Mekong Delta

Pte. de Ca Mau

Gulf of Thailand

Malay Peninsula

Straits of Malacca

Sumatra

Mentawai Is.

Kerinci 3805

Java

Andaman Sea

Andaman Is.

Nicobar Is.

Sri Lanka

Gulf of Mannar

C. Comorin

Maldives

Lakshadweep Is.

Eastern Ghats

Chagos Archipelago

INDIAN OCEAN

Madagascar

Equator

Scale 1:40 000 000

0 400 800 1200 1600 km

Lambert azimuthal equal area projection

Relief

Metres
5000
3000
2000
1000
500
200
0
Land Dep.

Sea level
200
4000
7000
Metres

© Collins ○ Longman Atlases

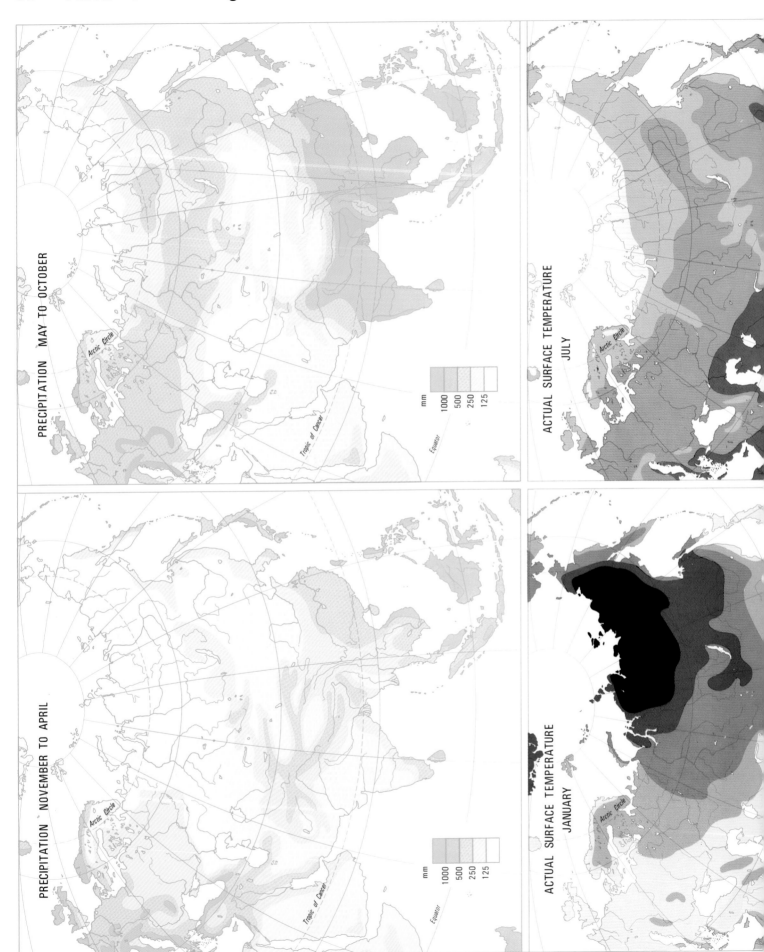

PRECIPITATION MAY TO OCTOBER

Arctic Circle

Tropic of Cancer

Equator

mm
1000
500
250
125

PRECIPITATION NOVEMBER TO APRIL

Arctic Circle

Tropic of Cancer

Equator

mm
1000
500
250
125

ACTUAL SURFACE TEMPERATURE
JULY

Arctic Circle

ACTUAL SURFACE TEMPERATURE
JANUARY

Arctic Circle

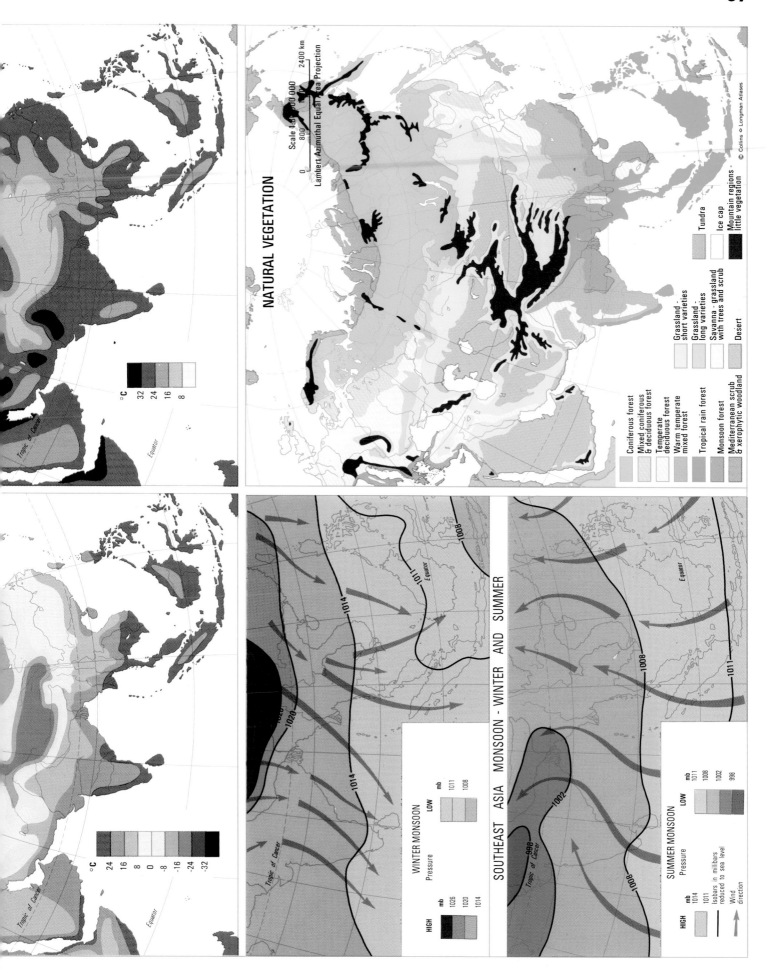

NATURAL VEGETATION

Scale 1:50 000 000
2400 km
800
0
Lambert Azimuthal Equal Area Projection

© Collins - Longman Atlases

Coniferous forest

Mixed coniferous
& deciduous forest

Temperate
deciduous forest

Warm temperate
mixed forest

Tropical rain forest

Monsoon forest

Mediterranean scrub
& xerophytic woodland

Grassland -
short varieties

Grassland -
long varieties

Savanna - grassland
with trees and scrub

Desert

Tundra

Ice cap

Mountain regions -
little vegetation

°C
32
24
16
8

°C
24
16
8
0
-8
-16
-24
-32

SOUTHEAST ASIA MONSOON - WINTER AND SUMMER

WINTER MONSOON

Pressure

HIGH

mb
1026
1020
1014

LOW

mb
1011
1008

1008
1011
1014
1020
1014

Equator

Tropic of Cancer

SUMMER MONSOON

Pressure

HIGH

mb
1014
1011

LOW

mb
1011
1008
1002
998

Isobars in millibars
reduced to sea level

Wind
direction

1008
1011
1008
1002
998

Equator

Tropic of Cancer

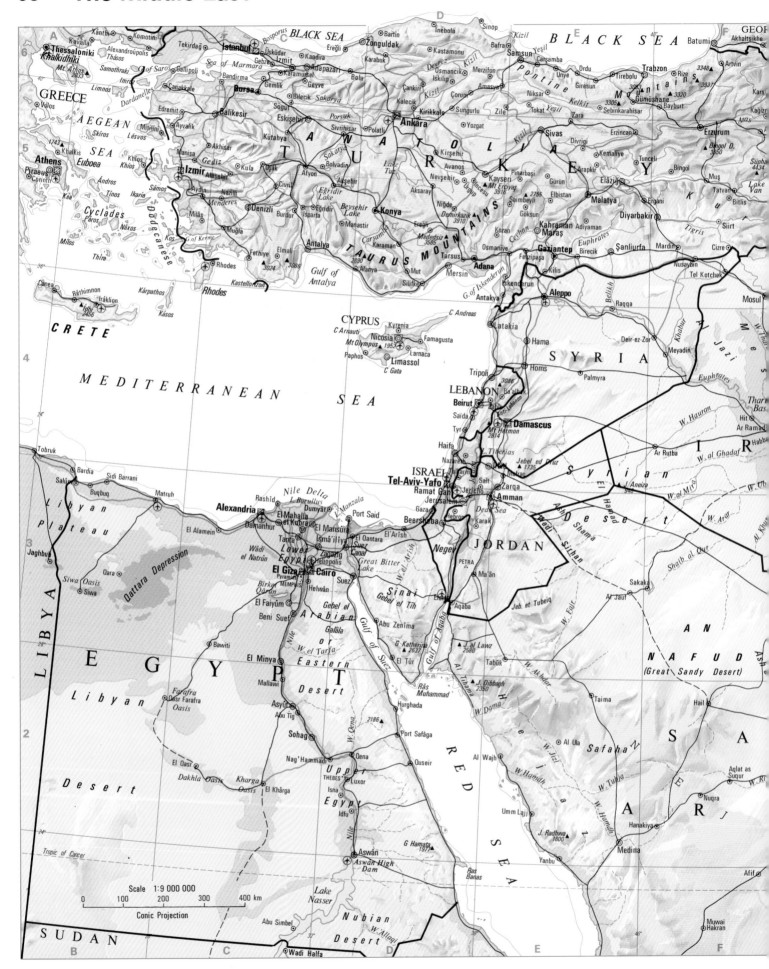

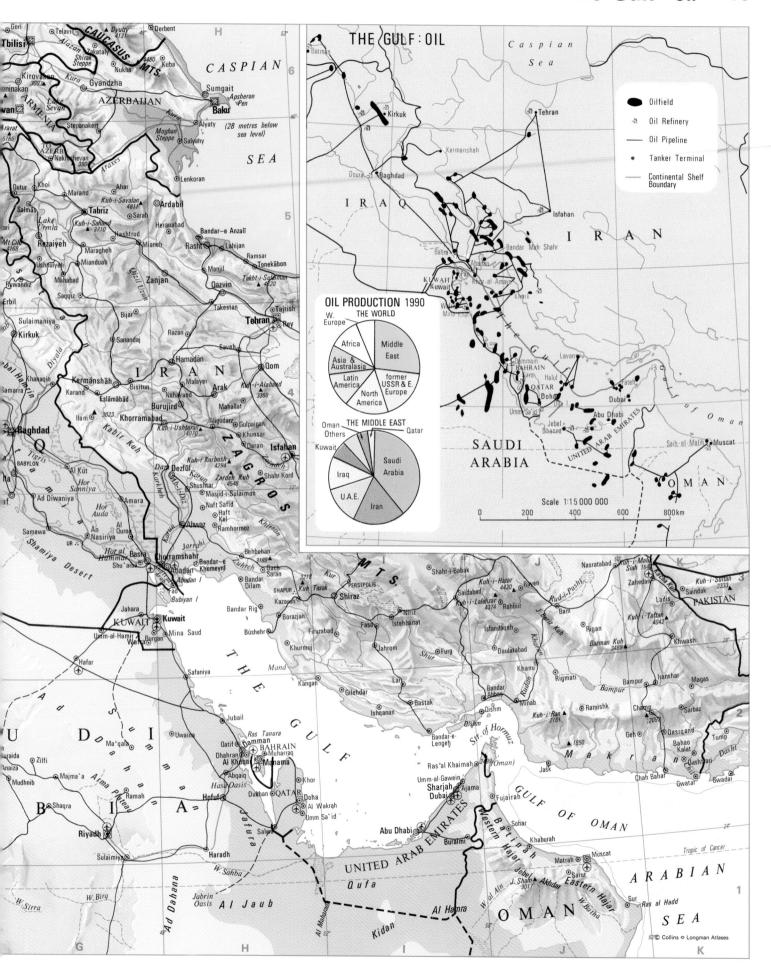

THE GULF: OIL

Legend:
- Oilfield
- Oil Refinery
- Oil Pipeline
- Tanker Terminal
- Continental Shelf Boundary

OIL PRODUCTION 1990

THE WORLD
- W. Europe
- Africa
- Asia & Australasia
- Latin America
- North America
- Middle East
- former USSR & E. Europe

THE MIDDLE EAST
- Oman
- Others
- Qatar
- Kuwait
- Iraq
- U.A.E.
- Iran
- Saudi Arabia

Scale 1:15 000 000
0 200 400 600 800km

FACT*file* — India

Total population	796.60 million
Total area	3 288 000 sq km
GDP per head	335 US$

EMPLOYMENT

Primary	66.4%
Secondary	12.6%
Tertiary	21.0%

PRINCIPAL IMPORTS

Non-electric machinery	19.1%
Fuels / Lubricants	18.2%
Precious stones	8.9%
Iron / Steel	5.7%

PRINCIPAL EXPORTS

Precious stones / Jewellery	16.6%
Clothing	11.4%
Machinery & metal products	9.1%
Leather & products	7.3%

NATURAL RESOURCES

Coal   Iron ore   Gold   Diamonds

FACT*file* — Pakistan

Total population	105.40 million
Total area	796 095 sq km
GDP per head	350 US$

EMPLOYMENT

Primary	49.5%
Secondary	19.2%
Tertiary	31.3%

PRINCIPAL IMPORTS

Non-electric machinery	17.6%
Mineral oils	16.2%
Chemicals	9.3%
Transport equipment	8.6%

PRINCIPAL EXPORTS

Raw cotton	16.2%
Cotton yarn	13.7%
Cotton fabric	9.3%
Rice	8.6%

NATURAL RESOURCES

Coal   Iron ore   Copper   Natural Gas

FACT*file* — Bangladesh

Total population	113.34 million
Total area	143 998 sq km
GDP per head	170 US$

EMPLOYMENT

Primary	56.5%
Secondary	12.0%
Tertiary	31.5%

PRINCIPAL IMPORTS

Minerals products	15.9%
Textiles	14.2%
Vegetable products	12.4%
Base metals	11.0%

PRINCIPAL EXPORTS

Clothing	33.8%
Prawns & shrimps	11.1%
Leather & products	10.6%
Raw jute	6.6%

NATURAL RESOURCES

Natural Gas   Crude oil

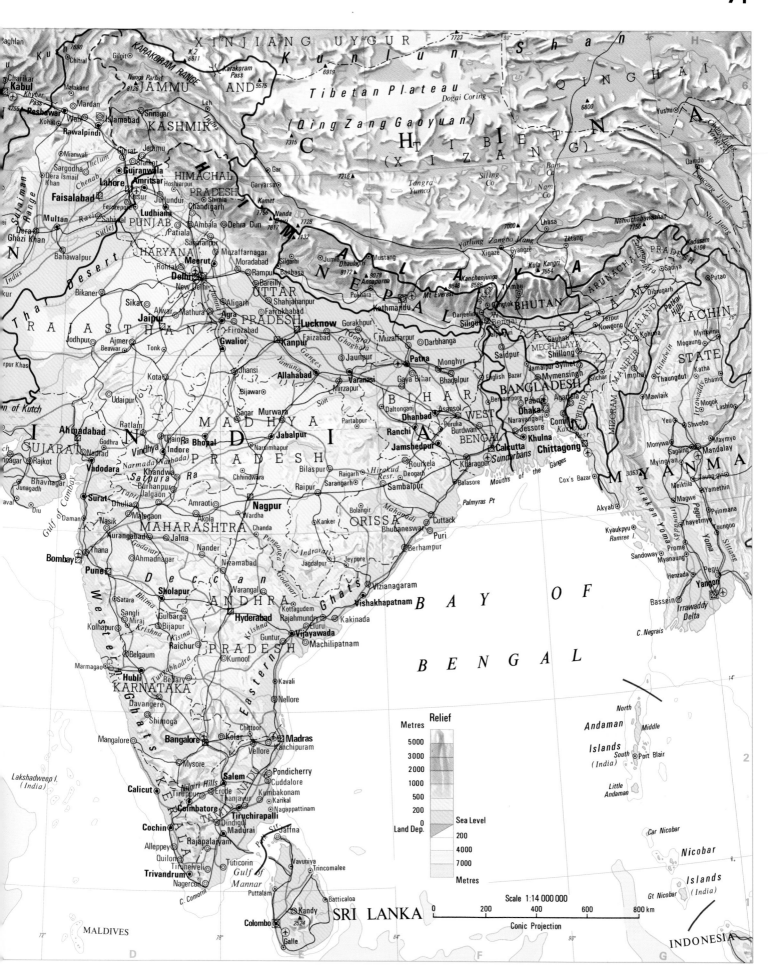

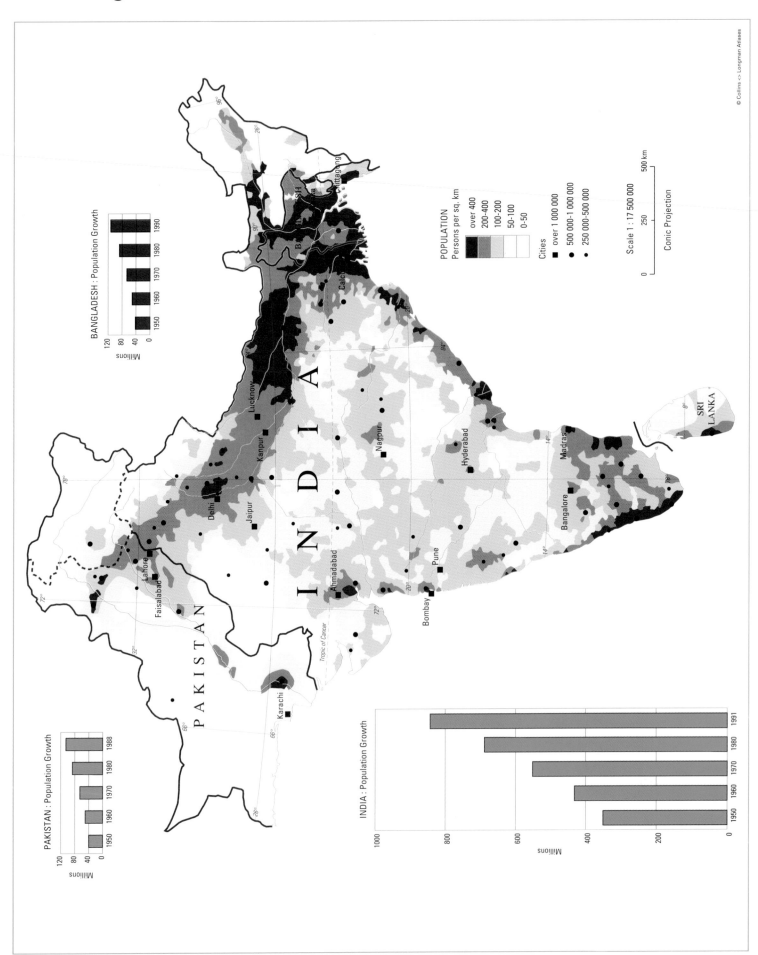

BANGLADESH : Population Growth

Millions

120
80
40
0

1950 1960 1970 1980 1990

POPULATION
Persons per sq. km

over 400
200-400
100-200
50-100
0-50

Cities
over 1 000 000
500 000-1 000 000
250 000-500 000

Scale 1 : 17 500 000

0   250   500 km

Conic Projection

PAKISTAN : Population Growth

Millions

120
80
40
0

1950 1960 1970 1980 1988

INDIA : Population Growth

Millions

1000 800 600 400 200 0

1950 1960 1970 1980 1991

PAKISTAN

INDIA

SRI LANKA

Karachi
Faisalabad
Lahore
Delhi
Jaipur
Lucknow
Kanpur
Ahmadabad
Bombay
Pune
Nagpur
Hyderabad
Bangalore
Madras
Calcutta
Chittagong

Tropic of Cancer

© Collins <> Longman Atlases

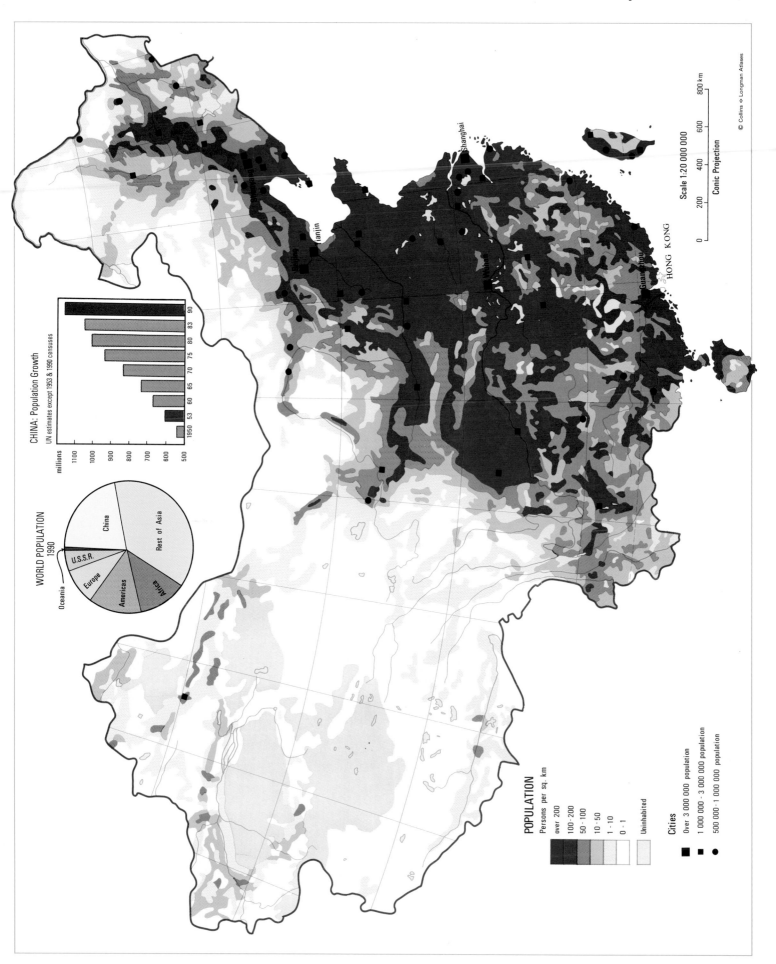

© Collins ◇ Longman Atlases

Scale 1:20 000 000

Conic Projection

| 0 | 200 | 400 | 600 | 800 km |

Shanghai

Tianjin

Wuhan

Guangzhou

HONG KONG

CHINA: Population Growth

UN estimates except 1953 & 1990 censuses

millions

1100
1000
900
800
700
600
500

1950 53 60 65 70 75 80 83 90

WORLD POPULATION
1990

China
Rest of Asia
U.S.S.R.
Europe
Americas
Africa
Oceania

POPULATION

Persons per sq. km

over 200
100 - 200
50 - 100
10 - 50
1 - 10
0 - 1
Uninhabited

Cities

■ Over 3 000 000 population

■ 1 000 000 - 3 000 000 population

● 500 000 - 1 000 000 population

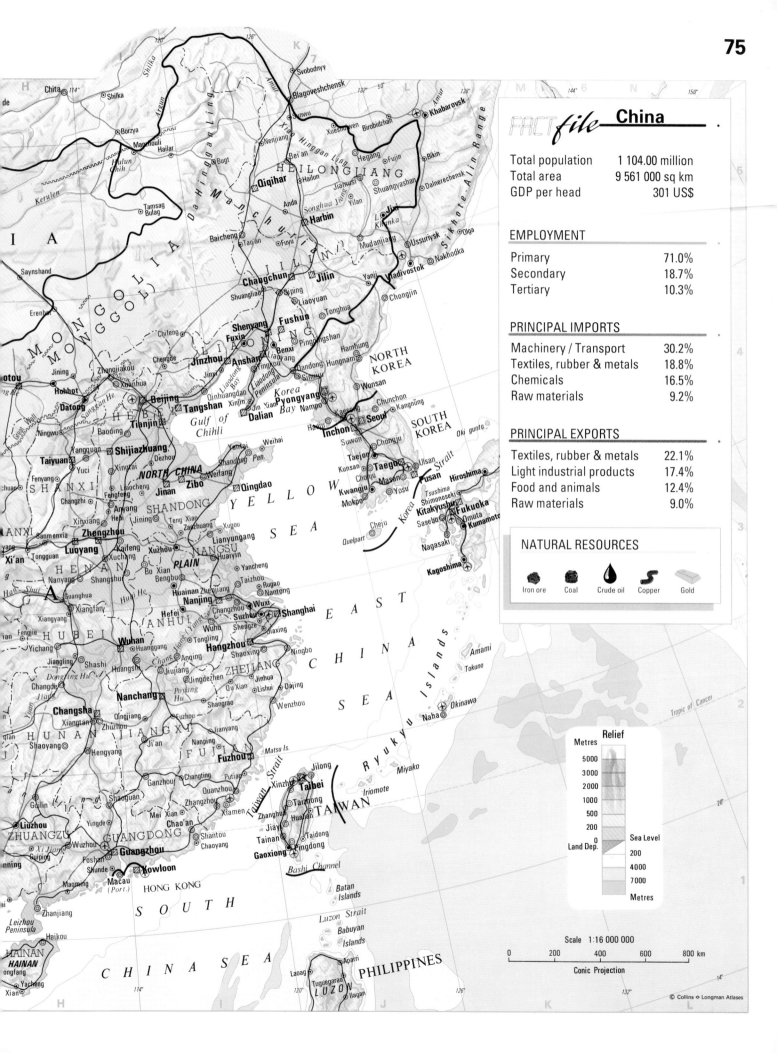

FACT *file* China

Total population	1 104.00 million
Total area	9 561 000 sq km
GDP per head	301 US$

EMPLOYMENT

Primary	71.0%
Secondary	18.7%
Tertiary	10.3%

PRINCIPAL IMPORTS

Machinery / Transport	30.2%
Textiles, rubber & metals	18.8%
Chemicals	16.5%
Raw materials	9.2%

PRINCIPAL EXPORTS

Textiles, rubber & metals	22.1%
Light industrial products	17.4%
Food and animals	12.4%
Raw materials	9.0%

NATURAL RESOURCES

Iron ore   Coal   Crude oil   Copper   Gold

Relief

Metres	
5000	
3000	
2000	
1000	
500	
200	
0	Sea Level
Land Dep.	200
	4000
	7000
	Metres

Scale 1:16 000 000

0   200   400   600   800 km

Conic Projection

© Collins ◇ Longman Atlases

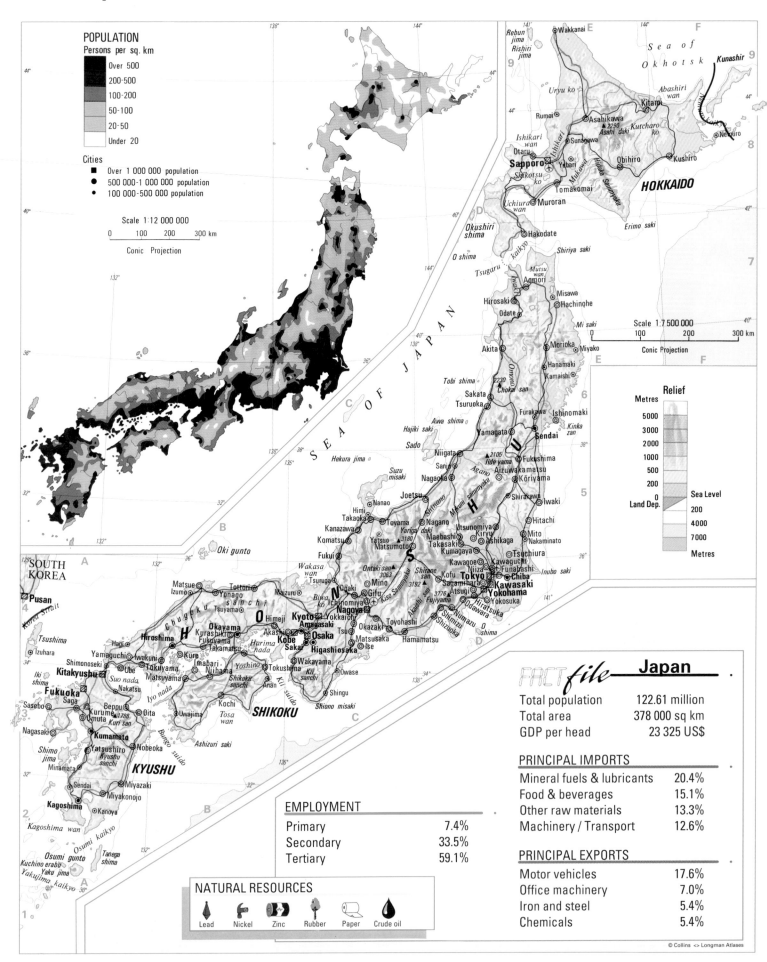

POPULATION

Persons per sq. km
- Over 500
- 200–500
- 100–200
- 50–100
- 20–50
- Under 20

Cities
- ■ Over 1 000 000 population
- ● 500 000–1 000 000 population
- • 100 000–500 000 population

Scale 1:12 000 000

0   100   200   300 km

Conic Projection

Scale 1:7 500 000

0   100   200   300 km

Conic Projection

Relief

Metres
5000
3000
2000
1000
500
200
0 Sea Level
Land Dep. 200
4000
7000

Metres

SEA OF JAPAN

Sea of Okhotsk

HOKKAIDO

HONSHU

SHIKOKU

KYUSHU

SOUTH KOREA

FACT file — Japan

Total population	122.61 million
Total area	378 000 sq km
GDP per head	23 325 US$

PRINCIPAL IMPORTS

Mineral fuels & lubricants	20.4%
Food & beverages	15.1%
Other raw materials	13.3%
Machinery / Transport	12.6%

PRINCIPAL EXPORTS

Motor vehicles	17.6%
Office machinery	7.0%
Iron and steel	5.4%
Chemicals	5.4%

EMPLOYMENT

Primary	7.4%
Secondary	33.5%
Tertiary	59.1%

NATURAL RESOURCES

Lead   Nickel   Zinc   Rubber   Paper   Crude oil

© Collins ◇ Longman Atlases

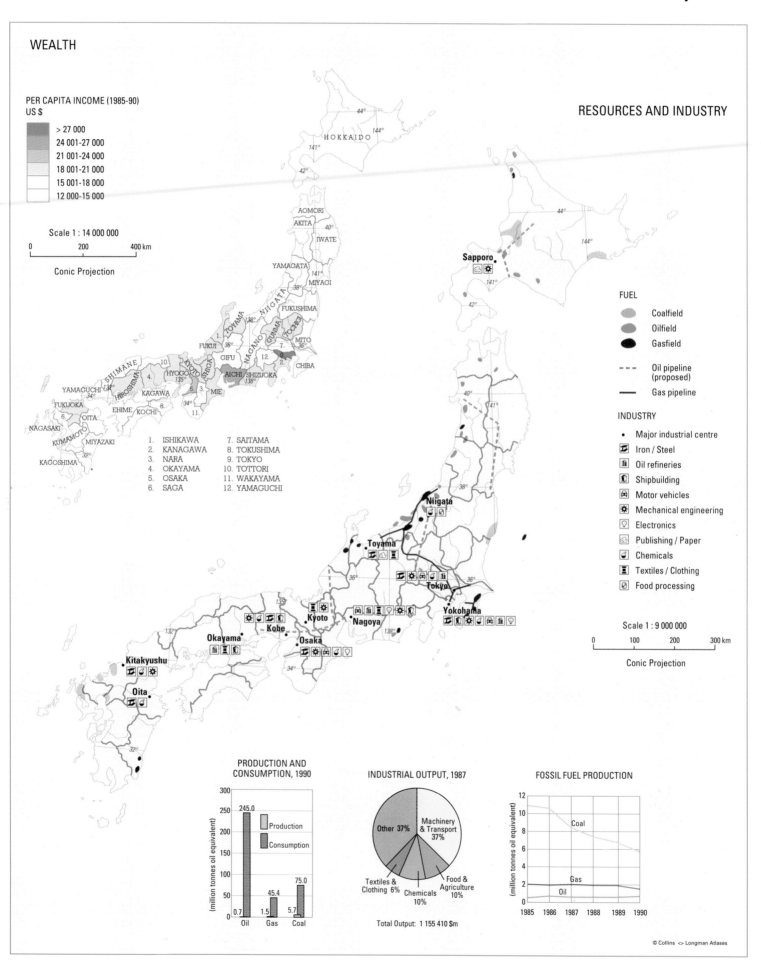

WEALTH

PER CAPITA INCOME (1985-90)
US $

- > 27 000
- 24 001-27 000
- 21 001-24 000
- 18 001-21 000
- 15 001-18 000
- 12 000-15 000

Scale 1 : 14 000 000

0　　　200　　　400 km

Conic Projection

RESOURCES AND INDUSTRY

FUEL

- Coalfield
- Oilfield
- Gasfield
- Oil pipeline (proposed)
- Gas pipeline

INDUSTRY

- Major industrial centre
- Iron / Steel
- Oil refineries
- Shipbuilding
- Motor vehicles
- Mechanical engineering
- Electronics
- Publishing / Paper
- Chemicals
- Textiles / Clothing
- Food processing

Scale 1 : 9 000 000

0　　100　　200　　300 km

Conic Projection

1. ISHIKAWA
2. KANAGAWA
3. NARA
4. OKAYAMA
5. OSAKA
6. SAGA
7. SAITAMA
8. TOKUSHIMA
9. TOKYO
10. TOTTORI
11. WAKAYAMA
12. YAMAGUCHI

PRODUCTION AND CONSUMPTION, 1990

(million tonnes oil equivalent)

- Production
- Consumption

Oil: Production 0.7, Consumption 245.0
Gas: Production 1.5, Consumption 45.4
Coal: Production 5.7, Consumption 75.0

INDUSTRIAL OUTPUT, 1987

- Machinery & Transport 37%
- Other 37%
- Chemicals 10%
- Food & Agriculture 10%
- Textiles & Clothing 6%

Total Output: 1 155 410 $m

FOSSIL FUEL PRODUCTION

(million tonnes oil equivalent)

- Coal
- Gas
- Oil

1985　1986　1987　1988　1989　1990

© Collins ⟨⟩ Longman Atlases

MYANMA

THAILAND

CAMBODIA

VIETNAM

CHINA

Gulf of Tongking

Hainan

S O U T H

C H I N A

S E A

Andaman
Islands
(India)

Nicobar
Islands
(India)

A N D A M A N

S E A

*Gulf of
Thailand*

*Gulf of
Martaban*

MALAYSIA

SUMATRA

BORNEO

KALIMANTAN

SARAWAK

SABAH

BRUNEI

SINGAPORE

I N D I A N

O C E A N

J A V A   S E A

INDON

JAVA

Jakarta
Bandung
Semarang
Surabaya

Lesser   Sunda

Bali
Lombok   Sumbawa

Scale 1:15 000 000

0   200   400   600   800 km

Bonne Projection

© Collins ◇ Longman Atlases

Taizhong
Zhanghua
Jiayi
Tainan
Pingdong

TAIWAN 125°

Batan Is

Luzon Strait 20°

Babuyan Is

eador C. Engaño

Laoag Aparri
Pulog ▲2929 Tuguegarao
Ilagan
San Fernando **LUZON**
Baguio Bayombong
Cagupan
San Carlos
Cabanatuan
Quezon City
Manila
San Pablo Daet
Lucena Naga
Vigas Legaspi
Mindoro Burias Irosin
Bulan
Masbate Catarman
Calbayog **Samar**
Panay Catbalogan
Iloilo Cadiz Guiuan
Bacolod Cebu Tacloban C. Johnson
Negros **Leyte** Depth
Dinagat 10497
Tanjay Bohol Siargao 10°
Dumaguete Tagbilaran Surigao
Dipolog Butuan
Ozamiz Cagayan de Oro
Pagadian Iligan
Zamboanga Cotabato **MINDANAO**
Basilan Moro Datu
Jolo Basilan Gulf Piang Davao
Sulu General
Arch Santos

PHILIPPINES

CHINA
Hanoi
**MACAU HONG TAIWAN
KONG**
MYANMA
Yangon **LAOS**
Vientiane
THAILAND
Bangkok
Andaman Is. **VIETNAM**
(India) **CAMBODIA**
Phnom
Penh **PHILIPPINES**
Manila

BRUNEI
Bandar Seri
Begawan
Kuala Lumpur
MALAYSIA
SINGAPORE

I N D O N E S I A

Jakarta

**PAPUA
NEW
GUINEA**
Port
Moresby

AUSTRALIA

Scale 1:40 000 000
0   500   1000 km

130° 135° Sorol 140° J Lamotrek
Ifalik
Koror
Palau Eauripik
(U.S.A)

Caroline Islands 5°

Sonsorol

Merir

Tobi

Helen Reef

P A C I F I C

O C E A N

Mapia Is

Karakelong Talaud
Is
Sangi
C E L E B E S Sangihe
Is
S E A

Morotai

Manado Tondano Tobelo
Buol Kuandang Belang Jailolo
Tomini ▲2207 Ternate **Halmahera**
Gorontalo ▲1970 Soasiu
Togian Is Weda
Poh
Poso Tuli Peleng Bacan
SI G. of Taliabu Obi
Tolo Banggai Is Sula Is
Tolo

Manokwari
Waigeo Biak Schouten Is
Dampier Str Kwoka Biak Bosnik
Sorong 3000 Mokmer
Klamono Arfak Japen
Vogelkop 2939
Misool Wasian Serui
Kokas **Teluk Berau** Babo Wasior **Teluk
Irian**
Fakfak ▲1340
Kaimana **Maoke**
Adi **Sudirman Mts. Range**
Puntjak Jaya Jayawijaya
Kokenau 5030 Mts. Mandala Pk
4702

Relief
Metres
5000
3000
2000
1000
500
200
0
Land Dep.
Sea Level
200
4000
7000
Metres

Equator 0°

Manus
Lorengau
Admiralty Is

Jayapura Vanimo
Sarmi Aitape
Serui Maprik Wewak
Mamberamo Sepik Angoram

IRIAN Bogia
JAYA Wabag Mt. Madang
Laiagam Hagen Goroka
Mendi Mt. Wilhelm Kainantu
4694 Huon Pen Finschhafen
PAPUA NEW Bulolo
GUINEA Wau
Bismarck Sea

**Bismarck
Sea**

MOLUCCA SEA

CERAM SEA
Binaija
Namlea 3055 Bula
Ambon **Ceram**
Buru Banda

Kendari
Mekongga
▲2790 Wowoni
Kolaka

BANDA SEA
Kai Is
Kabaena Butung Tukangbesi
Muna Baubau Is Wokam
Aru
Is Kobroör

Nila
Trangan
Damar
Jamdena
Wetar Roma Saumlaki Tanimbar
Islands Alor Leti Is Is
Maumere Dili Babar Is
Ende Sermate
Ngapu ▲2365 **Timor**
Baing Savu Sea Nikiniki Kupang
Sawu Roti 125°

N E W G U I N E A
Tanahmerah
Kokas Fakfak
Mappi
Kolepom Okaba
C. Vals Merauke
Daru

A R A F U R A S E A

Digoel
Fly
Kerema 3993
Popondetta
Gulf of
Papua
Kila Kila
Port Moresby 10°

Mulgrave Is Banks I
Torres Str.
Thursday I
Prince of Wales I C. York

**C o r a l
S e a**

130° 135° 140° 145°

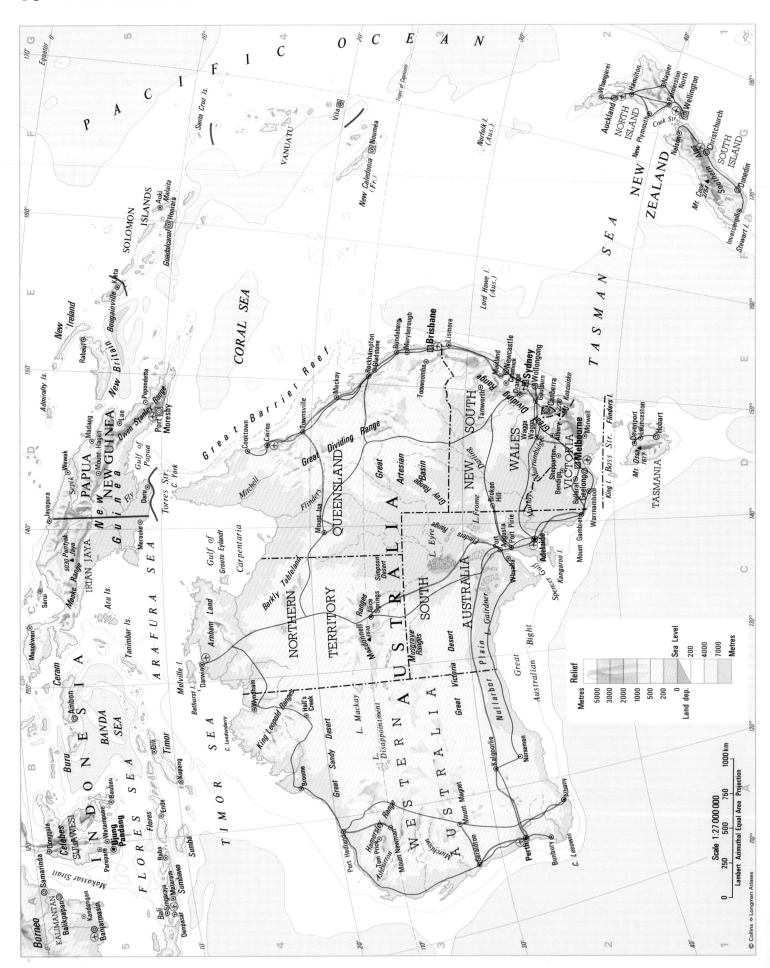

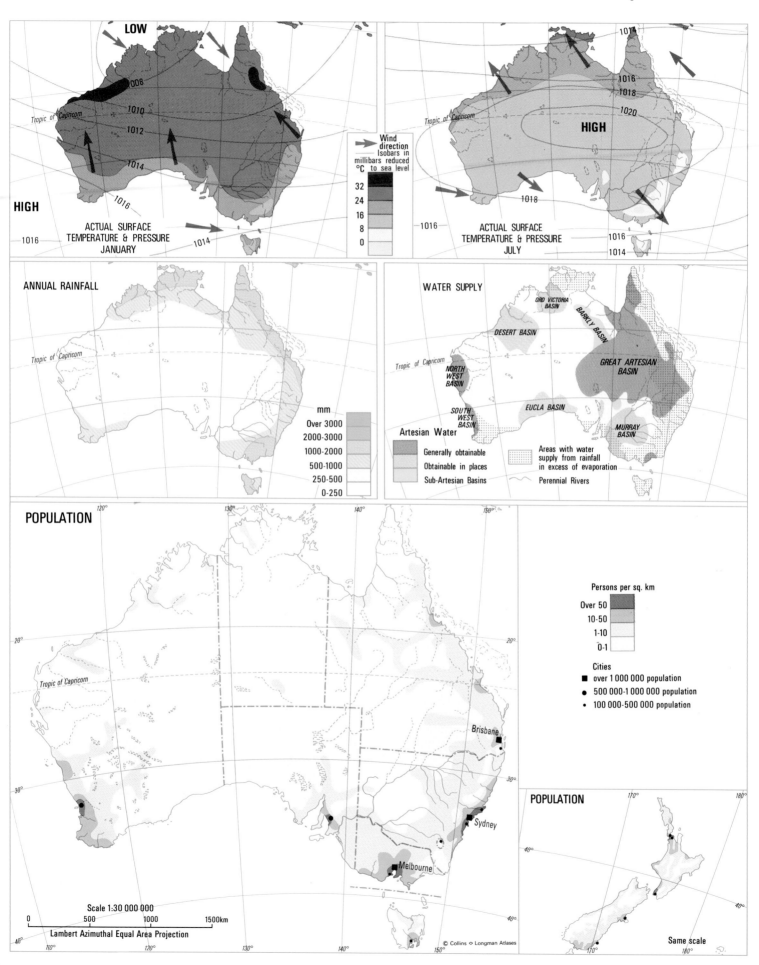

ACTUAL SURFACE TEMPERATURE & PRESSURE JANUARY

LOW
HIGH

1008
1010
1012
1014
1016

Tropic of Capricorn

Wind direction
Isobars in millibars reduced to sea level
°C
32
24
16
8
0

ACTUAL SURFACE TEMPERATURE & PRESSURE JULY

HIGH

1014
1016
1018
1020
1018
1016
1014

Tropic of Capricorn

ANNUAL RAINFALL

Tropic of Capricorn

mm
Over 3000
2000-3000
1000-2000
500-1000
250-500
0-250

WATER SUPPLY

ORD VICTORIA BASIN
BARKLY BASIN
DESERT BASIN
NORTH WEST BASIN
GREAT ARTESIAN BASIN
SOUTH WEST BASIN
EUCLA BASIN
MURRAY BASIN

Tropic of Capricorn

Artesian Water
Generally obtainable
Obtainable in places
Sub-Artesian Basins

Areas with water supply from rainfall in excess of evaporation
Perennial Rivers

POPULATION

120° 130° 140° 150°

20°
Tropic of Capricorn
30°
40°

Brisbane
Sydney
Melbourne

Persons per sq. km
Over 50
10-50
1-10
0-1

Cities
■ over 1 000 000 population
● 500 000-1 000 000 population
• 100 000-500 000 population

Scale 1:30 000 000
0   500   1000   1500km
Lambert Azimuthal Equal Area Projection

© Collins ◇ Longman Atlases

POPULATION

170° 180°
40°
40°

Same scale

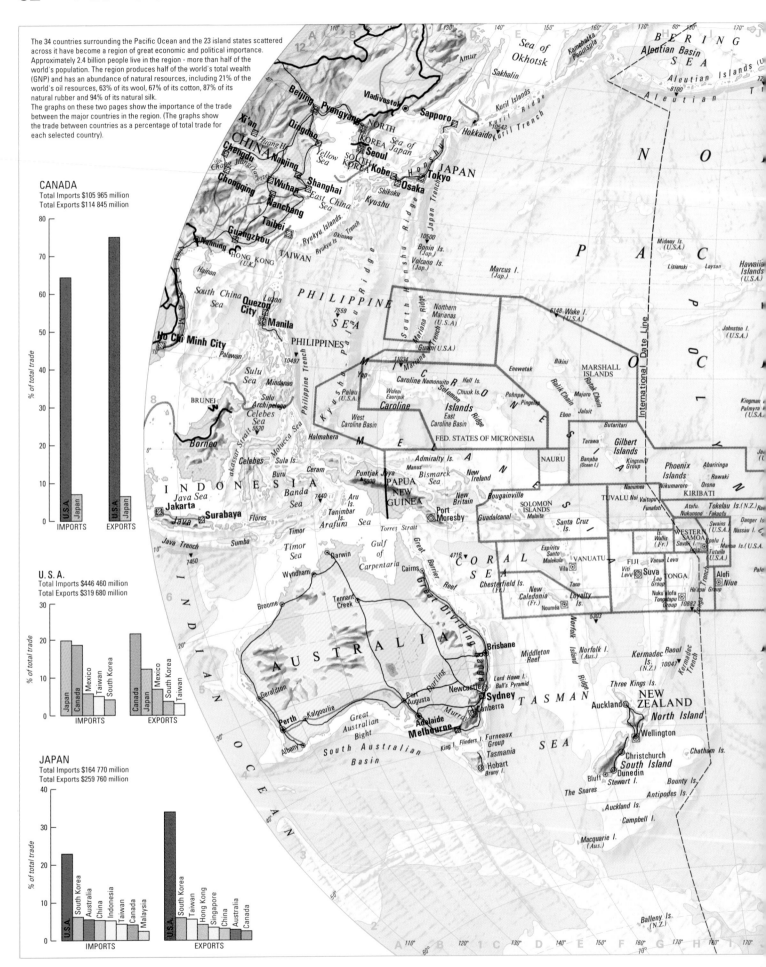

The 34 countries surrounding the Pacific Ocean and the 23 island states scattered across it have become a region of great economic and political importance. Approximately 2.4 billion people live in the region - more than half of the world's population. The region produces half of the world's total wealth (GNP) and has an abundance of natural resources, including 21% of the world's oil resources, 63% of its wool, 67% of its cotton, 87% of its natural rubber and 94% of its natural silk.

The graphs on these two pages show the importance of the trade between the major countries in the region. (The graphs show the trade between countries as a percentage of total trade for each selected country).

CANADA
Total Imports $105 965 million
Total Exports $114 845 million

U.S.A.
Total Imports $446 460 million
Total Exports $319 680 million

JAPAN
Total Imports $164 770 million
Total Exports $259 760 million

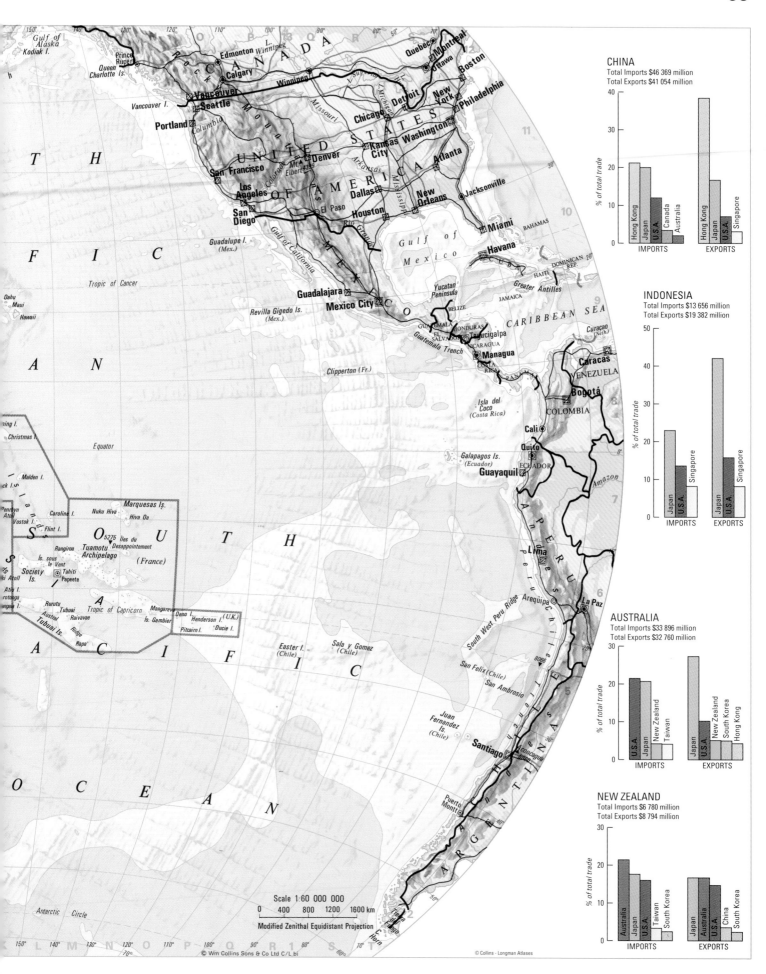

CHINA
Total Imports $46 369 million
Total Exports $41 054 million

INDONESIA
Total Imports $13 656 million
Total Exports $19 382 million

AUSTRALIA
Total Imports $33 896 million
Total Exports $32 760 million

NEW ZEALAND
Total Imports $6 780 million
Total Exports $8 794 million

Scale 1:60 000 000
0   400   800   1200   1600 km
Modified Zenithal Equidistant Projection

© Wm Collins Sons & Co Ltd C/L bi

© Collins - Longman Atlases

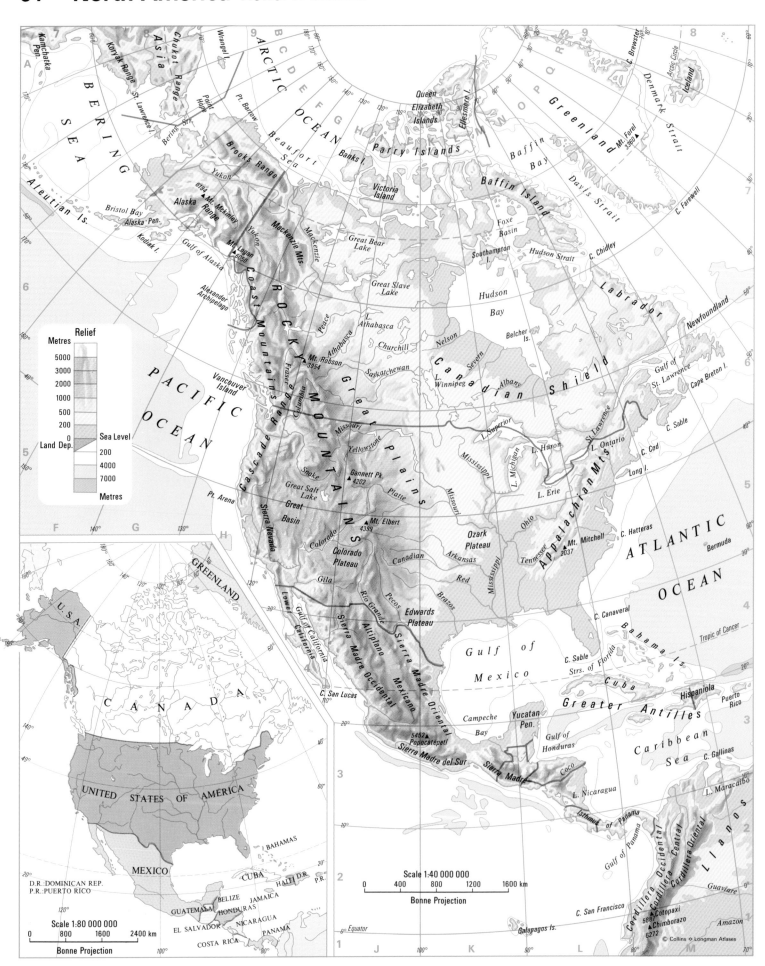

Relief

Metres
5000
3000
2000
1000
500
200
Land Dep. 0 Sea Level
200
4000
7000
Metres

Scale 1:40 000 000
0 400 800 1200 1600 km
Bonne Projection

D.R.:DOMINICAN REP.
P.R.:PUERTO RICO

Scale 1:80 000 000
0 800 1600 2400 km
Bonne Projection

© Collins ○ Longman Atlases

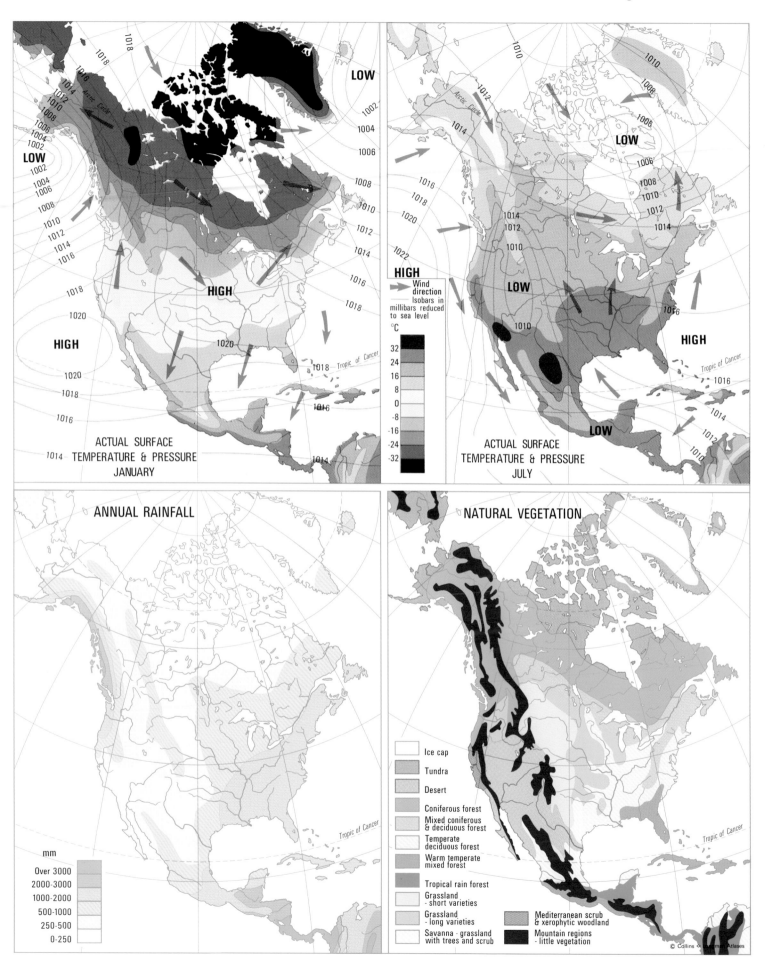

LOW

1018

Arctic Circle

LOW
1002
1004
1006
1008
1010
1012
1014
1016

HIGH
1020

1018
1016

LOW
1002
1004
1006
1008
1010
1012
1014
1016
1018
1020

HIGH

1020

1018

1016

1014

HIGH

1020

1018 Tropic of Cancer

1016

1014

ACTUAL SURFACE
TEMPERATURE & PRESSURE
JANUARY

LOW

1010

1008
1006

1004

1002

1004

1006

1008

1010

1012

1014

1016

1018

Wind
direction
Isobars in
millibars reduced
to sea level

°C
32
24
16
8
0
-8
-16
-24
-32

Arctic Circle

1010

1012

1014

1016
1018
1020
1022

HIGH

1010

1016
1014
1012

1010

LOW

LOW

1010

1016

1006

1008
1010
1012

1014

HIGH

Tropic of Cancer

1016

1014

1012

1010

LOW

ACTUAL SURFACE
TEMPERATURE & PRESSURE
JULY

ANNUAL RAINFALL

Tropic of Cancer

mm

Over 3000
2000-3000
1000-2000
500-1000
250-500
0-250

NATURAL VEGETATION

Tropic of Cancer

Ice cap

Tundra

Desert

Coniferous forest

Mixed coniferous
& deciduous forest

Temperate
deciduous forest

Warm temperate
mixed forest

Tropical rain forest

Grassland
- short varieties

Grassland
- long varieties

Savanna - grassland
with trees and scrub

Mediterranean scrub
& xerophytic woodland

Mountain regions
- little vegetation

© Collins

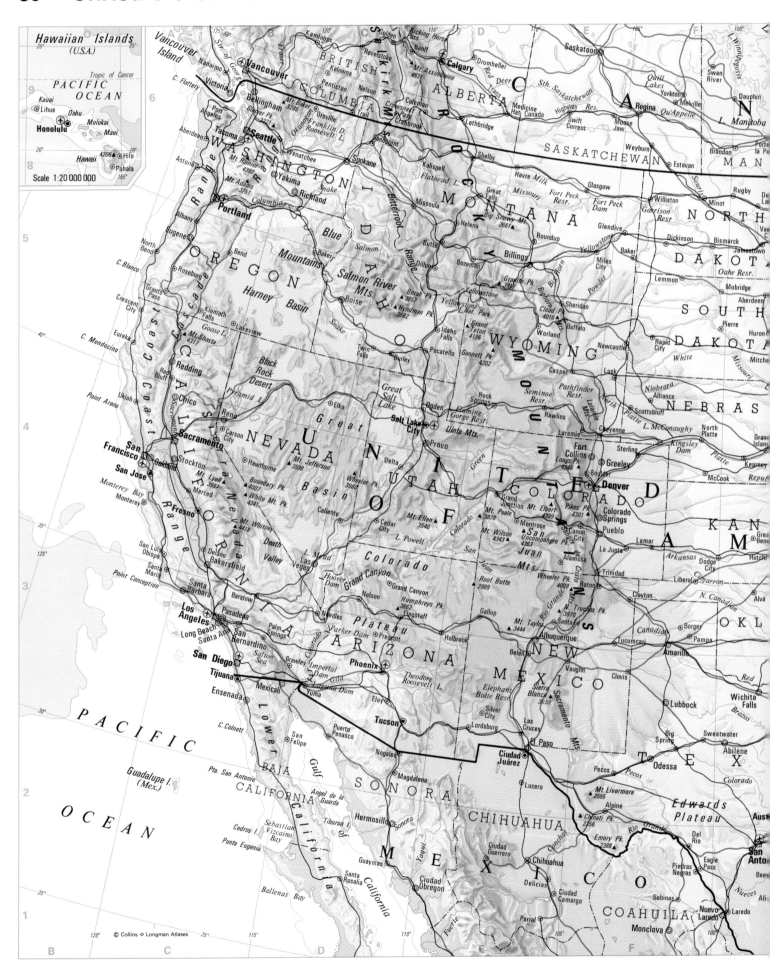

Hawaiian Islands
(U.S.A.)

PACIFIC OCEAN

Tropic of Cancer

Kauai
Lihue
Oahu
Molokai
Honolulu
Maui
Hawaii
4205
Hilo
Pahala

Scale 1:20 000 000

PACIFIC OCEAN

© Collins ◇ Longman Atlases

POPULATION

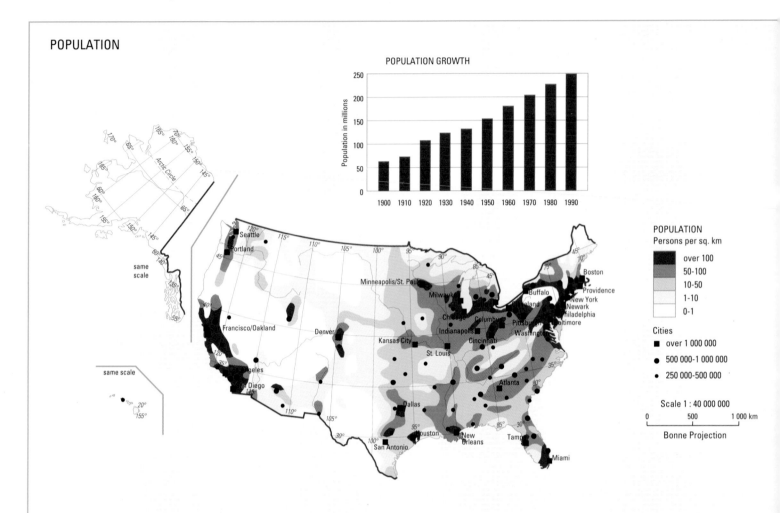

POPULATION GROWTH

POPULATION
Persons per sq. km

- over 100
- 50-100
- 10-50
- 1-10
- 0-1

Cities
- ■ over 1 000 000
- ● 500 000-1 000 000
- • 250 000-500 000

Scale 1 : 40 000 000

0   500   1 000 km

Bonne Projection

WEALTH

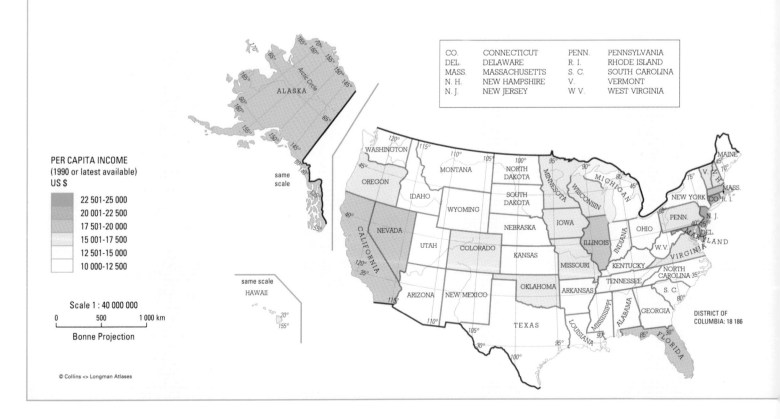

PER CAPITA INCOME
(1990 or latest available)
US $

- 22 501-25 000
- 20 001-22 500
- 17 501-20 000
- 15 001-17 500
- 12 501-15 000
- 10 000-12 500

Scale 1 : 40 000 000

0   500   1 000 km

Bonne Projection

CO.	CONNECTICUT	PENN.	PENNSYLVANIA
DEL.	DELAWARE	R. I.	RHODE ISLAND
MASS.	MASSACHUSETTS	S. C.	SOUTH CAROLINA
N. H.	NEW HAMPSHIRE	V.	VERMONT
N. J.	NEW JERSEY	W. V.	WEST VIRGINIA

DISTRICT OF
COLUMBIA: 18 186

© Collins <> Longman Atlases

RESOURCES AND INDUSTRY

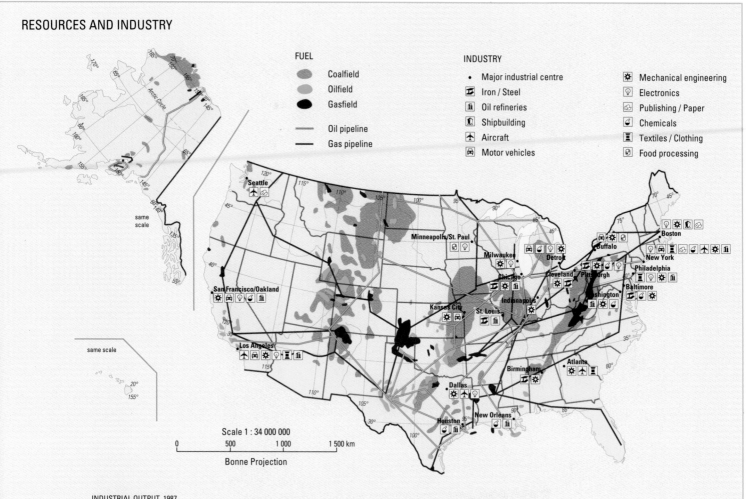

FUEL
- Coalfield
- Oilfield
- Gasfield
- —— Oil pipeline
- —— Gas pipeline

INDUSTRY
- • Major industrial centre
- Iron / Steel
- Oil refineries
- Shipbuilding
- Aircraft
- Motor vehicles
- Mechanical engineering
- Electronics
- Publishing / Paper
- Chemicals
- Textiles / Clothing
- Food processing

Scale 1 : 34 000 000

0   500   1 000   1 500 km

Bonne Projection

INDUSTRIAL OUTPUT, 1987

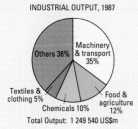

- Machinery & transport 35%
- Others 38%
- Textiles & clothing 5%
- Chemicals 10%
- Food & agriculture 12%

Total Output: 1 249 540 US$m

PROVED RESERVES, 1990

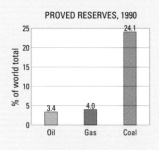

% of world total

Oil	Gas	Coal
3.4	4.0	24.1

FOSSIL FUEL PRODUCTION

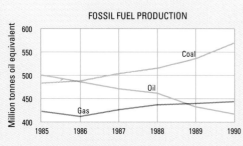

Million tonnes oil equivalent

Coal
Oil
Gas

1985 1986 1987 1988 1989 1990

FACTfile — USA

Total population	246.33 million
Total area	9 373 000 sq km
GDP per head	19 815 US$

EMPLOYMENT
Primary	2.9%
Secondary	26.7%
Tertiary	70.4%

PRINCIPAL IMPORTS
Machinery / Transport	43.5%
Manufactured goods	29.3%
Mineral fuels & lubricants	11.1%
Foods	4.4%

PRINCIPAL EXPORTS
Machinery	29.7%
Transport equipment	14.6%
Manufactured goods	15.7%
Chemicals	10.1%

NATURAL RESOURCES
- Coal
- Natural Gas
- Crude oil
- Gold
- Lead
- Copper
- Silver

© Collins ◇ Longman Atlases

Mexican States numbered on map
1. AGUASCALIENTES
2. DISTRICT FEDERAL
3. TLAXCALA

POPULATION

Cities
■ over 1 000 000
● 500 000–1 000 000
● 250 000–500 000

Scale 1:25 000 000

0   250   500   750   1000 km

Persons per sq. km

over 100
50–100
10–50
1–10
0–1

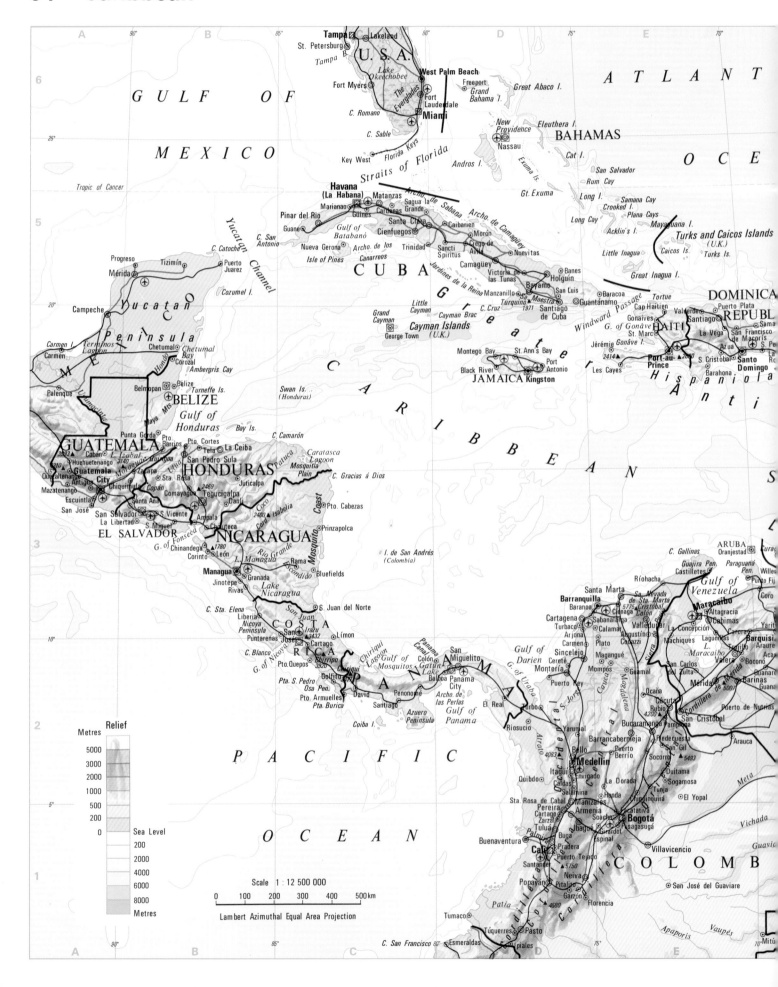

A   90°   B   85°   C   80°   D   75°   E   70°

Tampa ⊕ Lakeland
St. Petersburg
Tampa B.
U.S.A.
West Palm Beach
Fort Myers
Lake Okeechobee
The Everglades
Freeport
Grand Bahama I.
Great Abaco I.
Fort Lauderdale
⊕ **Miami**
C. Romano
C. Sable
New Providence
Nassau
BAHAMAS
Eleuthera I.
Cat I.
San Salvador
Rum Cay

GULF   OF

MEXICO

Tropic of Cancer

Key West
Florida Keys
Straits of Florida
Andros I.
Gt. Exuma
Exuma Is.
Long I.
Crooked I.
Plana Cays
Mayaguana I.
Acklin's I.
Little Inagua
Caicos Is.
Turks Is.
Turks and Caicos Islands
(U.K.)

ATLANT

OCE

Havana
(La Habana)   Matanzas
Marianao
Pinar del Rio   Güines   Cárdenas   Sagua la Grande   Archo. de Sabana
Guane   Santa Clara
Nueva Gerona   Cienfuegos   Caibarién   Morón   Archo. de Camagüey
Isle of Pines   Archo. de los   Trinidad   Sancti   Ciego de
Canarreos   Spíritus   Ávila   Nuevitas
CUBA   Camagüey
Victoria de   Banes
Jardines de la Reina   las Tunas   Holguín   San Luis
Little   Manzanillo   Bayamo   Baracoa
Grand   Cayman   C. Cruz   Maestra   Guantánamo
Cayman   Cayman Brac   Turquino   Santiago   Tortue
1971   de Cuba   Cap Haitien
George Town   **Cayman Islands**   Windward Passage   Gonaïves
(U.K.)   G. of Gonâve   St. Marc
Montego Bay   St. Ann's Bay   **HAITI**
Black River   Port   2414▲   **Port-au-**
Antonio   Jérémie   Gonâve I.   **Prince**
JAMAICA Kingston   Les Cayes

C. San
Antonio
Gulf of
Batabanó

Yucatán Channel

Cozumel I.

Progreso
Mérida   Tizimín
Campeche   Puerto
Juárez
Yucatán

Carmen I.   Terminos
Lagoon
Carmen
Palenque

DOMINICA
REPUBL
Puerto Plata
Valverde
Santiago
La Vega   San Francisco
de Macorís
Azua
S. Cristóbal   **Santo
Domingo**
Barahona
Hispaniola

Anti

C. Catoche

Peninsula

Chetumal
Corozal
Ambergris Cay
Belize
Turneffe Is.
Bay Is.

GREATER

Gulf of
Honduras

BELIZE
Belmopan

Swan Is.
(Honduras)

CARIBBEAN

C A R I B B E A N

Punta Gorda   Pto.
Barrios   Pto. Cortés   La Ceiba   C. Camarón
GUATEMALA   Cobán   L. Izabal   Tela   Caratasca
3893▲   San Pedro Sula   Patuca   Lagoon
Huehuetenango   3140   **HONDURAS**   Mosquitia
Quezaltenango   ▲**Guatemala**   Zacapa   Sta. Rosa   Juticalpa   Plain
Antigua   **City**   Chiquimula   Copán   Comayagua   2469▲   C. Gracias á Dios
Mazatenango   Escuintla⊕   Santa Ana   Tegucigalpa   Danlí   Pto. Cabezas
San José   San Salvador   S. Vicente   Ampala   2400   Coco
La Libertad   **EL SALVADOR**   S. Miguel   Choluteca   Cord. Isabelia   Prinzapolca
G. of Fonseca   **NICARAGUA**   Coast
Chinandega   1780▲   Río Grande
Corinto   León   L. Managua   Rama
Managua   Escondido   Bluefields
Jinotepe   Lake
Granada   Nicaragua
C. Sta. Elena   Rivas   San Juan   S. Juan del Norte
Liberia   **COSTA**   San Juan
Nicoya   Irazú   **RICA**   Límon
Peninsula   3432   Cartago
Puntarenas   José⊕   Chiriquí
C. Blanco   G. of Nicoya   Chirripó   Lagoon   Panama
Pto. Quepos   3920   Canal   San
Osa Pen.   Chiriquí   Gulf of   Gatún   Miguelito
Pta. S. Pedro   **PANAMA**   Mosquitos   Colón   Lake   Balboa Panama
David   Penonomé   **City**
Pto. Armuelles   Santiago   Archo. de
Pta. Burica   Azuero   las Perlas
Coiba I.   Peninsula   Gulf of   El Real
Panama   Riosucio

I. de San Andrés
(Colombia)

ARUBA
Oranjestad
C. Gallinas
Guajira Pen.
Sa. Nevada   Castilletes   Paraguaná
Santa Marta   de Sta. Marta   Pen.   Punto Fij
Barranquilla   Baranoa   5775 Cristóbal▲   Coro
Cartagena   Ciénaga   Colón   **Maracaibo**   Altagracia
Turbaco   Sabanalarga   Valledupar   La Concepción   Cabimas
Arjona   Calamar   Agustín   Machiques   Lagunillas   Yarit
Carmen   Plato   Codazzi   L.   **Barquisi**
Sincelejo   Magangué   Ocaña   del Zulia   Maracaibo   Trujillo   Araure
Gulf of   Montería   Cereté   San Carlos   **Mérida**   Barinas
Darien   Cauca   Mompós   Ocaña   Cúcuta   Valera   Bocono   Guana
Sincelejo   Geamal   4200▲   Rubio   Cordillera de   5007   Barinas
Turbo   Puerto Key   Pamplona   Bucaramanga   S. Cristóbal   Buanare
Yarumal   San Gil   Arauca
Medellín   Barrancabermeja   5493▲   Duitama
4083▲   Bello   Berrío   Socorro   Sogamosa   Arauca
Itagüí   Envigado   La Dorada   Chiquinquirá   Tunja   ⊙ El Yopal
Quibdó   Salamina   Honda   El Yopal
Sta. Rosa de Cabal   Manizales   Soacha   Facatativá   Meta
Pereira   Armenia   **Bogotá**   Vichada
Cartago   Soacha   Girardot   Fusagasugá
Zarzal   Buga   Espinal   Villavicencio   Guavi
Tuluá   Pradera   Neiva
Buenaventura   Palmira   COLOMB
Buga
Cali   Puerto Tejado   San José del Guaviare
Santander   5750▲
Popayán   Pitalito
Patía   4580   Florencia
Túquerres   Pasto   Apaporis   Vaupés
C. San Francisco   Esmeraldas   Mitú
Tumaco   Ipiales

PACIFIC

OCEAN

Relief
Metres
5000
3000
2000
1000
500
200
0   Sea Level
200
2000
4000
6000
8000
Metres

Scale   1 : 12 500 000
0   100   200   300   400   500 km

Lambert Azimuthal Equal Area Projection

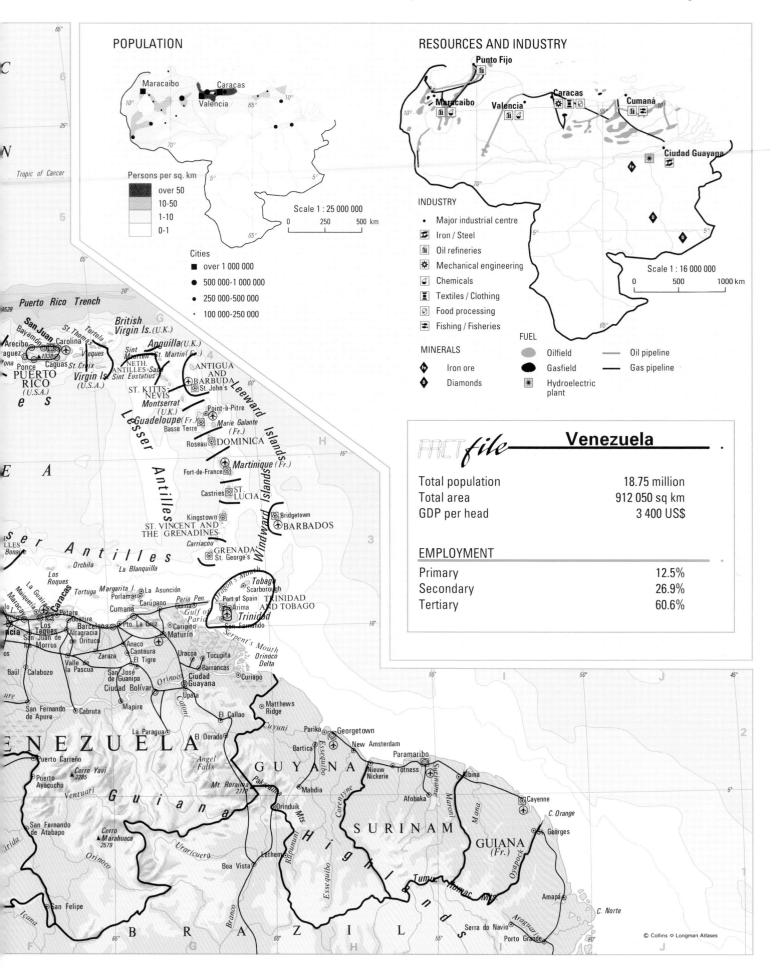

POPULATION

Maracaibo   Caracas
              Valencia

Persons per sq. km
- over 50
- 10-50
- 1-10
- 0-1

Scale 1 : 25 000 000

0   250   500 km

Cities
- ■ over 1 000 000
- ● 500 000-1 000 000
- • 250 000-500 000
- · 100 000-250 000

RESOURCES AND INDUSTRY

Punto Fijo
Maracaibo   Caracas   Cumaná
          Valencia
                    Ciudad Guayana

Scale 1 : 16 000 000

0   500   1000 km

INDUSTRY
- • Major industrial centre
- Iron / Steel
- Oil refineries
- Mechanical engineering
- Chemicals
- Textiles / Clothing
- Food processing
- Fishing / Fisheries

MINERALS
- Fe   Iron ore
- D   Diamonds

FUEL
- Oilfield
- Gasfield
- Hydroelectric plant
- Oil pipeline
- Gas pipeline

FACT*file* **Venezuela**

Total population	18.75 million
Total area	912 050 sq km
GDP per head	3 400 US$

EMPLOYMENT

Primary	12.5%
Secondary	26.9%
Tertiary	60.6%

Tropic of Cancer

Puerto Rico Trench

San Juan
Bayamón Carolina
Arecibo St. Thomas Tortola
aguez Vieques British Virgin Is.(U.K.)
Ponce Caguas St. Croix
PUERTO RICO Virgin Is.
(USA) (U.S.A.)

Anguilla(U.K.)
Sint Maarten St. Martin (Fr.)
NETH. ANTILLES Saba
Sint Eustatius ANTIGUA AND BARBUDA
ST. KITTS- St. John's
NEVIS
Montserrat (U.K.)
Point-à-Pitre
Guadeloupe (Fr.)
Basse Terre Marie Galante (Fr.)
Roseau DOMINICA

Martinique (Fr.)
Fort-de-France
Castries ST. LUCIA

ST. VINCENT AND Kingstown Bridgetown
THE GRENADINES BARBADOS
Carriacou GRENADA
St. George's

Antilles

Orchila La Blanquilla
Los Roques
La Guaira Margarita I. Tobago
Tortuga Porlamar La Asunción Scarborough
Maiquetía Caracas Cumaná Port of Spain TRINIDAD
Los Teques Petare Paria Pen. Carúpano AND TOBAGO
Guatire Güiria Arima Trinidad
ia San Juan de Barcelona Pto. La Cruz San Fernando
los Morros Altagracia Caripito
Baúl de Orituco Anaco Maturín Serpent's Mouth
Zaraza Cantaura Uracoa
Valle de El Tigre Tucupita Orinoco Delta
la Pascua San José Barrancas
Calabozo de Guanipa Ciudad Curiapo
San Fernando Ciudad Bolívar Guayana
de Apure Cabruta Upata
Mapire El Callao
La Paragua Matthews Ridge
San Juan de
ure Cuyuni
Baúl Parika Georgetown
Bartica New Amsterdam
El Dorado Paramaribo
VENEZUELA GUYANA Nieuw Nickerie Totness Albina
Puerto Carreño Angel Falls Mahdia Afobaka
Cerro Yavi Mt. Roraima Cayenne
2285 2772
Puerto Ayacucho Orinduik C. Orange
Venturi Guiana SURINAM St. Georges
San Fernando Cerro Lethem GUIANA
de Atabapo Marahuaca (Fr.)
2579
Orinoco Boa Vista Amapá
Uraricuera C. Norte
San Felipe Branco
Serra do Navio
Porto Grande
BRAZIL

© Collins ◇ Longman Atlases

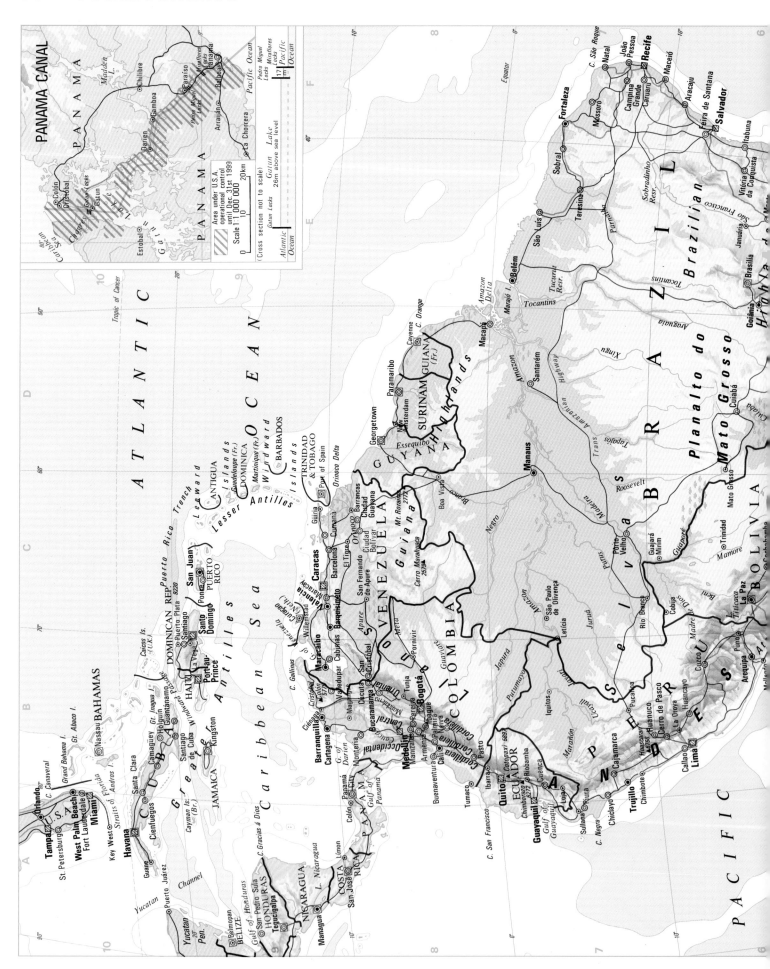

PANAMA CANAL

PANAMA

Pacific Ocean

Madden L.

Chilibre

Paraíso

Gamboa

Pedro Miguel Locks

Miraflores Locks

Balboa

Arraiján

La Chorrera

Gatún Lake

Gatún Locks

Darién

Colón

Cristóbal

Estobal

Caribbean Sea

Area under U.S.A. operational control until Dec. 31st 1999

Scale 1:1 000 000

0   10   20km

(Cross section not to scale)

Gatún Locks

Miraflores Locks

Pedro Miguel Locks

17m Pacific Ocean

Gatún Lake 26m above sea level

Atlantic Ocean

Tropic of Cancer

ATLANTIC OCEAN

Orlando

Tampa

St. Petersburg

C. Canaveral

West Palm Beach

Fort Lauderdale

Miami

U.S.A.

Key West

Straits of Florida

BAHAMAS

Nassau

Grand Bahama I.

Gt. Abaco I.

Gt. Inagua I.

Andros I.

Havana

Guane

Cienfuegos

Santa Clara

Camagüey

Holguín

CUBA

Santiago de Cuba

Guantánamo

Cayman Is. (Br.)

JAMAICA

Kingston

HAITI

Port-au-Prince

Gonaïves

La Vega

Santiago

DOMINICAN REP.

Puerto Plata

Santo Domingo

San Juan

PUERTO RICO

Ponce

Puerto Rico Trench

9220

Caicos Is. (U.K.)

Turks Is.

Windward Passage

Leeward Islands

ANTIGUA

Guadeloupe (Fr.)

DOMINICA

Martinique (Fr.)

BARBADOS

Windward Islands

Lesser Antilles

Greater Antilles

Caribbean Sea

TRINIDAD & TOBAGO

Port of Spain

Puerto Juárez

Yucatán Pen.

Yucatán Channel

Belmopan

BELIZE

San Pedro Sula

HONDURAS

Gulf of Honduras

Tegucigalpa

NICARAGUA

Managua

L. Nicaragua

COSTA RICA

San José

C. Gracias á Dios

Limón

Colón

PANAMA

Panamá

Gulf of Panamá

Gulf of Darién

C. Gallinas

Maracaibo

G. of Venezuela

Curaçao (Neth.)

Willemstad

Aruba (Neth.)

Coro

Valencia

Caracas

Barcelona

Cumaná

Güiria

Barrancas

Ciudad Guayana

Ciudad Bolívar

El Tigre

Orinoco Delta

Orinoco

VENEZUELA

San Fernando de Apure

Apure

Meta

San Cristóbal

Cúcuta

Cabimas

Valledupar

Barinas

Barquisimeto

Mérida

Ciénaga

Barranquilla

Cartagena

Montería

Medellín

Manizales

Bucaramanga

Tunja

COLOMBIA

Bogotá

Ibagué

Armenia

Pereira

Cali

Palmira

Villa de Leyva

Cordillera Occidental

Cordillera Central

Cordillera Oriental

Buenaventura

Pasto

Tumaco

Ipiales

Mt. Roraima 2772

Guiana Highlands

Cerro Maravaca 2579

GUYANA

Georgetown

Essequibo

New Amsterdam

SURINAM

Paramaribo

GUIANA (Fr.)

Cayenne

C. Orange

Macapá

Amazon Delta

Marajó I.

Belém

Tocantins

Tucuruí Resr.

Amazon

Santarém

Trans Amazon Highway

Xingu

Tapajós

Manaus

Negro

Boa Vista

Branco

Roosevelt

Madeira

Pôrto Velho

Guaporé

Trinidad

Mamoré

Mato Grosso

Cuiabá

Planalto do Mato Grosso

BRAZIL

Brazilian Highlands

São Francisco

São Luís

Teresina

Sobral

Fortaleza

Mossoró

C. São Roque

Natal

João Pessoa

Campina Grande

Caruaru

Recife

Maceió

Aracaju

Feira de Santana

Salvador

Itabuna

Vitória da Conquista

Januária

Brasília

Goiânia

Araguaia

Tocantins

Sobradinho Resr.

Parnaíba

Equator

São Paulo de Olivença

Leticia

Japurá

Putumayo

Içá

Juruá

Jutaí

Napo

Iquitos

Pucallpa

Ucayali

Marañón

B O L I V I A

La Paz

Cobija

Beni

Dios

Madre de Dios

Guajará Mirim

Riberalta

Cuzco

Titicaca

Puno

Arequipa

Cerro de Pasco

La Oroya

Huánuco

Huancayo

Huaraz

Huascarán 6768

P E R U

A N D E S

Cajamarca

Trujillo

Chimbote

Chiclayo

Callao

Lima

C. Negra

Sullana

Piura

Guayaquil

Gulf of Guayaquil

C. San Francisco

ECUADOR

Quito

Ibarra

Riobamba

Cotopaxi 5897

Chimborazo 6272

Cuenca

Loja

Macas

Ambato

PACIFIC OCEAN

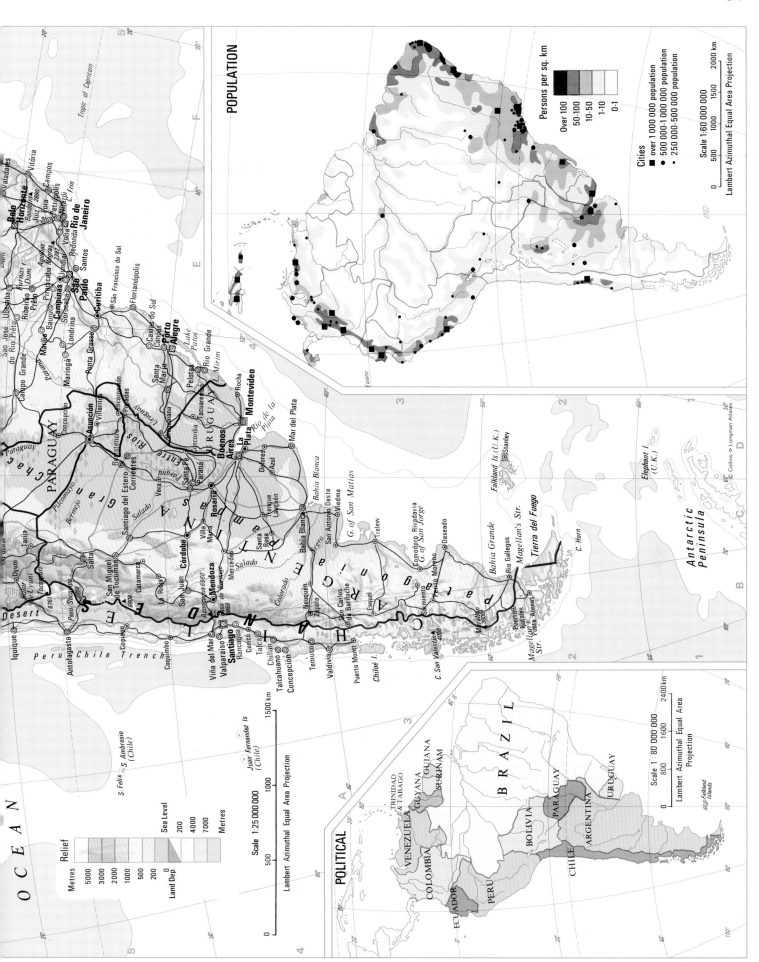

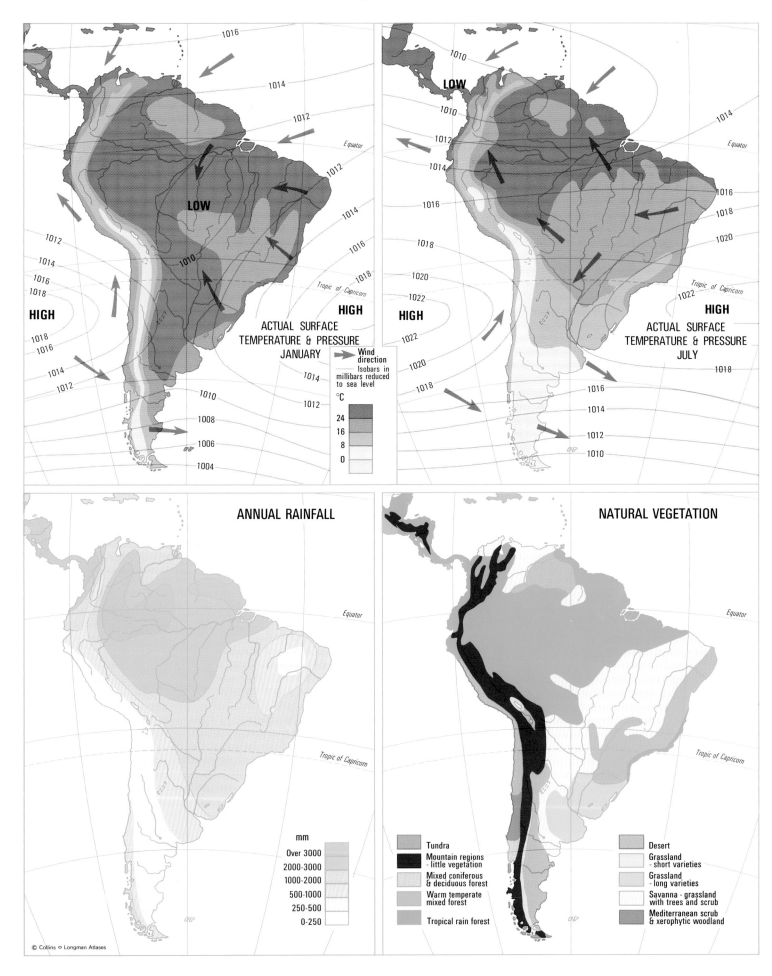

ACTUAL SURFACE
TEMPERATURE & PRESSURE
JANUARY

Wind direction
Isobars in millibars reduced to sea level

°C
24
16
8
0

ACTUAL SURFACE
TEMPERATURE & PRESSURE
JULY

ANNUAL RAINFALL

mm
Over 3000
2000-3000
1000-2000
500-1000
250-500
0-250

NATURAL VEGETATION

Tundra
Mountain regions - little vegetation
Mixed coniferous & deciduous forest
Warm temperate mixed forest
Tropical rain forest

Desert
Grassland - short varieties
Grassland - long varieties
Savanna - grassland with trees and scrub
Mediterranean scrub & xerophytic woodland

© Collins ◇ Longman Atlases

RESOURCES AND INDUSTRY

SELECTED MINERAL PRODUCTION

Legend:
- Lead
- Copper
- Zinc

thousand tonnes

700, 600, 500, 400, 300, 200, 100, 0

1970   1980   1987

MINERAL PRODUCTION
(Percentage of world total)

Zinc	rest of world
Lead	rest of world
Copper	rest of world

0 20 40 60 80 100
% world total

INDUSTRIAL OUTPUT, 1987

Other 44%
Food / agriculture 24%
Textiles / clothing 11%
Chemicals 11%
Machinery / transport 10%

Total output 12 090 US $m

INDUSTRY

- 🛢 Oil refineries
- ⚙ Iron / Steel
- ✸ Mechanical engineering
- ☰ Textiles
- ▨ Publishing / Paper
- ⇄ Fish processing
- ▦ Food processing

FUELS AND MINERALS

- Oilfield
- Gasfield
- Oil pipeline
- ◆ Cu Copper
- ◆ Pb Lead
- ◆ Zn Zinc
- ◆ Ag Silver

Map cities: Tarala, Chiclayo, Chimbote, Paramonga, Lima, Cuzco, Chincha Alta, Arequipa

Scale 1 : 16 000 000

0   150   300   450 km

POPULATION

POPULATION
Persons per sq. km

- over 100
- 50-100
- 10-50
- 1-10
- 0-1

Cities
- ■ over 1 million
- ● 500 000-1 000 000
- • 250 000-500 000
- · 100 000-250 000

Map cities: Iquitos, Piura, Chiclayo, Trujillo, Chimbote, Callao, Lima, Cuzco, Arequipa

Scale 1 : 21 000 000

0   200   400   600 km

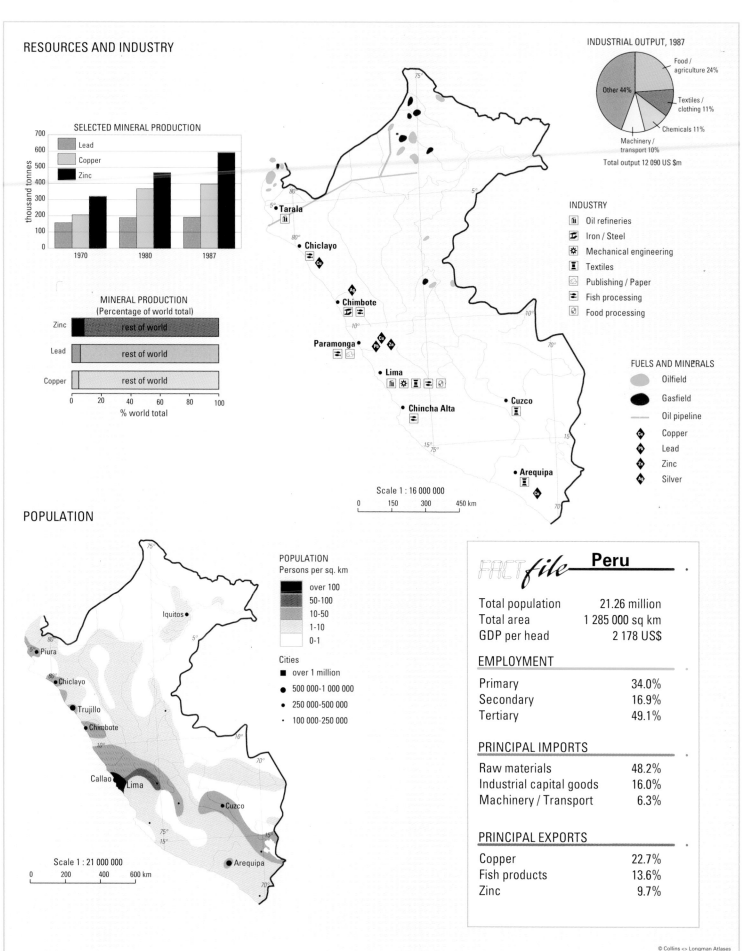

FACTfile Peru

Total population	21.26 million
Total area	1 285 000 sq km
GDP per head	2 178 US$

EMPLOYMENT

Primary	34.0%
Secondary	16.9%
Tertiary	49.1%

PRINCIPAL IMPORTS

Raw materials	48.2%
Industrial capital goods	16.0%
Machinery / Transport	6.3%

PRINCIPAL EXPORTS

Copper	22.7%
Fish products	13.6%
Zinc	9.7%

RESOURCES AND INDUSTRY

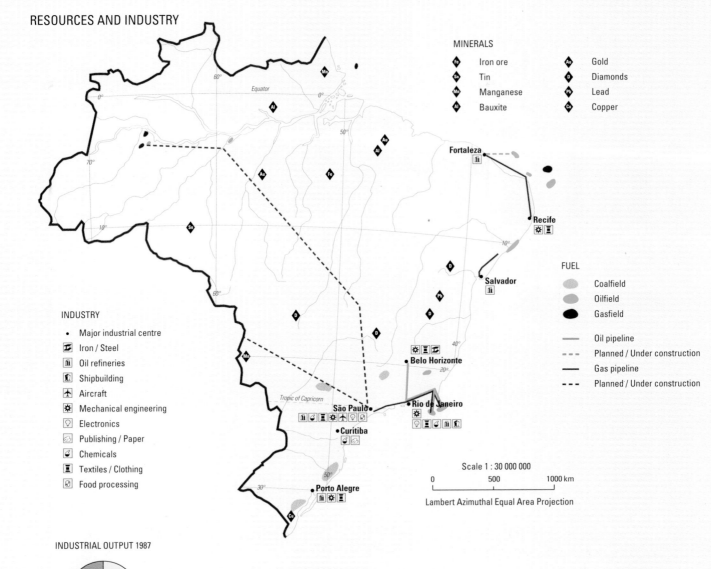

MINERALS

◆ Fe Iron ore ◆ Au Gold
◆ Sn Tin ◆ D Diamonds
◆ Mn Manganese ◆ Pb Lead
◆ Al Bauxite ◆ Cu Copper

FUEL

Coalfield
Oilfield
Gasfield

—— Oil pipeline
---- Planned / Under construction
—— Gas pipeline
---- Planned / Under construction

INDUSTRY

• Major industrial centre
▣ Iron / Steel
▣ Oil refineries
▣ Shipbuilding
✈ Aircraft
✹ Mechanical engineering
▣ Electronics
▣ Publishing / Paper
▣ Chemicals
▣ Textiles / Clothing
▣ Food processing

Scale 1 : 30 000 000

0   500   1000 km

Lambert Azimuthal Equal Area Projection

INDUSTRIAL OUTPUT 1987

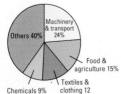

Machinery & transport 24%
Others 40%
Food & agriculture 15%
Chemicals 9%
Textiles & clothing 12

Total output: 116 130 US$m

GROWTH IN OIL PRODUCTION

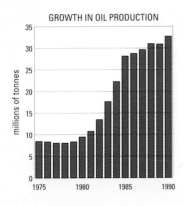

millions of tonnes

1975   1980   1985   1990

FACT*file*   **Brazil**

Total population	144.43 million
Total area	8 512 000 sq km
GDP per head	2 451 US$

EMPLOYMENT

Primary	25.2%
Secondary	23.6%
Tertiary	51.2%

PRINCIPAL IMPORTS

Minerals & petroleum	33.2%
Machinery & electrical equipment	24.2%
Industrial chemicals	16.0%

PRINCIPAL EXPORTS

Metals and products	17.5%
Processed food	16.5%
Machinery	9.7%
Nonmetallic minerals	9.3%
Fresh vegetables	9.1%

NATURAL RESOURCES

Gold   Iron ore   Tin

Quartz crystal   Silver   Diamonds

AMAZONIA

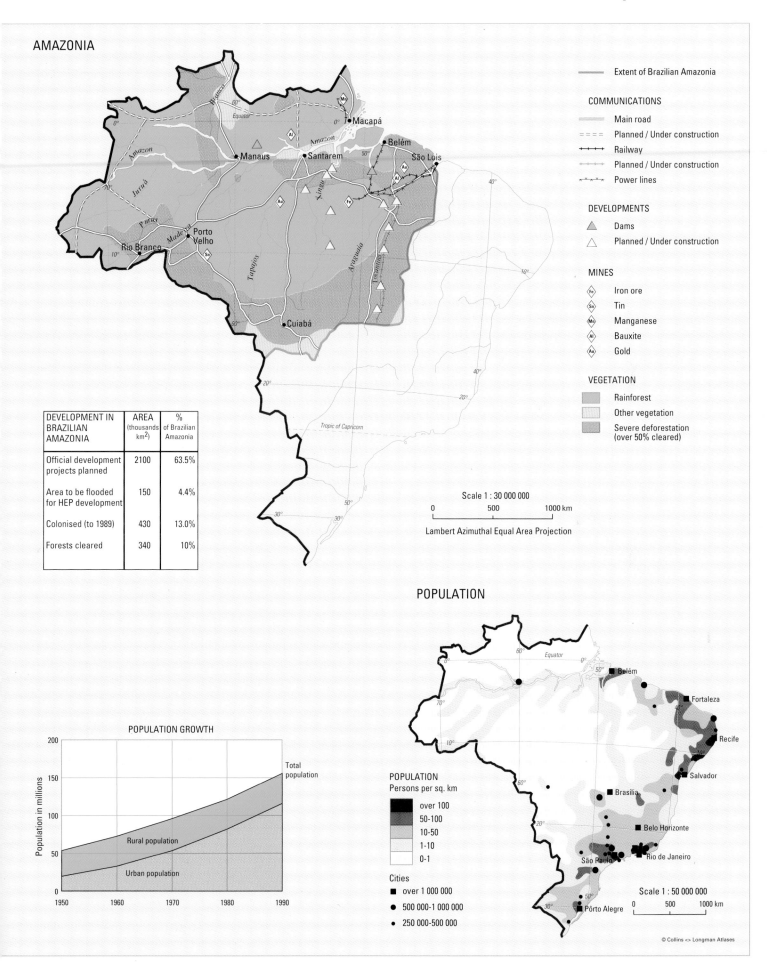

DEVELOPMENT IN BRAZILIAN AMAZONIA	AREA (thousands km²)	% of Brazilian Amazonia
Official development projects planned	2100	63.5%
Area to be flooded for HEP development	150	4.4%
Colonised (to 1989)	430	13.0%
Forests cleared	340	10%

Legend

Extent of Brazilian Amazonia

COMMUNICATIONS
Main road
Planned / Under construction
Railway
Planned / Under construction
Power lines

DEVELOPMENTS
Dams
Planned / Under construction

MINES
Fe Iron ore
Sn Tin
Mn Manganese
Al Bauxite
Au Gold

VEGETATION
Rainforest
Other vegetation
Severe deforestation (over 50% cleared)

Scale 1 : 30 000 000

0   500   1000 km

Lambert Azimuthal Equal Area Projection

POPULATION

POPULATION GROWTH

Population in millions

Total population

Rural population

Urban population

1950 1960 1970 1980 1990

POPULATION
Persons per sq. km

over 100
50-100
10-50
1-10
0-1

Cities
over 1 000 000
500 000-1 000 000
250 000-500 000

Scale 1 : 50 000 000

0   500   1000 km

© Collins <> Longman Atlases

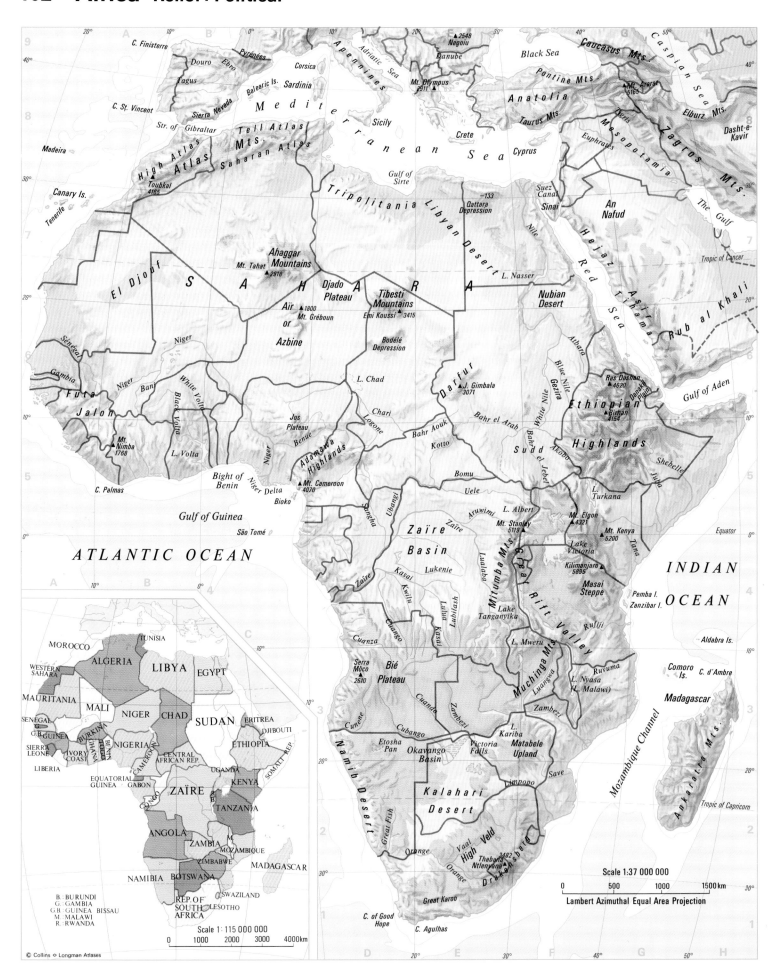

ATLANTIC OCEAN

INDIAN OCEAN

Mediterranean Sea

Black Sea

Caspian Sea

Red Sea

Gulf of Aden

Gulf of Guinea

Mozambique Channel

SAHARA

Zaïre Basin

Kalahari Desert

Namib Desert

Madagascar

C. Finisterre
Douro
Tagus
Ebro
Pyrénées
Corsica
Apennines
Adriatic Sea
Danube
▲2548 Negoiu
Caucasus Mts.
Pontine Mts.
Anatolia
Mt. Ararat ▲5165
Elburz Mts.
Dasht-e-Kavir
Sierra Nevada
Balearic Is.
Sardinia
Sicily
Crete
Mt. Olympus ▲2911
Taurus Mts.
Cyprus
Mesopotamia
Zagros Mts.
C. St. Vincent
Str. of Gibraltar
Tell Atlas Mts.
Saharan Atlas
High Atlas
Atlas
Toubkal 4165
Euphrates
Tigris
The Gulf
Madeira
Canary Is.
Tenerife
Tripolitania
Libyan Desert
Gulf of Sirte
Qattara Depression −133
Suez Canal
Sinai
An Nafud
Rub al Khali
Tropic of Cancer
L. Nasser
Nile
Hejaz
Asir
Tihama
Ahaggar Mountains
Mt. Tahat ▲2918
Djado Plateau
Tibesti Mountains
Emi Koussi ▲3415
Nubian Desert
El Djouf
Aïr or Azbine
Mt. Gréboun ▲1800
Bodélé Depression
Darfur
J. Gimbala ▲3071
Ras Dashan ▲4620
Danakil Plain
Sénégal
Gambia
Niger
Ban
White Volta
Black Volta
Futa Jalon
Mt. Nimba ▲1768
C. Palmas
Niger
Jos Plateau
L. Chad
Chari
Logone
Benue
Bahr Aouk
Kotto
Bahr el Arab
Blue Nile
White Nile
Gezira
Ethiopian Highlands
Birhan ▲4154
Shebelle
Bight of Benin
Niger Delta
Bioko
São Tomé
Adamawa Highlands
Mt. Cameroon ▲4070
Sangha
Ubangi
Uele
Bomu
Aruwimi
Zaïre
Sudd
Bahr el Jebel
Akobo
L. Albert
Mt. Stanley ▲5119
Mt. Elgon ▲4321
L. Turkana
Juba
Equator
Kasai
Lukenie
Lualaba
Mitumba Mts.
Lake Victoria
Mt. Kenya ▲5200
Tana
Kwilu
Luilaka
Lubilash
Kasai
Cuango
Lake Tanganyika
Kilimanjaro ▲5895
Masai Steppe
Pemba I.
Zanzibar I.
Aldabra Is.
Cuanza
Serra Môco ▲2610
Bié Plateau
Lake Mweru
Great Rift Valley
Rufiji
Comoro Is.
C. d'Ambre
Cuanda
Cunene
Muchinga Mts.
Luangwa
L. Nyasa (L. Malawi)
Ruvuma
Ankaratra Mts.
Etosha Pan
Okavango Basin
Cubango
Zambezi
Zambezi
Victoria Falls
Matabele Upland
L. Kariba
Save
Tropic of Capricorn
Kalahari Desert
Impopo
Great Fish
Orange
Vaal
High Veld
Thabana Ntlenyana ▲3482
Drakensberg
Great Karoo
C. of Good Hope
C. Agulhas

Scale 1:37 000 000

0   500   1000   1500 km

Lambert Azimuthal Equal Area Projection

MOROCCO
TUNISIA
WESTERN SAHARA
ALGERIA
LIBYA
EGYPT
MAURITANIA
MALI
NIGER
CHAD
SUDAN
ERITREA
DJIBOUTI
SENEGAL
G.B. GUINEA
SIERRA LEONE
LIBERIA
IVORY COAST
BURKINA
GHANA
TOGO
BENIN
NIGERIA
CAMEROON
CENTRAL AFRICAN REP.
ETHIOPIA
SOMALI REP.
EQUATORIAL GUINEA
GABON
CONGO
ZAÏRE
UGANDA
KENYA
R.
B.
TANZANIA
ANGOLA
ZAMBIA
M.
MOZAMBIQUE
ZIMBABWE
MADAGASCAR
NAMIBIA
BOTSWANA
SWAZILAND
REP. OF SOUTH AFRICA
LESOTHO

B.:BURUNDI
G.:GAMBIA
G.B.:GUINEA BISSAU
M.:MALAWI
R.:RWANDA

Scale 1: 115 000 000

0   1000   2000   3000   4000 km

© Collins ◇ Longman Atlases

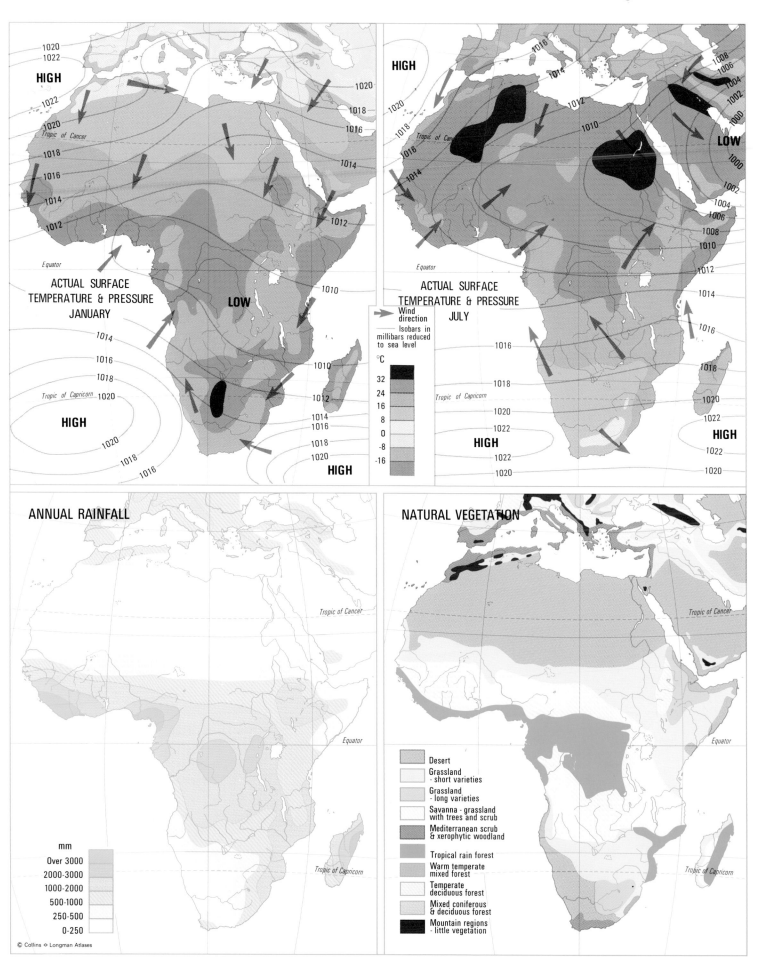

ACTUAL SURFACE
TEMPERATURE & PRESSURE
JANUARY

HIGH

1020
1022
1022
1020
Tropic of Cancer
1018
1016
1014
1012

Equator

LOW

1014
1016
1018
HIGH
1020
Tropic of Capricorn 1020
1018
1016

1010
1012
1014
1016
1018
1020
HIGH

ACTUAL SURFACE
TEMPERATURE & PRESSURE
JULY

HIGH

1016
1014
1012
Tropic of Cancer
1010
1014

LOW

1008
1006
1004
1002
1000
1002
1004
1006
1008
1010
1012
1014
1016
1018
1020
1022
HIGH

Equator

1016
1018
1020
1022
Tropic of Capricorn
HIGH

→ Wind
direction
Isobars in
millibars reduced
to sea level

°C
32
24
16
8
0
-8
-16

ANNUAL RAINFALL

Tropic of Cancer

Equator

Tropic of Capricorn

mm
Over 3000
2000-3000
1000-2000
500-1000
250-500
0-250

© Collins ○ Longman Atlases

NATURAL VEGETATION

Tropic of Cancer

Equator

Tropic of Capricorn

Desert

Grassland
- short varieties

Grassland
- long varieties

Savanna - grassland
with trees and scrub

Mediterranean scrub
& xerophytic woodland

Tropical rain forest

Warm temperate
mixed forest

Temperate
deciduous forest

Mixed coniferous
& deciduous forest

Mountain regions
- little vegetation

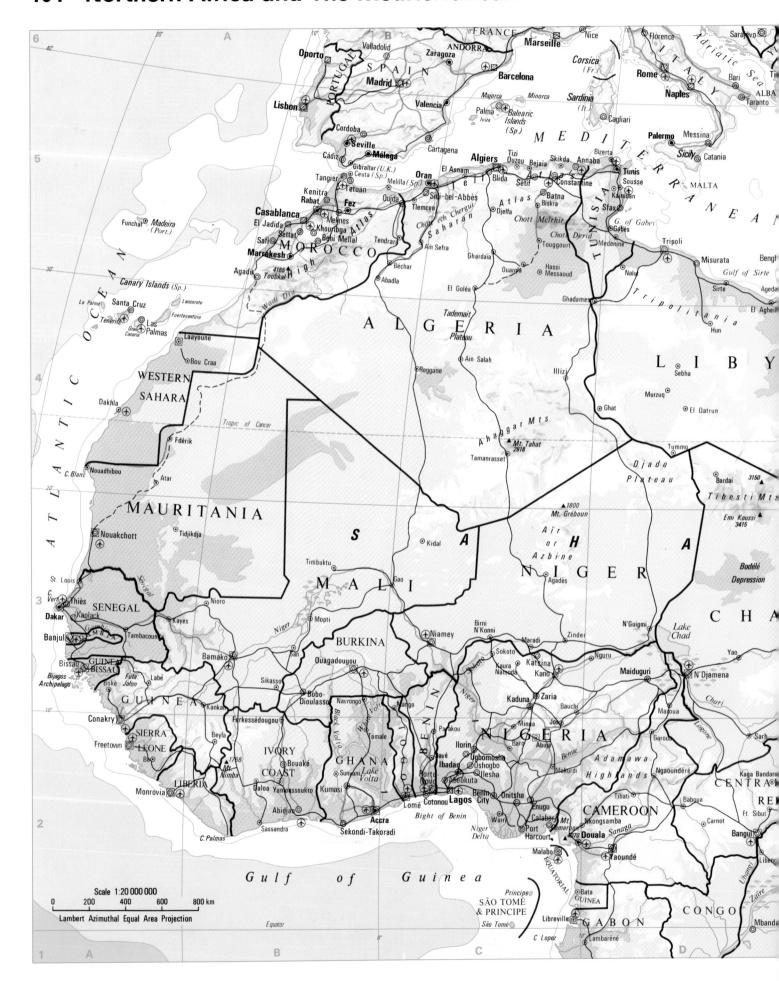

Scale 1:20 000 000

0   200   400   600   800 km

Lambert Azimuthal Equal Area Projection

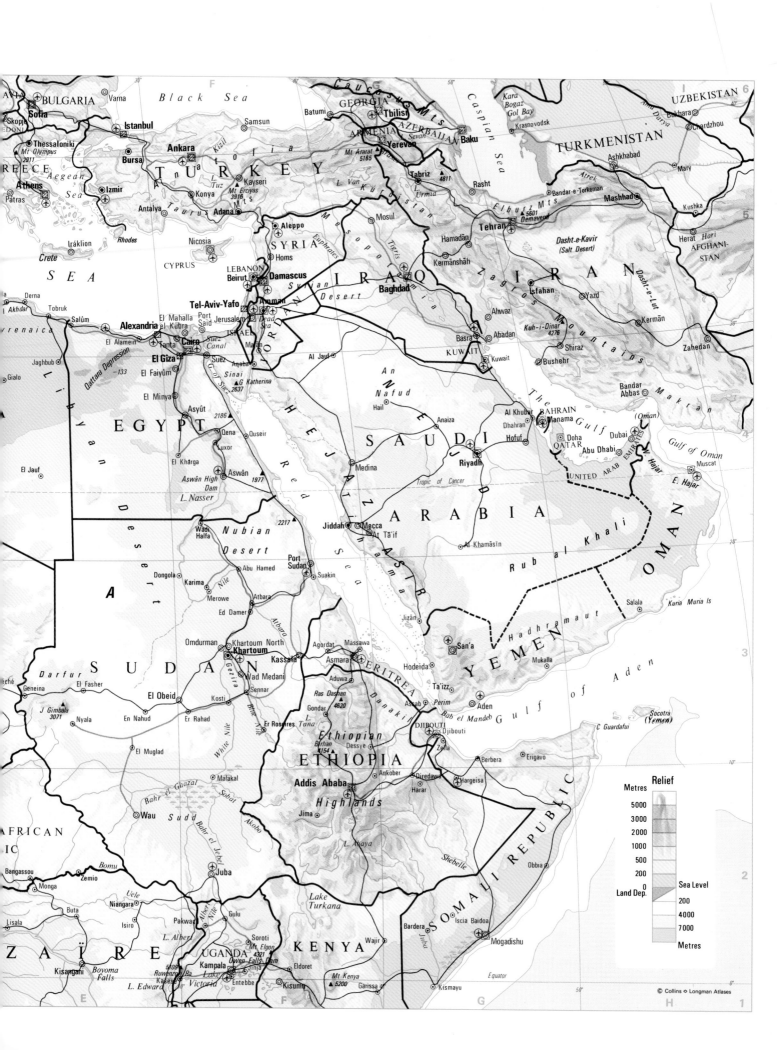

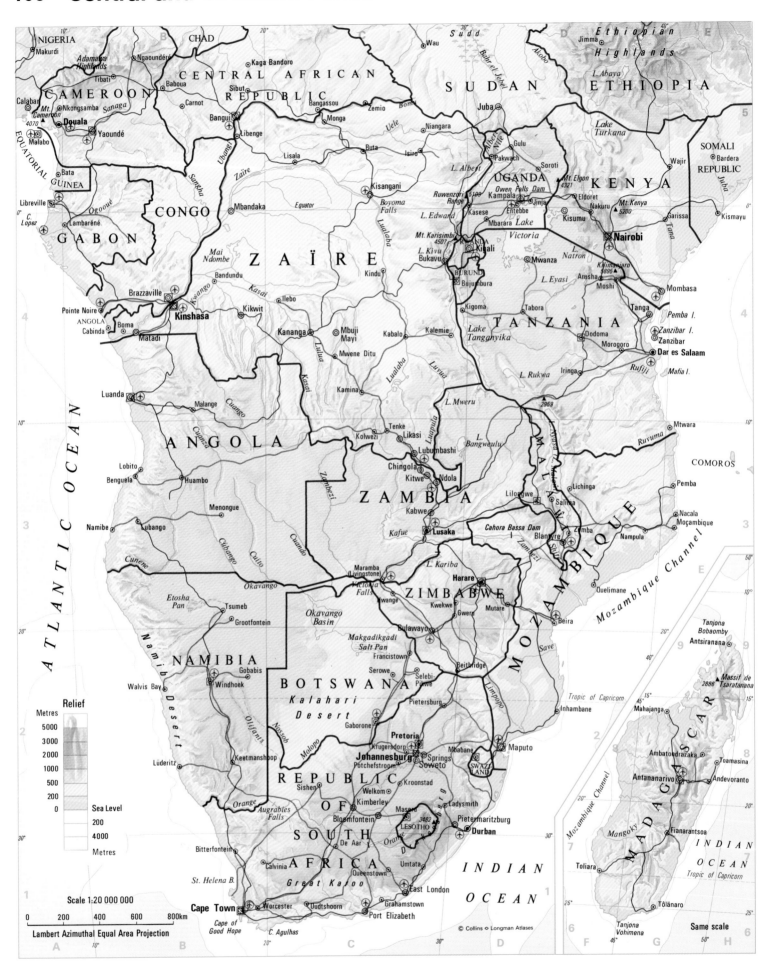

EGYPT

POPULATION

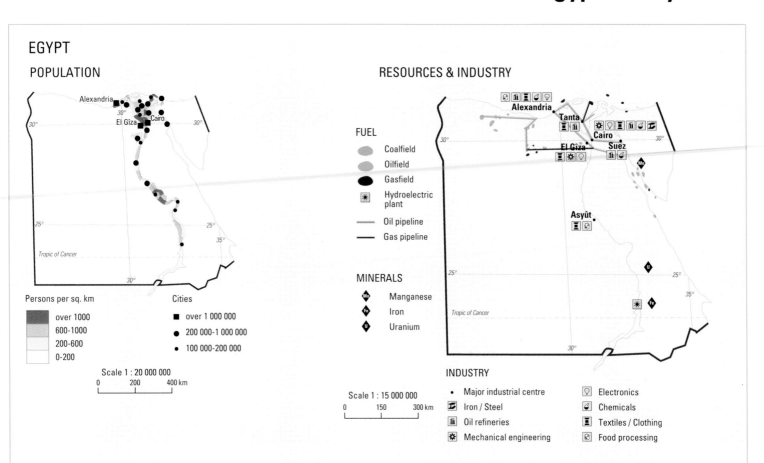

Persons per sq. km

- over 1000
- 600-1000
- 200-600
- 0-200

Cities

- ■ over 1 000 000
- ● 200 000-1 000 000
- • 100 000-200 000

Scale 1 : 20 000 000

0   200   400 km

RESOURCES & INDUSTRY

FUEL

- Coalfield
- Oilfield
- Gasfield
- ✳ Hydroelectric plant
- Oil pipeline
- Gas pipeline

MINERALS

- Mn Manganese
- Fe Iron
- U Uranium

Scale 1 : 15 000 000

0   150   300 km

INDUSTRY

- • Major industrial centre
- Iron / Steel
- Oil refineries
- ✳ Mechanical engineering
- Electronics
- Chemicals
- Textiles / Clothing
- Food processing

KENYA

RESOURCES AND INDUSTRY

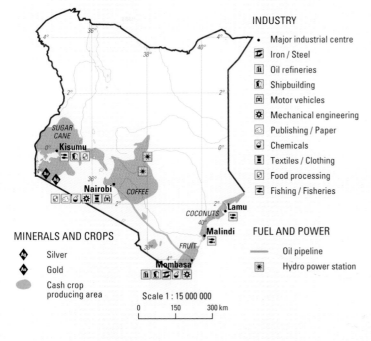

INDUSTRY

- • Major industrial centre
- Iron / Steel
- Oil refineries
- Shipbuilding
- Motor vehicles
- ✳ Mechanical engineering
- Publishing / Paper
- Chemicals
- Textiles / Clothing
- Food processing
- Fishing / Fisheries

FUEL AND POWER

- Oil pipeline
- ✳ Hydro power station

MINERALS AND CROPS

- Ag Silver
- Au Gold
- Cash crop producing area

Scale 1 : 15 000 000

0   150   300 km

POPULATION

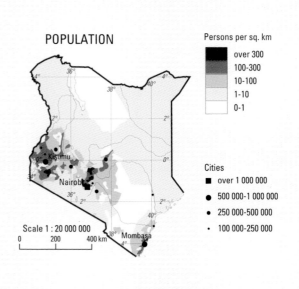

Persons per sq. km

- over 300
- 100-300
- 10-100
- 1-10
- 0-1

Cities

- ■ over 1 000 000
- ● 500 000-1 000 000
- ● 250 000-500 000
- • 100 000-250 000

Scale 1 : 20 000 000

0   200   400 km

Ghana and Nigeria

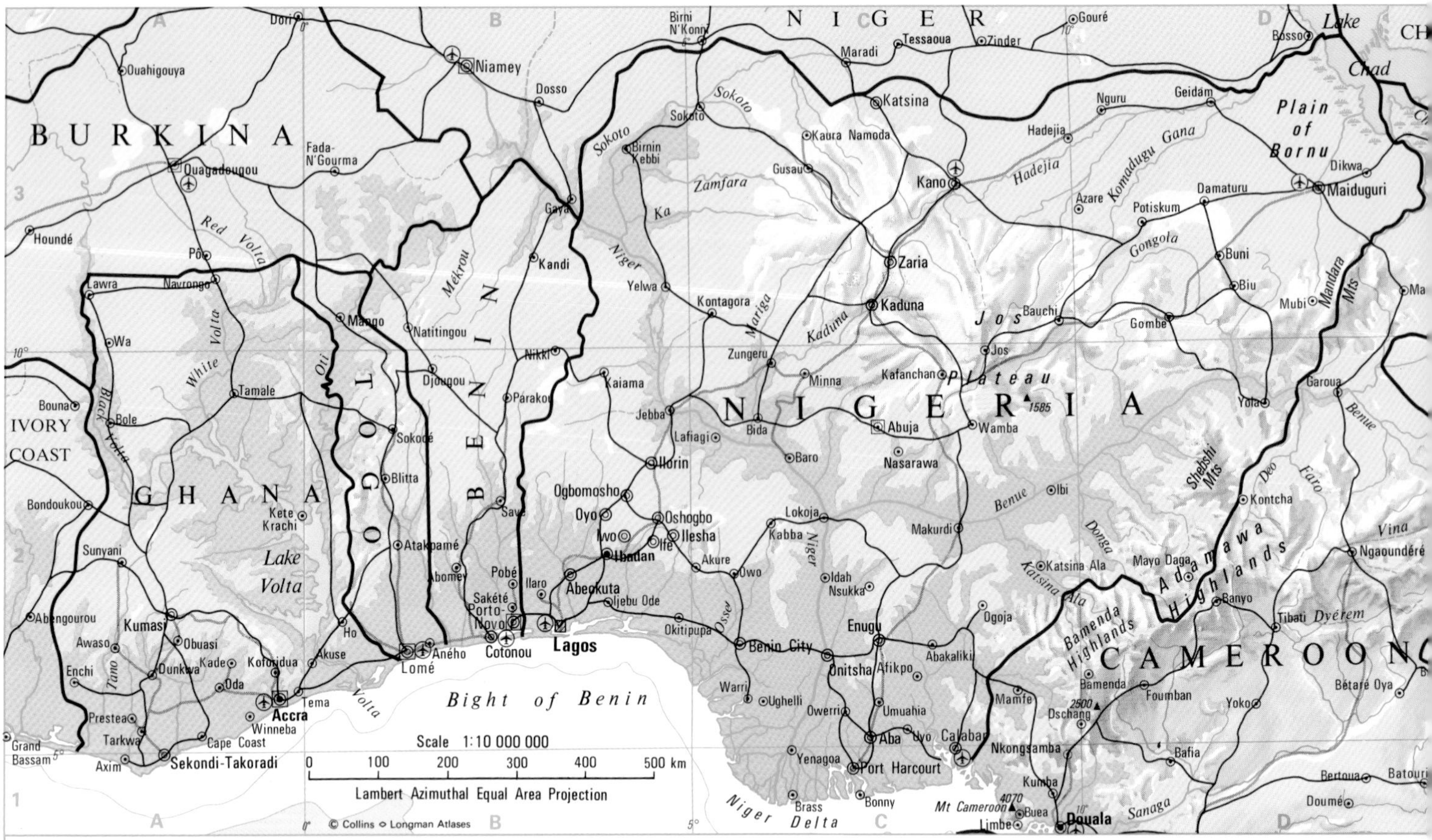

GHANA

POPULATION

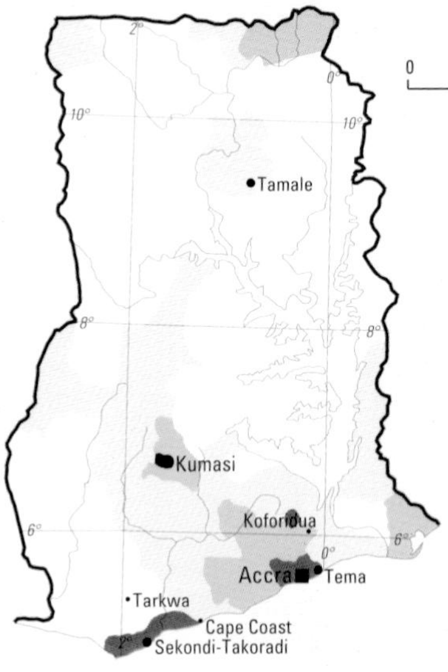

Scale 1 : 10 000 000
0 100 200 300 km

POPULATION
Persons per sq. km

- over 1000
- 200-1000
- 100-200
- 50-100
- 0-50

Cities

- 500 000-1 000 000
- 250 000-500 000
- 100 000-250 000
- 50 000- 100 000

URBAN POPULATION

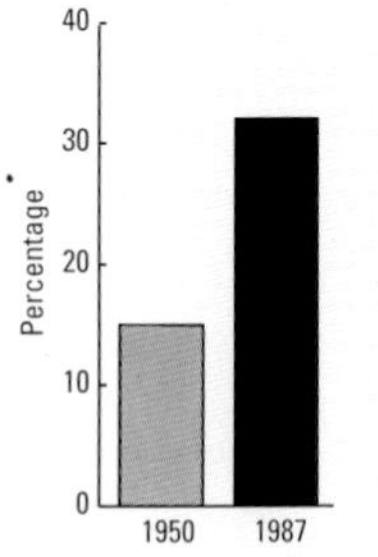

EMPLOYED IN AGRICULTURE

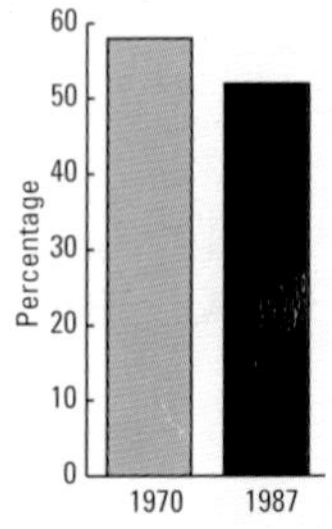

ENERGY CONSUMPTION PER HEAD

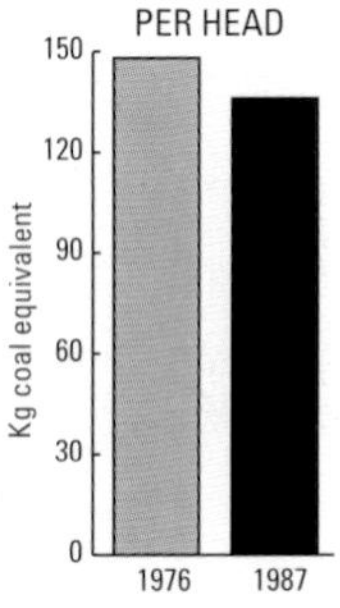

RESOURCES AND INDUSTRY

POWER

- Electricity transmission lines
- Proposed electricity transmission lines
- Hydro power station
- Oil fields

INDUSTRY

- Oil refineries
- Iron / Steel
- Mechanical engineering
- Publishing / Paper
- Textiles
- Food processing
- Fishing / Fisheries

MINERALS

- Gold
- Bauxite
- Diamond
- Manganese

TIMBER

- Major producing areas

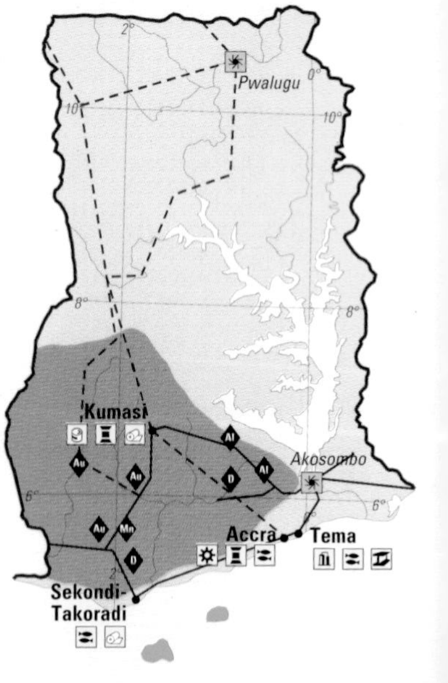

Scale 1 : 10 000 000
0 100 200 300 km

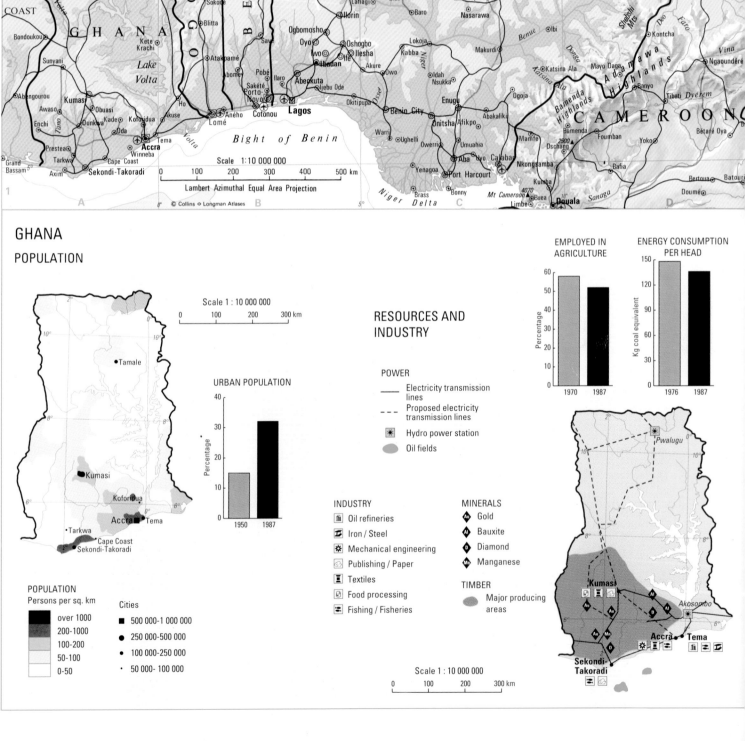

NIGERIA

POPULATION

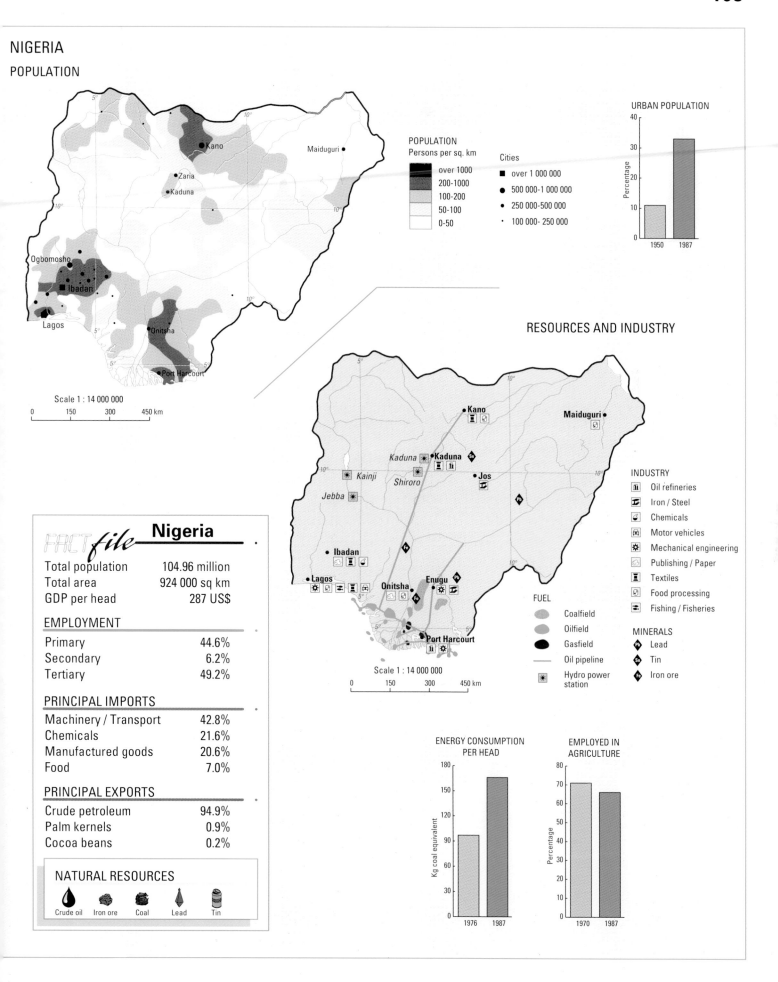

URBAN POPULATION

POPULATION
Persons per sq. km

	over 1000
	200-1000
	100-200
	50-100
	0-50

Cities

■ over 1 000 000
● 500 000-1 000 000
• 250 000-500 000
· 100 000- 250 000

Scale 1 : 14 000 000

0   150   300   450 km

RESOURCES AND INDUSTRY

INDUSTRY

🛢	Oil refineries
⚒	Iron / Steel
⚗	Chemicals
🚗	Motor vehicles
✺	Mechanical engineering
📄	Publishing / Paper
☰	Textiles
◔	Food processing
⮂	Fishing / Fisheries

MINERALS

◆ Pb	Lead
◆ Sn	Tin
◆ Fe	Iron ore

FUEL

Coalfield
Oilfield
Gasfield
Oil pipeline
✷ Hydro power station

Scale 1 : 14 000 000

0   150   300   450 km

FACT file — **Nigeria**

Total population	104.96 million
Total area	924 000 sq km
GDP per head	287 US$

EMPLOYMENT

Primary	44.6%
Secondary	6.2%
Tertiary	49.2%

PRINCIPAL IMPORTS

Machinery / Transport	42.8%
Chemicals	21.6%
Manufactured goods	20.6%
Food	7.0%

PRINCIPAL EXPORTS

Crude petroleum	94.9%
Palm kernels	0.9%
Cocoa beans	0.2%

NATURAL RESOURCES

Crude oil   Iron ore   Coal   Lead   Tin

ENERGY CONSUMPTION PER HEAD

Kg coal equivalent

1976   1987

EMPLOYED IN AGRICULTURE

Percentage

1970   1987

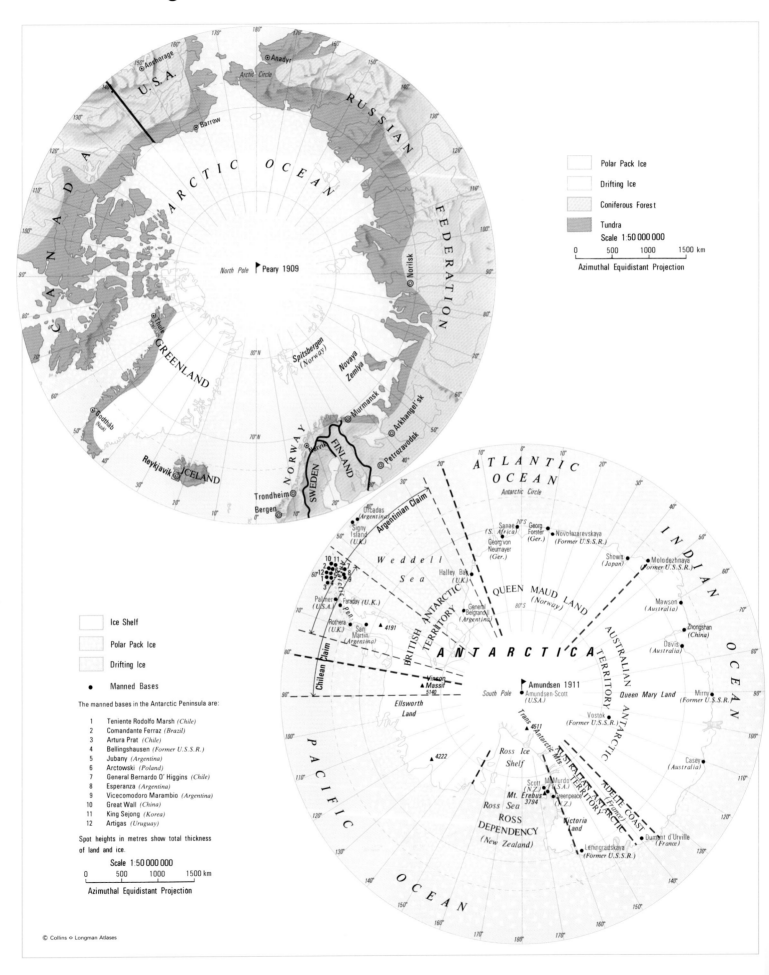

Polar Pack Ice

Drifting Ice

Coniferous Forest

Tundra

Scale 1:50 000 000

0   500   1000   1500 km

Azimuthal Equidistant Projection

Ice Shelf

Polar Pack Ice

Drifting Ice

•   Manned Bases

The manned bases in the Antarctic Peninsula are:

1   Teniente Rodolfo Marsh *(Chile)*
2   Comandante Ferraz *(Brazil)*
3   Artura Prat *(Chile)*
4   Bellingshausen *(Former U.S.S.R.)*
5   Jubany *(Argentina)*
6   Arctowski *(Poland)*
7   General Bernardo O' Higgins *(Chile)*
8   Esperanza *(Argentina)*
9   Vicecomodoro Marambio *(Argentina)*
10   Great Wall *(China)*
11   King Sejong *(Korea)*
12   Artigas *(Uruguay)*

Spot heights in metres show total thickness
of land and ice.

Scale 1:50 000 000

0   500   1000   1500 km

Azimuthal Equidistant Projection

© Collins ◇ Longman Atlases

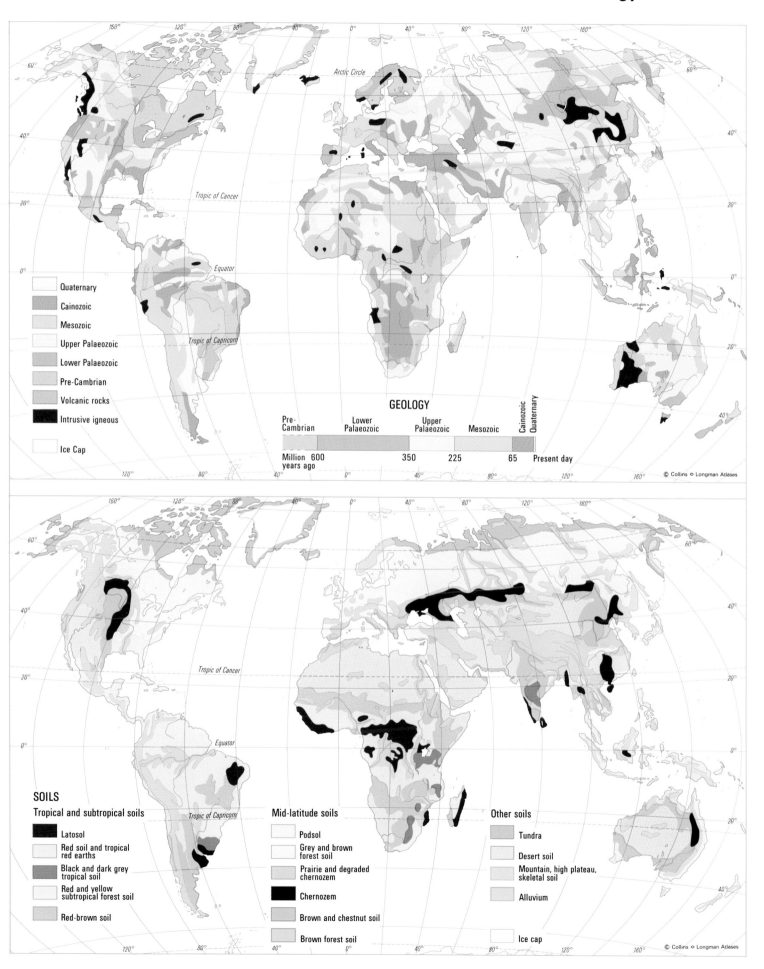

GEOLOGY

Pre-Cambrian	Lower Palaeozoic	Upper Palaeozoic	Mesozoic	Cainozoic Quaternary

Million 600   350   225   65   Present day
years ago

Quaternary

Cainozoic

Mesozoic

Upper Palaeozoic

Lower Palaeozoic

Pre-Cambrian

Volcanic rocks

Intrusive igneous

Ice Cap

© Collins ◇ Longman Atlases

SOILS

Tropical and subtropical soils

Latosol

Red soil and tropical red earths

Black and dark grey tropical soil

Red and yellow subtropical forest soil

Red-brown soil

Mid-latitude soils

Podsol

Grey and brown forest soil

Prairie and degraded chernozem

Chernozem

Brown and chestnut soil

Brown forest soil

Other soils

Tundra

Desert soil

Mountain, high plateau, skeletal soil

Alluvium

Ice cap

© Collins ◇ Longman Atlases

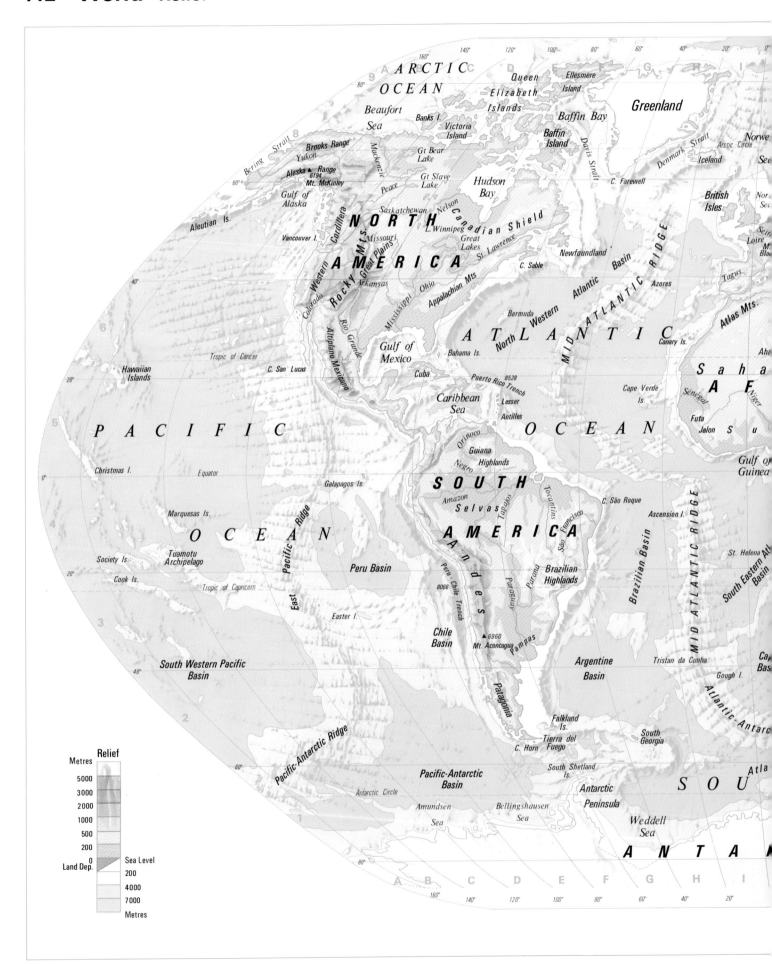

ARCTIC OCEAN

Queen
Elizabeth
Islands

Ellesmere
Island

Greenland

Beaufort
Sea

Banks I.

Victoria
Island

Baffin Bay

Baffin
Island

Davis Strait

Denmark Strait

Iceland

Arctic Circle

Norwe

Sea

British
Isles

Nor

Bering Strait

Brooks Range
Yukon

Mackenzie

Gt Bear
Lake

Hudson
Bay

C. Farewell

Alaska Range
6194
Mt. McKinley

Gt Slave
Lake

Seine
Loire
Bla

Gulf of
Alaska

Peace

Aleutian Is.

Vancouver I.

Saskatchewan

Nelson

Canadian Shield

Newfoundland

NORTH

Cordillera

Mts.

Missouri

L. Winnipeg

C. Sable

Western

Great Plains

Great
Lakes

St. Lawrence

AMERICA

Rocky

Colorado

Arkansas

Mississippi

Ohio

Appalachian Mts.

North Western Atlantic Basin

MID ATLANTIC RIDGE

Tagus

Atlas Mts.

Rio Grande

Tropic of Cancer

Bermuda

Azores

Hawaiian
Islands

Altiplano Mexicano

C. San Lucas

Gulf of
Mexico

Bahama Is.

ATLANTIC

Canary Is.

Saha

AF

Christmas I.

Cuba

Caribbean
Sea

Puerto Rico Trench

8528

Cape Verde
Is.

Senegal

Niger

PACIFIC

Lesser
Antilles

OCEAN

Futa
Jalon

Gulf of
Guinea

S u

Galapagos Is.

Orinoco

Guiana
Highlands

Negro

SOUTH

C. São Roque

Ascension I.

St. Helena

Marquesas Is.

Pacific Ridge

Amazon

Selvas

Tapajos

Tocantins

Brazilian Basin

OCEAN

Society Is.

Tuamotu
Archipelago

Peru Basin

AMERICA

São Francisco

Brazilian
Highlands

MID ATLANTIC RIDGE

South Eastern Atl
Basin

Cook Is.

Tropic of Capricorn

East

Easter I.

Peru-Chile Trench

8066

Andes

Paraná

Paraguay

Tristan da Cunha

Ca
Bas

Gough I.

Chile
Basin

Mt. Aconcagua
6960

Pampas

Argentine
Basin

Atlantic-Antarc

South Western Pacific
Basin

Patagonia

Falkland
Is.

South
Georgia

Pacific-Antarctic Ridge

C. Horn

Tierra del
Fuego

South Shetland
Is.

Atla

SOU

Pacific-Antarctic
Basin

Antarctic
Peninsula

Antarctic Circle

Amundsen
Sea

Bellingshausen
Sea

Weddell
Sea

ANTA

Equator

9
8
6
5
4
3
2
1

A B C D E F G H I

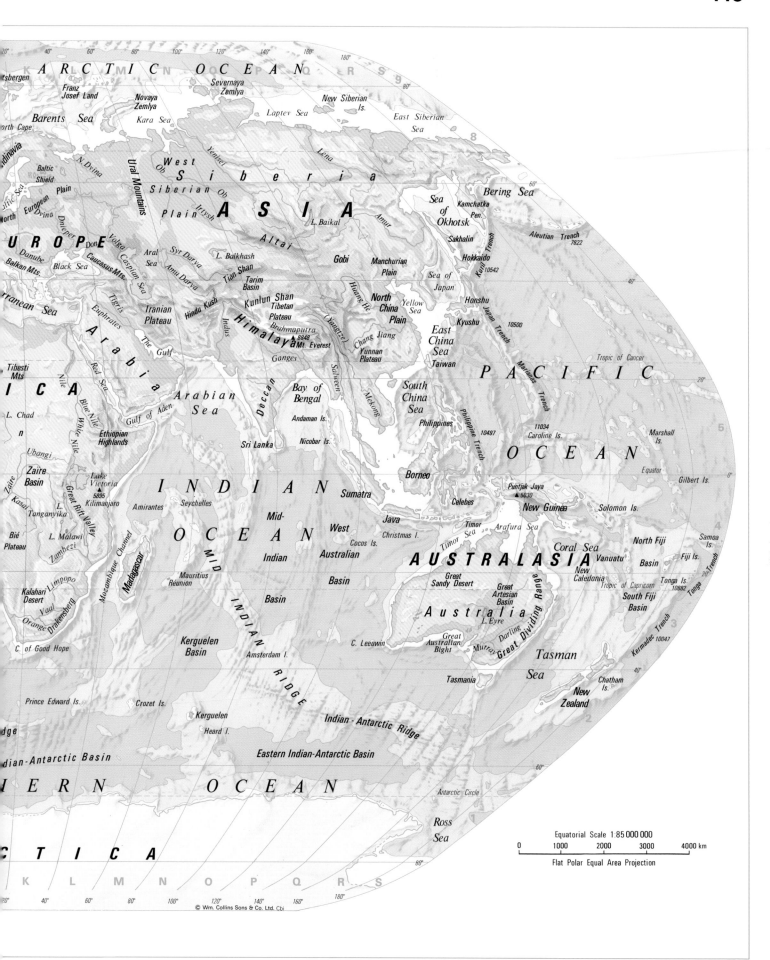

ARCTIC OCEAN

Spitsbergen
Franz Josef Land
Novaya Zemlya
Severnaya Zemlya
New Siberian Is.
Laptev Sea
East Siberian Sea

Barents Sea
North Cape
Kara Sea

Scandinavia
Baltic Shield
N. Dvina
Ural Mountains
West Siberian Plain
Yenisei
Ob
Ob
Irtysh
S i b e r i a
Lena
Bering Sea
Kamchatka Pen.
Aleutian Trench 7822

Baltic Sea
European Plain
Drina
Volga
Don
Aral Sea
Caspian Sea
Syr Darya
Amu Darya
L. Balkhash
Tian Shan
Altai
L. Baikal
A S I A
Amur
Sea of Okhotsk
Sakhalin
Hokkaido
Kuril Trench 10542

EUROPE
Dnieper
Danube
Balkan Mts.
Black Sea
Caucasus Mts.
Tigris
Euphrates
Iranian Plateau
Hindu Kush
Tarim Basin
Kunlun Shan
Tibetan Plateau
Gobi
Huang He
Manchurian Plain
North China Plain
Yellow Sea
Sea of Japan
Honshu
Kyushu
Japan Trench 10500

Mediterranean Sea
Arabia
Red Sea
The Gulf
Brahmaputra
8848 Mt. Everest
Himalaya
Ganges
(Yangtze)
Chang Jiang
Yunnan Plateau
East China Sea
Taiwan
PACIFIC
Tropic of Cancer
20°

AFRICA
Tibesti Mts
L. Chad
Nile
Blue Nile
White Nile
Gulf of Aden
Ethiopian Highlands
Arabian Sea
Indus
Deccan
Bay of Bengal
Andaman Is.
Nicobar Is.
Salween
Mekong
South China Sea
Philippines
Philippine Trench 10497
Caroline Is. 11034
Marshall Is.
Mariands Trench

Ubangi
Zaire Basin
Kasai
Tanganyika
Bié Plateau
L. Malawi
Zambezi
Great Rift Valley
Lake Victoria
5895 Kilimanjaro
Amirantes
Seychelles
Sri Lanka
Mid-Indian
West Australian
Cocos Is.
Christmas I.
Borneo
Sumatra
Celebes
Java
Timor
Arafura Sea
Puntjak Jaya 5030
New Guinea
Solomon Is.
Gilbert Is.
Equator
0°
OCEAN

Kalahari Desert
Vaal
Orange
Drakensberg
C. of Good Hope
Limpopo
Mozambique Channel
Madagascar
Mauritius
Réunion
Seychelles
I N D I A N
O C E A N
Basin
Basin
Indian
Basin
AUSTRALASIA
Great Sandy Desert
Great Artesian Basin
Australia
L. Eyre
Timor
Coral Sea
New Caledonia
Vanuatu
North Fiji Basin
Fiji Is.
South Fiji Basin
Tonga Trench 10882
Samoa Is.
Tropic of Capricorn
20°

Prince Edward Is.
Crozet Is.
Kerguelen Basin
Amsterdam I.
Kerguelen
Heard I.
MID INDIAN RIDGE
C. Leeuwin
Great Australian Bight
Murray
Darling
Great Dividing Range
Tasman Sea
Tasmania
New Zealand
Chatham Is.
Kermadec Trench 10047
40°

Indian-Antarctic Ridge
Indian-Antarctic Basin
Eastern Indian-Antarctic Basin
Antarctic Circle
Ross Sea
60°

SOUTHERN OCEAN
ANTARCTICA
80°

ARCTIC OCEAN

GREENLAND

• Godthåb · ICELAND
Reykjavík · *Faroe Is.*
(Den.)

C A N A D A

U.S.A.
ALASKA

Arctic Circle

UNITED DENM
KINGDOM
REP. OF Dublin Amst
IRELAND
London
Brussels
Paris Ber
FRANCE

• Edmonton

NORTH

• Vancouver · Winnipeg
• Seattle

Ottawa · Montreal
Chicago · Detroit · Toronto
Pittsburgh · Boston
• New York
San Francisco · St. Louis · Philadelphia
Washington

UNITED STATES

OF AMERICA

ATLANTIC

PORTUGAL
Lisbon
SPAIN
Madrid
Azores
(Port.)

• Dallas
• Houston

M
E
X
I
C
O

Rabat
Algiers
MOROCCO
ALGERI

OCEAN

Bermuda
(U.K.)

• Monterrey
Tropic of Cancer

Canary Is.
(Sp.)

Western Sahara

Hawaiian Is.
(U.S.A.)

• Guadalajara
Mexico
City

• Miami
Nassau
BAHAMAS
Havana · CUBA

JAMAICA HAITI
DOMINICAN
REP.
PUERTO
RICO
S.K.
ANTIGUA
DOMINICA
ST. LUCIA
BA.

MAURITANIA
Nouakchott

CAPE VERDE

MALI

Dakar
Bamako
SENEGAL
BURKIN
GAMBIA
GUINEA
Bissau
G.B.
Conakry
IVOR
Freetown
COAST
SIERRA LEONE
Monrovia
LIBERIA

NI
Niam
Ouagadougo
Abuj
Yamoussoukro
Accra
Lomé
Porto Novo
Malab
S.T
Libre

BELIZE
Belmopan
Guatemala City GUAT.
HONDURAS
EL SALVADOR · Tegucigalpa
Managua · NICARAGUA
COSTA · San José
RICA
PANAMA Panama
City

Kingston

Caracas
VENEZUELA
Georgetown
Paramaribo
Cayenne
S.V.
TRINIDAD
& TOBAGO
GUYANA
SURINAM
GUIANA (Fr.)

P A C I F I C

Bogotá

COLOMBIA

• Recife

Ascension I.
(U.K.)

KIRIBATI

Galapagos Is.
(Ec.)

Quito
ECUADOR

Marquesas Is.
(Fr.)

O C E A N

Tuamotu Archipelago

Samoa
(U.S.A.)

Cook Is.
(N.Z.)
Tahiti
Society Is.
(Fr.)

Tropic of Capricorn

P E R U

Lima

B R A Z I L

• Brasília

St. Helena
(U.K.)

• La Paz

SOUTH

BOLIVIA
Sucre

• Belo Horizonte

Easter I.
(Chile)

PARAGUAY

• Rio de Janeiro
São Paulo

(U.K.)

Asunción

A
R
G
E
N
T
I
N
A

URUGUAY

ATLANTIC

C
H
I
L
E

Santiago
Buenos
Aires
Montevideo

Tristan da Cunha (U.K.)

Gough I. (U.K.)

O C E A N

40°

Falkland Is.
(U.K.)

South Georgia
(U.K.)

A.: ANDORRA
ALB.: ALBANIA
AR.: ARMENIA
AUS.: AUSTRIA
AZ.: AZERBAIJAN
B.: BELGIUM
B.-H.: BOSNIA-HERZEGOVINA
BA.: BARBADOS
BANGLA.: BANGLADESH
BULG.: BULGARIA
C.: CROATIA
CAMB.: CAMBODIA
C.R.: CZECH REPUBLIC
E.: ESTONIA
EQ.G.: EQUATORIAL GUINEA
G.: GEORGIA
G.B.: GUINEA BISSAU
GERM.: GERMANY
GR.: GRENADA
GUAT.: GUATEMALA
H.: HUNGARY
KIRG.: KIRGHIZIA
L.: LUXEMBOURG
LA.: LATVIA
LEB.: LEBANON
LI.: LIECHTENSTEIN
LIT.: LITHUANIA
M.: MONACO
MA.: MALTA
MAC.: MACEDONIA
MOLD.: MOLDAVIA
NETH.: NETHERLANDS
R.F.: RUSSIAN FEDERATION

S.: SWITZERLAND
SA.: SLOVAKIA
S.K.: ST. KITTS-NEVIS
SL.: SLOVENIA
S.M.: SAN MARINO
S.T.: SÃO TOMÉ & PRINCIPE
S.V.: ST. VINCENT AND THE GRENADINES
T.: TURKEY (in Europe)
TAJ.: TAJIKISTAN
U.A.E.: UNITED ARAB EMIRATES
UZBEK.: UZBEKISTAN
V.C.: VATICAN CITY
YUGO.: YUGOSLAVIA

Antarctic Circle

Chilean Claim

Argentinian Claim

BRITISH ANTARCTIC TERRITORY

NORWEG

Anta

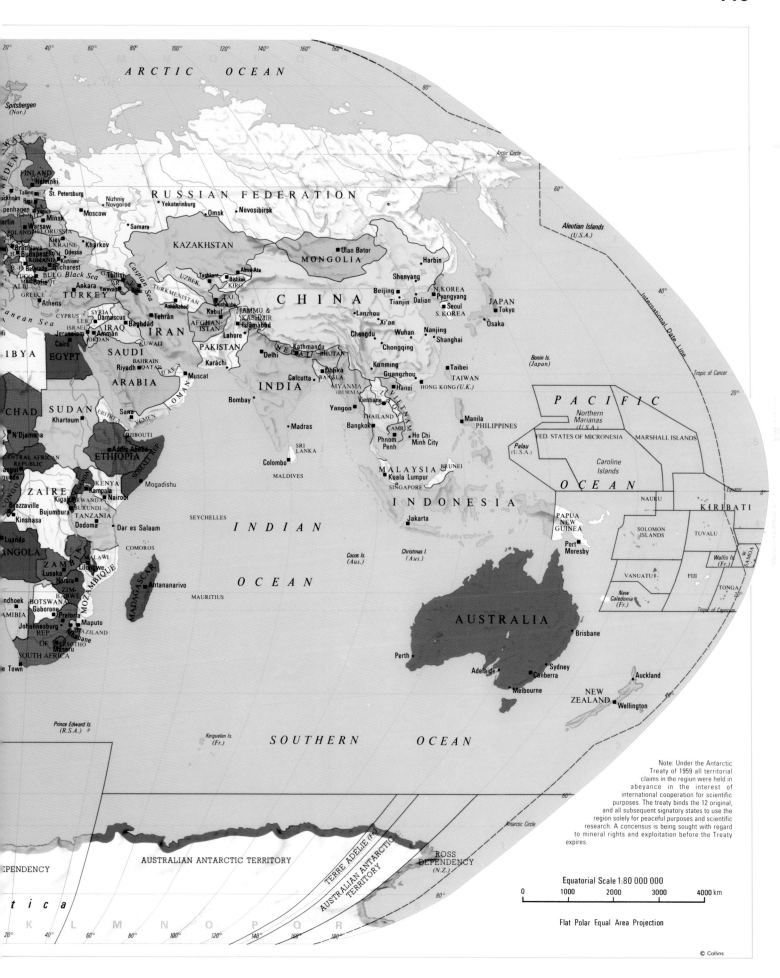

ARCTIC OCEAN

Spitsbergen (Nor.)

Arctic Circle

80°
60°
40°

RUSSIAN FEDERATION

SWEDEN
FINLAND
Helsinki
Tallinn
St. Petersburg
Riga
Stockholm
Nizhniy Novgorod
penhagen
Moscow
Yekaterinburg
Omsk
Novosibirsk
Berlin
Warsaw
Minsk
POLAND
BELORUSSIA
Kiev
UKRAINE
Kharkov
Samara
Bratislava
Budapest
ROMANIA
Kishinev
Odessa
Belgrade
Bucharest
BULG.
Sofia
Black Sea
Tbilisi
GEORGIA
Athens
GREECE
TURKEY
Ankara
Yerevan
ARM. AZ.
Caspian Sea
CYPRUS
LEB.
SYRIA
Damascus
ISRAEL
Jerusalem
JORDAN
Amman
Baghdad
IRAQ
KUWAIT
IRAN
Tehran
SAUDI
Riyadh
BAHRAIN
QATAR
U.A.E.
Muscat
ARABIA
OMAN

KAZAKHSTAN
Aral Sea
UZBEK.
Tashkent
Bishkek
KIRG.
TURKMENISTAN
Ashkhabad
Dushanbe
TAJ.
Kabul
AFGHAN-
ISTAN
JAMMU &
KASHMIR
Islamabad
PAKISTAN
Lahore
Karachi

MONGOLIA
Ulan Bator

CHINA
Lanzhou
Chengdu
Xi'an
Chongqing
Kunming

Delhi
NEPAL
Kathmandu
BHUTAN
BANGLA.
Dhaka
Calcutta
MYANMA
(BURMA)
Yangon

INDIA
Bombay
Madras

SRI
LANKA
Colombo
MALDIVES

Harbin
Shenyang
Beijing
Tianjin
Dalian
N.KOREA
Pyongyang
S.KOREA
Seoul
JAPAN
Tokyo
Osaka
Wuhan
Nanjing
Shanghai
Guangzhou
Taibei
Hong Kong (U.K.)
TAIWAN
Hanoi
VIETNAM
Vientiane
THAILAND
Bangkok
CAMB.
Phnom
Penh
Ho Chi
Minh City

Aleutian Islands (U.S.A.)

International Date Line

Arctic Circle

60°
40°
20°

Bonin Is. (Japan)

Tropic of Cancer

PACIFIC
Northern
Marianas
(U.S.A.)
FED. STATES OF MICRONESIA
Palau
(U.S.A.)
Caroline
Islands
OCEAN

MARSHALL ISLANDS

Manila
PHILIPPINES

MALAYSIA
Kuala Lumpur
BRUNEI
SINGAPORE

INDONESIA
Jakarta

NAURU

KIRIBATI

SOLOMON
ISLANDS
TUVALU
W.
SAMOA
Wallis Is.
(Fr.)
FIJI
TONGA

PAPUA
NEW
GUINEA
Port
Moresby
VANUATU
New
Caledonia
(Fr.)

Equator
20°

Tropic of Capricorn

LIBYA
EGYPT
Cairo
CHAD
SUDAN
Khartoum
N'Djamena
CENTRAL AFRICAN
REPUBLIC
ERITREA
Sana
YEMEN
DJIBOUTI
SOMALI REP.
Addis Abeba
ETHIOPIA
ZAIRE
Brazzaville
Kinshasa
UGANDA
Kampala
KENYA
Nairobi
RWANDA
Kigali
BURUNDI
Bujumbura
TANZANIA
Dodoma
Dar es Salaam
Mogadishu
SEYCHELLES
COMOROS

ANGOLA
Luanda
ZAMBIA
Lusaka
MALAWI
Lilongwe
MOZAMBIQUE
ZIM-
BABWE
Harare
NAMIBIA
Windhoek
BOTSWANA
Gaborone
Pretoria
Johannesburg
REP. OF
SOUTH AFRICA
Maputo
SWAZILAND
LESOTHO
Maseru
Cape Town

MADAGASCAR
Antananarivo
MAURITIUS

INDIAN

OCEAN

Cocos Is.
(Aus.)
Christmas I.
(Aus.)

AUSTRALIA
Perth
Adelaide
Brisbane
Sydney
Canberra
Melbourne

Auckland
NEW
ZEALAND
Wellington

40°

Prince Edward Is.
(R.S.A.)

Kerguelen Is.
(Fr.)

SOUTHERN   OCEAN

20°

Note: Under the Antarctic Treaty of 1959 all territorial claims in the region were held in abeyance in the interest of international cooperation for scientific purposes. The treaty binds the 12 original, and all subsequent signatory states to use the region solely for peaceful purposes and scientific research. A concensus is being sought with regard to mineral rights and exploitation before the Treaty expires.

60°

Antarctic Circle

DEPENDENCY
AUSTRALIAN ANTARCTIC TERRITORY
TERRE ADÉLIE (Fr.)
AUSTRALIAN ANTARCTIC
TERRITORY
ROSS
DEPENDENCY
(N.Z.)

tica

80°

Equatorial Scale 1:80 000 000

0   1000   2000   3000   4000 km

Flat Polar Equal Area Projection

© Collins

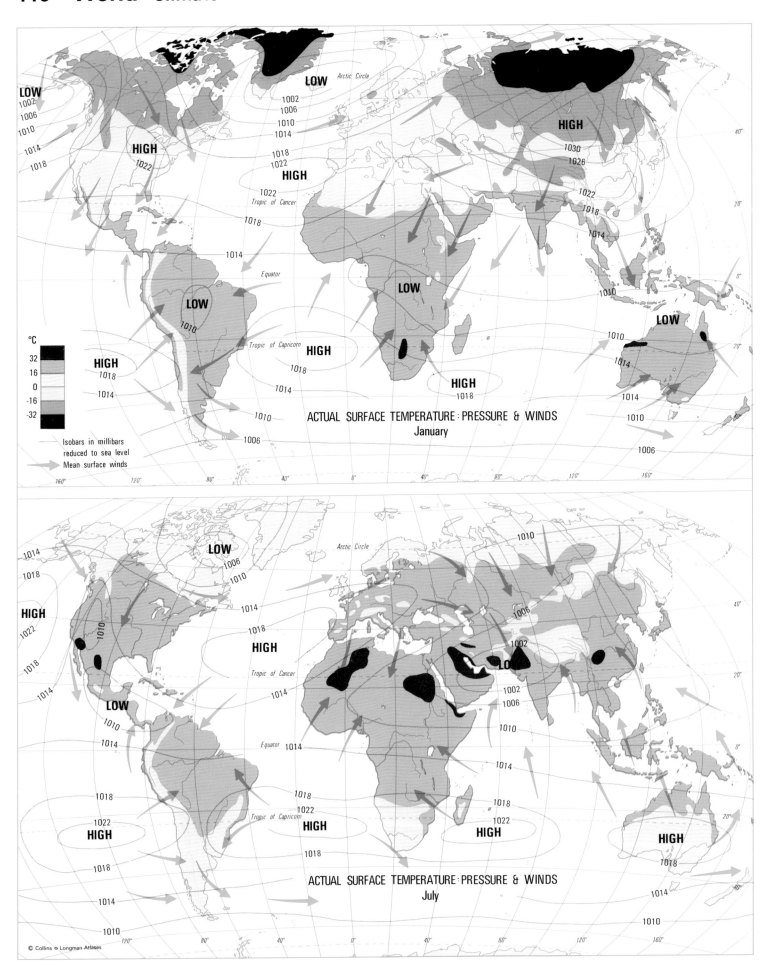

ACTUAL SURFACE TEMPERATURE: PRESSURE & WINDS
January

ACTUAL SURFACE TEMPERATURE: PRESSURE & WINDS
July

°C
32
16
0
-16
-32

Isobars in millibars
reduced to sea level
Mean surface winds

© Collins ◇ Longman Atlases

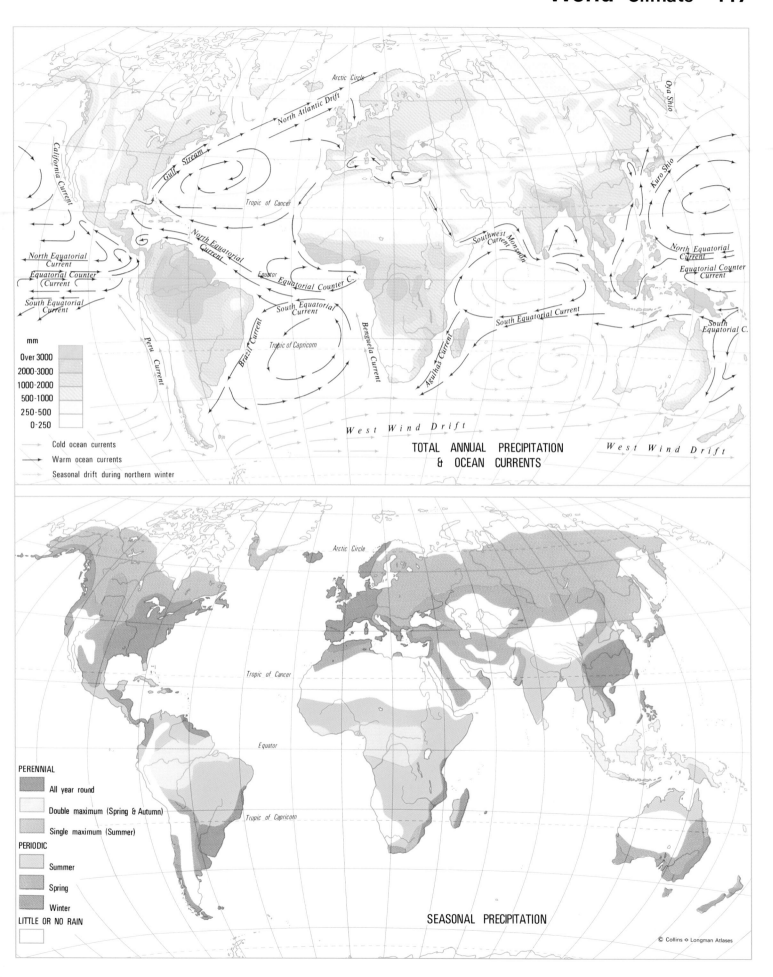

TOTAL ANNUAL PRECIPITATION & OCEAN CURRENTS

mm

Over 3000	
2000-3000	
1000-2000	
500-1000	
250-500	
0-250	

→ Cold ocean currents

→ Warm ocean currents

→ Seasonal drift during northern winter

SEASONAL PRECIPITATION

PERENNIAL

- All year round
- Double maximum (Spring & Autumn)
- Single maximum (Summer)

PERIODIC

- Summer
- Spring
- Winter

LITTLE OR NO RAIN

© Collins ◇ Longman Atlases

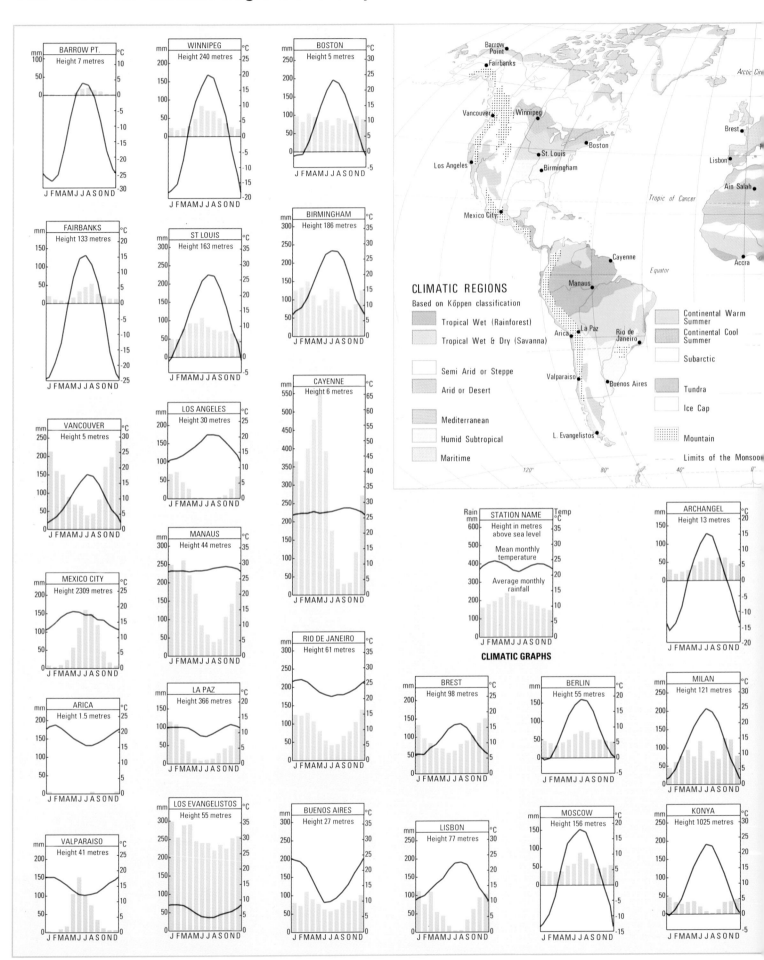

CLIMATIC REGIONS

Based on Köppen classification

- Tropical Wet (Rainforest)
- Tropical Wet & Dry (Savanna)
- Semi Arid or Steppe
- Arid or Desert
- Mediterranean
- Humid Subtropical
- Maritime
- Continental Warm Summer
- Continental Cool Summer
- Subarctic
- Tundra
- Ice Cap
- Mountain
- Limits of the Monsoon

CLIMATIC GRAPHS

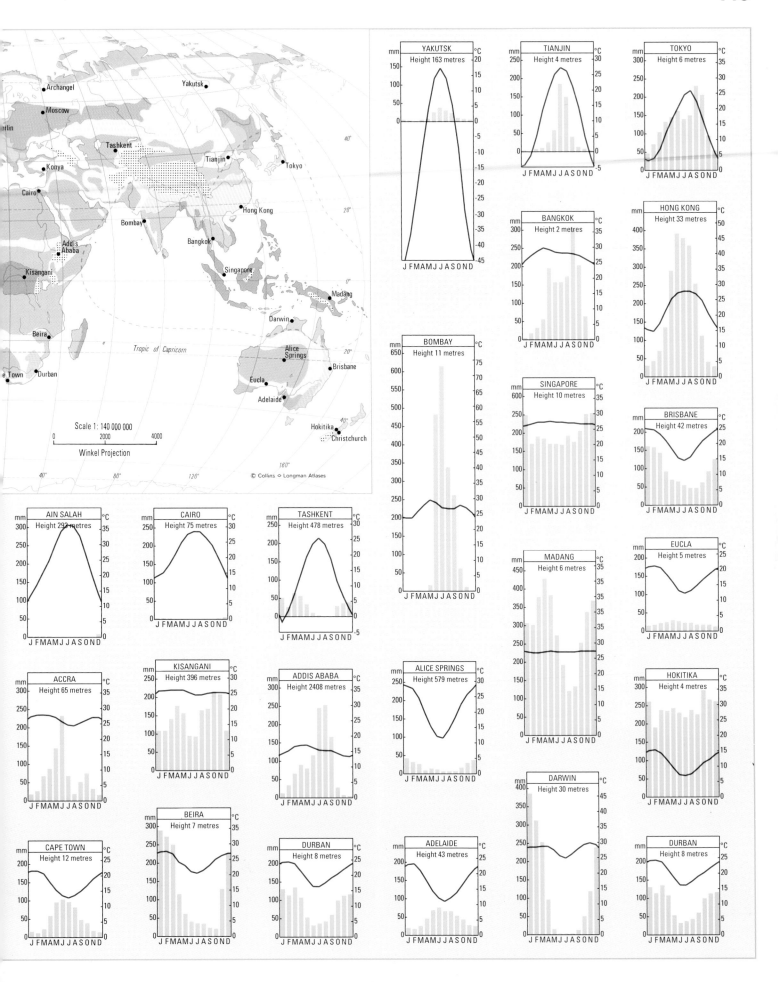

Scale 1: 140 000 000

Winkel Projection

© Collins ◇ Longman Atlases

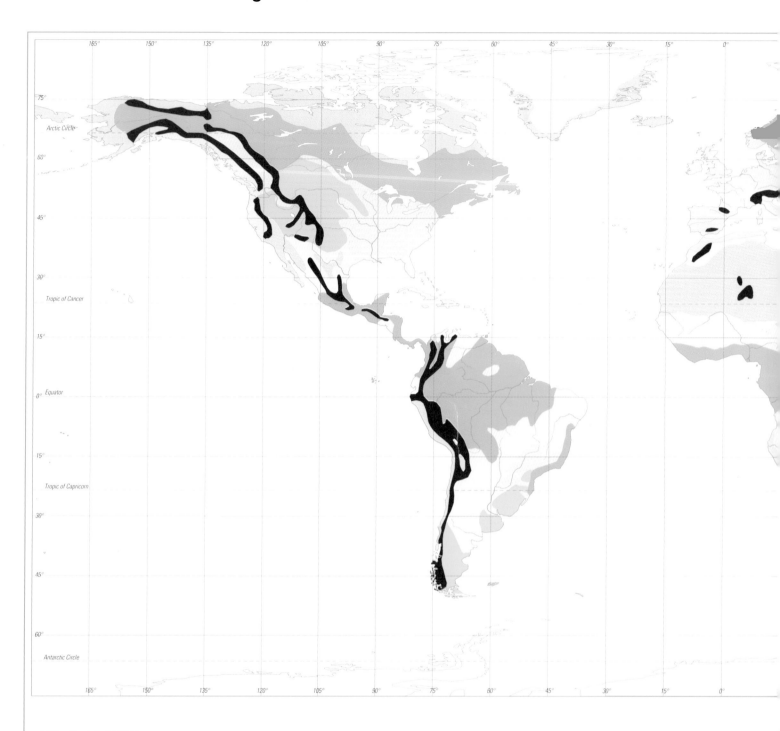

Ice cap, Antarctica

Tundra, Norway

Coniferous forest, Canada

Temperate deciduous forest, UK

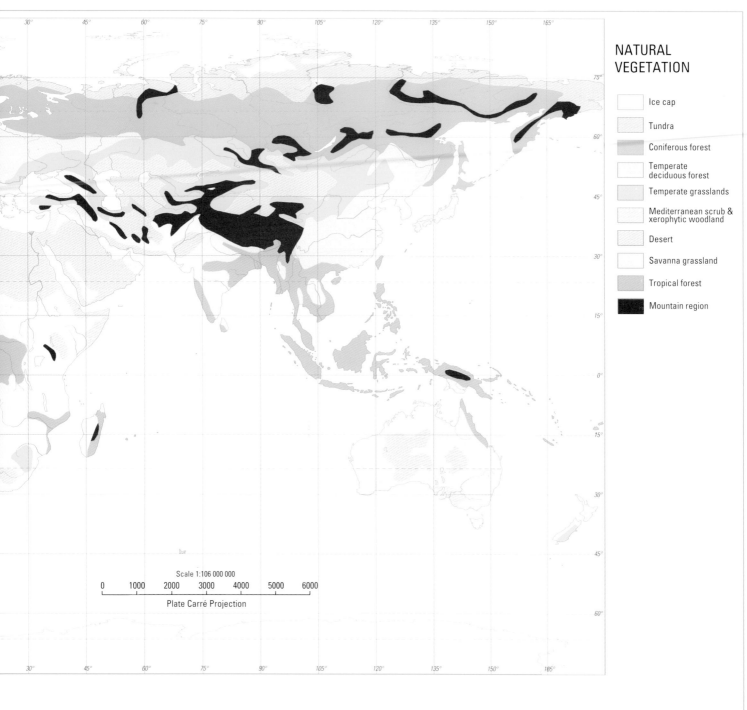

NATURAL VEGETATION

- Ice cap
- Tundra
- Coniferous forest
- Temperate deciduous forest
- Temperate grasslands
- Mediterranean scrub & xerophytic woodland
- Desert
- Savanna grassland
- Tropical forest
- Mountain region

Scale 1:106 000 000

0 1000 2000 3000 4000 5000 6000

Plate Carré Projection

...sert, Iran

Savanna grassland, Nigeria

Tropical forest, Malaysia

Mountain region, Nepal

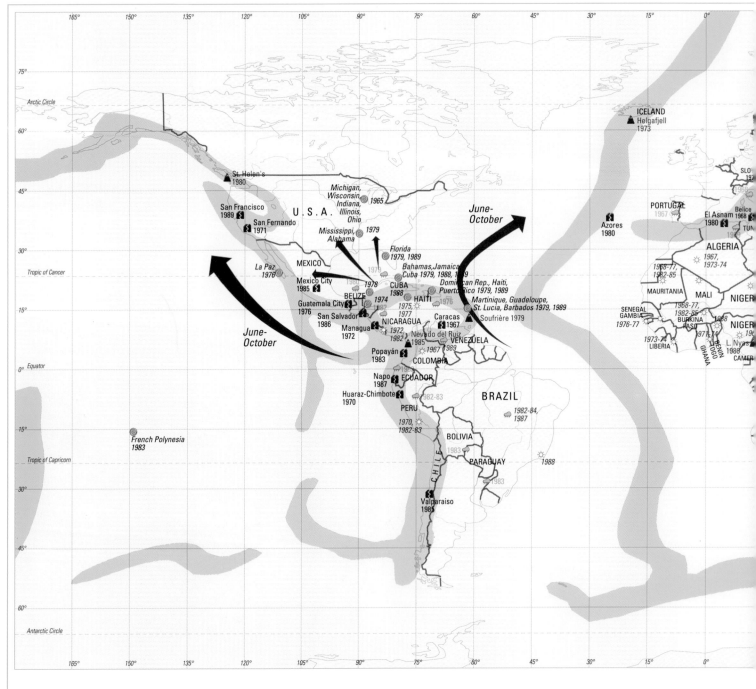

ICELAND
Helgafjell
1973

St. Helen's
1980

San Francisco
1989

San Fernando
1971

U.S.A.

Michigan,
Wisconsin,
Indiana,
Illinois,
Ohio

1965

Mississippi,
Alabama

1979

June-
October

PORTUGAL
1967

SLO
197

El Asnam
1980

Belice
1968

Azores
1980

ALGERIA
1967,
1973-74

La Paz
1976

MEXICO

Mexico City
1985

1979

1978

Florida
1979, 1989

Bahamas, Jamaica,
Cuba 1979, 1988, 1989

MAURITANIA

1968-77,
1982-85

MALI

NIGER

BELIZE

Guatemala City
1976

San Salvador
1986

Managua
1972

1980

CUBA
1988

1974

HAITI

1975,
1977

NICARAGUA

1972
1982

Caracas
1967

Popayán
1983

Napo
1987

Huaraz-Chimbote
1970

PERU

Nevado del Ruiz
1985

COLOMBIA

ECUADOR

1982-83

Dominican Rep., Haiti,
Puerto Rico 1979, 1989

Martinique, Guadeloupe,
St. Lucia, Barbados 1979, 1989

Soufrière 1979

VENEZUELA

1967 1989

June-
October

SENEGAL
GAMBIA
1976-77

1968-77,
1982-85

LIBERIA

1973-74

BURKINA
FASO

NIGER

1988

1971

1980

BENIN
TOGO

GHANA

L. Nyas

CAMER

French Polynesia
1983

BRAZIL

1982-84,
1987

1970,
1982-83

BOLIVIA

1983

PARAGUAY

1988

1983

Valparaiso
1985

C H I L E

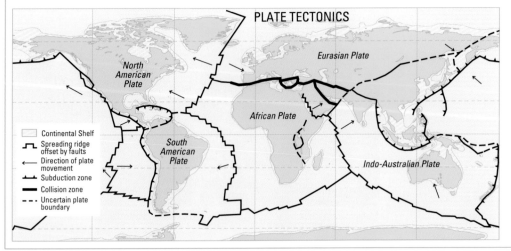

PLATE TECTONICS

Eurasian Plate

North
American
Plate

African Plate

South
American
Plate

Indo-Australian Plate

Continental Shelf

Spreading ridge
offset by faults

Direction of plate
movement

Subduction zone

Collision zone

Uncertain plate
boundary

Volcanic eruption, Mt. St. Helens, USA

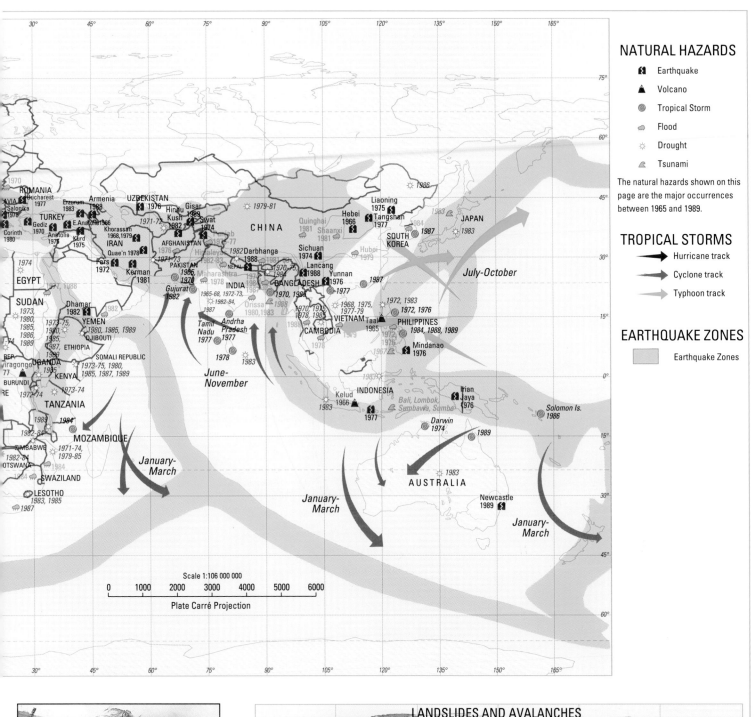

NATURAL HAZARDS

⚔ Earthquake

▲ Volcano

◎ Tropical Storm

☁ Flood

☼ Drought

◣ Tsunami

The natural hazards shown on this page are the major occurrences between 1965 and 1989.

TROPICAL STORMS

→ Hurricane track

→ Cyclone track

→ Typhoon track

EARTHQUAKE ZONES

Earthquake Zones

July-October

June-November

January-March

January-March

January-March

Earthquake damage, Armenia

LANDSLIDES AND AVALANCHES

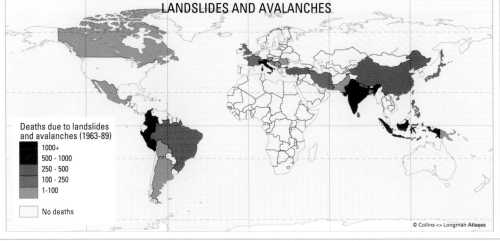

Deaths due to landslides and avalanches (1963-89)

1000+

500 - 1000

250 - 500

100 - 250

1 - 100

No deaths

© Collins <> Longman Atlases

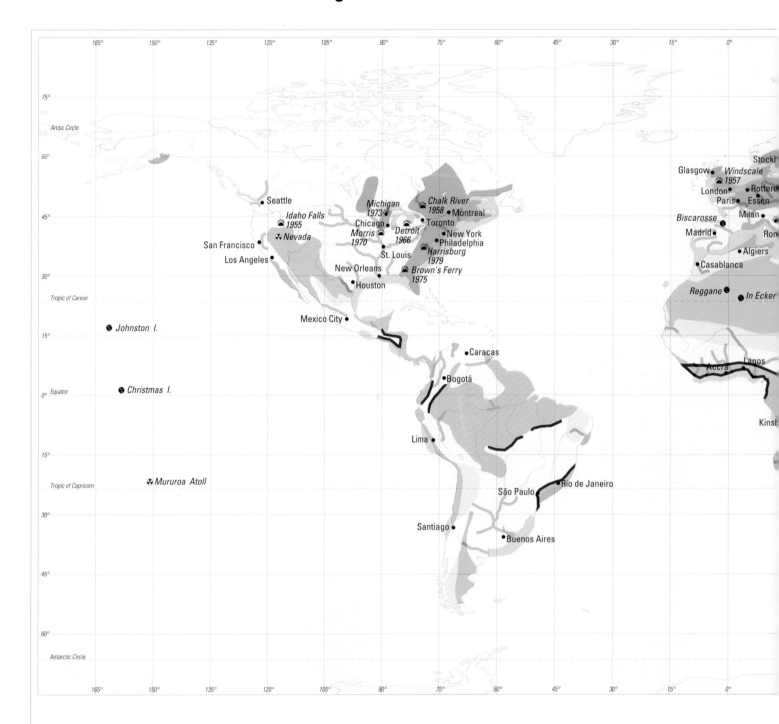

Deforestation in Amazonia, Brazil

Marine pollution in the North Sea

Industrial air pollution in Germany

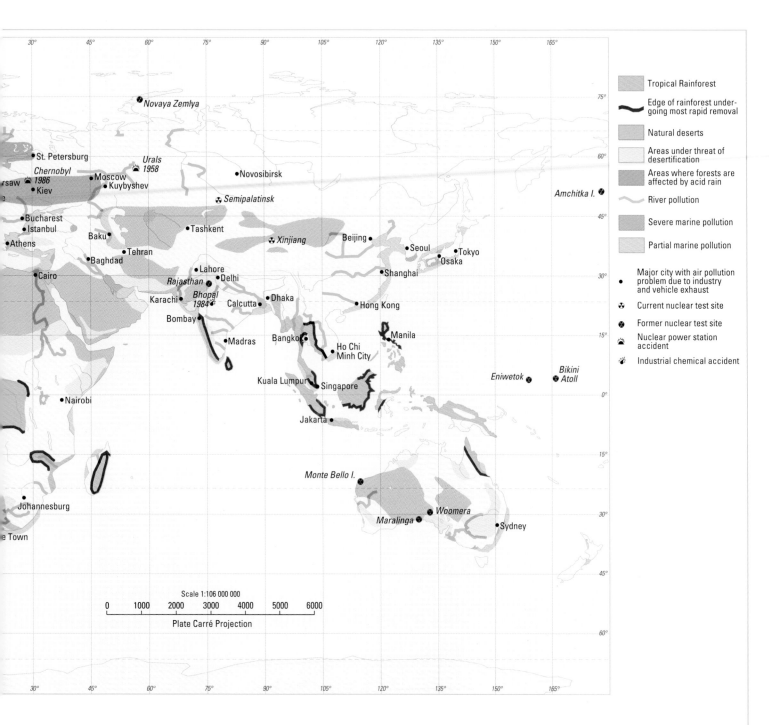

Tropical Rainforest

Edge of rainforest undergoing most rapid removal

Natural deserts

Areas under threat of desertification

Areas where forests are affected by acid rain

River pollution

Severe marine pollution

Partial marine pollution

• Major city with air pollution problem due to industry and vehicle exhaust

☢ Current nuclear test site

☢ Former nuclear test site

☢ Nuclear power station accident

☢ Industrial chemical accident

Novaya Zemlya

St. Petersburg
Chernobyl
1986
Warsaw
Kiev
Moscow
Kuybyshev
Urals
1958
Novosibirsk

Semipalatinsk

Amchitka I.

Bucharest
Istanbul
Athens
Baku
Tashkent
Tehran
Baghdad
Cairo
Lahore
Rajasthan
Delhi
Karachi
Bhopal
1984
Calcutta
Dhaka
Bombay
Madras
Bangkok
Ho Chi
Minh City
Kuala Lumpur
Singapore
Jakarta

Xinjiang
Beijing
Seoul
Tokyo
Osaka
Shanghai
Hong Kong
Manila

Nairobi

Eniwetok
Bikini
Atoll

Monte Bello I.

Johannesburg
e Town

Maralinga
Woomera
Sydney

Scale 1:106 000 000

0 1000 2000 3000 4000 5000 6000

Plate Carré Projection

Land at risk from desertification, Sudan

Vehicle fumes in Guatemala

Effect of acid rain on the trees of Czechoslovakia

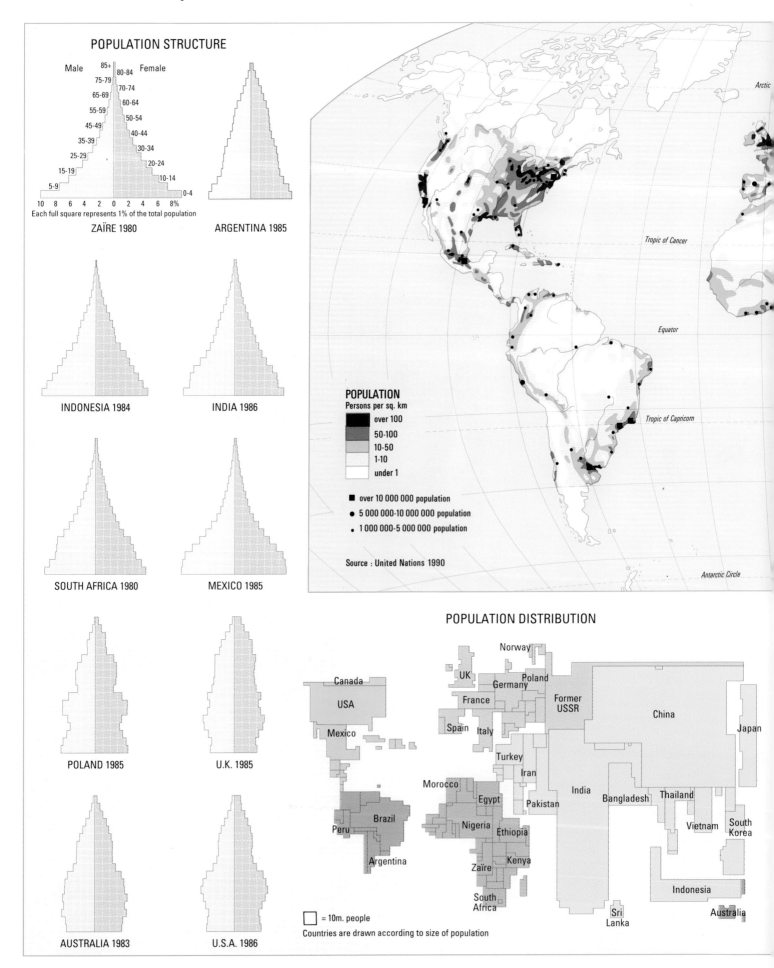

POPULATION STRUCTURE

Male Female

85+
80-84
75-79
70-74
65-69
60-64
55-59
50-54
45-49
40-44
35-39
30-34
25-29
20-24
15-19
10-14
5-9
0-4

10 8 6 4 2 0 2 4 6 8%
Each full square represents 1% of the total population

ZAÏRE 1980

ARGENTINA 1985

INDONESIA 1984

INDIA 1986

SOUTH AFRICA 1980

MEXICO 1985

POLAND 1985

U.K. 1985

AUSTRALIA 1983

U.S.A. 1986

POPULATION
Persons per sq. km

over 100
50-100
10-50
1-10
under 1

■ over 10 000 000 population
● 5 000 000-10 000 000 population
• 1 000 000-5 000 000 population

Source : United Nations 1990

Arctic

Tropic of Cancer

Equator

Tropic of Capricorn

Antarctic Circle

POPULATION DISTRIBUTION

Norway
Canada
UK
Poland
USA
Germany
France
Former USSR
China
Japan
Mexico
Spain
Italy
Turkey
Iran
India
Bangladesh
Thailand
Morocco
Pakistan
Vietnam
South Korea
Egypt
Nigeria
Ethiopia
Peru
Brazil
Zaïre
Kenya
Argentina
South Africa
Indonesia
Sri Lanka
Australia

□ = 10m. people
Countries are drawn according to size of population

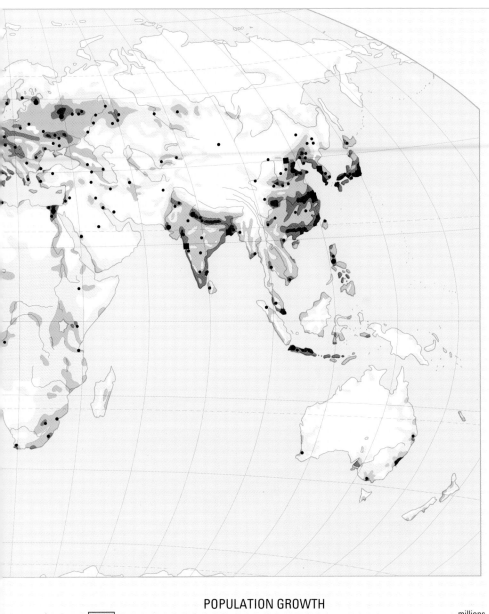

FACT*file* **Largest Cities**
Population figures in millions

AFRICA

Cairo	Egypt	9.0
Lagos	Nigeria	7.7
Alexandria	Egypt	3.7
Kinshasa	Zaïre	3.5
Casablanca	Morocco	3.2
Algiers	Algeria	3.0
Cape Town	South Africa	2.3
Abidjan	Ivory Coast	2.2
Tripoli	Libya	2.1
Khartoum	Sudan	1.9

ASIA

Tokyo	Japan	18.1
Shanghai	China	13.4
Calcutta	India	11.8
Bombay	India	11.2
Seoul	South Korea	11.0
Beijing	China	10.8
Tianjin	China	9.4
Jakarta	Indonesia	9.3
Delhi	India	8.8
Manila	Philippines	8.5

EUROPE

Moscow	Russian Federation	8.8
Paris	France	8.5
London	United Kingdom	7.5
Milan	Italy	5.3
Madrid	Spain	5.2
St. Petersburg	Russian Federation	5.1
Naples	Italy	3.6
Barcelona	Spain	3.4
Athens	Greece	3.4
Katowice	Poland	3.4

NORTH AMERICA

Mexico City	Mexico	20.2
New York	USA	16.2
Los Angeles	USA	11.9
Chicago	USA	7.0
Philadelphia	USA	4.3
Detroit	USA	3.7
San Francisco	USA	3.7
Toronto	Canada	3.5
Dallas	USA	3.4
Guadalajara	Mexico	3.2

SOUTH AMERICA

São Paulo	Brazil	17.4
Buenos Aires	Argentina	11.5
Rio de Janeiro	Brazil	10.7
Lima	Peru	6.2
Santiago	Chile	4.7
Caracas	Venezuela	4.1
Belo Horizonte	Brazil	3.6
Porto Alegre	Brazil	3.1
Recife	Brazil	2.5
Salvador	Brazil	2.4

AUSTRALASIA

Sydney	Australia	3.4
Melbourne	Australia	2.8
Brisbane	Australia	1.2
Perth	Australia	1.1

Note: Figures refer to urban agglomerations as defined by the U. N.

POPULATION GROWTH

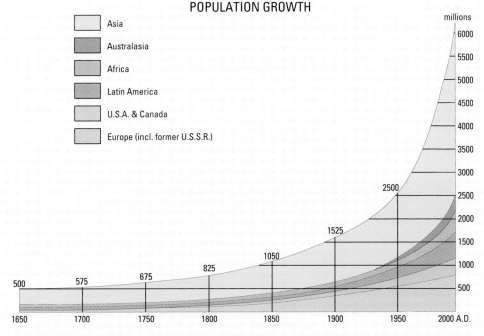

Asia

Australasia

Africa

Latin America

U.S.A. & Canada

Europe (incl. former U.S.S.R.)

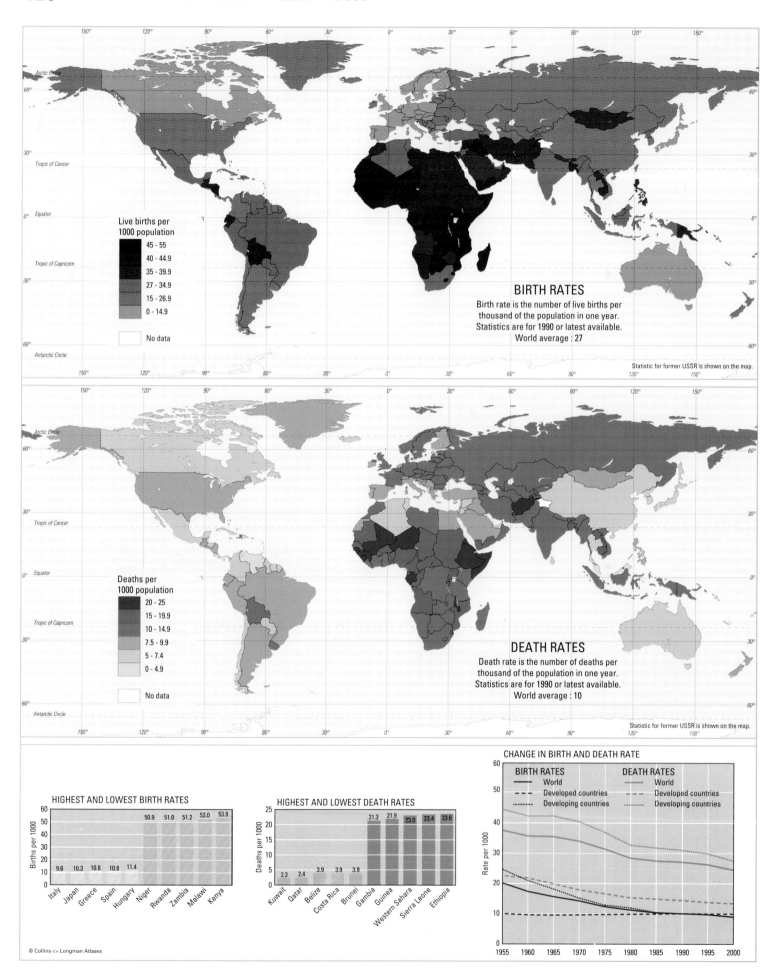

Live births per 1000 population

- 45 - 55
- 40 - 44.9
- 35 - 39.9
- 27 - 34.9
- 15 - 26.9
- 0 - 14.9

No data

BIRTH RATES

Birth rate is the number of live births per thousand of the population in one year. Statistics are for 1990 or latest available. World average : 27

Statistic for former USSR is shown on the map.

Deaths per 1000 population

- 20 - 25
- 15 - 19.9
- 10 - 14.9
- 7.5 - 9.9
- 5 - 7.4
- 0 - 4.9

No data

DEATH RATES

Death rate is the number of deaths per thousand of the population in one year. Statistics are for 1990 or latest available. World average : 10

Statistic for former USSR is shown on the map.

HIGHEST AND LOWEST BIRTH RATES

Country	Births per 1000
Italy	9.6
Japan	10.3
Greece	10.8
Spain	10.8
Hungary	11.4
Niger	50.9
Rwanda	51.0
Zambia	51.2
Malawi	53.0
Kenya	53.9

HIGHEST AND LOWEST DEATH RATES

Country	Deaths per 1000
Kuwait	2.3
Qatar	2.4
Belize	3.9
Costa Rica	3.9
Brunei	3.9
Gambia	21.3
Guinea	21.9
Western Sahara	23.0
Sierra Leone	23.4
Ethiopia	23.6

CHANGE IN BIRTH AND DEATH RATE

BIRTH RATES
- World
- Developed countries
- Developing countries

DEATH RATES
- World
- Developed countries
- Developing countries

Rate per 1000

1955 1960 1965 1970 1975 1980 1985 1990 1995 2000

© Collins ◇ Longman Atlases

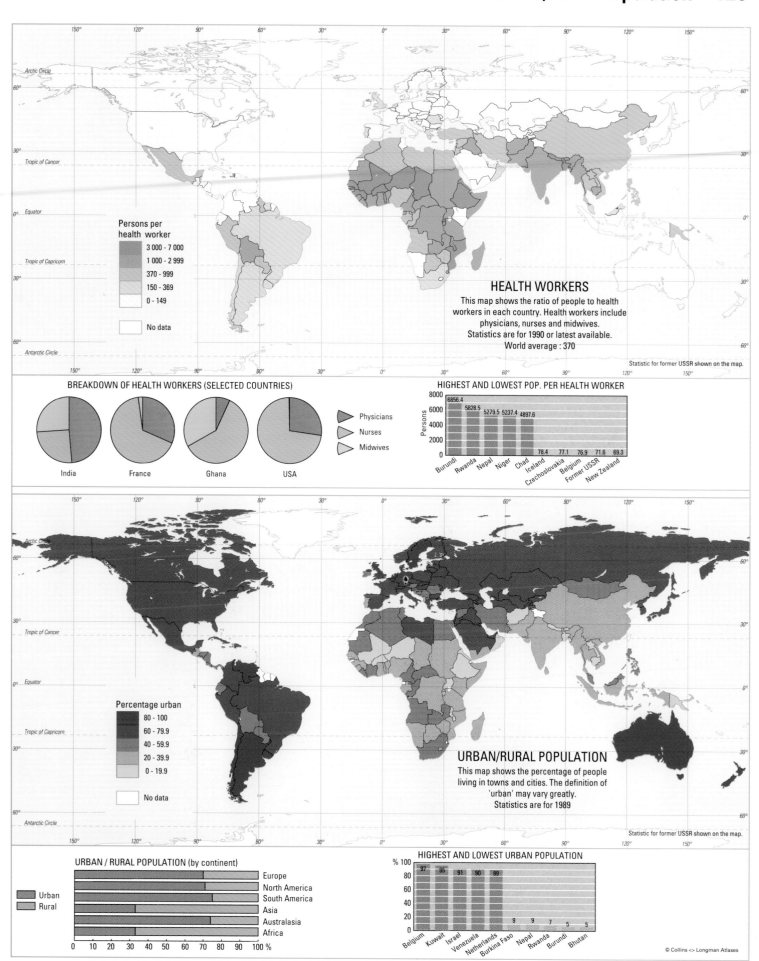

Persons per health worker
- 3 000 - 7 000
- 1 000 - 2 999
- 370 - 999
- 150 - 369
- 0 - 149
- No data

HEALTH WORKERS

This map shows the ratio of people to health workers in each country. Health workers include physicians, nurses and midwives. Statistics are for 1990 or latest available.
World average : 370

Statistic for former USSR shown on the map.

BREAKDOWN OF HEALTH WORKERS (SELECTED COUNTRIES)

- Physicians
- Nurses
- Midwives

India   France   Ghana   USA

HIGHEST AND LOWEST POP. PER HEALTH WORKER

Persons

| 6856.4 | 5828.5 | 5279.5 | 5237.4 | 4897.6 | 78.4 | 77.1 | 76.9 | 71.6 | 69.3 |

Burundi Rwanda Nepal Niger Chad Iceland Czechoslovakia Belgium Former USSR New Zealand

Percentage urban
- 80 - 100
- 60 - 79.9
- 40 - 59.9
- 20 - 39.9
- 0 - 19.9
- No data

URBAN/RURAL POPULATION

This map shows the percentage of people living in towns and cities. The definition of 'urban' may vary greatly.
Statistics are for 1989

Statistic for former USSR shown on the map.

URBAN / RURAL POPULATION (by continent)

- Urban
- Rural

Europe
North America
South America
Asia
Australasia
Africa

0 10 20 30 40 50 60 70 80 90 100 %

HIGHEST AND LOWEST URBAN POPULATION

% 100

| 97 | 95 | 91 | 90 | 89 | 9 | 9 | 7 | 5 | 5 |

Belgium Kuwait Israel Venezuela Netherlands Burkina Faso Nepal Rwanda Burundi Bhutan

© Collins <> Longman Atlases

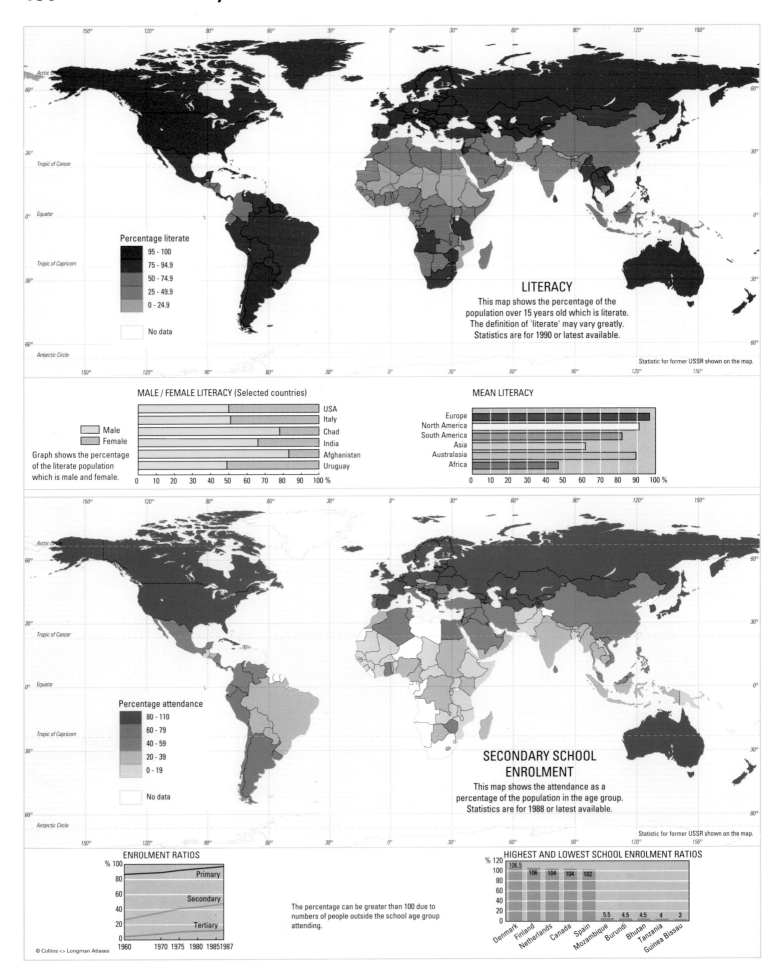

LITERACY
This map shows the percentage of the population over 15 years old which is literate. The definition of 'literate' may vary greatly. Statistics are for 1990 or latest available.

Percentage literate
- 95 - 100
- 75 - 94.9
- 50 - 74.9
- 25 - 49.9
- 0 - 24.9

No data

Statistic for former USSR shown on the map.

MALE / FEMALE LITERACY (Selected countries)
- Male
- Female

Graph shows the percentage of the literate population which is male and female.

USA
Italy
Chad
India
Afghanistan
Uruguay

0 10 20 30 40 50 60 70 80 90 100 %

MEAN LITERACY
Europe
North America
South America
Asia
Australasia
Africa

0 10 20 30 40 50 60 70 80 90 100 %

SECONDARY SCHOOL ENROLMENT
This map shows the attendance as a percentage of the population in the age group. Statistics are for 1988 or latest available.

Percentage attendance
- 80 - 110
- 60 - 79
- 40 - 59
- 20 - 39
- 0 - 19

No data

Statistic for former USSR shown on the map.

ENROLMENT RATIOS
% 100
80
60
40
20
0

Primary
Secondary
Tertiary

1960 1970 1975 1980 19851987

The percentage can be greater than 100 due to numbers of people outside the school age group attending.

HIGHEST AND LOWEST SCHOOL ENROLMENT RATIOS
% 120
100
80
60
40
20
0

Denmark	Finland	Netherlands	Canada	Spain	Mozambique	Burundi	Bhutan	Tanzania	Guinea Bissau
106.5	106	104	104	102	5.5	4.5	4.5	4	3

© Collins <> Longman Atlases

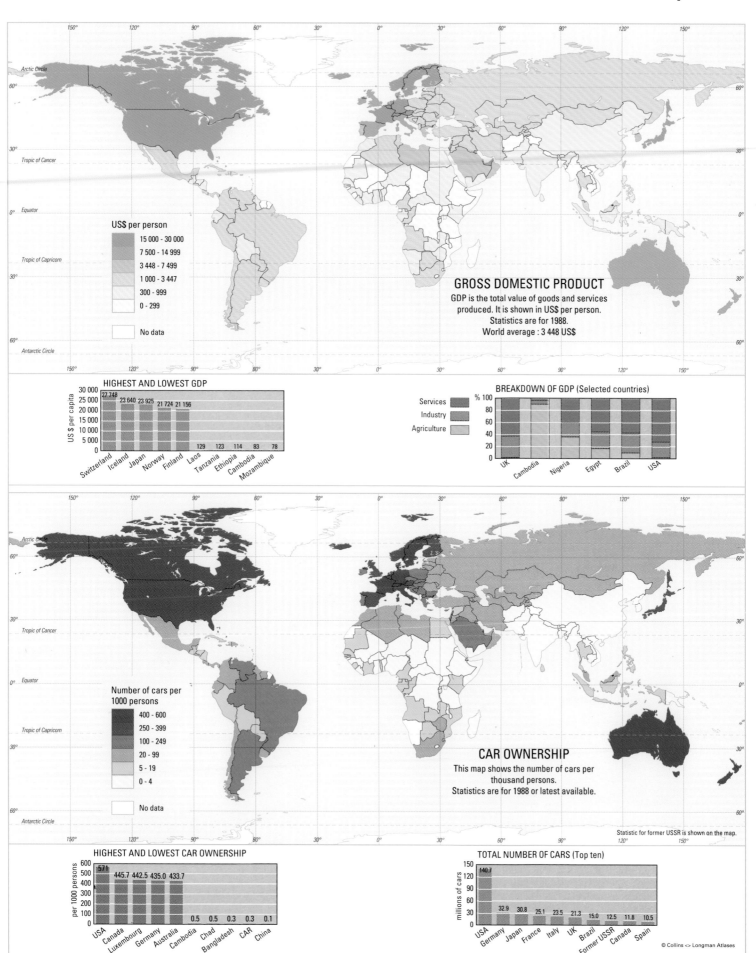

GROSS DOMESTIC PRODUCT

GDP is the total value of goods and services produced. It is shown in US$ per person. Statistics are for 1988.
World average : 3 448 US$

US$ per person
- 15 000 - 30 000
- 7 500 - 14 999
- 3 448 - 7 499
- 1 000 - 3 447
- 300 - 999
- 0 - 299
- No data

HIGHEST AND LOWEST GDP

US $ per capita

Switzerland	Iceland	Japan	Norway	Finland	Laos	Tanzania	Ethiopia	Cambodia	Mozambique
27.748	23 640	23 925	21 724	21 156	129	123	114	83	78

BREAKDOWN OF GDP (Selected countries)

Services
Industry
Agriculture

%: 100, 80, 60, 40, 20

UK, Cambodia, Nigeria, Egypt, Brazil, USA

CAR OWNERSHIP

This map shows the number of cars per thousand persons.
Statistics are for 1988 or latest available.

Number of cars per 1000 persons
- 400 - 600
- 250 - 399
- 100 - 249
- 20 - 99
- 5 - 19
- 0 - 4
- No data

Statistic for former USSR is shown on the map.

HIGHEST AND LOWEST CAR OWNERSHIP

per 1000 persons

USA	Canada	Luxembourg	Germany	Australia	Cambodia	Chad	Bangladesh	CAR	China
571	445.7	442.5	435.0	433.7	0.5	0.5	0.3	0.3	0.1

TOTAL NUMBER OF CARS (Top ten)

millions of cars

USA	Germany	Japan	France	Italy	UK	Brazil	Former USSR	Canada	Spain
140.7	32.9	30.8	25.1	23.5	21.3	15.0	12.5	11.8	10.5

© Collins <> Longman Atlases

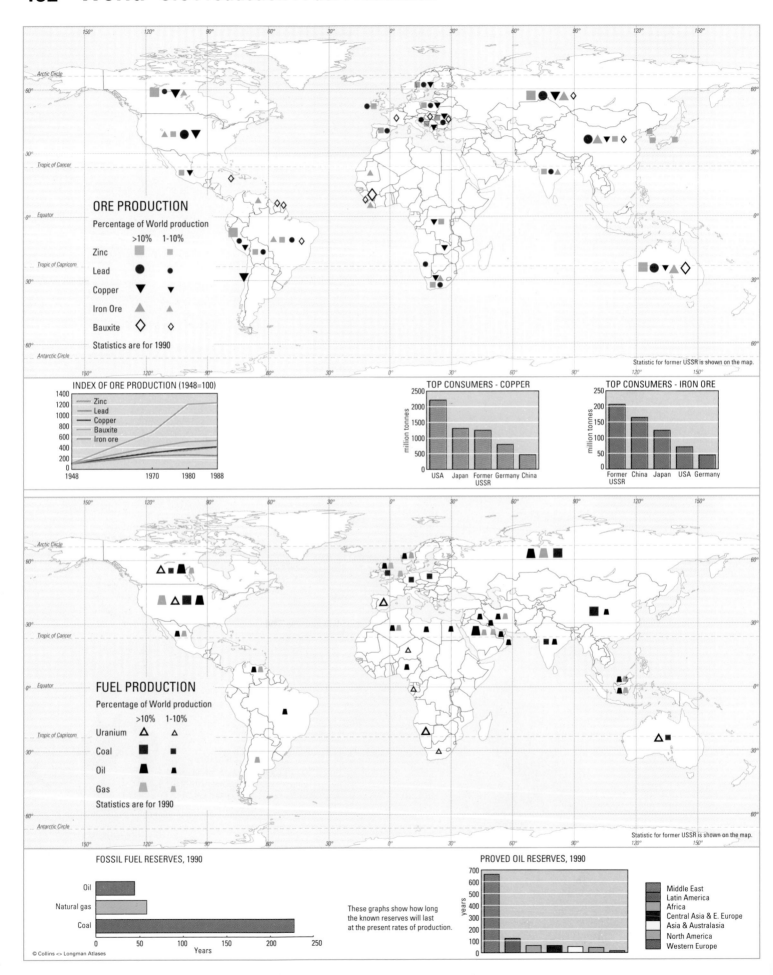

ORE PRODUCTION

Percentage of World production

	>10%	1-10%
Zinc	■	■
Lead	●	●
Copper	▼	▼
Iron Ore	▲	▲
Bauxite	◇	◇

Statistics are for 1990

Statistic for former USSR is shown on the map.

INDEX OF ORE PRODUCTION (1948=100)

Zinc
Lead
Copper
Bauxite
Iron ore

TOP CONSUMERS - COPPER

TOP CONSUMERS - IRON ORE

FUEL PRODUCTION

Percentage of World production

	>10%	1-10%
Uranium	△	△
Coal	■	■
Oil	▲	▲
Gas	▲	▲

Statistics are for 1990

Statistic for former USSR is shown on the map.

FOSSIL FUEL RESERVES, 1990

Oil
Natural gas
Coal

These graphs show how long
the known reserves will last
at the present rates of production.

© Collins <> Longman Atlases

PROVED OIL RESERVES, 1990

Middle East
Latin America
Africa
Central Asia & E. Europe
Asia & Australasia
North America
Western Europe

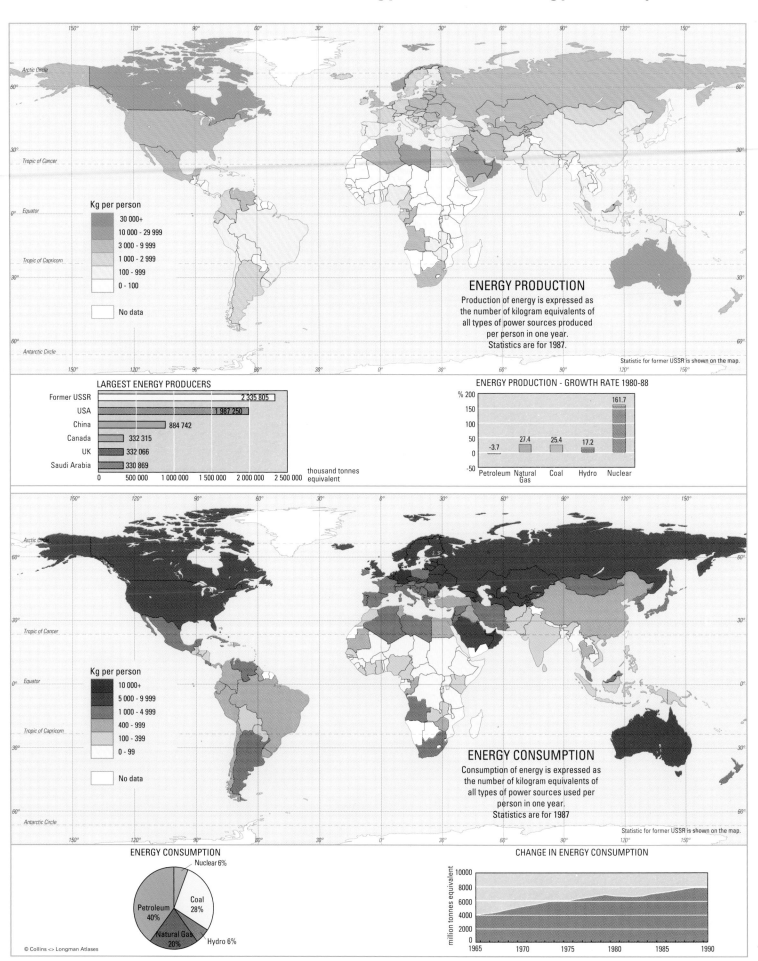

ENERGY PRODUCTION

Production of energy is expressed as the number of kilogram equivalents of all types of power sources produced per person in one year.
Statistics are for 1987.

Statistic for former USSR is shown on the map.

Kg per person
- 30 000+
- 10 000 - 29 999
- 3 000 - 9 999
- 1 000 - 2 999
- 100 - 999
- 0 - 100
- No data

LARGEST ENERGY PRODUCERS

	thousand tonnes equivalent
Former USSR	2 335 805
USA	1 987 250
China	884 742
Canada	332 315
UK	332 066
Saudi Arabia	330 869

0   500 000   1 000 000   1 500 000   2 000 000   2 500 000

ENERGY PRODUCTION - GROWTH RATE 1980-88

% 200

Petroleum	Natural Gas	Coal	Hydro	Nuclear
-3.7	27.4	25.4	17.2	161.7

ENERGY CONSUMPTION

Consumption of energy is expressed as the number of kilogram equivalents of all types of power sources used per person in one year.
Statistics are for 1987

Statistic for former USSR is shown on the map.

Kg per person
- 10 000+
- 5 000 - 9 999
- 1 000 - 4 999
- 400 - 999
- 100 - 399
- 0 - 99
- No data

ENERGY CONSUMPTION

- Nuclear 6%
- Coal 28%
- Hydro 6%
- Natural Gas 20%
- Petroleum 40%

CHANGE IN ENERGY CONSUMPTION

million tonnes equivalent

10000
8000
6000
4000
2000
0

1965   1970   1975   1980   1985   1990

© Collins <> Longman Atlases

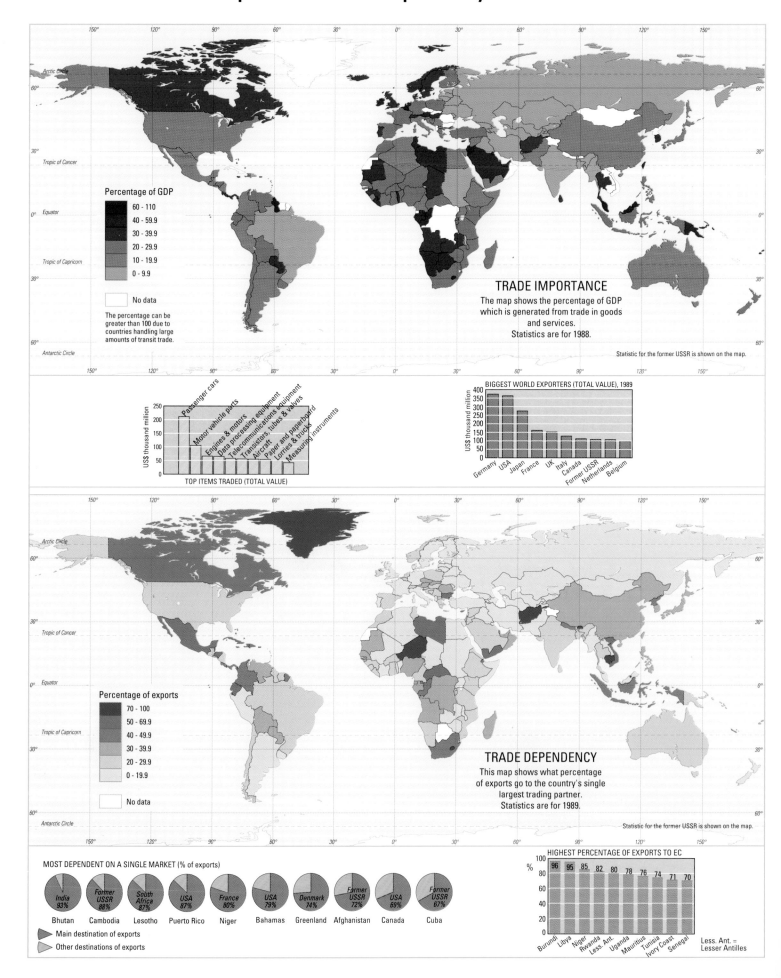

TRADE IMPORTANCE

The map shows the percentage of GDP which is generated from trade in goods and services.
Statistics are for 1988.

Statistic for the former USSR is shown on the map.

Percentage of GDP

- 60 - 110
- 40 - 59.9
- 30 - 39.9
- 20 - 29.9
- 10 - 19.9
- 0 - 9.9

No data

The percentage can be greater than 100 due to countries handling large amounts of transit trade.

TOP ITEMS TRADED (TOTAL VALUE)

US$ thousand million

- Passenger cars
- Motor vehicle parts
- Engines & motors
- Data processing equipment
- Telecommunications equipment
- Transistors, tubes & valves
- Aircraft
- Paper and paperboard
- Lorries & trucks
- Measuring instruments

BIGGEST WORLD EXPORTERS (TOTAL VALUE), 1989

US$ thousand million

Germany, USA, Japan, France, UK, Italy, Canada, Former USSR, Netherlands, Belgium

TRADE DEPENDENCY

This map shows what percentage of exports go to the country's single largest trading partner.
Statistics are for 1989.

Statistic for the former USSR is shown on the map.

Percentage of exports

- 70 - 100
- 50 - 69.9
- 40 - 49.9
- 30 - 39.9
- 20 - 29.9
- 0 - 19.9

No data

MOST DEPENDENT ON A SINGLE MARKET (% of exports)

Country	Market	%
Bhutan	India	93%
Cambodia	Former USSR	88%
Lesotho	South Africa	87%
Puerto Rico	USA	87%
Niger	France	80%
Bahamas	USA	79%
Greenland	Denmark	74%
Afghanistan	Former USSR	72%
Canada	USA	69%
Cuba	Former USSR	67%

Main destination of exports
Other destinations of exports

HIGHEST PERCENTAGE OF EXPORTS TO EC

%

Burundi	Libya	Niger	Rwanda	Less. Ant.	Uganda	Mauritius	Tunisia	Ivory Coast	Senegal
96	95	85	82	80	78	76	74	71	70

Less. Ant. = Lesser Antilles

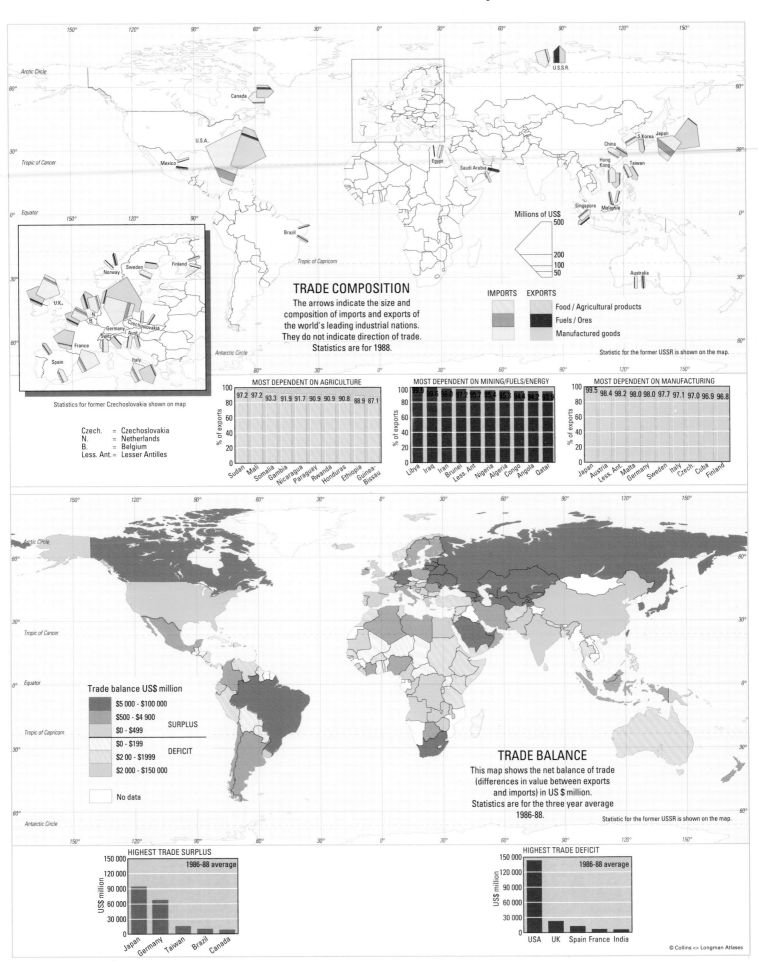

TRADE COMPOSITION

The arrows indicate the size and composition of imports and exports of the world's leading industrial nations. They do not indicate direction of trade. Statistics are for 1988.

Millions of US$
500
200
100
50

IMPORTS EXPORTS
Food / Agricultural products
Fuels / Ores
Manufactured goods

Statistic for the former USSR is shown on the map.

Statistics for former Czechoslovakia shown on map

Czech. = Czechoslovakia
N. = Netherlands
B. = Belgium
Less. Ant. = Lesser Antilles

MOST DEPENDENT ON AGRICULTURE

% of exports

Sudan	Mali	Somalia	Gambia	Nicaragua	Paraguay	Rwanda	Honduras	Ethiopia	Guinea-Bissau
97.2	97.2	93.3	91.9	91.7	90.9	90.9	90.8	88.9	87.1

MOST DEPENDENT ON MINING/FUELS/ENERGY

% of exports

Libya	Iraq	Iran	Brunei	Less. Ant	Nigeria	Algeria	Congo	Angola	Qatar
99.9	99.6	98.0	97.2	95.7	95.4	95.3	94.4	94.2	93.9

MOST DEPENDENT ON MANUFACTURING

% of exports

Japan	Austria	Less. Ant.	Malta	Germany	Sweden	Italy	Czech.	Cuba	Finland
99.5	98.4	98.2	98.0	98.0	97.7	97.1	97.0	96.9	96.8

TRADE BALANCE

This map shows the net balance of trade (differences in value between exports and imports) in US $ million. Statistics are for the three year average 1986-88.

Statistic for the former USSR is shown on the map.

Trade balance US$ million

- $5 000 - $100 000
- $500 - $4 900
- $0 - $499 — SURPLUS
- $0 - $199
- $2 00 - $1999 — DEFICIT
- $2 000 - $150 000
- No data

HIGHEST TRADE SURPLUS

US$ million — 1986-88 average

Japan, Germany, Taiwan, Brazil, Canada

HIGHEST TRADE DEFICIT

US$ million — 1986-88 average

USA, UK, Spain, France, India

© Collins <> Longman Atlases

SIZE OF SALES (TOP 20)

Company	Sales
Sumitomo	80 521
C. Itoh	77 244
Mitsui & Co.	76 369
General Motors	
Marubeni	68 650
Mitsubishi	62 502
Nissho Iwai	56 609
Ford Motor	54 212
Exxon Corp.	54 173
Royal Dutch / Shell	44 003
BP	37 394
IBM	35 359
Mobil	31 946
General Electric	30 786
Sears, Roebuck	30 332
Toyota Motors	
Daimler-Benz	
Philip Morris	25 238
Fiat	
Tomen	23 792

Sales in £million
Main interest of business

- Sogo shoshas (integrated marketing, finance, transport and information)
- Vehicles
- Oil industry
- Electrical and electronic
- Food and retailing

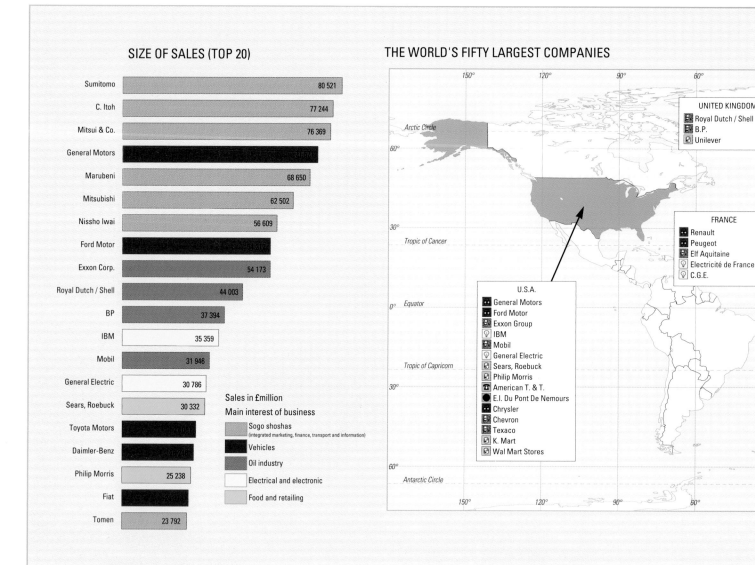

THE WORLD'S FIFTY LARGEST COMPANIES

UNITED KINGDOM
- Royal Dutch / Shell
- B.P.
- Unilever

FRANCE
- Renault
- Peugeot
- Elf Aquitaine
- Electricité de France
- C.G.E.

U.S.A.
- General Motors
- Ford Motor
- Exxon Group
- IBM
- Mobil
- General Electric
- Sears, Roebuck
- Philip Morris
- American T. & T.
- E.I. Du Pont De Nemours
- Chrysler
- Chevron
- Texaco
- K. Mart
- Wal Mart Stores

SIZE OF MULTINATIONALS

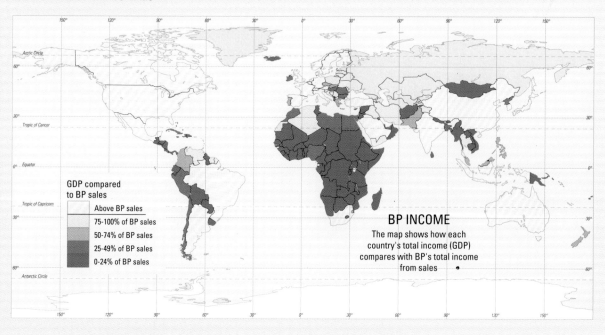

GDP compared to BP sales
- Above BP sales
- 75-100% of BP sales
- 50-74% of BP sales
- 25-49% of BP sales
- 0-24% of BP sales

BP INCOME
The map shows how each country's total income (GDP) compares with BP's total income from sales

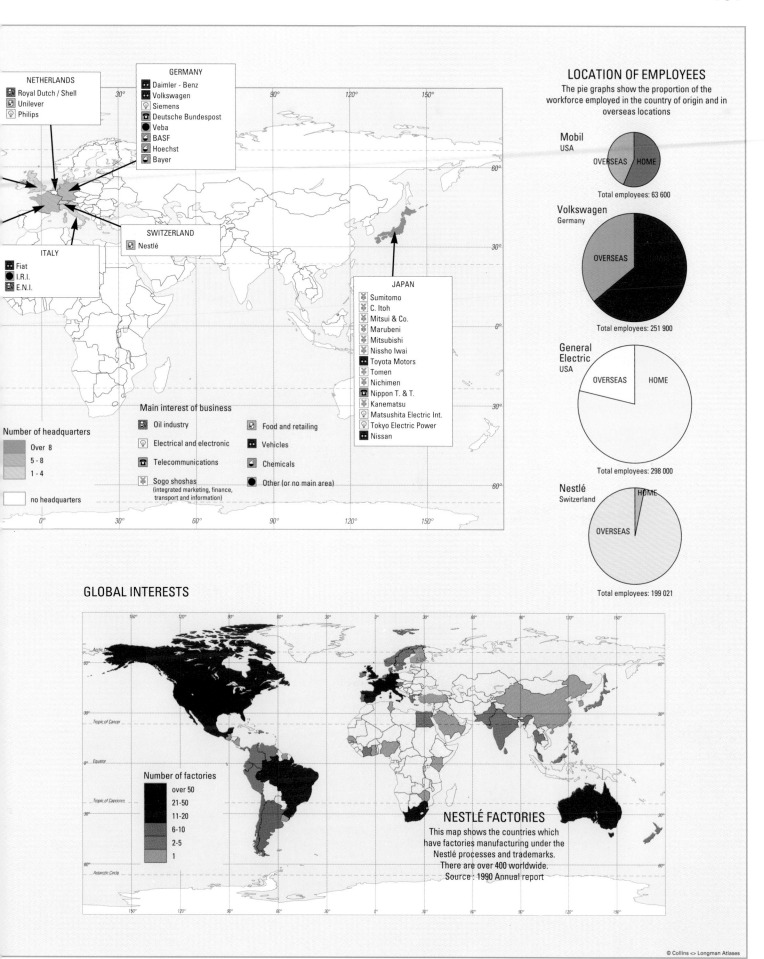

NETHERLANDS
- Royal Dutch / Shell
- Unilever
- Philips

GERMANY
- Daimler - Benz
- Volkswagen
- Siemens
- Deutsche Bundespost
- Veba
- BASF
- Hoechst
- Bayer

SWITZERLAND
- Nestlé

ITALY
- Fiat
- I.R.I.
- E.N.I.

JAPAN
- Sumitomo
- C. Itoh
- Mitsui & Co.
- Marubeni
- Mitsubishi
- Nissho Iwai
- Toyota Motors
- Tomen
- Nichimen
- Nippon T. & T.
- Kanematsu
- Matsushita Electric Int.
- Tokyo Electric Power
- Nissan

Main interest of business

- Oil industry
- Electrical and electronic
- Telecommunications
- Sogo shoshas (integrated marketing, finance, transport and information)
- Food and retailing
- Vehicles
- Chemicals
- Other (or no main area)

Number of headquarters
- Over 8
- 5 - 8
- 1 - 4
- no headquarters

LOCATION OF EMPLOYEES

The pie graphs show the proportion of the workforce employed in the country of origin and in overseas locations

Mobil
USA
OVERSEAS | HOME
Total employees: 63 600

Volkswagen
Germany
OVERSEAS | HOME
Total employees: 251 900

General Electric
USA
OVERSEAS | HOME
Total employees: 298 000

Nestlé
Switzerland
HOME
OVERSEAS
Total employees: 199 021

GLOBAL INTERESTS

Number of factories
- over 50
- 21-50
- 11-20
- 6-10
- 2-5
- 1

NESTLÉ FACTORIES

This map shows the countries which have factories manufacturing under the Nestlé processes and trademarks. There are over 400 worldwide.
Source : 1990 Annual report

© Collins <> Longman Atlases

KEY STATISTICS

COUNTRY	CAPITAL CITY	POPULATION in millions, 1992	AREA in sq. km	MAIN LANGUAGES	MAIN RELIGIONS	CURRENCY
AFGHANISTAN	Kabul	16.1	652 225	Pushtu, Dari	Sunni Muslim	Afghani
ALBANIA	Tiranë	3.3	28 750	Albanian	Muslim	Lek
ALGERIA	Algiers	25.0	2 381 745	Arabic	Sunni Muslim	Dinar
ANGOLA	Luanda	10.0	1 246 700	Portuguese	Roman Catholic	Kwanza
ARGENTINA	Buenos Aires	32.3	2 777, 815	Spanish	Roman Catholic	Austral
ARMENIA	Yerevan	3.3	29 800	Armenian	Orthodox	Rouble
AUSTRALIA	Canberra	17.1	7 682 300	English	Protestant, Roman Catholic	Dollar
AUSTRIA	Vienna	7.7	83 855	German	Roman Catholic	Schilling
AZERBAIJAN	Baku	7.2	86 600	Azerbaijani	Shi'a Muslim	Manat
BAHAMAS	Nassau	0.3	13 865	English	Protestant	Dollar
BAHRAIN	Manama	0.5	661	Arabic	Muslim	Dinar
BANGLADESH	Dhaka	115.6	144 000	Bengali	Muslim	Taka
BELGIUM	Brussels	9.8	30 520	French, Dutch	Roman Catholic	Franc
BELIZE	Belmopan	0.2	22 965	English	Roman Catholic	Dollar
BELORUSSIA	Minsk	10.3	208 000	Belorussian	Orthodox	Rouble
BENIN	Porto-Novo	4.7	112 620	French	Traditional	CFA Franc
BHUTAN	Thimbu	1.5	46 620	Dzongkha	Buddhist	Indian Rupee, Ngultrum
BOLIVIA	La Paz	7.4	1 098 575	Spanish	Roman Catholic	Boliviano
BOSNIA-HERZEGOVINA	Sarajevo	4.2	51 130	Serbo-Croat	Muslim, Orthodox, Roman Catholic	Dinar
BOTSWANA	Gaborone	1.3	600 372	English, Tswana	Traditional	Pula
BRAZIL	Brasilia	150.4	8 511 965	Portuguese	Roman Catholic	Cruzeiro
BRUNEI	Bandar Seri Begawan	0.3	5 765	Malay	Muslim	Dollar
BULGARIA	Sofia	9.0	110 910	Bulgarian	Orthodox	Lev
BURKINA	Ouagadougou	9.0	274 200	French	Traditional, Muslim	CFA Franc
BURUNDI	Bujumbura	5.5	27 834	French, Kirundi	Roman Catholic	Franc
CAMBODIA	Phnom Penh	8.2	181 000	Khmer	Buddhist	Riel
CAMEROON	Yaounde	11.8	475 500	French, English	Roman Catholic	CFA Franc
CANADA	Ottawa	26.6	9 922 385	English, French	Roman Catholic, Protestant	Dollar
CENTRAL AFRICAN REPUBLIC	Bangui	3.0	624 975	French, Sango	Traditional	CFA Franc
CHAD	N' Djamena	5.7	1 284 000	French, Arabic	Muslim	CFA Franc
CHILE	Santiago	13.2	751 625	Spanish	Roman Catholic	Peso
CHINA	Beijing	1 139.1	9 579 000	Mandarin	Confucian, Buddhist	Yuan
COLOMBIA	Bogota	33.0	1 138 915	Spanish	Roman Catholic	Peso
CONGO	Brazzaville	2.3	342 000	French	Traditional	CFA Franc
COSTA RICA	San Jose	3.0	50 900	Spanish	Roman Catholic	Colon
CROATIA	Zagreb	4.6	56 540	Serbo-Croat	Roman Catholic	Dinar
CUBA	Havana	10.6	114 525	Spanish	Roman Catholic	Peso
CYPRUS	Nicosia	0.7	9 250	Greek	Greek Orthodox	Pound
CZECH REPUBLIC	Prague	10.4	78 860	Czech	Roman Catholic	Koruna
DENMARK	Copenhagen	5.1	43 075	Danish	Protestant	Krone
DJIBOUTI	Djibouti	0.4	23 000	French, Somali	Muslim	Franc
DOMINICA	Roseau	0.1	751	English, French	Roman Catholic	EC Dollar
DOMINICAN REPUBLIC	Santo Domingo	7.2	48 440	Spanish	Roman Catholic	Peso
ECUADOR	Quito	10.8	461 475	Spanish	Roman Catholic	Sucre
EGYPT	Cairo	53.2	1 000 250	Arabic	Muslim	Pound
EL SALVADOR	San Salvador	5.3	21 395	Spanish	Roman Catholic	Colon
EQUATORIAL GUINEA	Malabo	0.3	28 050	Spanish	Roman Catholic	CFA Franc
ERITREA	Asmara	3.5	93 679	English, Arabic	Christian, Muslim	Ethiopian birr
ESTONIA	Tallinn	1.6	45 100	Estonian	Protestant	Kroon
ETHIOPIA	Addis Ababa	51.0	1 221 900	Amharic	Orthodox	Birr
FIJI	Suva	0.8	18 330	English, Fiji, Hindi	Christian, Hindu	Dollar
FINLAND	Helsinki	5.0	337 030	Finnish, Swedish	Protestant	Markka
FRANCE	Paris	56.4	543 965	French	Roman Catholic	Franc
GABON	Libreville	1.2	267 665	French	Roman Catholic	CFA Franc
GAMBIA	Banjul	0.9	10 690	English	Muslim	Dalasi
GEORGIA	Tbilisi	5.5	69 700	Georgian	Orthodox	Rouble
GERMANY	Berlin	79.5	357 868	German	Protestant, Roman Catholic	Mark

HEALTH AND EDUCATION

CALORIES PER CAPITA PER DAY mean daily calory intake, 1989	PEOPLE PER DOCTOR the ratio of people to doctors, 1990	POPULATION WITH ACCESS TO SAFE WATER % of population with access to clean water, 1990	PRIMARY SCHOOL ENROLMENT % of children attending first level education, 1990
2 110	5 452	29	17
2 700	583		96
2 699	1 262	88	89
1 806	15 298	30	66
3 168	337	71	96
	241		
3 347	467		98
3 474	347		91
	259		
2 680	835		
3 150	758		96
1 925	6 615	45	63
3 901	307		96
2 627	2 000		
	254		
2 115	19 899	18	50
2 400	10 683	19	8
2 096	2 331	63	83
2 251	8 276	88	
2 703	729		84
2 839	1 556		
3 650	324		98
2 002	32 146	49	27
2 320	20 066	61	46
2 162	27 215	53	
2 142	14 206	41	80
3 451	463		97
1 965	18 530	45	49
2 067	60 415		38
2 581	946		89
2 637	642		100
2 544	1 124	60	73
2 519	4 542	83	
2 781	1 179	80	85
3 103	305		96
3 150	604		100
3 540			
3 605	376		
	4 596		
2 884	2 677		
2 359	978	80	
2 302	977	62	73
3 196	725		
2 396	1 641	56	72
1 950	69 600		
	208		
1 715	41 075	46	27
2 785	2 361		100
3 120	519		
3 312	393		100
2 521	2 074	90	
2 339	13 045		61
	178		
3 598	365		

DEVELOPMENT

GROSS DOMESTIC PRODUCT total value of goods & services, US$ per person, 1989	LIFE EXPECTANCY years a new born child can expect to live given the mortality risk in the country, 1992	ADULT LITERACY % of people over 15 years who can read and write, 1990	UNDER 5 MORTALITY number of children of every 1000 live births who die before age 5, 1989
250	44	24	162
1 200	73	100	32
2 170	66	50	61
620	46	28	127
2 160	71	95	29
	72		20
14 440	77	100	7
17 360	75	100	9
	70		26
10 570	70	95	21
6 360	72	77	12
180	53	35	108
16 390	76	100	8
1 600	67	93	36
	72		12
380	48	23	85
190	50	18	118
600	56	78	93
	72		15
940	61	74	58
2 550	66	82	57
14 120	74	85	9
2 320	73	96	14
310	49	18	127
220	50	50	110
130	51	48	116
1 010	55	54	86
19 020	77	96	7
390	51	38	95
190	48	30	122
1 770	72	93	19
360	71	73	27
1 190	69	87	37
930	55	57	65
1 790	75	93	17
	72		10
2 000	76	96	13
7 050	77	95	10
3 140	72	100	11
20 510	76	100	6
1 070	49	34	112
1 650	74		14
790	68	83	57
1 040	67	69	57
630	62	48	57
1 040	67	73	53
430	48	32	117
	70	100	15
120	47	5	122
1 640	66	87	24
22 060	76	100	5
17 830	77	99	7
2 770	54	61	94
230	45	27	132
	72		20
20 750	76	100	8

KEY STATISTICS

COUNTRY	CAPITAL CITY	POPULATION in millions, 1992	AREA in sq. km	MAIN LANGUAGES	MAIN RELIGIONS	CURRENCY
GHANA	Accra	15.0	238 305	English	Christian	Cedi
GREECE	Athens	10.1	131 985	Greek	Orthodox	Drachma
GUATEMALA	Guatemala City	9.2	108 890	Spanish	Roman Catholic	Quetzal
GUINEA	Conakry	5.8	254 855	French	Muslim	Franc
GUINEA-BISSAU	Bissau	1.0	36 125	Portuguese	Traditional, Muslim	Peso
GUYANA	Georgetown	0.8	214 970	English	Protestant, Hindu	Dollar
HAITI	Port-au-Prince	6.5	27 750	French, Creole	Roman Catholic	Gourde
HONDURAS	Tegucigalpa	5.1	112 085	Spanish	Roman Catholic	Lempira
HONG KONG	Victoria	5.8	1 062	Cantonese, English	Buddhist, Taoist	Dollar
HUNGARY	Budapest	10.6	93 030	Hungarian	Roman Catholic	Forint
ICELAND	Reykjavik	0.3	102 820	Icelandic	Protestant	Krona
INDIA	New Delhi	827.1	3 166 830	Hindi, English	Hindu	Rupee
INDONESIA	Jakarta	179.3	1 919 445	Bahasa Indonesia	Muslim	Rupiah
IRAN	Tehran	54.6	1 648 000	Persian	Shi'a Muslim	Rial
IRAQ	Baghdad	18.9	438 445	Arabic, Kurdish	Muslim	Dinar
IRELAND	Dublin	3.5	68 895	English, Irish	Roman Catholic	Punt
ISRAEL	Jerusalem	4.7	20 770	Hebrew	Jewish	Shekel
ITALY	Rome	57.7	301 245	Italian	Roman Catholic	Lira
IVORY COAST	Yamoussoukro	12.0	322 465	French	Muslim, Roman Catholic	CFA Franc
JAMAICA	Kingston	2.4	11 425	English	Protestant	Dollar
JAPAN	Tokyo	123.5	369 700	Japanese	Shintoist, Buddhist	Yen
JORDAN	Amman	4.0	96 000	Arabic	Sunni Muslim	Dinar
KAZAKHSTAN	Alma-Ata	16.7	2 717 300	Kazakh	Sunni Muslim	Rouble
KENYA	Nairobi	24.0	582 645	Swahili, English	Roman Catholic, Protestant	Shilling
KIRGHIZIA	Bishkek	4.4	198 500	Kirgiz	Sunni Muslim	Rouble
KUWAIT	Kuwait City	2.1	24 280	Arabic	Sunni Muslim	Dinar
LAOS	Vientiane	4.1	236 725	Lao	Buddhist	Kip
LATVIA	Riga	2.7	63 700	Latvian	Protestant	Latvian Rouble
LEBANON	Beirut	2.7	10 400	Arabic	Muslim, Christian	Pound
LESOTHO	Maseru	1.8	30 345	English, Sesotho	Roman Catholic, Protestant	Loti
LIBERIA	Monrovia	2.6	111 370	English	Christian	Dollar
LIBYA	Tripoli	4.5	1 759 540	Arabic	Sunni Muslim	Dinar
LITHUANIA	Vilnius	3.7	65 200	Lithuanian	Roman Catholic	Rouble
LUXEMBOURG	Luxembourg	0.4	2 585	Lux., French, German	Roman Catholic	Franc
MACEDONIA	Skopje	2.0	25 713	Macedonian	Orthodox	Dinar
MADAGASCAR	Antananarivo	11.2	594 180	Malagasy, French	Christian, Traditional	Franc
MALAWI	Lilongwe	8.3	94 080	English, Chichewa	Christian	Kwacha
MALAYSIA	Kuala Lumpur	17.9	332 965	Bahasa Malay	Muslim	Ringgit
MALI	Bamako	8.2	1 240 140	French, Bambara	Sunni Muslim	CFA Franc
MAURITANIA	Nouakchott	2.0	1 030 700	Arabic, French	Sunni Muslim	Ouguiya
MAURITIUS	Port Louis	1.1	1 865	English	Hindu	Rupee
MEXICO	Mexico City	86.2	1 972 545	Spanish	Roman Catholic	Peso
MICRONESIA	Palikir on Pohnpei	0.1	702	English	Christian	US Dollar
MOLDAVIA	Kishinev	4.4	33 700	Romanian	Orthodox	Rouble
MONGOLIA	Ulan Bator	2.2	1 565 000	Khalka Mongol	Shamanist	Tugrik
MOROCCO	Rabat	25.1	446 550	Arabic	Sunni Muslim	Dirham
MOZAMBIQUE	Maputo	15.7	784 755	Portuguese	Roman Catholic	Metical
MYANMA	Yangon	41.7	678 030	Burmese	Buddhist	Kyat
NAMIBIA	Windhoek	1.8	824 295	Afrikaans, English	Protestant	SA Rand
NEPAL	Kathmandu	18.9	141 415	Nepali	Hindu	Rupee
NETHERLANDS	Amsterdam	14.9	41 160	Dutch	Roman Catholic, Protestant	Guilder
NEW ZEALAND	Wellington	3.3	265 150	English, Maori	Protestant, Roman Catholic	Dollar
NICARAGUA	Managua	3.9	148 000	Spanish	Roman Catholic	Cordoba
NIGER	Niamey	7.7	1 186 410	French	Sunni Muslim	CFA Franc
NIGERIA	Abuja	88.5	923 850	English	Muslim, Christian	Naira
NORTH KOREA	Pyongyang	21.8	122 310	Korean	Shamanist	Won
NORWAY	Oslo	4.2	323 895	Norwegian	Protestant	Krone

HEALTH AND EDUCATION

CALORIES PER CAPITA PER DAY	PEOPLE PER DOCTOR	POPULATION WITH ACCESS TO SAFE WATER	PRIMARY SCHOOL ENROLMENT
mean daily calory intake, 1989	the ratio of people to doctors, 1990	% of population with access to clean water, 1990	% of children attending first level education, 1990
2 167	25 047	60	
3 702	304		97
2 327	2 570	34	62
2 007	9 065		23
2 543	7 910		40
2 423	7 171	89	90
1 992	6 871	70	44
2 138	1 879	73	91
2 883	927		
3 635	323		93
3 361	378		
2 104	2 494		
2 645	7 767	75	100
3 124	3 228	78	96
2 950	4 273	93	84
3 688	676		89
3 133	392		92
3 571	235		96
2 405	23 900	30	
2 579	2 157		98
2 822	613		100
2 884	891	97	88
	254		
2 016	7 358		91
	295		
3 127	739	100	79
2 614	7 418		70
	200		
3 275	770		
2 275	17 223		71
2 344	29 292	39	
3 393	862		
	218		
3 901	537		
2 174	9 081	56	66
2 057	31 637	80	49
2 665	2 847		
2 114	23 370	15	18
2 465	11 912	30	33
2 690	1 194	100	95
3 123	663	45	100
	2 750		
	255		
2 481	413		95
2 808	5 067	70	57
1 604	45 778	30	45
2 545	3 947	33	65
1 900	6 338		
2 034	21 520		64
3 303	417		100
3 476	373		100
2 373	1 856	83	76
2 321	48 325	41	27
2 083	5 997	40	
3 172	377		
3 266	328		94

DEVELOPMENT

GROSS DOMESTIC PRODUCT	LIFE EXPECTANCY	ADULT LITERACY	UNDER 5 MORTALITY
total value of goods & services, US$ per person, 1989	years a new born child can expect to live given the mortality risk in the country, 1992	% of people over 15 years who can read and write, 1990	number of children of every 1000 live births who die before age 5, 1989
380	56	60	81
5 340	77	93	13
920	65	60	48
430	45	27	134
180	44	37	140
340	65	96	48
400	57	53	86
900	66	73	57
10 320	78	88	6
2 560	72	99	17
21 240	78	100	5
350	60	48	88
490	63	78	65
1 800	67	52	40
1 940	66	60	56
8 500	75	100	8
9 750	76	92	10
15 150	76	97	9
790	54	54	87
1 260	74	98	14
23 730	79	100	5
1 730	68	80	36
	69		26
380	61	60	64
	68		33
16 380	74	73	15
170	51	84	97
	70	98	11
690	67	77	40
470	59	74	89
450	55	40	126
5 410	63	64	68
	71	100	11
24 860	75	100	9
	72		35
230	56	80	110
180	49	41	138
2 130	71	73	20
260	46	32	159
490	48	34	117
1 950	70	82	20
1 990	70	87	36
1 500	73		26
	69		21
470	64	90	60
900	63	71	68
80	49	33	130
200	63	79	59
1 245	59	73	97
170	54	21	118
16 010	78	100	7
11 800	76	100	9
800	66	74	50
290	47	28	124
250	53	51	96
1 240	71	90	24
21 850	74	100	6

KEY STATISTICS

COUNTRY	CAPITAL CITY	POPULATION in millions, 1992	AREA in sq. km	MAIN LANGUAGES	MAIN RELIGIONS	CURRENCY
OMAN	Muscat	1.5	271 950	Arabic	Muslim	Rial
PAKISTAN	Islamabad	112.0	803 940	Urdu	Muslim	Rupee
PANAMA	Panama City	2.4	78 515	Spanish	Roman Catholic	Balboa
PAPUA NEW GUINEA	Port Moresby	3.7	462 840	English	Protestant, Roman Catholic	Kina
PARAGUAY	Asuncion	4.3	406 750	Spanish, Guarani	Roman Catholic	Guarani
PERU	Lima	21.6	1 285 215	Spanish, Quechua	Roman Catholic	Sol
PHILIPPINES	Manila	61.5	300 000	Filipino, English	Roman Catholic	Peso
POLAND	Warsaw	38.2	312 685	Polish	Roman Catholic	Zloty
PORTUGAL	Lisbon	10.5	88 940	Portuguese	Roman Catholic	Escudo
QATAR	Doha	0.5	11 435	Arabic	Muslim	Riyal
ROMANIA	Bucharest	23.2	237 500	Romanian	Orthodox	Leu
RUSSIAN FEDERATION	Moscow	148.3	17 078 000	Russian	Orthodox	Rouble
RWANDA	Kigali	7.2	26 330	Kinyarwanda, French	Roman Catholic	Franc
SAUDI ARABIA	Riyadh	14.9	2 400 900	Arabic	Sunni Muslim	Riyal
SENEGAL	Dakar	7.3	196 720	French	Sunni Muslim	CRA Franc
SIERRA LEONE	Freetown	4.2	72 325	English	Traditional, Sunni Muslim	Leone
SINGAPORE	Singapore	3.0	616	Bahasa Malay	Taoist, Buddhist, Christian	Dollar
SLOVAKIA	Bratislava	5.3	49 036	Slovak	Roman Catholic	Koruna
SLOVENIA	Ljubljana	1.9	20 250	Slovene	Roman Catholic	Tolar
SOLOMON ISLANDS	Honiara	0.3	29 790	English	Protestant	Dollar
SOMALIA	Mogadishu	7.5	630 000	Arabic, Somali	Sunni Muslim	Shilling
SOUTH AFRICA	Cape Town / Pretoria	35.3	1 184 825	Afrikaans, English	Christian	Rand
SOUTH KOREA	Seoul	42.8	98 445	Korean	Buddhist, Christian	Won
SPAIN	Madrid	39.0	504 880	Spanish	Roman Catholic	Peseta
SRI LANKA	Colombo	17.0	65 610	Sinhalese, Tamil	Buddhist, Hindu	Rupee
SUDAN	Khartoum	25.2	2 505 815	Arabic	Sunni Muslim	Pound
SURINAM	Paramaribo	0.4	163 820	Dutch, English	Hindu, Roman Catholic	Guilder
SWAZILAND	Mbabane	0.8	17 365	English, Siswati	Christian	Lilangeni
SWEDEN	Stockholm	8.6	449 790	Swedish	Protestant	Krona
SWITZERLAND	Berne	6.7	41 285	German, French, Italian	Roman Catholic, Protestant	Franc
SYRIA	Damascus	12.1	185 680	Arabic	Sunni Muslim	Pound
TAIWAN	Taibei	20.3	35 990	Mandarin	Buddhist, Taoist	Dollar
TAJIKISTAN	Dushanbe	5.3	143 100	Tajik	Sunni Muslim	Rouble
TANZANIA	Dodoma	25.6	939 760	Swahili, English	Christian, Muslim	Shilling
THAILAND	Bangkok	57.2	514 000	Thai	Buddhist	Baht
TOGO	Lome	3.5	56 785	French	Traditional	CFA Franc
TONGA	Nuku'alofa	0.1	699	English, Tongan	Protestant	Pa'anga
TRINIDAD AND TOBAGO	Port of Spain	1.2	5 130	English	Roman Catholic, Hindu	Dollar
TUNISIA	Tunis	8.2	164 150	Arabic	Sunni Muslim	Dinar
TURKEY	Ankara	56.1	779 450	Turkish	Sunni Muslim	Lira
TURKMENISTAN	Ashkhabad	3.7	488 100	Turkmenian	Sunni Muslim	Rouble
UGANDA	Kampala	18.8	236 580	Swahili, English	Roman Catholic	Shilling
UKRAINE	Kiev	51.9	603 700	Ukrainian, Russian	Orthodox	Rouble
UNITED ARAB EMIRATES	Abu Dhabi	1.6	75 150	Arabic	Sunni Muslim	Dirham
UNITED KINGDOM	London	57.4	244 755	English	Protestant, Roman Catholic	Pound
UNITED STATES	Washington	250.0	9 363 130	English	Protestant, Roman Catholic	Dollar
URUGUAY	Montevideo	3.1	186 925	Spanish	Roman Catholic	Peso
UZBEKISTAN	Tashkent	20.5	447 400	Uzbek	Sunni Muslim	Rouble
VENEZUELA	Caracas	19.7	912 045	Spanish	Roman Catholic	Bolivar
VIETNAM	Hanoi	66.2	329 565	Vietnamese	Buddhist	Dong
WESTERN SAHARA	Laayoune	0.2	266 000	Arabic	Sunni Muslim	Moroccan Dirham
WESTERN SAMOA	Apia	0.2	2 840	Samoan, English	Protestant	Tala
YEMEN	San'a	11.3	481 155	Arabic	Muslim	Rial, Dinar
YUGOSLAVIA	Belgrade	10.0	127 885	Serbo-Croat	Orthodox, Roman Catholic, Muslim	Dinar
ZAIRE	Kinshasa	35.6	2 345 410	French, Lingala	Roman Catholic	Zaire
ZAMBIA	Lusaka	7.8	752 615	English	Christian	Kwacha
ZIMBABWE	Harare	9.4	390 310	English	Christian, Traditional	Dollar

HEALTH AND EDUCATION · DEVELOPMENT

CALORIES PER CAPITA PER DAY (mean daily calory intake, 1989)	PEOPLE PER DOCTOR (the ratio of people to doctors, 1990)	POPULATION WITH ACCESS TO SAFE WATER (% of population with access to clean water, 1990)	PRIMARY SCHOOL ENROLMENT (% of children attending first level education, 1990)	GROSS DOMESTIC PRODUCT (total value of goods & services, US$ per person, 1989)	LIFE EXPECTANCY (years a new born child can expect to live given the mortality risk in the country, 1992)	ADULT LITERACY (% of people over 15 years who can read and write, 1990)	UNDER 5 MORTALITY (number of children of every 1000 live births who die before age 5, 1989)
	1 079	91	80	5 220	68	41	34
2 167	1 874	55		370	59	26	98
2 484	857	80	90	1 780	73	88	21
2 227	13 071			900	56	42	53
2 784	1 687	61	90	1 030	67	90	39
2 277	989		97	1 090	65	87	76
2 238	1 195		98	700	65	89	40
3 434	482		99	1 760	72	99	17
3 284	381		100	4 260	75	85	13
3 150	646		100	9 920	70	76	26
3 327	553			3 445	72	96	19
	215				70		18
1 817	40 343	27	64	310	51	50	112
2 805	969	97	56	6 230	66	62	58
2 162	18 002		50	650	49	38	80
1 813	13 837			200	43	21	143
2 882	950			10 450	75		7
				3 140	71	100	11
					73	100	9
2 140	10 355			570	61	54	74
1 781	16 660	27	11	170	47	24	122
2 963	1 597			2 460	63	50	62
2 867	1 076	93	100	4 400	71	93	21
3 494	280		100	9 150	77	93	9
2 297	7 337	93	100	430	72	86	24
1 981	11 620	51	49	540	52	27	99
2 775	1 927		96	3 020	70	95	28
2 554	9 600		82	900	58	67	107
3 031	322		100	21 710	78	100	6
3 623	334			30 270	78	100	7
3 142	1 439	75	99	1 100	67	65	39
2 749	974			7 990	74	92	6
	366				70		43
2 186	24 070	76	50	120	55	46	97
2 288	5 080	70		1 170	67	89	24
2 110	15 352	61	73	390	55	39	85
2 964	2 111			800	66		49
2 983	1 197		87	3 160	72	96	14
2 911	1 897	90	95	1 260	68	65	44
3 084	1 201		84	1 360	66	76	62
	296				65		55
2 034	26 850	61	53	250	53	57	94
	234				71		13
3 489	673	90	93	18 430	71	73	22
3 259	623		100	14 570	76	100	8
3 644	408		95	21 100	76	96	8
2 746	348	80	91	2 620	73	95	20
	292				69		38
2 534	605		89	2 450	70	91	33
2 217	3 108	80	88	215	64	88	54
	16 273				40		176
2 474	3 727			580	65	98	48
2 285	5 982		23	745	53	39	107
3 570			79	2 490	73	93	21
2 079	26 982	26	72	260	54	72	75
2 028	9 797	75	81	390	55	73	72
2 193	7 537	71	100	640	61	76	55

All the names on the maps in this atlas, except some of those on the special topic maps, are included in the index.

The names are arranged in **alphabetical order**. Where the name has more than one word the separate words are considered as one to decide the position of the name in the index:

Thetford
The Wash
The Weald
Thiers

Where there is more than one place with the same name, the country name is used to decide the order:

London Canada
London U.K.

If both places are in the same country, the county or state name is also used:

Avon *r.* Dorset U.K.
Avon *r.* Glos U.K.

Each entry in the index starts with the name of the place or feature, followed by the name of the country or region in which it is located. This is followed by the number of the most appropriate page on which the name appears, usually the largest scale map. Next comes the alphanumeric reference followed by the latitude and longitude.

Names of physical features such as rivers, capes, mountains etc are followed by a description. The descriptions are usually shortened to one or two letters, these abbreviations are keyed below. Town names are followed by a description only when the name may be confused with that of a physical feature:

Black River *town*

To help to distinguish the different parts of each entry, different styles of type are used:

place name	country name or region name	alphanumeric grid reference
description (if any)	page number	latitude/ longitude

Thames *r.* U.K. **15** **C2** 51.30N0.05E

To use the **alphanumeric grid reference** to find a feature on the map, first find the correct page and then look at the letters printed in blue along the top and bottom of the map and the numbers printed in blue at the sides of the map. When you have found the correct letter and number follow the grid boxes up and along until you find the correct grid box in which the feature appears. You must then search the grid box until you find the name of the feature.

The **latitude and longitude reference** gives a more exact description of the position of the feature.

Page 6 of the atlas describes lines of latitude and lines of longitude, and explains how they are numbered and divided into degrees and minutes. Each name in the index has a different latitude and longitude reference, so the feature can be located accurately. The lines of latitude and lines of longitude shown on each map are numbered in degrees. These numbers are printed black along the top, bottom and sides of the map.

The drawing above shows part of the map on page 28 and the lines of latitude and lines of longitude.

The index entry for Wexford is given as follows

Wexford Rep. of Ire. **28** **E2** 52.20N 6.25W

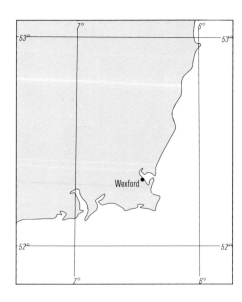

To locate Wexford, first find latitude 52N and estimate 20 minutes north from 52 degrees to find 52.20N, then find longitude 6W and estimate 25 minutes west from 6 degrees to find 6.25W. The symbol for the town of Wexford is where latitude 52.20N and longitude 6.25W meet.

On maps at a smaller scale than the map of Ireland, it is not possible to show every line of latitude and longitude. Only every 5 or 10 degrees of latitude and longitude may be shown. On these maps you must estimate the degrees and minutes to find the exact location of a feature.

Abbreviations

Afghan.	Afghanistan
Bangla.	Bangladesh
b., **B.**	bay, Bay
Beds.	Bedfordshire
Berks.	Berkshire
Bosnia.	Bosnia-Herzegovina
Bucks.	Buckinghamshire
Cambs.	Cambridgeshire
c., **C.**	cape, Cape
C.A.R.	Central African Republic
d.	internal division eg. county, state
Derbys.	Derbyshire
des.	desert
Dom. Rep.	Dominican Republic
D. and G.	Dumfries and Galloway
E. Sussex	East Sussex
Equat. Guinea	Equatorial Guinea
est.	estuary
f.	physical feature eg. valley, plain, geographic district
Glos.	Gloucestershire
G.L.	Greater London
G.M.	Greater Manchester
g., **G.**	Gulf
Hants.	Hampshire
H. and W.	Hereford and Worcester
Herts.	Hertfordshire
Humber.	Humberside

i., **I.**, *is.*, **Is.**	island, Island, islands, Islands
I.o.M.	Isle of Man
I.o.W.	Isle of Wight
l., **L.**	lake, Lake
Lancs.	Lancashire
Leics.	Leicestershire
Liech.	Liechtenstein
Lincs.	Lincolnshire
Lux.	Luxembourg
Mersey.	Merseyside
M.G.	Mid Glamorgan
Mt.	Mount
mtn., **Mtn.**	mountain, Mountain
mts., **Mts.**	mountains, Mountains
Neth.	Netherlands
N. Ireland	Northern Ireland
Northants.	Northamptonshire
Northum.	Northumberland
N. Korea	North Korea
N. Yorks.	North Yorkshire
Notts.	Nottinghamshire
Oxon.	Oxfordshire
P.N.G.	Papua New Guinea
pen., **Pen.**	peninsula, Peninsula
Phil.	Philippines
Pt.	Point
r., **R.**	river, River
Rep. of Ire.	Republic of Ireland
R.S.A.	Republic of South Africa

Resr.	Reservoir
Somali Rep.	Somali Republic
Sd.	Sound
S.G.	South Glamorgan
S. Korea	South Korea
S. Yorks.	South Yorkshire
Staffs.	Staffordshire
str., **Str.**	strait, Strait
Strath.	Strathclyde
Switz.	Switzerland
T. and W.	Tyne and Wear
U.A.E.	United Arab Emirates
U.K.	United Kingdom
U.S.A.	United States of America
Warwicks.	Warwickshire
W.G.	West Glamorgan
W. Isles	Western Isles
W. Midlands	West Midlands
W. Sahara	Western Sahara
W. Sussex	West Sussex
W. Yorks.	West Yorkshire
Wilts.	Wiltshire
Yugo.	Yugoslavia

A

Aachen Germany **47 E2** 50.46N 6.06E
Äänekoski Finland **58 F3** 62.36N 25.44E
Aarau Switz. **52 D2** 47.24N 8.04E
Aardenburg Neth. **47 B3** 51.16N 3.26E
Aare *r.* Switz. **52 D2** 47.37N 8.13E
Aarschot Belgium **47 C2** 50.59N 4.50E
Aba Nigeria **108 C2** 5.06N 7.21E
Abadan Iran **69 H3** 30.21N 48.15E
Abadan I. Iran **69 H3** 30.10N 48.30E
Abadla Algeria **104 B5** 31.01N 2.45W
Abakaliki Nigeria **108 C2** 6.17N 8.04E
Abakan Russian Fed. **61 H3** 53.43N 91.25E
Abariringa *i.* Kiribati **82 I7** 2.50S 171.40W
Abashiri wan *b.* Japan **76 F9** 44.02N 144.17E
Abaya, L. Ethiopia **82 F2** 6.20N 38.00E
Abbeville France **48 D6** 50.06N 1.51E
Abbey Town England **22 A1** 54.50N 3.18W
Abbotsbury England **13 E2** 50.40N 2.36W
Abéché Chad **105 E3** 13.49N 20.49E
Åbenrå Denmark **46 C3** 55.03N 9.26E
Abeokuta Nigeria **108 B2** 7.10N 3.26E
Aberaeron Wales **18 B2** 52.15N 4.16W
Abercarn Wales **18 C1** 51.39N 3.09W
Aberdare Wales **18 C1** 51.43N 3.27W
Aberdaron Wales **18 B2** 52.48N 4.41W
Aberdeen Scotland **24 F4** 57.08N 2.07W
Aberdeen S. Dak. U.S.A. **86 G6** 45.28N 98.30W
Aberdeen Wash. U.S.A. **86 B6** 46.58N 123.49W
Aberdovey Wales **18 B2** 52.33N 4.03W
Aberfan Wales **18 C1** 51.42N 3.20W
Aberfeldy Scotland **24 E3** 56.38N 3.52W
Aberffraw Wales **18 B3** 53.11N 4.28W
Aberfoyle Scotland **26 D3** 56.11N 4.23W
Abergavenny Wales **18 C1** 51.49N 3.01W
Abergele Wales **18 C3** 53.17N 3.34W
Abernethy Scotland **27 E3** 56.20N 3.19W
Aberporth Wales **18 B2** 52.08N 4.33W
Abersoch Wales **18 B2** 52.50N 4.31W
Abersychan Wales **18 C1** 51.44N 3.03W
Abertillery Wales **18 C1** 51.44N 3.09W
Aberystwyth Wales **18 B2** 52.25N 4.06W
Ab-i-Diz *r.* Iran **69 H3** 31.38N 48.54E
Abidjan Ivory Coast **104 B2** 5.19N 4.01W
Abilene U.S.A. **86 G3** 32.27N 99.45W
Abingdon England **14 A2** 51.40N 1.17W
Abington Scotland **27 E2** 55.29N 3.42W
Abitibi *r.* Canada **91 J3** 51.20N 80.30W
Abomey Benin **108 B2** 7.14N 2.00E
Aboyne Scotland **24 F4** 57.05N 2.49W
Abqaiq Saudi Arabia **69 H2** 25.55N 49.40E
Abrantes Portugal **50 A3** 39.28N 8.12W
Abu Dhabi U.A.E. **69 I2** 24.27N 54.23E
Abu Hamed Sudan **105 F3** 19.32N 33.20E
Abuja Nigeria **108 C2** 9.12N 7.11E
Abu Simbel Egypt **68 C1** 22.18N 31.40E
Abu Tig Egypt **68 C2** 27.06N 31.17E
Abu Zenîma Egypt **68 D3** 29.03N 33.06E
Acambaro Mexico **92 D4** 20.01N 101.42W
Acapulco Mexico **92 E3** 16.51N 99.56W
Acarigua Venezuela **94 F2** 9.35N 69.12W
Acatlán Mexico **92 E3** 18.12N 98.02W
Accra Ghana **108 A2** 5.33N 0.15W
Accrington England **20 C2** 53.46N 2.22W
Achahoish Scotland **26 C2** 55.57N 5.30W
Achill I. Rep. of Ire. **28 A3** 53.57N 10.00W
Achinsk Russian Fed. **60 H3** 56.10N 90.10E
Acklin's I. Bahamas **93 J4** 22.30N 74.10W
Ackworth Moor Top *town* England **21 D2** 53.39N 1.20W
Aconcagua *mtn.* Argentina **97 C4** 32.37S 70.00W
Acqui Italy **54 B6** 44.41N 8.28E
Adamawa Highlands Nigeria/Cameroon **108 D2** 7.05N 12.00E
Adams, Mt. U.S.A. **86 B6** 46.13N 121.29W
Adana Turkey **68 D5** 37.00N 35.19E
Adapazari Turkey **68 C6** 40.45N 30.23E
Adda *r.* Italy **54 B6** 45.08N 9.55E
Ad Dahana *des.* Saudi Arabia **69 G2** 26.00N 47.00E
Adderbury England **14 A3** 52.01N 1.19W
Addis Ababa Ethiopia **105 F2** 9.03N 38.42E
Ad Diwaniya Iraq **69 G3** 31.59N 44.57E
Adelaide Australia **80 C2** 34.56S 138.36E
Aden Yemen **105 G3** 12.50N 45.00E
Aden, G. of Indian Oc. **105 G3** 13.00N 50.00E
Adi *i.* Indonesia **79 I3** 4.10S 133.10E
Adige *r.* Italy **54 D6** 45.10N 12.20E
Adiyaman Turkey **68 E5** 37.46N 38.15E
Adlington England **20 C2** 53.37N 2.36W
Admiralty Is. P.N.G. **79 L3** 2.30S 147.20E
Adour *r.* France **48 C2** 43.28N 1.35W
Adrano Italy **54 E2** 37.39N 14.49E
Adriatic Sea Med. Sea **56 B5** 42.30N 16.00E
Aduwa Ethiopia **105 F3** 14.12N 38.56E
Adwick le Street England **21 D2** 53.35N 1.12W
Aegean Sea Med. Sea **56 G3** 39.00N 25.00E
Aerö *i.* Denmark **46 D2** 54.52N 10.25E
Aeron *r.* Wales **18 B2** 52.14N 4.16W
Afghanistan Asia **70 B6** 33.00N 65.30E
Afif Saudi Arabia **68 F1** 23.53N 42.59E
Afikpo Nigeria **108 C2** 5.53N 7.55E
Afobaka Surinam **95 H2** 5.00N 55.05W
Africa 113
Afyon Turkey **68 C5** 38.46N 30.32E
Agadès Niger **104 C3** 17.00N 7.56E
Agadir Morocco **104 B5** 30.26N 9.36W
Agana Guam **79 K6** 13.28N 144.45E
Agano *r.* Japan **76 D5** 37.58N 139.02E
Agartala India **71 G4** 23.49N 91.15E
Agedabia Libya **104 E5** 30.48N 20.15E
Agen France **48 D3** 44.12N 0.38E
Agger *r.* Germany **47 F2** 50.45N 7.06E
Aghada Rep. of Ire. **28 C1** 51.50N 8.14W
Agnew's Hill N. Ireland **23 D1** 54.51N 5.58W
Agordat Eritrea **105 F3** 15.35N 37.55E
Agra India **71 E5** 27.09N 78.00E
Agra *r.* Spain **50 E5** 42.12N 1.43W
Agreda Spain **50 E4** 41.51N 1.55W
Agri *r.* Italy **54 F4** 40.13N 16.45E
Agri Turkey **68 F5** 39.44N 43.04E
Agrigento Italy **54 D2** 37.19N 13.36E
Agrihan *i.* Mariana Is. **79 L7** 18.44N 145.39E
Aguascalientes Mexico **92 D4** 21.51N 102.18W
Aguascalientes *d.* Mexico **92 D4** 22.00N 102.00W
Águeda *r.* Spain **50 B4** 41.00N 6.56W
Aguilas Spain **50 E2** 37.25N 1.35W
Agulhas, C. R.S.A. **106 C1** 34.50S 20.00E
Agulhas Negras *mtn.* Brazil **97 E5** 22.20S 44.43W
Ahaggar Mts. Algeria **104 C4** 24.00N 5.50E
Ahar Iran **69 G5** 38.25N 47.07E
Ahaus Germany **47 F4** 52.04N 7.01E
Ahlen Germany **52 C4** 51.46N 7.53E
Ahmadabad India **71 D4** 23.03N 72.40E
Ahmadnagar India **71 D3** 19.08N 74.48E
Ahr *r.* Germany **47 F2** 50.34N 7.16E
Ahwaz Iran **69 H3** 31.17N 48.44E
Ailette *r.* France **47 B1** 49.35N 3.09E
Ailsa Craig *i.* Scotland **26 C2** 55.15N 5.07W
Ain *r.* France **48 F3** 45.47N 5.12E
Ain Salah Algeria **104 C4** 27.12N 2.29E
Aïn Sefra Algeria **104 B5** 32.45N 0.35W
Aïr *mts.* Niger **104 C3** 18.30N 8.30E
Airdrie Scotland **27 E2** 55.52N 3.59W
Aire *r.* England **21 E2** 53.42N 0.54W
Aire France **48 C2** 43.39N 0.15W
Airedale *f.* England **20 D2** 53.56N 1.54W
Aisne *r.* France **47 A1** 49.27N 2.51E
Aitape P.N.G. **79 K3** 3.10S 142.17E
Aitutaki Atoll Cook Is. **83 K6** 18.52S 159.46W
Aix-en-Provence France **48 F2** 43.31N 5.27E
Aíyina *i.* Greece **56 F2** 37.43N 23.30E
Aizuwakamatsu Japan **76 D5** 37.30N 139.58E
Ajaccio France **49 H1** 41.55N 8.43E
Ajama U.A.E. **69 I2** 25.23N 55.26E
Ajmer India **71 D5** 26.29N 74.40E
Akaishi san *mts.* Japan **76 D4** 35.20N 138.05E
Akashi Japan **76 C4** 34.39N 135.00E
Akhaltsikhe Georgia **68 F6** 41.37N 42.59E
Akhdar, Jebel *mts.* Libya **105 E5** 32.10N 22.00E
Akhdar, Jebel *mts.* Oman **69 J1** 23.10N 57.25E
Akhdar, Wadi *r.* Saudi Arabia **68 E3** 28.30N 36.48E
Akhelóös *r.* Greece **56 E3** 38.20N 21.04E
Akhisar Turkey **68 B5** 38.54N 27.49E
Akhtyrka Ukraine **59 C4** 50.19N 34.54E
Akimiski I. Canada **91 J3** 53.00N 81.20W
Akita Japan **76 D6** 39.44N 140.05E
Akkajaure *l.* Sweden **58 D4** 67.40N 17.30E
Akobo *r.* Sudan/Ethiopia **105 F2** 8.30N 33.15E
Akola India **71 D4** 20.44N 77.00E
Akpatok I. Canada **91 L4** 60.30N 68.30W
Akron U.S.A. **87 J5** 41.04N 81.31W
Aksaray Turkey **68 D5** 38.22N 34.02E
Akşehir Turkey **68 C5** 38.22N 31.24E
Aksu China **74 C5** 42.10N 80.00E
Aktogay Kazakhstan **74 C6** 46.59N 79.42E
Aktyubinsk Kazakhstan **60 E2** 50.16N 57.13E
Akure Nigeria **108 C2** 7.14N 5.08E
Akureyri Iceland **58 J7** 65.41N 18.04W
Akuse Ghana **108 B2** 6.04N 0.12E
Akyab Myanma **71 G4** 20.09N 92.55E
Alabama *d.* U.S.A. **87 I3** 33.00N 87.00W
Alabama *r.* U.S.A. **87 I3** 31.05N 87.55W
Alagez *mtn.* Armenia **69 G6** 40.32N 44.11E
Al Ain, Wadi *r.* Oman **69 I1** 22.18N 55.35E
Alakol, L. Kazakhstan **74 C6** 46.00N 81.40E
Alakurtti Russian Fed. **58 G4** 67.00N 30.23E
Alamagan *i.* Mariana Is. **79 L7** 17.35N 145.50E
Alamosa U.S.A. **86 E4** 37.28N 105.54W
Åland Is. Finland **58 E3** 60.20N 20.00E
Alanya Turkey **68 D5** 36.32N 32.02E
Alaşehir Turkey **68 C5** 38.22N 28.29E
Alaska *d.* U.S.A. **90 C4** 65.00N 153.00W
Alaska, G. of U.S.A. **90 D3** 58.45N 145.00W
Alaska Pen. U.S.A. **90 B3** 56.00N 160.00W
Alaska Range *mts.* U.S.A. **90 C4** 62.10N 152.00W
Alazan *r.* Georgia **69 G6** 41.06N 46.40E
Albacete Spain **50 E3** 39.00N 1.52W
Ålbaek Denmark **46 D5** 57.38N 10.26E
Alba-Iulia Romania **56 F7** 46.04N 23.33E
Albania Europe **56 E4** 41.00N 20.00E
Albany Australia **80 A2** 34.57S 117.54E
Albany *r.* Canada **91 J3** 52.10N 82.00W
Albany Ga. U.S.A. **87 J3** 31.37N 84.10W
Albany N.Y. U.S.A. **87 L5** 42.40N 73.49W
Albany Oreg. U.S.A. **86 B5** 44.38N 123.07W
Albemarle Sd. U.S.A. **87 K4** 36.10N 76.00W
Alberche *r.* Spain **50 C4** 40.00N 4.45W
Albert France **48 E6** 50.00N 2.40E
Alberta *d.* Canada **90 G3** 55.00N 115.00W
Albert Canal Belgium **47 D3** 51.00N 5.15E
Albert, L. Africa **105 F2** 1.45N 31.00E
Albert Nile *r.* Uganda **105 F2** 3.30N 32.00E
Albi France **48 E2** 43.56N 2.08E
Albina Surinam **95 I2** 5.30N 54.03W
Alborán, Isla de *i.* Spain **50 D1** 35.55N 3.10W
Ålborg Denmark **46 C5** 57.03N 9.56E
Ålborg Bugt *b.* Denmark **46 D4** 56.50N 10.30E
Albuquerque U.S.A. **86 E4** 35.05N 106.38W
Alburquerque Spain **50 B3** 39.13N 6.59W
Alcácer do Sal Portugal **50 A3** 38.22N 8.30W
Alcalá de Chisvert Spain **50 F4** 40.19N 0.13E
Alcalá de Henares Spain **50 D4** 40.28N 3.22W
Alcalá la Real Spain **50 D2** 37.28N 3.55W
Alcamo Italy **54 D2** 37.59N 12.58E
Alcañiz Spain **50 E4** 41.03N 0.09W
Alcaudete Spain **50 C2** 37.35N 4.05W
Alcázar de San Juan Spain **50 D3** 39.24N 3.12W
Alcester England **16 C2** 52.13N 1.52W
Alcira Spain **50 E3** 39.10N 0.27W
Alcoy Spain **50 E3** 38.42N 0.29W
Alcubierre, Sierra de *mts.* Spain **50 E4** 41.40N 0.20W
Alcudia Spain **51 G3** 39.51N 3.09E
Aldabra Is. Indian Oc. **102 G4** 9.00S 47.00E
Aldan Russian Fed. **61 K3** 58.44N 125.22E
Aldan *r.* Russian Fed. **61 K3** 63.30N 130.00E
Aldbourne England **13 F3** 51.28N 1.38W
Aldbrough England **21 E2** 53.50N 0.07W
Aldeburgh England **15 D3** 52.09N 1.35E
Alderney *i.* Channel Is. **48 B5** 49.42N 2.11W
Aldershot England **15 B2** 51.15N 0.47W
Aldridge England **16 C2** 52.36N 1.55W
Aldsworth England **13 F3** 51.48N 1.46W
Aleksandrovsk Sakhalinskiy Russian Fed. **61 L2** 50.55N 142.12E
Alençon France **48 D5** 48.25N 0.05E
Aleppo Syria **68 E5** 36.14N 37.10E
Aléria France **49 H2** 42.05N 9.30E
Alès France **48 F3** 44.08N 4.05E
Alessandria Italy **54 B6** 44.54N 8.37E
Ålestrup Denmark **46 C4** 56.41N 9.30E
Ålesund Norway **58 A3** 62.28N 6.11E
Aleutian Basin Bering Sea **82 H13** 57.00N 179.00E
Aleutian Is. U.S.A. **84 C7** 52.00N 176.00W
Aleutian Range *mts.* U.S.A. **90 C3** 58.00N 156.00W
Aleutian Trench Pacific Oc. **82 J13** 50.00N 176.00W
Alexander Archipelago *is.* U.S.A. **90 E3** 56.30N 134.30W
Alexandria Egypt **68 C3** 31.13N 29.55E
Alexandria Scotland **26 D2** 55.59N 4.35W
Alexandria La. U.S.A. **87 H3** 31.19N 92.29W
Alexandroúpolis Greece **56 G4** 40.50N 25.53E
Alfaro Spain **50 E5** 42.11N 1.45W
Alfiós *r.* Greece **56 E2** 37.37N 21.27E
Alford Scotland **24 F4** 57.14N 2.43W
Alfreton England **16 C3** 53.06N 1.22W
Algeciras Spain **50 C2** 36.08N 5.27W
Algeria Africa **104 C4** 28.00N 2.00E
Al Ghadaf, Wadi *r.* Iraq **68 F4** 32.54N 43.33E
Alghero Italy **54 B4** 40.33N 8.20E
Algiers Algeria **104 C5** 36.50N 3.00E
Al Hamra *des.* U.A.E. **69 I1** 22.45N 55.10E
Aliákmon *r.* Greece **56 F4** 40.30N 22.38E
Alicante Spain **50 E3** 38.21N 0.29W
Alice U.S.A. **86 G2** 27.45N 98.06W
Alice Springs *town* Australia **80 C3** 23.42S 133.52E
Aligarh India **71 E5** 27.54N 78.04E
Aligudarz Iran **69 H4** 33.25N 49.38E
Alingsås Sweden **58 C2** 57.55N 12.30E
Al Jaub *f.* Saudi Arabia **69 H1** 23.00N 50.00E
Al Jauf Saudi Arabia **68 E3** 29.49N 39.52E
Al Jazi *des.* Iraq **68 F4** 35.00N 41.00E
Al Khamāsīn Saudi Arabia **105 G4** 20.29N 44.49E
Al Khubar Saudi Arabia **69 H2** 26.18N 50.06E
Al Khurr *r.* Iraq **68 F3** 32.00N 44.15E
Alkmaar Neth. **47 C4** 52.37N 4.44E
Al Kut Iraq **69 G4** 32.30N 45.51E
Allahabad India **71 E4** 25.57N 81.50E
Allakaket U.S.A. **90 C4** 66.30N 152.45W
'Allaqi, Wadi *r.* Egypt **68 D1** 22.55N 33.02E
Al Lawz, Jebel *mtn.* Saudi Arabia **68 D3** 28.40N 35.20E
Allegheny Mts. U.S.A. **87 K5** 40.00N 79.00W
Allen, Lough Rep. of Ire. **28 C4** 54.07N 8.04W
Allentown U.S.A. **87 K5** 40.37N 75.30W
Alleppey India **71 D2** 9.30N 76.22E
Aller *r.* Germany **52 D5** 52.57N 9.11E
Alliance Nebr. U.S.A. **86 F5** 42.08N 103.00W
Allier *r.* France **48 E4** 46.58N 3.04E
Allingåbro Denmark **46 D4** 56.29N 10.20E
Alloa Scotland **27 E3** 56.07N 3.49W
Alma-Ata Kazakhstan **74 B5** 43.19N 76.55E
Almadén Spain **50 C3** 38.47N 4.50W
Al Maharadh *des.* Saudi Arabia **69 I1** 22.00N 52.30E
Almansa Spain **50 E3** 38.52N 1.06W
Almanzora *r.* Spain **50 E2** 37.16N 1.49W
Almanzor, Pico de *mtn.* Spain **50 C4** 40.20N 5.22W
Almazán Spain **50 D4** 41.29N 2.31W
Almeirim Portugal **50 A3** 39.12N 8.37W
Almelo Neth. **47 E4** 52.21N 6.40E
Almería Spain **50 D2** 36.50N 2.26W
Almetyevsk Russian Fed. **60 E3** 54.50N 52.22E
Älmhult Sweden **58 C2** 56.32N 14.10E
Al Mira, Wadi *r.* Iraq **68 F4** 32.27N 41.21E
Almond *r.* Scotland **27 E3** 56.25N 3.28W
Almuñécar Spain **50 D2** 36.44N 3.41W
Aln *r.* England **22 C2** 55.23N 1.36W
Alnwick England **22 C2** 55.25N 1.41W
Alofi Niue **82 J6** 19.03S 169.55W
Alor *i.* Indonesia **79 G2** 8.20S 124.30E
Alor Setar Malaysia **78 C5** 6.06N 100.23E
Alost Belgium **47 C2** 50.57N 4.03E
Alpes Maritimes *mts.* France **48 G3** 44.07N 7.08E
Alphen Neth. **47 C4** 52.08N 4.40E
Alpine U.S.A. **86 F3** 30.22N 103.40W
Alps *mts.* Europe **48 G4** 46.00N 7.30E
Al Qurna Iraq **69 G3** 31.00N 47.26E
Als *i.* Denmark **46 C2** 54.56N 9.55E
Alsager England **20 C2** 53.07N 2.20W
Alsasua Spain **50 D5** 42.54N 2.10W
Alston England **22 B1** 54.48N 2.26W
Alta Norway **58 E5** 69.57N 23.10E
Alta *r.* Norway **58 E5** 70.00N 23.15E
Altagracia Venezuela **94 E3** 10.44N 71.30W
Altagracia de Orituco Venezuela **95 F2** 9.45N 66.24W
Altai *mts.* Mongolia **74 E6** 46.30N 93.30E
Altaj Mongolia **74 F6** 46.20N 97.00E
Altamaha *r.* U.S.A. **87 J3** 31.15N 81.23W
Altamura Italy **54 F4** 40.50N 16.32E
Altay China **74 D6** 47.48N 88.07E
Altea Spain **50 E3** 38.37N 0.03W
Altenburg Germany **52 F4** 50.59N 12.27E
Altenkirchen Germany **47 F2** 50.41N 7.40E
Al Tihama *des.* Saudi Arabia **68 D2** 27.50N 35.30E
Altiplano Mexicano *mts.* N. America **84 J4** 24.00N 105.00W
Altnaharra Scotland **24 D5** 58.16N 4.27W
Alton England **15 B2** 51.08N 0.59W
Altoona U.S.A. **87 K5** 40.32N 78.23W
Altrincham England **20 C2** 53.25N 2.21W
Altun Shan *mts.* China **74 D5** 38.10N 87.50E
Al Ula Saudi Arabia **68 E2** 26.39N 37.58E
Alva Scotland **27 E3** 56.09N 3.49W
Alva U.S.A. **86 G4** 36.48N 98.40W
Alvarado Mexico **92 E3** 18.49N 95.46W
Älvsbyn Sweden **58 E4** 65.41N 21.00E
Al Wajh Saudi Arabia **68 E2** 26.16N 36.28E
Al Wakrah Qatar **69 H2** 25.09N 51.36E
Alwar India **71 D5** 27.32N 76.35E
Alyaty Azerbaijan **69 H5** 39.59N 49.20E
Alyth Scotland **27 E3** 56.38N 3.14W
Alytus Lithuania **57 I7** 54.24N 24.03E
Alzette *r.* Lux. **47 E1** 49.52N 6.07E
Amagasaki Japan **76 C4** 34.43N 135.20E
Amager *i.* Denmark **46 F3** 55.34N 12.30E
Amami *i.* Japan **75 K3** 28.20N 129.30E
Amara Iraq **69 G3** 31.52N 47.50E
Amarillo U.S.A. **86 F4** 35.14N 101.50W
Amaro, Monte *mtn.* Italy **54 E5** 42.06N 14.04E
Amasya Turkey **68 D6** 40.37N 35.50E
Amazon *r.* Brazil **96 D7** 2.00S 50.00W
Amazon Delta *f.* Brazil **96 E8** 0.00 50.00W
Ambala India **71 D5** 30.19N 76.49E
Ambarchik Russian Fed. **61 N4** 69.39N 162.27E
Ambatondrazaka Madagascar **106 G8** 17.20S 48.30E
Amberg Germany **52 E3** 49.27N 11.52E
Ambergris Cay *i.* Belize **94 B4** 18.00N 87.58W
Amberley England **15 B1** 50.54N 0.33W
Amble England **22 C2** 55.20N 1.34W
Ambleside England **22 B1** 54.26N 2.58W
Ambon Indonesia **79 H3** 3.50S 128.10E
Ambre, Cap d' *c.* Madagascar **106 G9** 11.58S 49.14E
Ameland *i.* Neth. **47 D5** 53.28N 5.48E
Amersfoort Neth. **47 D4** 52.10N 5.23E
Amesbury England **13 F3** 51.10N 1.46W
Amga Russian Fed. **61 K3** 60.51N 131.59E
Amga *r.* Russian Fed. **61 L3** 62.40N 135.20E
Amgun *r.* Russian Fed. **61 L3** 53.10N 139.47E
Amiata *mtn.* Italy **54 C5** 42.53N 11.37E
Amiens France **48 E5** 49.54N 2.18E
Amirantes *is.* Indian Oc. **113 L4** 6.00S 52.00E
Amlwch Wales **18 B3** 53.24N 4.21W
Amman Jordan **68 D3** 31.57N 35.56E
Ammanford Wales **18 C1** 51.48N 4.00W
Ammassalik Greenland **91 O4** 65.40N 38.00W
Ampala Honduras **93 G2** 13.16N 87.39W
Ampthill England **15 B3** 52.03N 0.30W
Amraoti India **71 D4** 20.58N 77.50E
Amritsar India **71 D5** 31.35N 74.56E
Amrum *i.* Germany **46 B2** 54.40N 8.20E
Amsterdam Neth. **47 C4** 52.22N 4.54E
Amsterdam I. Indian Oc. **113 M3** 37.00S 79.00E
Amu Darya *r.* Asia **60 E2** 43.50N 59.00E
Amundsen G. Canada **90 F5** 70.30N 122.00W
Amundsen Sea Antarctica **112 D1** 70.00S 116.00W
Amuntai Indonesia **78 F3** 2.24S 115.14E
Amur *r.* Russian Fed. **61 L3** 53.17N 140.00E
Anabar *r.* Russian Fed. **61 J4** 72.40N 113.30E
Anaco Venezuela **95 G2** 9.27N 64.28W
Anadyr Russian Fed. **61 O4** 64.40N 177.32E
Anadyr *r.* Russian Fed. **61 O4** 65.00N 176.00E
Anadyr, G. of Russian Fed. **61 P4** 64.30N 177.50W
Anaiza Saudi Arabia **69 F2** 26.05N 43.57E
Anambas Is. Indonesia **78 D4** 3.00N 106.10E
Anan Japan **76 B3** 33.55N 134.39E
Anatahan *i.* Mariana Is. **79 L7** 16.22N 145.38E
Anatolia *f.* Turkey **68 D5** 38.00N 35.00E
Anchorage U.S.A. **90 D4** 61.10N 150.00W
Ancona Italy **54 D5** 43.37N 13.33E
Ancroft England **22 B2** 55.42N 2.00W
Anda China **75 J6** 46.25N 125.20E
Andalsnes Norway **58 A3** 62.33N 7.43E
Andalucia *d.* Spain **50 C2** 38.00N 4.00W
Andaman Is. India **71 G2** 12.00N 93.00E
Andaman Sea Indian Oc. **78 B6** 11.00N 96.00E
Andernach Germany **47 F2** 50.25N 7.24E
Anderson *r.* Canada **90 F4** 69.45N 129.00W
Andes *mts.* S. America **96 B6** 15.00S 72.00W
Andevoranto Madagascar **106 G8** 18.56S 49.07E
Andfjorden *est.* Norway **58 D5** 69.10N 16.20E
Andhra Pradesh *d.* India **71 E3** 17.00N 79.00E
Andikíthira *i.* Greece **56 F1** 35.52N 23.18E
Andizhan Uzbekistan **74 B5** 40.48N 72.23E
Andorra *town* Andorra **48 D2** 42.30N 1.31E
Andorra Europe **48 D2** 42.30N 1.32E
Andover England **14 A2** 51.13N 1.29W
Andöy *i.* Norway **58 C5** 69.00N 15.30E
Andreas I.o.M. **20 A3** 54.22N 4.26W
Andreas, C. Cyprus **68 D4** 35.40N 34.35E
Andropov Russian Fed. **59 D5** 58.01N 38.52E
Ándros *i.* Greece **56 G2** 37.50N 24.50E
Andros I. Bahamas **93 I4** 24.30N 78.00W
Andújar Spain **50 C3** 38.02N 4.03W
Anegada *i.* B.V.Is. **93 L3** 18.46N 64.24W
Aného Togo **108 B2** 6.17N 1.40E
Aneiza, Jebel *mtn.* Asia **68 E4** 32.15N 39.19E
Aneto, Pico de *mtn.* Spain **50 F5** 42.40N 0.19E
Angara *r.* Russian Fed. **61 I3** 58.00N 93.00E
Angarsk Russian Fed. **61 I3** 52.31N 103.55E
Ånge Sweden **58 C3** 62.31N 15.40E
Angel de la Guarda *i.* Mexico **92 B5** 29.10N 113.20W
Angel Falls *f.* Venezuela **95 G2** 5.55N 62.30W
Ängelholm Sweden **58 C2** 56.15N 12.50E
Ångerman *r.* Sweden **58 D3** 62.52N 17.45E
Angers France **48 C4** 47.29N 0.32W
Angkor *ruins* Cambodia **78 C6** 13.26N 103.50E

Angle Wales **18 A1** 51.40N 5.03W
Anglesey *i.* Wales **18 B3** 53.16N 4.25W
Angola Africa **106 B3** 12.00S 18.00E
Angoram P.N.G. **79 K3** 4.04S 144.04E
Angoulême France **48 D3** 45.40N 0.10E
Anguilar de Campóo Spain **50 C5** 42.55N 4.15W
Anguilla *i.* Leeward Is. **93 L3** 18.14N 63.05W
Anholt *i.* Denmark **46 E4** 56.42N 11.35E
Anholt Germany **47 E3** 51.51N 6.26E
Anhui *d.* China **75 I3** 31.30N 116.45E
Aniak U.S.A. **90 C4** 61.32N 159.40W
Ankara Turkey **68 D5** 39.55N 32.50E
Ankaratra Mts. Madagascar **102 G2** 20.00S 47.00E
Ankober Ethiopia **105 F2** 9.32N 39.43E
Annaba Algeria **104 C5** 36.55N 7.47E
An Nafud *des.* Saudi Arabia **68 F3** 28.40N 41.30E
An Najaf Iraq **69 G3** 31.59N 44.19E
Annalong N. Ireland **23 D1** 54.06N 5.55W
Annam Highlands *mts.* Asia **78 D7** 17.40N 105.30E
Annan Scotland **27 E1** 54.59N 3.16W
Annan *r.* Scotland **27 E1** 54.58N 3.16W
Annandale *f.* Scotland **27 E2** 55.12N 3.25W
Annapurna *mtn.* Nepal **71 E5** 28.34N 83.50E
An Nasiriya Iraq **69 G3** 31.04N 46.16E
Annecy France **48 G3** 45.54N 6.07E
Annfield Plain *town* England **22 C1** 54.52N 1.45W
Annonay France **48 F3** 45.15N 4.40E
Anqing China **75 I3** 30.20N 116.50E
Ansbach Germany **52 E3** 49.18N 10.36E
Anshan China **75 J5** 41.05N 122.58E
Anshun China **74 G3** 26.15N 105.51E
Anston England **21 D2** 53.22N 1.13W
Anstruther Scotland **27 F3** 56.14N 2.42W
Antakya Turkey **68 E5** 36.12N 36.10E
Antalya Turkey **68 C5** 36.53N 30.42E
Antalya, G. of Turkey **68 C5** 36.38N 31.00E
Antananarivo Madagascar **106 G8** 18.52S 47.30E
Antarctica 112
Antarctic Pen. Antarctica **97 C1** 65.00S 64.00W
Antequera Spain **50 C2** 37.01N 4.34W
Anticosti I. Canada **91 L2** 49.20N 63.00W
Antigua Guatemala **92 F2** 14.33N 90.42W
Antigua *i.* Leeward Is. **93 L3** 17.09N 61.49W
Anti-Lebanon *mts.* Lebanon **68 E4** 34.00N 36.25E
Antipodes Is. Pacific Oc. **82 H3** 49.42S 178.50E
Antofagasta Chile **97 B5** 23.40S 70.23W
Antrim N. Ireland **23 C1** 54.43N 6.14W
Antrim *d.* N. Ireland **23 C1** 54.45N 6.15W
Antrim, Mts. of N. Ireland **23 C2** 55.00N 6.10W
Antsiranana Madagascar **106 G9** 12.19S 49.17E
Antwerp Belgium **47 C3** 51.13N 4.25E
Antwerp *d.* Belgium **47 C3** 51.16N 4.45E
Anvik U.S.A. **90 B4** 62.38N 160.20W
Anxi China **74 E5** 40.32N 95.57E
Anyang China **75 I4** 36.04N 114.20E
Anzhero-Sudzhensk Russian Fed. **60 H3** 56.10N 86.10E
Aomori Japan **76 D7** 40.50N 140.43E
Aosta Italy **54 A6** 45.43N 7.19E
Apalachee B. U.S.A. **87 J2** 29.30N 84.00W
Aparri Phil. **79 G7** 18.22N 121.40E
Apatity Russian Fed. **58 H4** 67.32N 33.21E
Apeldoorn Neth. **47 D4** 52.13N 5.57E
Apennines *mts.* Italy **54 C6** 42.00N 13.30E
Apia W. Samoa **82 I6** 13.48S 171.45W
Apostle Is. U.S.A. **87 H6** 47.00N 90.30W
Appalachian Mts. U.S.A. **87 K4** 39.30N 78.00W
Appingedam Neth. **47 E5** 53.18N 6.52E
Appleby England **22 B1** 54.35N 2.29W
Apsheron Pen. Azerbaijan **69 H6** 40.28N 50.00E
Apure *r.* Venezuela **95 F2** 7.44N 66.38W
Aqaba Jordan **68 D3** 29.32N 35.00E
Aqaba, G. of Asia **68 D3** 28.45N 34.45E
Aqlat as Suqur Saudi Arabia **68 F2** 25.50N 42.12E
Aquila Mexico **92 D3** 18.30N 103.50W
Arabia Asia **113 L6** 25.00N 45.00E
Arabian Desert Egypt **68 C3** 28.15N 31.55E
Arabian Sea Asia **70 B3** 16.00N 65.00E
Aracaju Brazil **96 F6** 10.54S 37.07W
Arad Romania **57 G3** 46.12N 21.19E
Arafura Sea Austa. **79 I2** 9.00S 135.00E
Aragon *d.* Spain **50 E4** 42.00N 1.00W
Aragón *r.* Spain **50 E5** 42.20N 1.45W
Araguaia *r.* Brazil **96 E7** 5.30S 48.05W
Araguari Brazil **97 E6** 18.38S 48.13W
Arak Iran **69 H4** 34.06N 49.44E
Arakan Yoma *mts.* Myanma **71 G4** 20.00N 94.00E
Aral Sea Asia **60 E2** 45.00N 60.00E
Aralsk Kazakhstan **60 F2** 46.56N 61.43E
Aranda de Duero Spain **50 D4** 41.40N 3.41W
Aran Fawddwy *mtn.* Wales **18 C2** 52.48N 3.42W
Aran I. Rep. of Ire. **28 C5** 55.00N 8.32W
Aran Is. Rep. of Ire. **28 B3** 53.07N 9.38W
Aranjuez Spain **50 D4** 40.02N 3.37W
Arapkir Turkey **68 E5** 39.03N 38.29E
Ararat, Mt. Turkey **69 G5** 39.45N 44.15E
Arar, Wadi *r.* Iraq **68 F3** 32.00N 42.30E
Aras *r. see* Araxes *r.* Turkey **68**
Arauca Colombia **94 E2** 7.04N 70.41W
Araure Venezuela **94 F2** 9.36N 69.15W
Araxes *r.* Asia **69 H5** 40.00N 48.28E
Arbatax Italy **54 B3** 39.56N 9.41E
Arbroath Scotland **27 F3** 56.34N 2.35W
Arcachon France **48 C3** 44.40N 1.11W
Arctic Ocean 112
Arctic Red *r.* Canada **90 E4** 67.26N 133.48W
Arda *r.* Greece **56 H4** 41.39N 26.30E
Ardabil Iran **69 H5** 38.15N 48.18E
Ardara Rep. of Ire. **28 C4** 54.45N 8.28W
Ardèche *r.* France **48 F3** 44.31N 4.40E
Ardennes *mts.* Belgium **47 D2** 50.10N 5.30E
Ardentinny Scotland **26 D3** 56.03N 4.55W
Ardfert Rep. of Ire. **28 B2** 52.19N 9.49W
Ardglass N. Ireland **23 D1** 54.16N 5.37W
Ardila *r.* Portugal **50 B3** 38.10N 7.30W
Ardlamont Pt. Scotland **26 C2** 55.49N 5.12W
Ardlui Scotland **26 D3** 56.18N 4.43W
Ardmore Rep. of Ire. **28 D1** 51.58N 7.43W
Ardmore Pt. Strath. Scotland **26 B2** 55.42N 6.01W
Ardmore Pt. Strath. Scotland **26 B3** 56.39N 6.08W
Ardnamurchan, Pt. of Scotland **24 B3** 56.44N 6.14W
Ardnave Pt. Scotland **26 B2** 55.54N 6.20W
Ardrishaig Scotland **26 C3** 56.00N 5.26W
Ardrossan Scotland **26 D2** 55.38N 4.49W
Ards Pen. N. Ireland **23 D1** 54.30N 5.30W
Arecibo Puerto Rico **93 K3** 18.29N 66.44W
Arena, Pt. U.S.A. **86 B4** 38.58N 123.44W
Arendal Norway **58 B2** 58.27N 8.56E
Arequipa Peru **96 B6** 16.25S 71.32W
Arès France **48 C3** 44.47N 1.08W
Arezzo Italy **54 C5** 43.27N 11.52E
Arfak *mtn.* Indonesia **79 I3** 1.30S 133.50E
Arganda Spain **50 D4** 40.19N 3.26W
Argens *r.* France **48 G2** 43.10N 6.45E
Argentan France **48 C5** 48.45N 0.01W
Argentina S. America **97 C4** 35.00S 65.00W
Argentine Basin Atlantic Oc. **112 G3** 40.00S 40.00W
Argenton France **48 D4** 46.36N 1.30E
Argeș *r.* Romania **56 H6** 44.13N 26.22E
Árgos Greece **56 F2** 37.37N 22.45E
Argun *r.* Russian Fed. **75 J7** 53.30N 121.48E
Argyll *f.* Scotland **26 C3** 56.12N 5.15W
Århus Denmark **46 D4** 56.10N 10.13E
Århus *d.* Denmark **46 D4** 56.20N 10.20E
Ariano Italy **54 E4** 41.04N 15.00E
Arica Chile **97 B6** 18.30S 70.20W
Arild Sweden **46 F4** 56.16N 12.32E
Arima Trinidad **95 G3** 10.38N 61.17W
Arinagour Scotland **26 B3** 56.37N 6.31W
Arisaig Scotland **24 C3** 56.55N 5.51W
Ariza Spain **50 D4** 41.19N 2.03W
Arizona *d.* U.S.A. **86 D3** 34.00N 112.00W
Arjona Colombia **94 D3** 10.14N 75.22W
Arkaig, L. Scotland **24 C3** 56.59N 5.10W
Arkansas *d.* U.S.A. **87 H4** 35.00N 92.00W
Arkansas *r.* U.S.A. **87 H3** 33.50N 91.00W
Arkansas City U.S.A. **87 G4** 37.03N 97.02W
Arkhangel'sk Russian Fed. **60 D4** 64.32N 41.10E
Arklow Rep. of Ire. **28 E2** 52.47N 6.10W
Arlberg Pass Austria **57 B3** 47.00N 10.05E
Arles France **48 F2** 43.41N 4.38E
Arlon Belgium **47 D1** 49.41N 5.49E
Armadale Scotland **27 E2** 55.54N 3.41W
Armagh N. Ireland **23 C1** 54.21N 6.40W
Armagh *d.* N. Ireland **23 C1** 54.15N 6.45W
Arma Plateau Saudi Arabia **69 G2** 25.30N 46.30E
Armavir Russian Fed. **59 E2** 44.59N 41.10E
Armenia Asia **69 G6** 40.00N 45.00E
Armenia Colombia **94 D1** 4.32N 75.40W
Armentières France **47 A2** 50.41N 2.53E
Armoy N. Ireland **23 C2** 55.08N 6.20W
Arnaud *r.* Canada **91 L3** 60.00N 69.45W
Arnauti, C. Cyprus **68 D4** 35.06N 32.17E
Arnborg Denmark **46 B4** 56.02N 8.59E
Arnhem Neth. **47 D4** 52.00N 5.55E
Arnhem Land *f.* Australia **80 C4** 13.00S 132.30E
Arno *r.* Italy **54 C5** 43.43N 10.17E
Arnold England **16 C2** 53.00N 1.08W
Arnsberg Germany **47 G3** 51.24N 8.03E
Ar Ramadi Iraq **68 F4** 33.27N 43.19E
Arran *i.* Scotland **26 C2** 55.35N 5.14W
Arras France **47 A2** 50.17N 2.46E
Arrochar Scotland **26 D3** 56.12N 4.44W
Arrow, Lough Rep. of Ire. **28 C4** 54.03N 8.20W
Ar Rutba Iraq **68 F4** 33.03N 40.18E
Års Denmark **46 C4** 56.50N 9.30E
Árta Greece **56 E3** 39.10N 20.57E
Artois *f.* France **47 A2** 50.16N 2.50E
Artux China **74 B5** 39.40N 75.49E
Artvin Turkey **68 F6** 41.12N 41.48E
Aruba *i.* Neth. Ant. **93 J2** 12.30N 70.00W
Aru Is. Indonesia **79 I2** 6.00S 134.30E
Arun *r.* England **15 B1** 50.48N 0.32W
Arunachal Pradesh *d.* India **71 G5** 28.40N 94.60E
Arundel England **15 B1** 50.52N 0.32W
Årup Denmark **46 D3** 55.23N 10.06E
Arusha Tanzania **106 D4** 3.21S 36.40E
Aruwimi *r.* Zaïre **102 E5** 1.20N 23.26E
Arvagh Rep. of Ire. **28 D3** 53.56N 7.36W
Arvidsjaur Sweden **58 D4** 65.37N 19.10E
Arvika Sweden **58 C2** 59.41N 12.38E
Arzamas Russian Fed. **59 E5** 55.24N 43.48E
Asahi dake *mtn.* Japan **76 E8** 43.42N 142.54E
Asahikawa Japan **76 E8** 43.46N 142.23E
Asansol India **71 F4** 23.40N 87.00E
Ascension I. Atlantic Oc. **114 I4** 8.00S 14.00W
Aschendorf Germany **47 F5** 53.03N 7.20E
Aschersleben Germany **52 E4** 51.46N 11.28E
Ascoli Piceno Italy **54 D5** 42.52N 13.36E
Ascot England **15 B2** 51.25N 0.41W
Åseda Sweden **58 C2** 57.10N 15.20E
Ashbourne England **16 C3** 53.02N 1.44W
Ashbourne Rep. of Ire. **28 E3** 53.31N 6.25W
Ashburton *r.* Australia **80 A3** 21.15S 115.00E
Ashburton England **13 D2** 50.31N 3.45W
Ashby de la Zouch England **16 C2** 52.45N 1.29W
Ashdown Forest England **15 C2** 51.03N 0.05E
Asheville U.S.A. **87 J4** 35.35N 82.35W
Ashford Kent England **15 C2** 51.08N 0.53E
Ashikaga Japan **76 D5** 36.21N 139.26E
Ashington England **22 C2** 55.11N 1.34W
Ashizuri saki *c.* Japan **76 B3** 32.45N 133.05E
Ashkhabad Turkmenistan **60 E1** 37.58N 58.24E
Ashland Ky. U.S.A. **87 J4** 38.28N 82.40W
Ashland Wisc. U.S.A. **87 H6** 46.34N 90.45W
Ash Sham *des.* Saudi Arabia **68 F3** 28.15N 43.05E
Ash Shama *des.* Saudi Arabia **68 E3** 31.20N 38.00E
Ashton-in-Makerfield England **20 C2** 53.29N 2.39W
Ashton-under-Lyne England **20 C2** 53.30N 2.08W
Asia 113
Asinara *i.* Italy **54 B4** 41.04N 8.18E
Asinara, G. of Med. Sea **54 B4** 41.00N 8.32E
Asir *f.* Saudi Arabia **105 G3** 19.00N 42.00E
Askeaton Rep. of Ire. **28 C2** 52.35N 8.59W
Askern England **21 D2** 53.37N 1.09W
Askersund Sweden **58 C2** 58.55N 14.55E
Askim Norway **58 B2** 59.33N 11.20E
Asmara Eritrea **105 F3** 15.20N 38.58E
Aspatria England **22 A1** 54.45N 3.20W
Assab Eritrea **105 G3** 13.01N 42.47E
Assam *d.* India **71 G5** 26.30N 93.00E
Assen Neth. **47 E5** 53.00N 6.34E
Assens Denmark **46 C3** 55.14N 9.54E
Åsted Denmark **46 B4** 56.48N 8.59E
Asti Italy **54 B6** 44.54N 8.13E
Astorga Spain **50 B5** 42.30N 6.02W
Astoria U.S.A. **86 B6** 46.12N 123.50W
Astrakhan Russian Fed. **59 F3** 46.22N 48.00E
Åstrup Denmark **46 C3** 55.57N 9.40E
Asturias *d.* Spain **50 B5** 43.30N 6.00W
Asuncion *i.* Mariana Is. **79 L7** 19.34N 145.24E
Asunción Paraguay **97 D5** 25.15S 57.40W
Aswân Egypt **68 D2** 24.05N 32.56E
Aswân High Dam Egypt **68 D1** 23.59N 32.54E
Asyût Egypt **68 C2** 27.14N 31.07E
Atacama Desert S. America **97 C6** 20.00S 69.00W
Atafu Pacific Oc. **82 I7** 8.40S 172.40W
Atakpamé Togo **108 B2** 7.34N 1.14E
Atar Mauritania **104 A4** 20.32N 13.08W
Atbara Sudan **105 F3** 17.42N 34.00E
Atbara *r.* Sudan **105 F3** 17.47N 34.00E
Atchafalaya B. U.S.A. **87 H2** 29.30N 92.00W
Ath Belgium **47 B2** 50.38N 3.45E
Athabasca Canada **90 G3** 54.44N 113.15W
Athabasca *r.* Canada **90 G3** 58.30N 111.00W
Athabasca, L. Canada **90 H3** 59.30N 109.00W
Athea Rep. of Ire. **28 B2** 52.28N 9.18W
Athenry Rep. of Ire. **28 C3** 53.18N 8.48W
Athens Greece **56 F2** 37.59N 23.42E
Atherstone England **16 C2** 52.35N 1.32W
Atherton England **20 C2** 53.32N 2.30W
Athlone Rep. of Ire. **28 D3** 53.26N 7.57W
Áthos, Mt. Greece **56 G4** 40.09N 24.19E
Atkarsk Russian Fed. **59 E4** 51.55N 45.00E
Atlanta U.S.A. **87 J3** 33.45N 84.23W
Atlantic-Antarctic Ridge Atlantic Oc. **112 I2** 53.00S 0.00
Atlantic City U.S.A. **87 L4** 39.23N 74.27W
Atlantic-Indian-Antarctic Basin Atl. Oc./Ind. Oc. **113 J1** 61.00S 0.00
Atlantic Ocean 112
Atlas Mts. Africa **102 B8** 33.00N 4.00W
Atouguia Portugal **50 A3** 39.20N 9.20W
Ätran *r.* Sweden **58 C2** 56.54N 12.30E
Atrato *r.* Colombia **94 D2** 8.15N 76.58W
Atrek *r.* Asia **105 H5** 37.23N 54.00E
Atsugi Japan **76 D4** 35.27N 139.22E
At Tā'if Saudi Arabia **105 G4** 21.15N 40.21E
Attleborough England **15 D3** 52.31N 1.01E
Attopeu Laos **78 D6** 14.51N 106.56E
Atui I. Cook Is. **83 K5** 20.00S 158.07W
Aubagne France **48 F2** 43.17N 5.35E
Aube *r.* France **48 E5** 48.30N 3.37E
Aubigny-sur-Nère France **48 E4** 47.29N 2.26E
Aubin France **48 E3** 44.32N 2.14E
Auch France **48 D2** 43.40N 0.36E
Auchinleck Scotland **26 D2** 55.28N 4.17W
Auchterarder Scotland **27 E3** 56.18N 3.43W
Auchtermuchty Scotland **27 E3** 56.17N 3.15W
Auckland New Zealand **80 G2** 36.52S 174.45E
Auckland Is. Pacific Oc. **82 G2** 50.35S 166.00E
Aude *r.* France **48 E2** 43.13N 2.20E
Audlem England **20 C1** 52.59N 2.31W
Augher N. Ireland **23 B1** 54.26N 7.08W
Aughnacloy N. Ireland **23 C1** 54.25N 6.59W
Augrabies Falls *f.* R.S.A. **106 C2** 28.45S 20.00E
Augsburg Germany **52 E3** 48.21N 10.54E
Augusta Ga. U.S.A. **87 J3** 33.29N 82.00W
Augusta Maine U.S.A. **87 M5** 44.20N 69.50W
Augustín Codazzi Colombia **94 E3** 10.01N 73.10W
Auki Solomon Is. **80 F5** 8.45S 160.46E
Aulne *r.* France **48 A5** 48.30N 4.11W
Aumale France **48 D5** 49.46N 1.45E
Aurangabad India **71 D3** 19.52N 75.22E
Aurich Germany **47 F5** 53.28N 7.29E
Aurillac France **48 E3** 44.56N 2.26E
Austin Tex. U.S.A. **86 G3** 30.18N 97.47W
Australasia 113
Australia Austa. **80 B3** 25.00S 135.00E
Austral Ridge Pacific Oc. **83 L5** 24.00S 148.00W
Austria Europe **57 C3** 47.30N 14.00E
Autun France **48 F4** 46.58N 4.18E
Auxerre France **48 E4** 47.48N 3.35E
Auzances France **48 E4** 46.02N 2.29E
Avallon France **48 E4** 47.30N 3.54E
Avanos Turkey **68 D5** 38.44N 34.51E
Avarua Rarotonga Cook Is. **82 J5** 21.12S 159.46W
Aveiro Portugal **50 A4** 40.40N 8.35W
Avellino Italy **54 E4** 40.55N 14.46E
Avesnes France **47 B2** 50.08N 3.57E
Avesta Sweden **58 D3** 60.09N 16.10E
Aveyron *r.* France **48 D3** 44.09N 1.10E
Avezzano Italy **54 D5** 42.03N 13.26E
Aviemore Scotland **24 E4** 57.11N 3.51W
Avignon France **48 F2** 43.56N 4.48E
Ávila Spain **50 C4** 40.39N 4.42W
Avon *d.* England **13 E3** 51.35N 2.40W
Avon *r.* Avon England **13 E3** 51.30N 2.43W
Avon *r.* Devon England **13 D2** 50.17N 3.52W
Avon *r.* Dorset England **14 A1** 50.43N 1.45W
Avon *r.* Glos. England **13 B2** 52.00N 2.10W
Avonmouth England **13 E3** 51.30N 2.42W
Avranches France **48 C5** 48.42N 1.21W
Awa shima *i.* Japan **76 D6** 38.30N 139.20E
Awaso Ghana **108 A2** 6.20N 2.22W
Awe, Loch Scotland **26 C3** 56.18N 5.24W
Axel Heiberg I. Canada **91 I5** 79.30N 90.00W
Axim Ghana **108 A1** 4.53N 2.14W
Axiós *r.* Greece **40 J3** 40.31N 22.43E
Axminster England **13 D2** 50.47N 3.01W
Ayaguz Kazakhstan **74 C6** 47.59N 80.27E
Ayan Russian Fed. **61 L3** 56.29N 138.00E
Aydin Turkey **68 B5** 37.52N 27.50E
Áyios Evstrátios *i.* Greece **56 G3** 39.30N 25.00E
Aylesbury England **15 B2** 51.48N 0.49W
Aylesford England **15 C2** 51.18N 0.29E
Aylesham England **15 D2** 51.14N 1.12E
Aylsham England **15 D3** 52.48N 1.16E
Ayr Scotland **26 D2** 55.28N 4.37W
Ayr *r.* Scotland **26 D2** 55.28N 4.38W
Ayre, Pt. of I.o.M. **20 A3** 54.25N 4.22W
Aysgarth England **20 C3** 54.18N 2.00W
Ayutthaya Thailand **78 C6** 14.25N 100.30E
Ayvalik Turkey **68 B5** 39.19N 26.42E
Azare Nigeria **108 D3** 11.40N 10.08E
Azbine *mts. see* Aïr *mts.* Niger **104**
Azerbaijan Asia **69 G6** 40.10N 47.50E
Azores *is.* Atlantic Oc. **112 H6** 38.00N 28.00W
Azov, Sea of Ukraine **59 D3** 46.00N 36.30E
Azua Dom. Rep. **93 J3** 18.29N 70.44W
Azuaga Spain **50 C3** 38.16N 5.40W
Azuero Pen. Panama **93 H1** 7.30N 80.30W
Azul Argentina **97 D4** 36.46S 59.50W

B

Ba'albek Lebanon **68 E4** 34.00N 36.12E
Baarle-Hertog Neth. **47 C3** 51.26N 4.56E
Babar Is. Indonesia **79 H2** 8.00S 129.30E
Babbacombe B. England **13 D2** 50.30N 3.28W
Bab el Mandeb *str.* Asia **105 G3** 13.00N 43.10E
Babia Gora *mtn.* Slovakia/Poland **57 F4** 49.38N 19.38E
Babo Indonesia **79 I3** 2.33S 133.25E
Baboua C.A.R. **104 D2** 5.49N 14.51E
Babuyan Is. Phil. **79 G7** 19.20N 121.30E
Babylon *ruins* Iraq **69 G4** 32.33N 44.25E
Bacan *i.* Indonesia **79 H3** 0.30S 127.30E
Bacău Romania **59 B3** 46.32N 26.59E
Bac Can Vietnam **78 D8** 22.08N 105.49E
Baccarat France **48 G5** 48.27N 6.45E
Back *r.* Canada **91 I4** 66.37N 96.00W
Bac Ninh Vietnam **78 D8** 21.10N 106.04E
Bacolod Phil. **79 G6** 10.38N 122.58E
Bacton England **15 D3** 52.50N 1.29E
Bacup England **20 C2** 53.42N 2.12W
Badajoz Spain **50 B3** 38.53N 6.58W
Badalona Spain **50 G4** 41.27N 2.15E
Bad Bramstedt Germany **46 C1** 53.56N 9.59E
Bad Doberan Germany **46 E2** 54.06N 11.57E
Baden-Baden Germany **52 D3** 48.45N 8.15E
Baden-Württemberg *d.* Germany **52 D3** 48.30N 9.00E
Badgastein Austria **57 C3** 47.07N 13.09E
Bad Ischl Austria **57 C3** 47.43N 13.38E
Bad Kreuznach Germany **47 F1** 49.51N 7.52E
Bad Schwartau Germany **46 D1** 53.56N 10.43E
Bad Segeberg Germany **46 D1** 53.58N 10.19E
Bad Sülze Germany **46 F2** 54.07N 12.41E
Baffin *d.* Canada **91 K4** 66.00N 72.00W
Baffin B. Canada **91 L5** 74.00N 70.00W
Baffin I. Canada **91 L4** 68.50N 70.00W
Bafra Turkey **68 D6** 41.34N 35.56E
Baggy Pt. England **12 C3** 51.08N 4.15W
Baghdad Iraq **69 G4** 33.20N 44.26E
Baghlan Afghan. **71 C6** 36.11N 68.44E
Baguio Phil. **79 G7** 16.25N 120.37E
Bahamas C. America **94 D5** 23.30N 75.00W
Bahao Kalat Iran **69 K2** 25.42N 61.28E
Bahawalpur Pakistan **71 C5** 29.24N 71.47E
Bahía Blanca Argentina **97 C4** 38.45S 62.15W
Bahrain Asia **69 H2** 26.00N 50.35E
Bahr el Arab *r.* Sudan **102 F5** 9.12N 29.28E
Bahr el Ghazal *r.* Sudan **105 F2** 9.30N 31.30E
Bahr el Jebel *r.* Sudan **105 F2** 9.30N 30.20E
Baicheng China **75 J6** 45.40N 122.52E
Baie Comeau Canada **91 L2** 49.12N 68.10W
Baikal, L. Russian Fed. **61 I3** 53.30N 108.00E
Bailleul France **47 A2** 50.44N 2.44E
Baimuru P.N.G. **79 K2** 7.30S 144.49E
Baing Indonesia **79 G1** 10.15S 120.34E
Baise *r.* France **48 D3** 44.15N 0.20E
Baja Hungary **56 D7** 46.12N 18.58E
Baja California Norte *d.* Mexico **92 B5** 30.00N 115.00W
Baja California Sur *d.* Mexico **92 B5** 26.00N 112.00W
Baker Mont. U.S.A. **86 F6** 46.23N 104.16W
Baker Oreg. U.S.A. **86 C5** 44.46N 117.50W
Baker, Mt. U.S.A. **86 B6** 48.48N 121.10W
Bakersfield U.S.A. **86 C4** 35.25N 119.00W
Bakewell England **16 C3** 53.13N 1.40W
Baku Azerbaijan **69 H6** 40.22N 49.53E
Bala Wales **18 C2** 52.54N 3.36W
Balabac Str. Malaysia/Phil. **78 F5** 7.30N 117.00E
Balakovo Russian Fed. **59 F4** 52.04N 47.46E
Balashov Russian Fed. **59 E4** 51.30N 43.10E
Balasore India **71 F4** 21.31N 86.59E
Balaton, L. Hungary **57 E3** 46.55N 17.50E
Balboa Panama **93 I1** 8.37N 79.33W
Balbriggan Rep. of Ire. **28 E3** 53.36N 6.12W
Baldock England **15 B2** 51.59N 0.11W
Balearic Is. Spain **50 F3** 39.30N 2.30E
Balerno Scotland **27 E2** 55.53N 3.10W
Balfron Scotland **26 D3** 56.04N 4.20W
Bali *i.* Indonesia **78 F2** 8.30S 115.05E
Balikesir Turkey **68 B5** 39.38N 27.51E
Balikpapan Indonesia **78 F3** 1.15S 116.50E

Balkan Mts. Bulgaria **56 F5** 42.50N 24.30E
Balkhash Kazakhstan **74 B6** 46.51N 75.00E
Balkhash, L. Kazakhstan **74 B6** 46.40N 75.00E
Ballachulish Scotland **24 C3** 56.41N 5.08W
Ballantrae Scotland **26 C2** 55.06N 5.01W
Ballarat Australia **80 D2** 37.36S 143.58E
Ballater Scotland **24 E4** 57.03N 3.04W
Ballenas B. Mexico **92 B5** 26.40N 113.30W
Balleny Is. Antarctica **82 G1** 66.35S 162.50E
Ballina Rep. of Ire. **28 B4** 54.08N 9.10W
Ballinasloe Rep. of Ire. **28 C3** 53.20N 8.15W
Ballinderry *r.* N. Ireland **23 C1** 54.40N 6.32W
Ballingeary Rep. of Ire. **28 B1** 51.50N 9.17W
Balloch Scotland **26 D3** 56.00N 4.36W
Ball's Pyramid *i.* Pacific Oc. **82 F4** 31.45S 159.15E
Ballybay *town* Rep. of Ire. **28 E4** 54.08N 6.55W
Ballycastle N. Ireland **23 C2** 55.12N 6.16W
Ballyclare N. Ireland **23 C1** 54.45N 6.00W
Ballyconnell Rep. of Ire. **28 D4** 54.06N 7.36W
Ballydehob Rep. of Ire. **28 B1** 51.34N 9.28W
Ballydonegan Rep. of Ire. **28 A1** 51.38N 10.03W
Ballygar Rep. of Ire. **28 C3** 53.31N 8.20W
Ballygawley N. Ireland **23 B1** 54.28N 7.03W
Ballykelly N. Ireland **23 B2** 55.03N 7.00W
Ballymena N. Ireland **23 C1** 54.52N 6.17W
Ballymoney N. Ireland **23 C2** 55.04N 6.32W
Ballynahinch N. Ireland **23 D1** 54.24N 5.54W
Ballyquintin Pt. N. Ireland **23 D1** 54.20N 5.30W
Ballyragget Rep. of Ire. **28 D2** 52.47N 7.20W
Ballyshannon Rep. of Ire. **28 C4** 54.30N 8.11W
Ballyvaughan Rep. of Ire. **28 B3** 53.07N 9.10W
Ballyvourney Rep. of Ire. **28 B1** 51.57N 9.10W
Ballywalter N. Ireland **23 D1** 54.34N 5.30W
Balsas *r.* Mexico **92 D3** 18.10N 102.05W
Balta Ukraine **59 B3** 47.58N 29.39E
Baltic Sea Europe **58 D1** 56.30N 19.00E
Baltic Shield *f.* Europe **113 K8** 63.00N 30.00E
Baltimore U.S.A. **87 K4** 39.18N 76.38W
Baltiysk Russian Fed. **58 D1** 54.41N 19.59E
Baluchistan *f.* Pakistan **70 B5** 29.00N 66.00E
Bam Iran **69 J3** 29.07N 58.20E
Bamako Mali **104 B3** 12.40N 7.59W
Bamberg Germany **52 E3** 49.54N 10.53E
Bamburgh England **22 C2** 55.36N 1.41W
Bampton Devon England **13 D2** 51.00N 3.29W
Bampton Oxon. England **14 A2** 51.44N 1.33W
Bampur Iran **69 K2** 27.13N 60.29E
Bampur *r.* Iran **69 J2** 27.18N 59.02E
Banaba *i.* Kiribati **82 H7** 0.52S 169.35E
Banagher Rep. of Ire. **28 C3** 53.11N 8.01W
Banbasa Nepal **71 E5** 29.17N 80.36E
Banbridge N. Ireland **23 C1** 54.21N 6.16W
Banbury England **14 A3** 52.04N 1.21W
Banchory Scotland **24 F4** 57.04N 2.28W
Banda *i.* Indonesia **79 H3** 4.30S 129.55E
Banda Aceh Indonesia **78 B5** 5.35N 95.20E
Bandar Abbas Iran **69 J2** 27.10N 56.15E
Bandar Dilam Iran **69 H3** 30.05N 50.11E
Bandar-e Anzalī Iran **69 H5** 37.26N 49.29E
Bandar-e Khomeynī Iran **69 H3** 30.26N 49.03E
Bandar-e-Lengeh Iran **69 I2** 26.34N 54.52E
Bandar-e Torkeman Iran **105 H5** 36.55N 54.05E
Bandar Rig Iran **69 H3** 29.30N 50.40E
Bandar Seri Begawan Brunei **78 E4** 4.56N 114.58E
Banda Sea Indonesia **79 H2** 5.00S 128.00E
Bandeira *mtn.* Brazil **97 E5** 20.25S 41.45W
Bandirma Turkey **68 C6** 40.22N 28.00E
Bandon Rep. of Ire. **28 C1** 51.45N 8.45W
Bandon *r.* Rep. of Ire. **28 C1** 51.43N 8.38W
Bandundu Zaïre **106 B4** 3.20S 17.24E
Bandung Indonesia **78 D2** 6.57S 107.34E
Banes Cuba **94 D5** 20.59N 75.24W
Banff Canada **90 G3** 51.10N 115.34W
Banff Scotland **24 F4** 57.40N 2.31W
Bangalore India **71 D2** 12.58N 77.35E
Bangassou C.A.R. **105 E2** 4.41N 22.48E
Banggai Is. Indonesia **79 G3** 1.30S 123.10E
Bangka *i.* Indonesia **78 D3** 2.20S 106.10E
Bangkok Thailand **78 C6** 13.45N 100.35E
Bangladesh Asia **71 F4** 24.00N 90.00E
Bangor N. Ireland **23 D1** 54.39N 5.41W
Bangor Rep. of Ire. **28 B4** 54.09N 9.46W
Bangor U.S.A. **87 M5** 44.49N 68.47W
Bangor Wales **18 B3** 53.13N 4.09W
Bangui C.A.R. **104 D2** 4.23N 18.37E
Bangweulu, L. Zambia **106 C3** 11.15S 29.45E
Ban Hat Yai Thailand **78 C5** 7.00N 100.28E
Ban Houei Sai Laos **78 C8** 20.21N 100.26E
Bani *r.* Mali **102 B6** 14.30N 4.15W
Banjak Is. Indonesia **78 B4** 2.15N 97.10E
Banja Luka Bosnia. **56 C6** 44.47N 17.10E
Banjarmasin Indonesia **78 E3** 3.22S 114.36E
Banjul Gambia **104 A3** 13.28N 16.39W
Bankfoot Scotland **27 E3** 56.30N 3.32W
Banks I. Australia **79 K1** 10.15S 142.15E
Banks I. Canada **90 F5** 73.00N 122.00W
Ban Me Thuot Vietnam **78 D6** 12.41N 108.02E
Bann *r.* N. Ireland **23 C2** 55.10N 6.47W
Bannockburn Scotland **27 E3** 56.06N 3.55W
Banská Bystrica Slovakia **57 F4** 48.44N 19.07E
Banstead England **15 B2** 51.19N 0.12W
Bantry Rep. of Ire. **28 B1** 51.41N 9.27W
Bantry B. Rep. of Ire. **28 B1** 51.40N 9.40W
Banyuwangi Indonesia **78 E2** 8.12S 114.22E
Baoding China **75 I5** 38.54N 115.26E
Baoji China **74 G4** 34.23N 107.16E
Baoshan China **74 F2** 25.07N 99.08E
Baotou China **75 H5** 40.38N 109.59E
Bapaume France **47 A2** 50.07N 2.51E
Bar Yugo. **56 D5** 42.05N 19.06E
Baracoa Cuba **93 J4** 20.23N 74.31W
Barahona Dom. Rep. **94 E4** 18.13N 71.07W
Baranoa Colombia **94 E3** 10.50N 74.55W
Baranof I. U.S.A. **90 E3** 57.05N 135.00W
Baranovichi Belorussia **59 B4** 53.09N 26.00E
Barbados Lesser Antilles **93 M2** 13.20N 59.40W
Barbastro Spain **50 F5** 42.02N 0.07E
Barbezieux France **48 C3** 45.28N 0.09W
Barbuda *i.* Leeward Is. **93 L3** 17.41N 61.48W
Barcellona Italy **54 E3** 38.10N 15.13E
Barcelona Spain **50 G4** 41.25N 2.10E
Barcelona Venezuela **95 G3** 10.08N 64.43W
Bardai Chad **104 D4** 21.21N 16.56E
Bardejov Slovakia **57 G4** 49.18N 21.16E
Bardera Somali Rep. **105 G2** 2.18N 42.18E
Bardney England **17 D3** 53.13N 0.19W
Bardsey *i.* Wales **18 B2** 52.45N 4.48W
Bardsey Sd. Wales **18 B2** 52.45N 4.48W
Bardu Norway **58 D5** 68.54N 18.20E
Bareilly India **71 E5** 28.20N 79.24E
Barents Sea Arctic Oc. **60 D4** 73.00N 40.00E
Bari Italy **54 F4** 41.08N 16.52E
Barinas Venezuela **94 E2** 8.36N 70.15W
Barisan Range *mts.* Indonesia **78 C3** 3.30S 102.30E
Barito *r.* Indonesia **78 E3** 3.35S 114.35E
Bariz Kuh, Jebel *mts.* Iran **69 J3** 28.40N 58.10E
Barkly Tableland *f.* Australia **80 C4** 19.00S 136.40E
Bar-le-Duc France **48 E5** 48.46N 5.10E
Barletta Italy **54 F4** 41.20N 16.15E
Barmouth Wales **18 B2** 52.44N 4.03W
Barnard Castle *town* England **22 C1** 54.33N 1.55W
Barnaul Russian Fed. **60 G3** 53.21N 83.15E
Barnet England **15 B2** 51.39N 0.11W
Barneveld Neth. **47 D4** 52.10N 5.39E
Barnoldswick England **20 C2** 53.55N 2.11W
Barnsley England **21 D2** 53.33N 1.29W
Barnstaple England **13 C3** 51.05N 4.03W
Barnstaple B. England **12 C3** 51.04N 4.20W
Baro Nigeria **108 C2** 8.37N 6.19E
Barquisimeto Venezuela **94 F3** 10.03N 69.18W
Barra *i.* Scotland **24 A3** 56.59N 7.28W
Barrancabermeja Colombia **94 E2** 7.06N 73.54W
Barrancas Venezuela **95 G2** 8.45N 62.13W
Barranquilla Colombia **94 E3** 11.00N 74.50W
Barra, Sd. of Scotland **24 A4** 57.03N 7.25W
Barreiro Portugal **50 A3** 38.40N 9.05W
Barrhead Scotland **26 D2** 55.47N 4.24W
Barrow *r.* Rep. of Ire. **28 D2** 52.17N 7.00W
Barrow U.S.A. **90 C5** 71.16N 156.50W
Barrow-in-Furness England **22 A1** 54.08N 3.15W
Barrow, Pt. U.S.A. **84 E9** 71.30N 156.00W
Barry Wales **18 C1** 51.23N 3.19W
Barstow U.S.A. **86 C3** 34.55N 117.01W
Bar-sur-Aube France **48 F5** 48.14N 4.43E
Barth Germany **46 F2** 54.22N 12.43E
Bartica Guyana **95 H2** 6.22N 58.37W
Bartin Turkey **68 D6** 41.37N 32.20E
Barton on Sea England **14 A1** 50.44N 1.40W
Barton-upon-Humber England **21 E2** 53.41N 0.27W
Basel Switz. **52 C2** 47.33N 7.36E
Bashi Channel Phil./Taiwan **75 J2** 21.40N 121.20E
Basilan Phil. **79 G5** 6.40N 121.59E
Basilan *i.* Phil. **79 G5** 6.40N 122.10E
Basildon England **15 C2** 51.34N 0.25E
Basingstoke England **14 A2** 51.15N 1.05W
Basra Iraq **69 G3** 30.33N 47.50E
Bassein Myanma **71 G3** 16.45N 94.30E
Basse Terre Guadeloupe **95 G4** 16.00N 61.43W
Bass Rock *i.* Scotland **27 F3** 56.05N 2.38W
Bass Str. Australia **80 D2** 39.45S 146.00E
Bastak Iran **69 I2** 27.15N 54.26E
Bastelica France **49 H2** 42.00N 9.03E
Bastia France **49 H2** 42.41N 9.26E
Bastogne Belgium **47 D2** 50.00N 5.43E
Bata Equat. Guinea **104 C2** 1.51N 9.49E
Batabanó, G. of Cuba **94 C5** 23.15N 82.30W
Batang China **74 F3** 30.02N 99.01E
Batangas Phil. **79 G6** 13.46N 121.01E
Batan Is. Phil. **79 G8** 20.50N 121.55E
Bath England **13 E3** 51.22N 2.22W
Batha, Wadi *r.* Oman **69 J1** 22.01N 59.39E
Bathgate Scotland **27 E2** 55.44N 3.38W
Bathurst Canada **91 L2** 47.37N 65.40W
Bathurst, C. Canada **90 F5** 70.30N 128.00W
Bathurst I. Canada **91 H5** 76.00N 100.00W
Bathurst Inlet *town* Canada **90 H4** 66.48N 108.00W
Batinah *f.* Oman **69 J2** 24.25N 56.50E
Batley England **20 D2** 53.43N 1.38W
Batna Algeria **104 C5** 35.34N 6.11E
Baton Rouge U.S.A. **87 H3** 30.30N 91.10W
Battambang Cambodia **78 C6** 13.06N 103.13E
Batticaloa Sri Lanka **71 E1** 7.43N 81.42E
Battle England **15 C1** 50.55N 0.30E
Battle Harbour Canada **91 M3** 52.16N 55.36W
Batu Is. Indonesia **78 B3** 0.30S 98.20E
Batumi Georgia **68 F6** 41.37N 41.36E
Batu Pahat Malaysia **78 C4** 1.50N 102.48E
Baturaja Indonesia **78 C3** 4.10S 104.10E
Baubau Indonesia **79 G2** 5.30S 122.37E
Bauchi Nigeria **108 C3** 10.16N 9.50E
Baugé France **48 C4** 47.33N 0.06W
Bauld, C. Canada **91 M3** 51.30N 55.45W
Bauru Brazil **97 E5** 22.19S 49.07W
Bautzen Germany **52 G4** 51.11N 14.29E
Bavay France **47 B2** 50.18N 3.48E
Bawdsey England **15 D3** 52.01N 1.27E
Bawean *i.* Indonesia **78 E2** 5.50S 112.35E
Bawiti Egypt **68 C3** 28.21N 28.51E
Bawtry England **21 D2** 53.25N 1.01W
Bayamo Cuba **94 D5** 20.23N 76.39W
Bayamón Puerto Rico **95 F4** 18.24N 66.10W
Bayan Har Shan *mts.* China **74 F4** 34.00N 97.20E
Bayburt Turkey **68 F6** 40.15N 40.16E
Bay City U.S.A. **87 J5** 43.35N 83.52W
Baydaratskaya B. Russian Fed. **60 F4** 70.00N 66.00E
Bayern *d.* Germany **52 E3** 48.30N 11.30E
Bayeux France **48 C5** 49.16N 0.42W
Bay Is. Honduras **93 G3** 16.10N 86.30W
Bayombong Phil. **79 G7** 16.27N 121.10E
Bayonne France **48 C2** 43.30N 1.28W
Bayreuth Germany **52 E3** 49.56N 11.35E
Baza Spain **50 D2** 37.30N 2.45W
Bazman Kuh *mtn.* Iran **69 J3** 28.06N 60.00E
Beachy Head England **15 C1** 50.43N 0.15E
Beacon Hill England **13 F3** 51.12N 1.42W
Beacon Hill Wales **18 C2** 52.23N 3.14W
Beaconsfield England **15 B2** 51.37N 0.39W
Beaminster England **13 E2** 50.48N 2.44W
Bearsden Scotland **26 D2** 55.56N 4.20W
Beaufort Sea N. America **90 D5** 72.00N 141.00W
Beauly Scotland **24 D4** 57.29N 4.28W
Beauly *r.* Scotland **24 D4** 57.29N 4.27W
Beaumaris Wales **18 B3** 53.16N 4.07W
Beaumont Belgium **47 C2** 50.14N 4.16E
Beaumont U.S.A. **87 H3** 30.04N 94.06W
Beaune France **48 F4** 47.02N 4.50E
Beauvais France **48 E5** 49.26N 2.05E
Beawar India **71 D5** 26.02N 74.20E
Bebington England **20 C2** 53.23N 2.58W
Beccles England **15 D3** 52.27N 1.33E
Béchar Algeria **104 B5** 31.35N 2.17W
Beckum Germany **47 G3** 51.45N 8.02E
Bedale England **21 D3** 54.18N 1.35W
Bédarieux France **48 E2** 43.35N 3.10E
Bedford England **15 B3** 52.08N 0.29W
Bedford Levels *f.* England **15 C3** 52.35N 0.08E
Bedfordshire *d.* England **15 B3** 52.04N 0.28W
Bedlington England **22 C2** 55.08N 1.34W
Bedwas Wales **18 C1** 51.36N 3.10W
Bedworth England **16 C2** 52.28N 1.29W
Beersheba Israel **68 D3** 31.15N 34.47E
Beeston England **16 C2** 52.55N 1.11W
Beeville U.S.A. **86 G2** 28.25N 97.47W
Beg, Lough N. Ireland **23 C1** 54.48N 6.29W
Begna *r.* Norway **58 B3** 60.06N 10.15E
Behbehan Iran **69 H3** 30.35N 50.17E
Bei'an China **75 K6** 48.17N 126.33E
Beida Libya **105 E5** 32.50N 21.50E
Beihai China **75 H2** 21.29N 109.10E
Beijing China **75 I5** 39.55N 116.25E
Beilen Neth. **47 E4** 52.51N 6.31E
Beinn an Tuirc *mtn.* Scotland **26 C2** 55.24N 5.33W
Beinn Bheigeir *mtn.* Scotland **26 B2** 55.44N 6.08W
Beinn Dearg *mtn.* Scotland **24 D4** 57.49N 4.55W
Beira Mozambique **106 D3** 19.49S 34.52E
Beirut Lebanon **68 D4** 33.52N 35.30E
Beitbridge Zimbabwe **106 C2** 22.10S 29.59E
Beith Scotland **26 D2** 55.45N 4.37W
Beja Portugal **50 B3** 38.01N 7.52W
Bejaïa Algeria **104 C5** 36.45N 5.05E
Béjar Spain **50 C4** 40.24N 5.45W
Békéscsaba Hungary **57 G3** 46.41N 21.06E
Bela Pakistan **70 C5** 26.12N 66.20E
Belalcázar Spain **50 C3** 38.35N 5.10W
Belang Indonesia **79 G4** 0.58N 124.56E
Belaya *r.* Russian Fed. **60 E3** 55.40N 52.30E
Belaya Tserkov Ukraine **59 B3** 49.49N 30.10E
Belcher Is. Canada **91 K3** 56.00N 79.00W
Belcoo N. Ireland **23 B1** 54.18N 7.53W
Belém Brazil **96 E7** 1.27S 48.29W
Belen U.S.A. **86 E3** 34.39N 106.48W
Belfast N. Ireland **23 D1** 54.36N 5.57W
Belfast Lough N. Ireland **23 D1** 54.41N 5.49W
Belford England **22 C2** 55.36N 1.48W
Belfort France **48 G4** 47.38N 6.52E
Belgaum India **71 D3** 15.54N 74.36E
Belgium Europe **47 C2** 51.00N 4.30E
Belgorod Russian Fed. **59 D4** 50.38N 36.36E
Belgorod-Dnestrovskiy Ukraine **59 C3** 46.10N 30.19E
Belgrade Yugo. **56 E6** 44.49N 20.28E
Belikh *r.* Syria **68 E4** 35.58N 39.05E
Belitung *i.* Indonesia **78 D3** 3.00S 108.00E
Belize Belize **94 B4** 17.29N 88.20W
Belize C. America **94 B4** 17.00N 88.30W
Bellac France **48 D4** 46.07N 1.04E
Bellary India **71 D3** 15.11N 76.54E
Belleek N. Ireland **23 A1** 54.29N 8.06W
Belle Île France **48 B4** 47.20N 3.10W
Belle-Isle-Str. Canada **91 M3** 50.45N 58.00W
Bellingham England **22 B2** 55.09N 2.15W
Bellingham U.S.A. **86 B6** 48.45N 122.29W
Bellingshausen Sea Antarctica **112 E1** 70.00S 84.00W
Bello Colombia **94 D2** 6.20N 75.41W
Bell Rock *i. see* Inchcape *i.* Scotland **27**
Belmopan Belize **93 G3** 17.25N 88.46W
Belmullet Rep. of Ire. **28 A4** 54.13N 10.00W
Belo Horizonte Brazil **97 E6** 19.45S 43.53W
Belorussia Europe **59 B4** 53.00N 28.00E
Beloye, L. Russian Fed. **59 D6** 60.12N 37.45E
Belozersk Russian Fed. **59 D6** 60.00N 37.49E
Belper England **16 C3** 53.02N 1.29W
Beltsy Moldavia **59 B3** 47.45N 27.59E
Belukha, Mt. Russian Fed. **74 D6** 49.46N 86.40E
Bełżec Poland **57 H5** 50.24N 23.26E
Bembridge England **14 A1** 50.41N 1.04W
Bemidji U.S.A. **87 H6** 47.29N 94.52W
Benavente Spain **50 C5** 42.00N 5.40W
Benbane Head N. Ireland **23 C2** 55.15N 6.29W
Benbecula *i.* Scotland **24 A4** 57.26N 7.18W
Ben Chonzie *mtn.* Scotland **27 E3** 56.27N 4.00W
Ben Cruachan *mtn.* Scotland **26 C3** 56.26N 5.18W
Bend U.S.A. **86 B5** 44.04N 121.20W
Bendery Moldavia **59 B3** 46.50N 29.29E
Bendigo Australia **80 D2** 36.48S 144.21E
Beneraird *mtn.* Scotland **26 D2** 55.04N 4.56W
Benevento Italy **54 E4** 41.07N 14.46E
Bengal *d.* India **74 D2** 23.15N 88.00E
Bengal, B. of Indian Oc. **71 F3** 17.00N 89.00E
Bengbu China **75 I4** 32.56N 117.27E
Benghazi Libya **104 E5** 32.07N 20.05E
Bengkulu Indonesia **78 C3** 3.46S 102.16E
Benguela Angola **106 B3** 12.34S 13.24E
Ben Hope *mtn.* Scotland **24 D5** 58.24N 4.36W
Beni *r.* Bolivia **96 C6** 10.30S 66.00W
Benicarló Spain **50 F4** 40.25N 0.25E
Benidorm Spain **50 E3** 38.33N 0.09W
Beni Mellal Morocco **104 B5** 32.21N 6.21W
Benin Africa **108 B2** 9.00N 2.30E
Benin, Bight of Africa **108 B2** 5.30N 3.00E
Benin City Nigeria **108 C2** 6.19N 5.41E
Beni Suef Egypt **68 C3** 29.05N 31.05E
Ben Lawers *mtn.* Scotland **24 D3** 56.33N 4.14W
Benllech Wales **18 B3** 53.18N 4.15W
Ben Lomond *mtn.* Scotland **26 D3** 56.12N 4.38W
Ben Lui *mtn.* Scotland **26 D3** 56.23N 4.49W
Ben Macdhui *mtn.* Scotland **24 E4** 57.04N 3.40W
Ben More *mtn.* Central Scotland **26 D3** 56.23N 4.31W
Ben More *mtn.* Strath. Scotland **26 B3** 56.26N 6.02W
Ben More Assynt *mtn.* Scotland **24 D5** 58.07N 4.52W
Bennane Head Scotland **26 C2** 55.08N 5.00W
Ben Nevis *mtn.* Scotland **24 D3** 56.48N 5.00W
Benue *r.* Nigeria **108 C2** 7.52N 6.45E
Ben Vorlich *mtn.* Scotland **26 D3** 56.21N 4.13W
Ben Wyvis *mtn.* Scotland **24 D4** 57.40N 4.35W
Benxi China **75 J5** 41.21N 123.45E
Beppu Japan **76 A3** 33.18N 131.30E
Beragh N. Ireland **23 B1** 54.33N 7.11W
Berat Albania **56 D4** 40.42N 19.59E
Berau, Teluk *b.* Indonesia **79 I3** 2.20S 133.00E
Berbera Somali Rep. **105 G3** 10.28N 45.02E
Berchem Belgium **47 B2** 50.48N 3.32E
Berdichev Ukraine **59 B3** 49.54N 28.39E
Berdyansk Ukraine **59 D3** 46.45N 36.47E
Berezniki Russian Fed. **60 E3** 59.26N 56.49E
Berezovka Ukraine **59 C3** 47.12N 30.56E
Bergamo Italy **54 B6** 45.42N 9.40E
Bergen Germany **46 G2** 54.27N 13.27E
Bergen Norway **58 A3** 60.23N 5.20E
Bergen op Zoom Neth. **47 C3** 51.30N 4.17E
Bergerac France **48 D3** 44.50N 0.29E
Bergheim Germany **47 E2** 50.58N 6.39E
Bergisch Gladbach Germany **47 F2** 50.59N 7.10E
Berhampore India **71 F4** 24.06N 88.18E
Berhampur India **71 F3** 19.21N 84.51E
Bering Sea N. America/Asia **90 A4** 60.00N 170.00W
Bering Str. Russian Fed./U.S.A. **90 A4** 65.00N 170.00W
Berislav Ukraine **59 C3** 46.51N 33.26E
Berkel *r.* Neth. **47 E4** 52.10N 6.12E
Berkhamsted England **15 B2** 51.46N 0.35W
Berkshire *d.* England **14 A2** 51.25N 1.03W
Berkshire Downs *hills* England **14 A2** 51.32N 1.36W
Berlin Germany **52 F5** 52.32N 13.25E
Berlin *d.* Germany **52 F5** 52.35N 13.20E
Bermejo *r.* Tucumán Argentina **97 D5** 26.47S 58.30W
Bermuda *i.* Atlantic Oc. **84 N5** 32.18N 65.00W
Bernburg Germany **52 E4** 51.48N 11.44E
Berne Switz. **52 C2** 46.57N 7.26E
Bernina *mtn.* Italy/Switz. **54 B7** 46.22N 9.57E
Bernkastel Germany **47 F1** 49.55N 7.05E
Berry Head England **13 D2** 50.24N 3.28W
Bertnaghboy Bay Rep. of Ire. **28 B3** 53.23N 9.55W
Berwick-upon-Tweed England **22 B2** 55.46N 2.00W
Berwyn *mts.* Wales **18 C2** 52.55N 3.25W
Besançon France **48 G4** 47.14N 6.02E
Bessarabia *f.* Moldavia **59 B3** 47.00N 29.00E
Bessbrook N. Ireland **23 C1** 54.12N 6.25W
Betanzos Spain **50 A5** 43.17N 8.13W
Bethersden England **15 C2** 51.08N 0.46E
Bethesda Wales **18 B3** 53.11N 4.03W
Béthune France **47 A2** 50.32N 2.38E
Betws-y-Coed Wales **18 C3** 53.05N 3.48W
Beult *r.* England **15 C2** 51.13N 0.26E
Beverley England **21 E2** 53.52N 0.26W
Beverwijk Neth. **47 C4** 52.29N 4.40E
Bewcastle England **22 B2** 55.03N 2.45W
Bewcastle Fells *hills* England **22 B2** 55.05N 2.50W
Bewdley England **16 B2** 52.23N 2.19W
Bexhill England **15 C1** 50.51N 0.29E
Bexley England **15 C2** 51.26N 0.10E
Beyla Guinea **104 B2** 8.42N 8.39W
Beysehir L. Turkey **68 C5** 37.47N 31.30E
Bezhetsk Russian Fed. **59 D5** 57.49N 36.40E
Bezhitsa Russian Fed. **59 C4** 53.19N 34.17E
Béziers France **48 E2** 43.21N 3.13E
Bhagalpur India **71 F4** 25.14N 86.59E
Bhamo Myanma **71 H4** 24.15N 97.15E
Bhatpara India **74 D2** 22.51N 88.31E
Bhavnagar India **71 D4** 21.46N 72.14E
Bhima *r.* India **71 D3** 16.30N 77.10E
Bhopal India **71 D4** 23.17N 77.28E
Bhubaneswar India **71 F4** 20.15N 85.50E
Bhuj India **71 C4** 23.12N 69.54E
Bhutan Asia **71 G5** 27.25N 90.00E
Biak Indonesia **79 J3** 1.10S 136.05E
Biak *i.* Indonesia **79 J3** 0.55S 136.00E
Białogard Poland **57 D7** 54.00N 16.00E
Białystok Poland **57 H6** 53.09N 23.10E
Biarritz France **48 C2** 43.29N 1.33W
Bicester England **14 A2** 51.53N 1.09W
Bida Nigeria **108 C2** 9.06N 5.59E
Biddulph England **16 B3** 53.08N 2.11W
Bidean nam Bian *mtn.* Scotland **26 C3** 56.39N 5.02W
Bideford England **12 C3** 51.01N 4.13W
Bideford B. England **12 C3** 51.04N 4.20W
Biel Switz. **52 C2** 47.09N 7.16E
Bielefeld Germany **52 D5** 52.02N 8.32E
Bielsko-Biała Poland **57 F4** 49.49N 19.02E
Bié Plateau *f.* Angola **102 D3** 13.00S 16.00E
Bigbury B. England **13 D2** 50.15N 3.56W

Biggar Scotland 27 E2 55.38N 3.31W
Biggleswade England 15 B3 52.06N 0.16W
Bighorn r. U.S.A. 86 E6 46.05N 107.20W
Bighorn Mts. U.S.A. 86 E5 44.00N 107.30W
Big Snowy Mt. U.S.A. 86 E6 46.46N 109.31W
Big Spring town U.S.A. 86 F3 32.15N 101.30W
Bihać Bosnia. 56 B6 44.49N 15.53E
Bihar India 71 F4 25.13N 85.31E
Bihar d. India 71 F4 24.15N 86.00E
Bihor mtn. Romania 57 H3 46.26N 22.43E
Bijagos Archipelago is. Guinea Bissau 104 A3 11.30N 16.00W
Bijapur India 71 D3 16.52N 75.47E
Bijar Iran 69 G4 35.52N 47.39E
Bijawar India 71 E4 24.36N 79.30E
Bikaner India 71 D5 28.01N 73.22E
Bikin Russian Fed. 75 L6 46.52N 134.15E
Bikini i. Pacific Oc. 82 G9 11.35N 165.23E
Bilaspur India 71 E4 22.03N 82.12E
Bilauktaung Range mts. Asia 78 B6 13.20N 99.30E
Bilbao Spain 50 D5 43.15N 2.56W
Bilecik Turkey 68 C6 40.10N 29.59E
Billericay England 15 C2 51.38N 0.25E
Billingham England 22 C1 54.36N 1.18W
Billings U.S.A. 86 E6 45.47N 108.30W
Billingshurst England 15 B2 51.02N 0.28W
Biloxi U.S.A. 87 I3 30.30N 88.53W
Binaija mtn. Indonesia 79 H3 3.10S 129.30E
Binche Belgium 47 C2 50.25N 4.10E
Binderup Denmark 46 C4 56.46N 9.35E
Bingen Germany 47 F1 49.58N 7.55E
Bingham England 16 D2 52.57N 0.57W
Binghamton U.S.A. 87 K5 42.06N 75.55W
Bingkor Malaysia 78 F5 5.26N 116.15E
Bingley England 20 D2 53.51N 1.50W
Bingöl Turkey 68 F5 38.54N 40.29E
Bingol Dağlari mtn. Turkey 68 F5 39.21N 41.22E
Binh Dinh Vietnam 78 D6 13.55N 109.07E
Binjai Indonesia 78 B4 3.37N 98.25E
Bintan i. Indonesia 78 C4 1.10N 104.30E
Bintulu Malaysia 78 E4 3.12N 113.01E
Bioko i. Equat. Guinea 102 C5 3.25N 8.45E
Birecik Turkey 68 E5 37.03N 37.59E
Birhan mtn. Ethiopia 105 F3 11.00N 37.50E
Birjand Iran 70 A6 32.54N 59.10E
Birkenfeld Germany 47 F1 49.39N 7.10E
Birkenhead England 20 B2 53.24N 3.01W
Birket Qârûn l. Egypt 68 C3 29.30N 30.40E
Bîrlad Romania 59 B3 46.14N 27.40E
Birmingham England 16 C2 52.30N 1.55W
Birmingham Ala. U.S.A. 87 I3 33.30N 86.55W
Birnin Kebbi Nigeria 108 B3 12.30N 4.11E
Birni N'Konni Niger 104 C3 13.49N 5.19E
Birobidzhan Russian Fed. 75 L6 48.49N 132.54E
Birq, Wadi r. Saudi Arabia 69 G2 24.08N 47.35E
Birr Rep. of Ire. 28 D3 53.06N 7.56W
Biscay, B. of France 48 B3 45.30N 4.00W
Bishkek Kirghizia 74 B5 42.53N 74.46E
Bishop Auckland England 22 C1 54.40N 1.40W
Bishopbriggs Scotland 26 D2 55.55N 4.12W
Bishop's Castle England 16 A2 52.29N 3.00W
Bishop's Lydeard England 13 D3 51.04N 3.12W
Bishop's Stortford England 15 C2 51.53N 0.09E
Bishops Waltham England 14 A1 50.57N 1.13W
Bisitun Iran 69 G4 34.22N 47.29E
Biskra Algeria 104 C5 34.48N 5.40E
Bismarck U.S.A. 86 F6 46.50N 100.48W
Bismarck Range mts. P.N.G. 79 L2 6.00S 145.00E
Bismarck Sea Pacific Oc. 79 L3 4.00S 146.30E
Bissau Guinea Bissau 104 A3 11.52N 15.39W
Bistriţa Romania 59 A3 47.08N 24.30E
Bistriţa r. Romania 59 B3 46.30N 26.54E
Bitburg Germany 47 E1 49.58N 6.31E
Bitlis Turkey 68 F5 38.23N 42.04E
Bitola Macedonia 56 E4 41.02N 21.21E
Bitterfontein R.S.A. 106 B1 31.03S 18.16E
Bitterroot Range U.S.A. 86 D6 47.06N 115.00W
Biu Nigeria 108 D3 10.36N 12.11E
Biwa ko l. Japan 76 C4 35.20N 136.10E
Biysk Russian Fed. 60 H3 52.35N 85.16E
Bizerta Tunisia 104 C5 37.17N 9.51E
Bjärred Sweden 46 F3 55.43N 12.59E
Bjerringbro Denmark 46 C4 56.23N 9.39E
Black r. Ark. U.S.A. 87 H4 35.30N 91.20W
Black r. Vietnam 78 D8 21.20N 105.45E
Blackburn England 20 C2 53.44N 2.30W
Black Combe mtn. England 22 A1 54.15N 3.20W
Blackcraig Hill Scotland 26 D2 55.19N 4.08W
Black Down Hills England 13 D2 50.55N 3.10W
Blackford Scotland 27 E3 56.16N 3.48W
Black Forest f. Germany 52 D4 48.00N 8.00E
Black Head N. Ireland 23 D1 54.46N 5.41W
Blackmoor Vale f. England 13 E2 50.55N 2.25W
Black Mtn. Wales 18 C1 51.52N 3.50W
Black Mts. Wales 18 C1 51.52N 3.09W
Blackpool England 20 B2 53.48N 3.03W
Black River town Jamaica 94 D4 18.02N 77.52W
Black Rock Desert U.S.A. 86 C5 41.10N 118.45W
Black Sea Europe 59 C2 43.00N 35.00E
Blacksod B. Rep. of Ire. 28 A4 54.04N 10.00W
Black Volta r. Ghana 108 A2 8.14N 2.11W
Blackwater r. England 15 C2 51.43N 0.42E
Blackwater r. N. Ireland 23 E1 54.31N 6.35W
Blackwater r. Waterford Rep. of Ire. 28 D1 51.58N 7.52W
Blackwood Wales 18 C1 51.38N 3.13W
Blaenau Ffestiniog Wales 18 C2 53.00N 3.57W
Blaenavon Wales 18 C1 51.46N 3.05W
Blagoevgrad Bulgaria 56 F5 42.02N 23.04E
Blagoveshchensk Russian Fed. 75 K7 50.19N 127.30E
Blaina Wales 18 C1 51.46N 3.10W
Blair Atholl Scotland 24 E3 56.48N 3.50W
Blairgowrie Scotland 27 E3 56.36N 3.21W
Blanca, Bahía b. Argentina 97 C4 39.15S 61.00W
Blanca, Sierra mtn. U.S.A. 86 E3 33.23N 105.49W
Blanc, Cap c. Mauritania 104 A4 20.44N 17.05W
Blanc, Mont mtn. Europe 48 G3 45.50N 6.52E
Blanco, C. Costa Rica 94 B2 9.36N 85.06W
Blanco, C. U.S.A. 86 B5 42.50N 124.29W
Blandford Forum England 13 E2 50.52N 2.10W
Blankenberge Belgium 47 B3 51.18N 3.08E
Blantyre Malaŵi 106 D3 15.46S 35.00E
Blarney Rep. of Ire. 28 C1 51.56N 8.34W
Blavet r. France 48 B4 47.43N 3.18W
Blaydon England 22 C1 54.58N 1.42W
Blaye France 48 C3 45.08N 0.40W
Bleaklow Hill England 16 C3 53.27N 1.50W
Bletchley England 15 B2 51.59N 0.45W
Blida Algeria 104 C5 36.30N 2.50E
Blidworth England 16 C3 53.06N 1.07W
Blitar Indonesia 78 E2 8.06S 112.12E
Blitta Togo 108 B2 8.23N 1.06E
Bloemfontein R.S.A. 106 C2 29.07S 26.14E
Blois France 48 D4 47.36N 1.20E
Bloody Foreland c. Rep. of Ire. 28 C5 55.09N 8.17W
Bluefield U.S.A. 87 J4 37.14N 81.17W
Bluefields Nicaragua 94 C3 12.00N 83.49W
Blue Mts. U.S.A. 86 C6 45.00N 118.00W
Blue Nile r. Sudan 105 F3 15.45N 32.25E
Blue Stack Mts. Rep. of Ire. 28 C4 54.44N 8.09W
Blyth Northum. England 22 C2 55.07N 1.29W
Blyth Bridge town Scotland 27 E2 55.42N 3.23W
Bo Sierra Leone 104 A2 7.58N 11.45W
Boa Vista Brazil 96 C8 2.51N 60.43W
Bobo-Dioulasso Burkina Faso 104 B3 11.11N 4.18W
Bobruysk Belorussia 59 B4 53.08N 29.10E
Bocholt Germany 47 E3 51.49N 6.37E
Bochum Germany 47 F3 51.28N 7.11E
Boconó Venezuela 94 E2 9.17N 70.17W
Bodélé Depression f. Chad 104 D3 16.50N 17.10E
Boden Sweden 58 E4 65.50N 21.44E
Bodenham England 16 B2 52.09N 2.41W
Bodmin England 12 C2 50.28N 4.44W
Bodmin Moor England 12 C2 50.35N 4.35W
Bodö Norway 58 C4 67.18N 14.26E
Bogense Denmark 46 D3 55.34N 10.07E
Boggeragh Mts. Rep. of Ire. 28 C2 52.04N 8.50W
Bogia P.N.G. 79 L3 4.16S 145.00E
Bognor Regis England 15 B1 50.47N 0.40W
Bog of Allen f. Rep. of Ire. 28 D3 53.17N 7.00W
Bogor Indonesia 78 D2 6.34S 106.45E
Bogotá Colombia 94 E1 4.38N 74.05W
Bohain France 47 B1 49.59N 3.28E
Bohemian Forest mts. Germany/Czech Rep. 57 C4 49.20N 13.10E
Bohol i. Phil. 79 G5 9.45N 124.10E
Boise U.S.A. 86 C5 43.38N 116.12W
Bojeador, C. Phil. 79 G7 18.30N 120.50E
Boké Guinea 104 A3 10.57N 14.13W
Boknafjorden est. Norway 58 A2 59.15N 5.50E
Bolangir India 71 E4 20.41N 83.30E
Bolbec France 48 D5 49.34N 0.28E
Bole Ghana 108 A2 9.03N 2.23W
Bolgrad Ukraine 59 B3 45.42N 28.40E
Bolivia S. America 96 C6 17.00S 65.00W
Bollin r. England 20 C2 53.23N 2.29W
Bollnäs Sweden 58 D3 61.20N 16.25E
Bolmen l. Sweden 58 C2 57.00N 13.45E
Bologna Italy 54 C6 44.30N 11.20E
Bologoye Russian Fed. 59 C5 57.58N 34.00E
Bolsena, L. Italy 54 C5 42.36N 11.55E
Bolshevik i. Russian Fed. 61 I5 78.30N 102.00E
Bolshoi Lyakhovskiy i. Russian Fed. 61 L4 73.30N 142.00E
Bolshoy Uzen r. Russian Fed./Kazakhstan 59 F3 49.00N 49.40E
Bolsover England 16 C3 53.14N 1.18W
Bolt Head c. England 13 D2 50.13N 3.48W
Bolton England 20 C2 53.35N 2.26W
Bolu Turkey 68 C6 40.45N 31.38E
Bolus Hd. Rep. of Ire. 28 A1 51.48N 10.21W
Bolvadin Turkey 68 C5 38.43N 31.02E
Bolzano Italy 54 C7 46.30N 11.20E
Boma Zaïre 106 B4 5.50S 13.03E
Bombay India 71 D3 18.56N 72.51E
Bomu r. C.A.R. 105 E2 4.05N 22.27E
Bonaire i. Neth. Antilles 95 F3 12.15N 68.27W
Bonar-Bridge Scotland 24 D4 57.53N 4.22W
Bonavista Canada 91 M2 48.38N 53.08W
Bone, G. of Indonesia 79 G3 4.00S 120.50E
Bo'ness Scotland 27 E3 56.01N 3.36W
Bonifacio, Str. of Med. Sea 54 B4 41.18N 9.10E
Bonin Is. Japan 82 E10 27.00N 142.10E
Bonn Germany 47 F2 50.44N 7.06E
Bonny Nigeria 108 C1 4.25N 7.10E
Bonnyrigg Scotland 27 E2 55.52N 3.07W
Bontang Indonesia 78 F4 0.05N 117.31E
Bonthain Indonesia 78 F2 5.32S 119.58E
Boothia, G. of Canada 91 J4 70.00N 90.00W
Bootle Cumbria England 22 A1 54.17N 3.24W
Bootle Mersey. England 20 B2 53.28N 3.01W
Boppard Germany 47 F2 50.13N 7.35E
Borah Peak mtn. U.S.A. 86 D5 44.09N 113.47W
Borås Sweden 58 C2 57.44N 12.55E
Borazjan Iran 69 H3 29.14N 51.12E
Bordeaux France 48 C3 44.50N 0.34W
Borden I. Canada 90 G5 78.30N 111.00W
Borders d. Scotland 27 F2 55.30N 2.53W
Bordesholm Germany 46 C2 54.11N 10.00E
Bordö i. Faroe Is. 58 M9 62.10N 7.13W
Bordon Camp England 15 B2 51.06N 0.52W
Borgå Finland 58 F3 60.24N 25.40E
Börgefjell mtn. Norway 58 C4 65.15N 13.50E
Borger U.S.A. 86 F4 35.39N 101.24W
Borislav Ukraine 57 H4 49.18N 23.28E
Borisoglebsk Russian Fed. 59 E4 51.23N 42.02E
Borisov Belorussia 59 B4 54.09N 28.30E
Borken Germany 47 E3 51.50N 6.52E
Borkum Germany 47 E5 53.34N 6.41E
Borkum i. Germany 47 E5 53.35N 6.45E
Borlänge Sweden 58 C3 60.29N 15.25E
Borneo i. Asia 78 E4 1.00N 114.00E
Bornholm i. Denmark 58 C1 55.02N 15.00E
Bornu, Plain of f. Nigeria 108 D3 12.30N 13.00E
Boroughbridge England 21 D3 54.06N 1.23W
Borough Green England 15 C2 51.17N 0.19E
Borovichi Russian Fed. 59 C5 58.22N 34.00E
Borth Wales 18 B2 52.29N 4.03W
Borzya Russian Fed. 75 I7 50.24N 116.35E
Bosa Italy 54 B4 40.18N 8.29E
Boscastle England 12 C2 50.42N 4.42W
Bosna r. Bosnia./Croatia 56 D6 45.04N 18.27E
Bosnia-Herzegovina Europe 56 C6 44.00N 18.00E
Bosnik Indonesia 79 J3 1.09S 136.14E
Bosporus str. Turkey 68 C6 41.07N 29.04E
Bosten Hu l. China 74 D5 42.00N 87.00E
Boston England 17 D2 52.59N 0.02W
Boston U.S.A. 87 L5 42.15N 71.05W
Botevgrad Bulgaria 56 F5 42.55N 23.57E
Bothnia, G. of Europe 58 D3 63.30N 20.30E
Botoşani Romania 59 B3 47.44N 26.41E
Botrange mtn. Belgium 47 E2 50.30N 6.04E
Botswana Africa 106 C2 22.00S 24.00E
Bottesford England 16 D2 52.56N 0.48W
Bottrop Germany 47 E3 51.31N 6.55E
Bouaké Ivory Coast 104 B2 7.42N 5.00W
Bou Craa Western Sahara 104 A4 26.21N 12.57W
Bougainville i. P.N.G. 80 E5 6.00S 155.00E
Boughton England 16 D2 53.13N 0.59W
Boulder U.S.A. 86 E5 40.02N 105.16W
Boulogne France 48 D6 50.43N 1.37E
Boundary Peak mtn. U.S.A. 86 C4 37.51N 118.23W
Bounty Is. Pacific Oc. 82 H3 48.00S 178.30E
Bourg France 48 F4 46.12N 5.13E
Bourganeuf France 48 D3 45.57N 1.44E
Bourges France 48 E4 47.05N 2.23E
Bourg Madame France 48 D2 42.26N 1.55E
Bourne England 17 D2 52.46N 0.23W
Bourne End England 15 B2 51.34N 0.42W
Bournemouth England 13 F2 50.43N 1.53W
Bowes England 22 B1 54.31N 2.01W
Bowmore Scotland 26 B2 55.45N 6.17W
Bowness-on-Solway England 22 A1 54.57N 3.11W
Bo Xian China 75 I4 33.40N 115.50E
Boxtel Neth. 47 D3 51.36N 5.20E
Boyle Rep. of Ire. 28 C3 53.58N 8.20W
Boyne r. Rep. of Ire. 28 E3 53.43N 6.18W
Boyoma Falls f. Zaïre 106 C5 0.18N 25.30E
Bozeman U.S.A. 86 D6 45.40N 111.00W
Braan r. Scotland 27 E3 56.34N 3.36W
Braband Denmark 46 D4 56.09N 10.08E
Brabant d. Belgium 47 C2 50.47N 4.30E
Brač i. Croatia 56 C5 43.20N 16.38E
Bracadale, L. Scotland 24 B4 57.20N 6.32W
Bräcke Sweden 58 C3 62.44N 15.30E
Bracknell England 15 B2 51.26N 0.46W
Brad Romania 56 F7 46.06N 22.48E
Bradano r. Italy 54 F4 40.23N 16.52E
Bradford England 20 D2 53.47N 1.45W
Bradford-on-Avon England 13 E3 51.20N 2.15W
Bradwell-on-Sea England 15 C2 51.44N 0.55E
Bradworthy England 12 C2 50.54N 4.22W
Braemar Scotland 24 E3 56.59N 3.27W
Braga Portugal 50 A4 41.32N 8.26W
Bragança Portugal 50 B4 41.47N 6.46W
Brahmaputra r. Asia 71 F4 23.50N 89.45E
Brăila Romania 59 B3 45.18N 27.58E
Brailsford England 16 C2 52.58N 1.35W
Braintree England 15 C2 51.53N 0.32E
Bramming Denmark 46 B3 55.28N 8.44E
Brampton England 22 B1 54.56N 2.43W
Branco r. Brazil 96 C7 1.30S 62.00W
Brande Denmark 46 C3 55.56N 9.09E
Brandenburg Germany 52 F5 52.25N 12.34E
Brandenburg d. Germany 52 F5 52.30N 13.50E
Brandon Canada 91 I2 49.50N 99.57W
Brandon Durham England 22 C1 54.46N 1.37W
Brandon Suffolk England 15 C3 52.27N 0.37E
Brandon Mtn. Rep. of Ire. 28 A2 52.14N 10.15W
Brandon Pt. Rep. of Ire. 28 A2 52.17N 10.11W
Braniewo Poland 57 F7 54.24N 19.50E
Brasília Brazil 96 E6 15.54S 47.50W
Braşov Romania 56 G6 45.40N 25.35E
Brass Nigeria 108 C1 4.20N 6.15E
Bratislava Slovakia 57 E4 48.10N 17.10E
Bratsk Russian Fed. 61 I3 56.20N 101.15E
Bratsk Resr. Russian Fed. 61 I3 54.40N 103.00E
Braunschweig Germany 52 E5 52.15N 10.30E
Braunton England 12 C3 51.06N 4.09W
Brawley U.S.A. 86 C3 33.10N 115.30W
Bray Rep. of Ire. 28 E3 53.12N 6.07W
Bray Hd. Kerry Rep. of Ire. 28 A1 51.52N 10.28W
Brazil S. America 96 D7 10.00S 52.00W
Brazilian Basin Atlantic Oc. 112 H4 15.00S 25.00W
Brazilian Highlands Brazil 96 E6 14.00S 45.00W
Brazos r. U.S.A. 87 G2 28.55N 95.20W
Brazzaville Congo 106 B4 4.14S 15.14E
Brda r. Poland 57 F6 53.07N 18.08E
Breadalbane f. Scotland 26 D3 56.30N 4.20W
Breaksea Pt. Wales 18 C1 51.24N 3.25W
Brechin Scotland 27 F3 56.44N 2.40W
Breckland f. England 15 C3 52.28N 0.40E
Brecon Wales 18 C1 51.57N 3.23W
Brecon Beacons mts. Wales 18 C1 51.53N 3.27W
Breda Neth. 47 C3 51.35N 4.46E
Bredstedt Germany 46 B2 54.37N 8.58E
Bregenz Austria 57 A3 47.31N 9.46E
Breidhafjördhur est. Iceland 58 I7 65.15N 23.00W
Bremen Germany 52 D5 53.05N 8.48E
Bremerhaven Germany 52 D5 53.33N 8.35E
Brendon Hills England 13 D3 51.05N 3.25W
Brenner Pass Italy/Austria 57 B3 47.00N 11.30E
Brenta r. Italy 54 D6 45.25N 12.15E
Brentwood England 15 C2 51.38N 0.18E
Brescia Italy 54 C6 45.33N 10.12E
Breskens Neth. 47 B3 51.24N 3.34E
Bressay i. Scotland 24 G7 60.08N 1.05W
Bressuire France 48 C4 46.50N 0.28W
Brest Belorussia 59 A4 52.08N 23.40E
Brest France 48 A5 48.23N 4.30W
Brewster, C. Greenland 84 R9 70.00N 22.00W
Briançon France 48 G3 44.53N 6.39E
Bride I.o.M. 20 A3 54.23N 4.24W
Bridgend Wales 18 C1 51.30N 3.35W
Bridge of Allan town Scotland 27 E3 56.09N 3.58W
Bridge of Earn town Scotland 27 E3 56.24N 3.25W
Bridgeport U.S.A. 87 L5 41.12N 73.12W
Bridgetown Barbados 93 M2 13.06N 59.37W
Bridgetown Rep. of Ire. 28 E2 52.14N 6.32W
Bridgnorth England 16 B2 52.33N 2.25W
Bridgwater England 13 E3 51.08N 3.00W
Bridgwater B. England 13 D3 51.15N 3.10W
Bridlington England 21 E3 54.06N 0.11W
Bridlington B. England 21 E3 54.03N 0.10W
Bridport England 13 E2 50.43N 2.45W
Brienne-le-Château France 48 F5 48.24N 4.32E
Brierfield England 20 C2 53.49N 2.15W
Brig Switz. 52 C2 46.19N 8.00E
Brigg England 21 E2 53.33N 0.30W
Brighouse England 20 D2 53.42N 1.47W
Brightlingsea England 15 D2 51.49N 1.01E
Brighton England 15 B1 50.50N 0.09W
Brindisi Italy 54 F4 40.38N 17.57E
Brisbane Australia 80 E3 27.30S 153.00E
Bristol England 13 E3 51.26N 2.35W
Bristol B. U.S.A. 90 C3 58.00N 158.50W
Bristol Channel England/Wales 13 D3 51.17N 3.20W
British Columbia d. Canada 90 F3 55.00N 125.00W
British Isles Europe 112 I7 54.00N 5.00W
Briton Ferry town Wales 18 C1 51.37N 3.50W
Brittany f. France 40 E4 48.00N 3.00W
Brive France 48 D3 45.09N 1.32E
Briviesca Spain 50 D5 42.33N 3.19W
Brixham England 13 D2 50.24N 3.31W
Brno Czech Rep. 57 E4 49.11N 16.39E
Broad B. Scotland 24 B5 58.15N 6.15W
Broad Law mtn. Scotland 27 E3 55.30N 3.21W
Broadstairs England 15 D2 51.22N 1.27E
Broadstone England 13 E2 50.45N 2.00W
Brockenhurst England 14 A1 50.49N 1.34W
Brod Croatia 56 D6 45.09N 18.02E
Brodick Scotland 26 C2 55.34N 5.09W
Brody Ukraine 59 A4 50.05N 25.08E
Broken Hill town Australia 80 D2 31.57S 141.30E
Bromley England 15 C2 51.24N 0.02E
Bromsgrove England 16 B2 52.20N 2.03W
Bromyard England 16 B2 52.12N 2.30W
Brönderslev Denmark 46 C5 57.16N 9.58E
Brookes Point town Phil. 78 F5 8.50N 117.52E
Brooks Range mts. U.S.A. 90 C4 68.50N 152.00W
Broom, L. Scotland 24 C4 57.55N 5.15W
Brora Scotland 24 E5 58.01N 3.52W
Brora r. Scotland 24 E4 57.59N 3.51W
Brosna r. Rep. of Ire. 28 D3 53.12N 7.59W
Brotton England 22 D1 54.34N 0.55W
Brough Cumbria England 22 B1 54.32N 2.19W
Brough Shetland Scotland 24 G7 60.29N 1.11W
Broughton England 21 D3 54.26N 1.08W
Broughton Scotland 27 E2 55.37N 3.25W
Broughton Wales 18 D3 53.10N 3.00W
Broughton in Furness England 22 A1 54.17N 3.12W
Brovary Ukraine 59 C4 50.30N 30.45E
Brovst Denmark 46 C5 57.06N 9.31E
Brownhills England 16 C2 52.38N 1.57W
Brown Willy hill England 12 C2 50.36N 4.36W
Bruay-en-Artois France 47 A2 50.29N 2.36E
Bruges Belgium 47 B3 51.13N 3.14E
Brühl Germany 47 E2 50.50N 6.55E
Brunei Asia 78 E4 4.56N 114.58E
Brunsbüttel Germany 46 C1 53.54N 9.10E
Brunssun Neth. 47 D2 50.57N 5.59E
Brunswick U.S.A. 87 J3 31.09N 81.21W
Bruny I. Australia 82 E2 43.15S 147.16E
Brussels Belgium 47 C2 50.50N 4.23E
Bruton England 13 E3 51.06N 2.28W
Bryansk Russian Fed. 59 C4 53.15N 34.09E
Bryn Brawd mtn. Wales 18 C2 52.08N 3.54W
Brynmawr Wales 18 C1 51.48N 3.10W
Bubiyan I. Kuwait 69 H3 29.45N 48.15E
Bucaramanga Colombia 94 E2 7.08N 73.01W
Buchan Ness c. Scotland 24 G4 57.28N 1.47W
Bucharest Romania 56 H6 44.25N 26.06E
Buckfastleigh England 13 D2 50.28N 3.47W
Buckhaven and Methil Scotland 27 E3 56.11N 3.03W
Buckie Scotland 24 F4 57.40N 2.58W
Buckingham England 15 B2 52.00N 0.59W
Buckinghamshire d. England 15 B2 51.50N 0.48W
Buckley Wales 18 C3 53.11N 3.04W
Budapest Hungary 57 F3 47.30N 19.03E
Buddon Ness c. Scotland 27 F3 56.29N 2.42W
Bude England 12 C2 50.49N 4.33W
Bude B. England 12 C2 50.50N 4.40W
Budleigh Salterton England 13 D2 50.37N 3.19W
Buenaventura Colombia 94 D1 3.54N 77.02W
Buenos Aires Argentina 97 D4 34.40S 58.30W
Buffalo N.Y. U.S.A. 87 K5 42.52N 78.55W
Buffalo Wyo. U.S.A. 86 E5 44.21N 106.40W
Bug r. Poland 57 G6 52.29N 21.11E
Bug r. Ukraine 59 C3 46.55N 31.59E
Buga Colombia 94 D1 3.53N 76.17W
Buggs Island L. U.S.A. 87 K4 36.35N 78.20W
Bugt China 75 J6 48.45N 121.58E
Bugulma Russian Fed. 59 G4 54.32N 52.46E
Buie, Loch Scotland 26 C3 56.20N 5.53W
Builth Wells Wales 18 C2 52.09N 3.24W
Buitenpost Neth. 47 E5 53.15N 6.09E

Bujumbura Burundi 106 C4 3.22S 29.21E
Bukavu Zaïre 106 C4 2.30S 28.49E
Bukhara Uzbekistan 60 F1 39.47N 64.26E
Bukittinggi Indonesia 78 C3 0.18S 100.20E
Bula Indonesia 79 I3 3.07S 130.27E
Bulagan Mongolia 74 G6 48.34N 103.12E
Bulan Phil. 79 G6 12.40N 123.53E
Bulawayo Zimbabwe 106 C2 20.10S 28.43E
Bulbjerg *mtn.* Denmark 46 C5 57.09N 9.04E
Bulgaria Europe 56 G5 42.30N 25.00E
Bulkington England 16 C2 52.29N 1.25W
Bulolo P.N.G. 79 L2 7.13S 146.35E
Bulu, Gunung *mtn.* Indonesia 78 F4 3.00N 116.00E
Bulun Russian Fed. 61 K4 70.50N 127.20E
Bunbury Australia 80 A2 33.20S 115.34E
Buncrana Rep. of Ire. 28 D5 55.08N 7.28W
Bundaberg Australia 80 E3 24.50S 152.21E
Bunde Germany 47 F5 53.12N 7.16E
Bundoran Rep. of Ire. 28 C4 54.28N 8.20W
Bunessan Scotland 26 B3 56.18N 6.14W
Bungay England 15 D3 52.27N 1.26E
Bungo suido *str.* Japan 76 B3 32.52N 132.30E
Bunguran *i.* Indonesia 78 D4 4.00N 108.20E
Bunguran Selatan *i.* Indonesia 78 D4 3.00N 108.50E
Buni Nigeria 108 D3 11.20N 11.59E
Buntingford England 15 B2 51.57N 0.01W
Buol Indonesia 79 G4 1.12N 121.28E
Buqbuq Egypt 68 B3 31.30N 25.32E
Buraida Saudi Arabia 69 F2 26.18N 43.58E
Buraimi U.A.E. 69 I2 24.15N 55.45E
Burdur Turkey 68 C5 37.44N 30.17E
Burdwan India 71 F4 23.15N 87.52E
Bure *r.* England 15 D3 52.36N 1.44E
Bures England 15 C2 51.59N 0.46E
Burford England 14 A2 51.48N 1.38W
Burg Germany 52 E5 52.17N 11.51E
Burgan Kuwait 69 G3 28.58N 47.58E
Burgas Bulgaria 59 B2 42.30N 27.29E
Burgenland *d.* Austria 57 E3 47.30N 16.20E
Burgess Hill *town* England 15 B1 50.57N 0.07W
Burgh le Marsh England 17 E3 53.10N 0.15E
Burgos Spain 50 D5 42.21N 3.41W
Burgsteinfurt Germany 47 F4 52.09N 7.21E
Burgsvik Sweden 58 D2 57.03N 18.19E
Burhanpur India 71 D4 21.18N 76.08E
Burias *i.* Phil. 79 G6 12.50N 123.10E
Burica, Punta Panama 94 C2 8.05N 82.50W
Burkina Faso Africa 104 B3 12.15N 1.30W
Burley U.S.A. 86 D5 42.32N 113.48W
Burlington Vt. U.S.A. 87 L5 44.25N 73.14W
Burnham Market England 15 C3 52.57N 0.43E
Burnham-on-Crouch England 15 C2 51.37N 0.50E
Burnham-on-Sea England 13 D3 51.15N 3.00W
Burnley England 20 C2 53.47N 2.15W
Burntisland Scotland 27 E3 56.03N 3.15W
Burntwood England 16 C2 52.42N 1.54W
Burriana Spain 50 E3 39.54N 0.05W
Burrow Head Scotland 26 D1 54.41N 4.24W
Burry Port Wales 18 B1 51.41N 4.17W
Bursa Turkey 68 C6 40.11N 29.04E
Burscough England 20 C2 53.37N 2.51W
Burton Agnes England 21 E3 54.04N 0.18W
Burton Latimer England 16 D2 52.23N 0.41W
Burton upon Trent England 16 C2 52.58N 1.39W
Buru *i.* Indonesia 79 H3 3.30S 126.30E
Burujird Iran 69 H4 33.54N 48.47E
Burullus, L. Egypt 68 C3 31.30N 30.45E
Burundi Africa 106 C4 3.30S 30.00E
Burwell Cambs. England 15 C3 52.17N 0.20E
Burwell Lincs. England 17 E3 53.19N 0.02E
Bury England 20 C2 53.36N 2.19W
Bury St. Edmunds England 15 C3 52.15N 0.42E
Bush *r.* N. Ireland 23 C2 55.13N 6.33W
Būshehr Iran 69 H3 28.57N 50.52E
Bushmills N. Ireland 23 C2 55.12N 6.32W
Bussum Neth. 47 D4 52.17N 5.10E
Büsum Germany 46 B2 54.09N 8.52E
Buta Zaïre 105 E2 2.49N 24.50E
Butaritari *i.* Kiribati 82 H8 3.07N 172.48E
Bute *i.* Scotland 26 C2 55.51N 5.07W
Bute, Sd. of Scotland 26 C2 55.44N 5.10W
Butser Hill England 15 B1 50.58N 0.58W
Butte U.S.A. 86 D6 46.00N 112.31W
Butterworth Malaysia 78 C5 5.24N 100.22E
Buttevant Rep. of Ire. 28 C2 52.13N 8.40W
Butt of Lewis *c.* Scotland 24 B5 58.31N 6.15W
Butuan Phil. 79 H5 8.56N 125.31E
Butung *i.* Indonesia 79 G2 5.00S 122.50E
Bützow Germany 46 E1 53.52N 11.59E
Buxton England 16 C3 53.16N 1.54W
Buy Russian Fed. 59 E5 58.23N 41.27E
Buzău Romania 56 H6 45.10N 26.49E
Bydgoszcz Poland 57 E6 53.16N 17.33E
Byfield England 16 C2 52.10N 1.15W
Bylot I. Canada 91 K5 73.00N 78.30W
Byrranga Mts. Russian Fed. 61 H4 74.50N 101.00E
Byske *r.* Sweden 58 E4 64.58N 21.10E
Bytom Poland 57 F5 50.22N 18.54E

C

Cabanatuan Phil. 79 G7 15.30N 120.58E
Cabimas Venezuela 94 E3 10.26N 71.27W
Cabinda Angola 106 B4 5.34S 12.12E
Cabot Str. Canada 91 M2 47.00N 59.00W
Cabrera *i.* Spain 51 G3 39.08N 2.56E
Cabrera, Sierra *mts.* Spain 50 B5 42.10N 6.30W
Cabriel *r.* Spain 50 E3 39.13N 1.07W
Cabruta Venezuela 95 F2 7.40N 66.16W
Cáceres Spain 50 B3 39.29N 6.23W
Cacín *r.* Spain 50 C2 37.10N 4.01W
Cader Idris *mtn.* Wales 18 C2 52.40N 3.55W
Cadillac U.S.A. 87 I5 44.15N 85.23W
Cadí, Sierra del *mts.* Spain 50 F5 42.12N 1.35E
Cadiz Phil. 79 G6 10.57N 123.18E
Cádiz Spain 50 B2 36.32N 6.18W
Cádiz, G. of Spain 50 B2 37.00N 7.10W
Caen France 48 C5 49.11N 0.22W
Caerleon Wales 18 D1 51.36N 2.57W
Caernarfon Wales 18 B3 53.08N 4.17W
Caernarfon B. Wales 18 B3 53.05N 4.25W
Caerphilly Wales 18 C1 51.34N 3.13W
Cagayan de Oro Phil. 79 G5 8.29N 124.40E
Cagliari Italy 54 B3 39.14N 9.07E
Cagliari, G. of Med. Sea 54 B3 39.07N 9.15E
Caguas Puerto Rico 93 K3 18.08N 66.00W
Caha Mts. Rep. of Ire. 28 B1 51.44N 9.45W
Caherciveen Rep. of Ire. 28 A1 51.51N 10.14W
Cahir Rep. of Ire. 28 D2 52.21N 7.56W
Cahora Bassa Dam Mozambique 106 D3 15.33S 32.42E
Cahore Pt. Rep. of Ire. 28 E2 52.33N 6.11W
Cahors France 48 D3 44.28N 0.26E
Caibarien Cuba 93 I4 22.31N 79.28W
Caicos Is. Turks & Caicos Is. 93 J4 21.30N 72.00W
Cairngorms *mts.* Scotland 24 E4 57.04N 3.30W
Cairns Australia 80 D4 16.51S 145.43E
Cairnsmore of Carsphairn *mtn.* Scotland 26 D2 55.15N 4.12W
Cairn Table *mtn.* Scotland 27 D2 55.29N 4.02W
Cairo Egypt 68 C3 30.03N 31.15E
Cairo U.S.A. 87 I4 37.02N 89.02W
Caister-on-Sea England 15 D3 52.38N 1.43E
Caistor England 17 D3 53.29N 0.20W
Cajamarca Peru 96 B7 7.09S 78.32W
Calabar Nigeria 108 C1 4.56N 8.22E
Calabozo Venezuela 95 F2 8.58N 67.28W
Calafat Romania 56 F5 43.59N 22.57E
Calahorra Spain 50 D5 42.18N 1.58W
Calais France 48 D6 50.57N 1.50E
Calamar Colombia 94 E3 10.16N 74.55W
Calamian Group *is.* Phil. 79 G6 12.00N 120.05E
Calamocha Spain 50 E4 40.54N 1.18W
Calapan Phil. 79 G6 13.23N 121.10E
Calatayud Spain 50 E4 41.21N 1.39W
Calbayog Phil. 79 G6 12.04N 124.58E
Calcutta India 71 F4 22.35N 88.21E
Caldas Colombia 94 D2 6.05N 75.36W
Caldas da Rainha Portugal 50 A3 39.24N 9.08W
Caldbeck England 22 A1 54.45N 3.03W
Caldy *i.* Wales 18 B1 51.38N 4.43W
Caledon N. Ireland 23 C1 54.21N 6.51W
Calgary Canada 90 G3 51.05N 114.05W
Cali Colombia 94 D1 3.24N 76.30W
Calicut India 71 D2 11.15N 75.45E
Caliente U.S.A. 86 D4 37.36N 114.31W
California *d.* U.S.A. 86 B4 37.00N 120.00W
California, G. of Mexico 92 B5 28.30N 112.30W
Callander Scotland 26 D3 56.15N 4.13W
Callao Peru 96 B6 12.05S 77.08W
Callington England 12 C2 50.30N 4.19W
Calne England 13 F3 51.26N 2.00W
Caloocan Phil. 79 G6 14.38N 120.58E
Caltagirone Italy 54 E2 37.14N 14.30E
Caltanissetta Italy 54 E2 37.30N 14.05E
Calvi France 49 H2 42.34N 8.44E
Calvinia R.S.A. 106 B1 31.25S 19.47E
Cam *r.* England 15 C3 52.34N 0.21E
Camagüey Cuba 94 D5 21.25N 77.55W
Camagüey, Archipelago de Cuba 94 D5 22.30N 78.00W
Camarón, C. Honduras 93 H3 15.59N 85.00W
Ca Mau, Pointe de *c.* Vietnam 78 C5 8.30N 104.35E
Cambay, G. of India 71 D4 20.30N 72.00E
Camberley England 15 B2 51.21N 0.45W
Cambodia Asia 78 C6 12.00N 105.00E
Camborne England 12 B2 50.12N 5.19W
Cambrai France 48 E6 50.10N 3.14E
Cambrian Mts. Wales 18 C2 52.33N 3.33W
Cambridge England 15 C3 52.13N 0.08E
Cambridge Bay *town* Canada 90 H4 69.09N 105.00W
Cambridgeshire *d.* England 15 C3 52.15N 0.05E
Camelford England 12 C2 50.37N 4.41W
Cameroon Africa 104 D2 6.00N 12.30E
Cameroon, Mt. Cameroon 104 C2 4.20N 9.05E
Campbell I. Pacific Oc. 82 G2 52.30S 169.02E
Campbeltown Scotland 26 C2 55.25N 5.36W
Campeche Mexico 92 F3 19.50N 90.30W
Campeche *d.* Mexico 92 F3 19.00N 90.00W
Campeche B. Mexico 92 F3 19.30N 94.00W
Campina Grande Brazil 96 F7 7.15S 35.53W
Campinas Brazil 97 E5 22.54S 47.06W
Campine *f.* Belgium 47 C3 51.05N 5.00E
Campobasso Italy 54 E4 41.34N 14.39E
Campo Grande Brazil 97 D5 20.24S 54.35W
Campo Maior Portugal 50 B3 39.01N 7.04W
Campos Brazil 97 E5 21.46S 41.21W
Campsie Fells *hills* Scotland 26 D3 56.02N 4.15W
Cam Ranh Vietnam 78 D6 11.54N 109.14E
Camrose Canada 90 G3 53.01N 112.48W
Canada N. America 90 H3 60.00N 105.00W
Canadian *r.* U.S.A. 87 G4 35.20N 95.40W
Canadian Shield *f.* N. America 84 L7 50.00N 80.00W
Çanakkale Turkey 68 B6 40.09N 26.26E
Canal du Midi France 48 D2 43.18N 2.00E
Canary Is. Atlantic Oc. 104 A4 29.00N 15.00W
Canaveral, C. U.S.A. 87 J2 28.28N 80.28W
Canberra Australia 80 D2 35.18S 149.08E
Candeleda Spain 50 C4 40.10N 5.14W
Canea Greece 56 G1 35.30N 24.02E
Çankiri Turkey 68 D6 40.35N 33.37E
Canna *i.* Scotland 24 B4 57.03N 6.30W
Cannes France 48 G2 43.33N 7.00E
Cannich Scotland 24 D4 57.21N 4.42W
Cannock England 16 B2 52.42N 2.02W
Cannock Chase *f.* England 16 C2 52.45N 2.00W
Canõas Brazil 97 D5 29.55S 51.10W
Canonbie Scotland 27 F2 55.05N 2.56W
Canon City U.S.A. 86 E4 38.27N 105.14W
Cantabria *d.* Spain 50 C5 43.00N 4.00W
Cantabrian Mts. Spain 50 B5 42.55N 5.10W
Cantabria, Sierra de *mts.* Spain 50 D5 42.40N 2.30W
Cantaura Venezuela 95 G2 9.22N 64.24W
Canterbury England 15 D2 51.17N 1.05E
Can Tho Vietnam 78 D6 10.03N 105.46E
Canvey England 15 C2 51.32N 0.35E
Cao Bang Vietnam 78 D8 22.40N 106.16E
Caoles Scotland 26 B3 56.32N 6.44W
Caolisport, Loch Scotland 26 C2 55.54N 5.38W
Cape Basin Atlantic Oc. 112 J3 38.00S 10.00E
Cape Breton I. Canada 91 L2 46.00N 61.00W
Cape Coast *town* Ghana 108 A2 5.10N 1.13W
Cape Johnson Depth Pacific Oc. 79 H6 10.20N 127.20E
Capel England 15 B2 51.08N 0.18W
Cape Town R.S.A. 106 B1 33.56S 18.28E
Cape Verde Is. Atlantic Oc. 112 H5 15.00N 24.00W
Cap Haïtien *town* Haiti 93 J3 19.47N 72.17W
Cappoquin Rep. of Ire. 28 D2 52.09N 7.52W
Capraia *i.* Italy 54 B5 43.03N 9.50E
Caprera *i.* Italy 54 B4 41.48N 9.27E
Capri *i.* Italy 54 E4 40.33N 14.13E
Cara *i.* Scotland 26 C2 55.58N 5.45W
Caracal Romania 56 G6 44.08N 24.18E
Caracas Venezuela 95 F3 10.35N 66.56W
Caratasca Lagoon Honduras 93 H3 15.10N 84.00W
Caravaca Spain 50 E3 38.06N 1.51W
Carbonara, C. Italy 54 B3 39.06N 9.32E
Carcassonne France 48 E2 43.13N 2.21E
Carcross Canada 90 E4 60.11N 134.41W
Cardenas Cuba 93 H4 23.02N 81.12W
Cardenete Spain 50 E3 39.46N 1.42W
Cardiff Wales 18 C1 51.28N 3.11W
Cardigan Wales 18 B2 52.06N 4.41W
Cardigan B. Wales 18 B2 52.30N 4.30W
Carei Romania 57 H3 47.42N 22.28E
Carentan France 48 C5 49.18N 1.14W
Carhaix France 48 B5 48.16N 3.35W
Caribbean Sea C. America 93 I3 15.00N 75.00W
Caribou Mts. Canada 90 G3 58.30N 115.00W
Carignan France 47 D1 49.38N 5.10E
Caripito Venezuela 95 G3 10.07N 63.07W
Carlingford Rep. of Ire. 28 E4 54.02N 6.12W
Carlingford Lough Rep. of Ire./N. Ireland 23 D1 54.03N 6.09W
Carlisle England 22 B1 54.54N 2.55W
Carlow Rep. of Ire. 28 E2 52.50N 6.54W
Carlow *d.* Rep. of Ire. 28 E2 52.43N 6.50W
Carlton England 16 C2 52.58N 1.06W
Carluke Scotland 27 E2 55.44N 3.51W
Carmacks Canada 90 E4 62.04N 136.21W
Carmarthen Wales 18 B1 51.52N 4.20W
Carmarthen B. Wales 18 B1 51.40N 4.30W
Carmel Head Wales 18 B3 53.24N 4.35W
Carmen Colombia 94 D2 9.46N 75.06W
Carmen Mexico 92 F3 18.38N 91.50W
Carmen I. Baja Calif.Sur Mexico 92 B5 25.55N 111.10W
Carmen I. Campeche Mexico 92 F3 18.35N 91.40W
Carmona Spain 50 C2 37.28N 5.38W
Carmyllie Scotland 27 F3 56.36N 2.41W
Carndonagh Rep. of Ire. 28 D5 55.15N 7.17W
Carnedd y Filiast *mtn.* Wales 18 C2 52.56N 3.40W
Carnew Rep. of Ire. 28 E2 52.41N 6.31W
Carnforth England 20 C3 54.08N 2.47W
Carnic Alps *mts.* Italy/Austria 57 C3 46.40N 12.48E
Car Nicobar *i.* India 71 G2 9.06N 92.57E
Carnot C.A.R. 104 D2 4.59N 15.56E
Carnoustie Scotland 27 F3 56.30N 2.44W
Carnsore Pt. Rep. of Ire. 28 E2 52.10N 6.21W
Carnwath Scotland 27 E2 55.43N 3.37W
Carolina Puerto Rico 95 F4 18.23N 65.57W
Caroline I. Kiribati 83 K7 10.00S 150.30W
Caroline Is. Pacific Oc. 79 K5 7.50N 145.00E
Caroline-Solomon Ridge Pacific Oc. 82 F8 8.00N 150.00E
Caroní *r.* Venezuela 95 G2 8.20N 62.45W
Carora Venezuela 94 E3 10.12N 70.07W
Carpathians *mts.* Europe 59 A3 48.45N 23.45E
Carpentaria, G. of Australia 80 C4 14.00S 140.00E
Carpentras France 48 F3 44.03N 5.03E
Carpio Spain 50 C4 41.13N 5.07W
Carradale Scotland 26 C2 55.35N 5.28W
Carra, Lough Rep. of Ire. 28 B3 53.40N 9.15W
Carrara Italy 54 C6 44.04N 10.06E
Carrauntoohil *mtn.* Rep. of Ire. 28 B2 52.00N 9.45W
Carriacou *i.* Grenada 95 G3 12.30N 61.35W
Carrick *f.* Scotland 26 D2 55.12N 4.38W
Carrickfergus N. Ireland 23 D1 54.43N 5.49W
Carrick Forest *hills* Scotland 26 D2 55.11N 4.29W
Carrickmacross Rep. of Ire. 28 E3 53.59N 6.44W
Carrick-on-Shannon Rep. of Ire. 28 C3 53.57N 8.06W
Carrick-on-Suir Rep. of Ire. 28 D2 52.21N 7.26W
Carrowmore Lough Rep. of Ire. 28 B4 54.11N 9.48W
Carşamba Turkey 68 E6 41.13N 36.43E
Çarşamba *r.* Turkey 68 C5 37.52N 31.48E
Carse of Gowrie *f.* Scotland 27 E3 56.25N 3.15W
Carson City U.S.A. 86 C4 39.10N 119.46W
Carsphairn Scotland 26 D2 55.13N 4.15W
Carstairs Scotland 27 E2 55.42N 3.41W
Cartagena Colombia 94 D3 10.24N 75.33W
Cartagena Spain 50 E2 37.36N 0.59W
Cartago Colombia 94 D1 4.45N 75.55W
Cartago Costa Rica 93 H1 9.50N 83.52W
Caruaru Brazil 96 F7 8.15S 35.55W
Carúpano Venezuela 95 G3 10.39N 63.14W
Carvin France 47 A2 50.30N 2.58E
Casablanca Morocco 104 B5 33.39N 7.35W
Cascade Range *mts.* U.S.A. 86 B5 44.00N 121.30W
Caserta Italy 54 E4 41.06N 14.21E
Cashel Rep. of Ire. 28 D2 52.31N 7.54W
Caspe Spain 50 E4 41.14N 0.03W
Casper U.S.A. 86 E5 42.50N 106.20W
Caspian Depression *f.* Russian Fed./Kazakhstan 60 E2 47.00N 48.00E
Caspian Sea Asia 60 E2 42.00N 51.00E
Castaños Mexico 92 D5 26.48N 101.26W
Casteljaloux France 48 D3 44.19N 0.06W
Castellón de la Plana Spain 50 E3 39.59N 0.03W
Castelo Branco Portugal 50 B3 39.50N 7.30W
Castilla la Mancha *d.* Spain 50 C3 39.00N 4.00W
Castilla y León *d.* Spain 50 C4 42.00N 5.00W
Castilletes Colombia 94 E3 11.55N 71.20W
Castlebar Rep. of Ire. 28 B3 53.52N 9.19W
Castleblayney Rep. of Ire. 28 E4 54.08N 6.46W
Castle Cary England 13 E3 51.06N 2.31W
Castledawson N. Ireland 23 C1 54.47N 6.35W
Castlederg N. Ireland 23 B1 54.43N 7.37W
Castle Douglas Scotland 27 E1 54.56N 3.56W
Castleford England 21 D2 53.43N 1.21W
Castleisland *town* Rep. of Ire. 28 B2 52.14N 9.29W
Castlerea Rep. of Ire. 28 C3 53.45N 8.30W
Castlerock N. Ireland 23 C2 55.10N 6.49W
Castletown I.o.M. 20 A3 54.04N 4.38W
Castletownshend Rep. of Ire. 28 B1 51.31N 9.11W
Castlewellan N. Ireland 23 D1 54.15N 5.57W
Castres France 48 E2 43.36N 2.14E
Castries St. Lucia 93 L2 14.01N 60.59W
Cataluna *d.* Spain 50 F4 42.00N 2.00E
Catamarca Argentina 97 C5 28.28S 65.46W
Catanduanes *i.* Phil. 79 G6 13.45N 124.20E
Catania Italy 54 E2 37.31N 15.05E
Catanzaro Italy 54 F3 38.55N 16.35E
Catarman Phil. 79 G6 12.28N 124.50E
Catbalogan Phil. 79 G6 11.46N 124.55E
Caterham England 15 B2 51.17N 0.04W
Cat I. Bahamas 93 I4 24.30N 75.30W
Catoche, C. Mexico 93 G4 21.38N 87.08W
Catterick England 20 D3 54.23N 1.38W
Cauca *r.* Colombia 94 E2 8.57N 74.30W
Caucasus Mts. Europe 59 E2 43.00N 44.00E
Cauldcleuch Head *mtn.* Scotland 27 F2 55.18N 2.50W
Cavan Rep. of Ire. 28 D3 53.59N 7.22W
Cavan *d.* Rep. of Ire. 28 D3 54.00N 7.15W
Cawood England 21 D2 53.50N 1.07W
Caxias do Sul Brazil 97 D5 29.14S 51.10W
Cayenne Guiana 95 I1 4.55N 52.18W
Cayman Brac *i.* Cayman Is. 93 I3 19.44N 79.48W
Cayman Is. C. America 93 H3 19.00N 81.00W
Cebollera, Sierra de *mts.* Spain 50 D4 41.58N 2.30W
Cebu Phil. 79 G6 10.17N 123.56E
Cebu *i.* Phil. 79 G6 10.15N 123.45E
Cecina Italy 54 C5 43.18N 10.30E
Cedar City U.S.A. 86 D4 37.40N 113.04W
Cedar Rapids *town* U.S.A. 87 H5 41.59N 91.31W
Cedros I. Mexico 92 A5 28.15N 115.15W
Cefalù Italy 54 E3 38.01N 14.03E
Cegléd Hungary 57 F3 47.10N 19.48E
Celaya Mexico 92 D4 20.32N 100.48W
Celebes *i.* Indonesia 79 G3 2.00S 120.30E
Celebes Sea Indonesia 79 G4 3.00N 122.00E
Celje Slovenia 56 B7 46.15N 15.16E
Celle Germany 52 E5 52.37N 10.05E
Celtic Sea U.K. 40 D5 51.00N 9.00W
Cemaes Bay *town* Wales 18 B3 53.24N 4.27W
Cemaes Head Wales 18 B2 52.08N 4.42W
Central *d.* Scotland 26 D3 56.10N 4.20W
Central African Republic Africa 104 D2 6.30N 20.00E
Central, Cordillera *mts.* Colombia 94 D1 5.00N 75.20W
Central Russian Uplands *f.* Russian Fed. 59 D4 53.00N 37.00E
Central Siberian Plateau *f.* Russian Fed. 61 I4 66.00N 108.00E
Ceram *i.* Indonesia 79 H3 3.10S 129.30E
Ceram Sea Pacific Oc. 79 H3 2.50S 128.00E
Cereté Colombia 94 D2 8.54N 75.51W
Cerignola Italy 54 E4 41.17N 15.53E
Cerne Abbas England 13 E2 50.49N 2.29W
Cerro de Pasco Peru 96 B6 10.43S 76.15W
Çervera Spain 50 F4 41.40N 1.16E
České Budějovice Czech Rep. 57 D4 49.00N 14.30E
Cetinje Yugo. 56 D5 42.24N 18.55E
Ceuta Spain 50 C1 35.53N 5.19W
Cévennes *mts.* France 48 E3 44.25N 4.05E
Ceyhan *r.* Turkey 68 D5 36.54N 34.58E
Chad Africa 104 D3 13.00N 19.00E
Chad, L. Africa 104 D3 13.30N 14.00E
Chagford England 13 D2 50.40N 3.50W
Chagos Archipelago *is.* Indian Oc. 65 J2 7.00S 72.00E
Chah Bahar Iran 69 K2 25.17N 60.41E
Chalfont St. Peter England 15 B2 51.37N 0.33W
Challans France 48 C4 46.51N 1.52W
Challenger Depth Pacific Oc. 79 K6 11.19N 142.15E
Châlons-sur-Marne France 48 F5 48.58N 4.22E
Chalon-sur-Saône France 48 F4 46.47N 4.51E
Chamai Thailand 78 B5 8.10N 99.41E
Chambal *r.* India 74 C3 26.30N 79.20E
Chambéry France 48 F3 45.34N 5.55E
Chamonix France 48 G3 45.55N 6.52E
Champ Iran 69 K2 26.40N 60.31E
Champlain, L. U.S.A. 87 L5 44.45N 73.20W
Chanda India 71 E4 19.58N 79.21E
Chandeleur Is. U.S.A. 87 I2 29.50N 88.50W
Chandigarh India 71 D5 30.44N 76.54E

D

Et Tubeiq, Jebel *mts.* Saudi Arabia **68 E3** 29.30N 37.15E
Euboea *i.* Greece **56 G3** 38.30N 23.50E
Eufaula Resr. U.S.A. **87 G4** 35.15N 95.35W
Eugene U.S.A. **86 B5** 44.03N 123.07W
Eugenia, Punta *c.* Mexico **92 A5** 27.50N 115.50W
Eupen Belgium **47 E2** 50.38N 6.04E
Euphrates *r.* Asia **69 G3** 31.00N 47.27E
Eureka U.S.A. **86 B5** 40.49N 124.10W
Europa, Picos de *mts.* Spain **50 C5** 43.10N 4.40W
Europe 113
Europoort Neth. **47 C3** 51.56N 4.08E
Euskirchen Germany **47 E2** 50.40N 6.47E
Eutin Germany **46 D2** 54.08N 10.38E
Evansville U.S.A. **87 I4** 38.02N 87.24W
Evercreech England **13 E3** 51.08N 2.30W
Everest, Mt. Asia **71 F5** 27.59N 86.56E
Evesham England **16 C2** 52.06N 1.57W
Evje Norway **58 A2** 58.36N 7.51E
Évora Portugal **50 B3** 38.34N 7.54W
Évreux France **48 D5** 49.03N 1.11E
Ewe, L. Scotland **24 C4** 57.52N 5.40W
Exe *r.* England **13 D2** 50.40N 3.28W
Exeter England **13 D2** 50.43N 3.31W
Exmoor Forest *hills* England **13 D3** 51.08N 3.45W
Exmouth England **13 D2** 50.37N 3.24W
Extremadura *d.* Spain **50 B3** 39.00N 6.00W
Exuma Is. Bahamas **93 I4** 24.00N 76.00W
Eyasi, L. Tanzania **106 D4** 3.40S 35.00E
Eye England **15 D3** 52.19N 1.09E
Eyemouth Scotland **27 F2** 55.52N 2.05W
Eygurande France **48 E3** 45.40N 2.26E
Eyre, L. Australia **80 C3** 28.30S 137.25E

F

Fåborg Denmark **46 D3** 55.06N 10.15E
Facatativá Colombia **94 E1** 4.48N 74.32W
Faenza Italy **54 C6** 44.17N 11.52E
Fagernes Norway **58 B3** 60.59N 9.17E
Fagersta Sweden **58 C3** 59.59N 15.49E
Fairbanks U.S.A. **90 D4** 64.50N 147.50W
Fairbourne Wales **18 B2** 52.42N 4.03W
Fair Head N. Ireland **23 C2** 55.14N 6.10W
Fair Isle Scotland **24 G6** 59.32N 1.38W
Fairweather, Mt. U.S.A. **90 E3** 59.00N 137.30W
Faisalabad Pakistan **71 D5** 31.25N 73.09E
Faizabad India **71 E5** 26.46N 82.08E
Fajr, Wadi *r.* Saudi Arabia **68 E3** 30.00N 38.25E
Fakaofu Pacific Oc. **82 I7** 9.30S 171.15W
Fakenham England **15 C3** 52.50N 0.51E
Fakfak Indonesia **79 I3** 2.55S 132.17E
Fakse Bugt *b.* Denmark **46 F3** 55.10N 12.20E
Falaise France **48 C5** 48.54N 0.11W
Falcarragh Rep. of Ire. **28 C5** 55.09N 8.09W
Falcone, C. Italy **54 B4** 40.57N 8.12E
Falkenberg Sweden **58 C2** 56.55N 12.30E
Falkirk Scotland **27 E2** 56.00N 3.48W
Falkland Scotland **27 E3** 56.15N 3.13W
Falkland Is. S. America **97 C2** 52.00S 60.00W
Falmouth England **12 B2** 50.09N 5.05W
Falmouth B. England **12 B2** 50.06N 5.05W
Falster *i.* Denmark **46 F2** 54.30N 12.00E
Falun Sweden **58 C3** 60.37N 15.40E
Famagusta Cyprus **68 D4** 35.07N 33.57E
Fannich, L. Scotland **24 D4** 57.38N 4.58W
Fanö *i.* Denmark **46 B3** 55.25N 8.25E
Fao Iraq **69 H3** 29.57N 48.30E
Faradofay Madagascar **106 G6** 25.01S 47.00E
Farafra Oasis Egypt **68 C2** 27.00N 28.20E
Farah Afghan. **70 B6** 32.23N 62.07E
Farah *r.* Afghan. **70 B5** 31.25N 61.30E
Farallon de Medinilla *i.* Mariana Is. **79 L7** 16.01N 146.04E
Farallon de Pajaros *i.* Mariana Is. **79 K8** 20.33N 144.59E
Faraulep *is.* Mariana Is. **79 K5** 8.36N 144.33E
Farcet Fen England **15 B3** 52.32N 0.11W
Fareham England **14 A1** 50.52N 1.11W
Farewell, C. Greenland **91 N3** 60.00N 44.20W
Fargo U.S.A. **87 G6** 46.52N 96.59W
Faringdon England **14 A2** 51.39N 1.34W
Farnborough Hants. England **15 B2** 51.17N 0.46W
Farndon England **20 C2** 53.06N 2.53W
Farne Is. England **22 C2** 55.38N 1.36W
Farnham England **15 B2** 51.13N 0.49W
Farnworth England **20 C2** 53.33N 2.33W
Faro Portugal **50 B2** 37.01N 7.56W
Faroe Is. Europe **58 L8** 62.00N 7.00W
Fårösund Sweden **58 D2** 57.51N 19.05E
Farrukhabad India **71 E5** 27.23N 79.35E
Fársala Greece **56 F3** 39.17N 22.22E
Farsö Denmark **46 C4** 56.47N 9.20E
Farsund Norway **58 A2** 58.05N 6.49E
Farum Denmark **46 F3** 55.49N 12.20E
Fasa Iran **69 I3** 28.55N 53.38E
Fastov Ukraine **59 B4** 50.08N 29.59E
Fauldhouse Scotland **27 E2** 55.49N 3.41W
Fauske Norway **58 C4** 67.17N 15.25E
Faversham England **15 C2** 51.18N 0.54E
Favignana *i.* Italy **54 D2** 37.57N 12.19E
Fawley England **14 A1** 50.49N 1.20W
Faxaflói *b.* Iceland **58 I7** 64.30N 22.50W
Faxe *r.* Sweden **58 D3** 63.15N 17.15E
Fayetteville U.S.A. **87 K4** 35.03N 78.53W
Fdérik Mauritania **104 A4** 22.30N 12.30W
Feale *r.* Rep. of Ire. **28 B2** 52.28N 9.38W
Fear, C. U.S.A. **87 K3** 33.51N 77.59W
Fécamp France **48 D5** 49.45N 0.23E
Feeagh, Lough Rep. of Ire. **28 B3** 53.55N 9.35W
Fehmarn *i.* Germany **52 E6** 54.30N 11.05E
Feira de Santana Brazil **96 F6** 12.17S 38.53W
Felanitx Spain **51 G3** 39.27N 3.08E
Feldkirch Austria **57 A3** 47.15N 9.38E
Felixstowe England **15 D2** 51.58N 1.20E
Felton England **22 C2** 55.18N 1.42W
Femer Baelt *str.* Denmark/Germany **46 E2** 54.35N 11.20E
Femunden *l.* Norway **58 B3** 62.05N 11.55E
Fengfeng China **75 I4** 36.34N 114.19E
Fengjie China **75 H3** 31.00N 109.30E
Fenyang China **75 H4** 37.14N 111.43E
Feodosiya Ukraine **59 D3** 45.03N 35.23E
Fergana Uzbekistan **60 F2** 40.23N 71.19E
Fergus Falls *town* U.S.A. **87 G6** 46.18N 96.00W
Ferkéssédougou Ivory Coast **104 B2** 9.30N 5.10W
Fermanagh *d.* N. Ireland **23 B1** 54.15N 7.45W
Fermoselle Spain **50 B4** 41.19N 6.24W
Fermoy Rep. of Ire. **28 C2** 52.08N 8.17W
Ferndown England **13 F2** 50.48N 1.55W
Ferozepore India **71 D5** 30.55N 74.38E
Ferrara Italy **54 C6** 44.49N 11.38E
Ferret, Cap *c.* France **48 C3** 44.42N 1.16W
Ferryhill England **22 C1** 54.41N 1.33W
Fethiye Turkey **68 C5** 36.37N 29.06E
Fetlar *i.* Scotland **24 H7** 60.37N 0.52W
Fevzipaşa Turkey **68 E5** 37.07N 36.38E
Fez Morocco **104 B5** 34.05N 5.00W
Ffestiniog Wales **18 C2** 52.58N 3.56W
Ffostrasol Wales **18 B2** 52.06N 4.23W
Fianarantsoa Madagascar **106 G7** 21.27S 47.05E
Fife *d.* Scotland **27 E3** 56.10N 3.10W
Fife Ness *c.* Scotland **27 F3** 56.17N 2.36W
Figeac France **48 E3** 44.32N 2.01E
Figueira da Foz Portugal **50 A4** 40.09N 8.51W
Figueras Spain **51 G5** 42.16N 2.57E
Fiji Pacific Oc. **82 H6** 18.00S 178.00E
Filey England **21 E3** 54.13N 0.18W
Findhorn *r.* Scotland **24 E4** 57.37N 3.40W
Finisterre, C. Spain **50 A5** 42.54N 9.16W
Finland Europe **58 F3** 64.30N 27.00E
Finland, G. of Finland/Estonia **58 F2** 60.00N 26.50E
Finlay *r.* Canada **90 F3** 56.30N 124.40W
Finn *r.* Rep. of Ire. **28 D4** 54.50N 7.30W
Finschhafen P.N.G. **79 L2** 6.35S 147.51E
Fintona N. Ireland **23 B1** 54.29N 7.19W
Fionnphort Scotland **26 B3** 56.19N 6.23W
Firozabad India **71 E5** 27.09N 78.24E
Firth of Clyde *est.* Scotland **26 D2** 55.35N 4.53W
Firth of Forth *est.* Scotland **27 F3** 56.05N 3.00W
Firth of Lorn *est.* Scotland **26 C3** 56.20N 5.40W
Firth of Tay *est.* Scotland **27 E3** 56.24N 3.08W
Firuzabad Iran **69 I3** 28.50N 52.35E
Fisher Str. Canada **91 J4** 63.00N 84.00W
Fishguard Wales **18 B1** 51.59N 4.59W
Fishguard B. Wales **18 B2** 52.06N 4.54W
Flagstaff U.S.A. **86 D4** 35.12N 111.38W
Flåm Norway **58 A3** 60.51N 7.08E
Flamborough England **21 E3** 54.07N 0.07W
Flamborough Head England **21 E3** 54.06N 0.05W
Flaming Gorge Resr. U.S.A. **86 E5** 41.10N 109.30W
Flanders *f.* Belgium **47 B2** 50.52N 3.00E
Flanders East *d.* Belgium **47 B3** 51.00N 3.45E
Flanders West *d.* Belgium **47 A2** 51.00N 3.00E
Flannan Is. Scotland **24 A5** 58.16N 7.40W
Flathead L. U.S.A. **86 D6** 47.50N 114.05W
Flat Holm *i.* England **18 C1** 51.23N 3.08W
Flattery, C. U.S.A. **86 B6** 48.23N 124.43W
Fleet England **15 B2** 51.16N 0.50W
Fleetwood England **20 B2** 53.55N 3.01W
Flekkefjord *town* Norway **58 A2** 58.17N 6.40E
Flen Sweden **58 D2** 59.04N 16.39E
Flensburg Germany **52 D6** 54.47N 9.27E
Flensburg Fjord *b.* Denmark/Germany **46 C2** 54.50N 9.50E
Flers France **48 C5** 48.45N 0.34W
Flimby England **22 A1** 54.42N 3.31W
Flinders *r.* Australia **80 D4** 15.12S 141.40E
Flinders I. Australia **80 D2** 40.00S 148.00E
Flinders Range *mts.* Australia **80 C2** 31.00S 138.30E
Flin Flon Canada **91 H3** 54.47N 101.51W
Flint U.S.A. **87 J5** 43.03N 83.40W
Flint *r.* U.S.A. **87 J3** 30.52N 84.35W
Flint Wales **18 C3** 53.15N 3.07W
Flint I. Kiribati **83 K6** 11.26S 151.48W
Flitwick England **15 B3** 51.59N 0.30W
Florence Italy **54 C5** 43.46N 11.15E
Florence U.S.A. **87 K3** 34.12N 79.44W
Florencia Colombia **94 D1** 1.37N 75.37W
Florenville Belgium **47 D1** 49.42N 5.19E
Flores *i.* Indonesia **79 G2** 8.40S 121.20E
Flores Sea Indonesia **79 G2** 7.00S 121.00E
Florianópolis Brazil **97 E5** 27.35S 48.31W
Florida *d.* U.S.A. **87 J2** 29.00N 82.00W
Florida, Straits of U.S.A. **94 C5** 24.00N 81.00W
Flórina Greece **56 E4** 40.48N 21.25E
Florö Norway **58 A3** 61.45N 4.55E
Flushing Neth. **47 B3** 51.27N 3.35E
Fly *r.* P.N.G. **79 K2** 8.22S 142.23E
Focşani Romania **59 B3** 45.40N 27.12E
Foggia Italy **54 E4** 41.28N 15.33E
Föhr *i.* Germany **46 B2** 54.44N 8.30E
Foix France **48 D2** 42.57N 1.35E
Folda *est.* N. Trönd. Norway **58 B4** 64.45N 11.20E
Foligno Italy **54 D5** 42.56N 12.43E
Folkestone England **15 D2** 51.05N 1.11E
Folkingham England **17 D2** 52.54N 0.24W
Fond du Lac Canada **90 H3** 59.20N 107.09W
Fonseca, G. of Honduras **93 G2** 13.10N 87.30W
Fontainebleau France **48 E5** 48.24N 2.42E
Fontenay France **48 C4** 46.28N 0.48W
Ford Scotland **26 C3** 56.10N 5.26W
Fordingbridge England **14 A1** 50.56N 1.48W
Foreland *c.* England **14 A1** 50.42N 1.06W
Foreland Pt. England **13 D3** 51.15N 3.47W
Forel, Mt. Greenland **91 O4** 67.00N 37.00W
Forest of Atholl *f.* Scotland **24 E3** 56.53N 3.55W
Forest of Bowland *hills* England **20 C2** 53.57N 2.30W
Forest of Dean *f.* England **13 E3** 51.48N 2.32W
Forest of Rossendale *f.* England **20 C2** 53.43N 2.15W
Forest Row England **15 C2** 51.06N 0.03E
Forfar Scotland **27 F3** 56.38N 2.54W
Forlì Italy **54 D6** 44.13N 12.02E
Formby England **20 B2** 53.34N 3.04W
Formby Pt. England **20 B2** 53.34N 3.07W
Formentera *i.* Spain **50 F3** 38.41N 1.30E
Fornaes *c.* Denmark **46 D4** 56.28N 10.58E
Forres Scotland **24 E4** 57.37N 3.38W
Forssa Finland **58 E3** 60.49N 23.40E
Forst Germany **52 G4** 51.46N 14.39E
Fort Albany Canada **91 J3** 52.15N 81.35W
Fortaleza Brazil **96 F7** 3.45S 38.45W
Fort Augustus Scotland **24 D4** 57.09N 4.41W
Fort Chimo Canada **91 L3** 58.10N 68.15W
Fort Chipewyan Canada **90 G3** 58.46N 111.09W
Fort Collins U.S.A. **86 E5** 40.35N 105.05W
Fort-de-France Martinique **93 L2** 14.36N 61.05W
Fort Frances Canada **91 I2** 48.37N 93.23W
Fort George Canada **91 K3** 53.50N 79.01W
Fort Good Hope Canada **90 F4** 66.16N 128.37W
Forth Scotland **27 E2** 55.46N 3.42W
Forth *r.* Scotland **27 E3** 56.06N 3.48W
Fort Lauderdale U.S.A. **87 J2** 26.08N 80.08W
Fort Liard Canada **90 F4** 60.14N 123.28W
Fort McMurray Canada **90 G3** 56.45N 111.27W
Fort McPherson Canada **90 E4** 67.29N 134.50W
Fort Myers U.S.A. **87 J2** 26.39N 81.51W
Fort Nelson Canada **90 F3** 58.48N 122.44W
Fort Norman Canada **90 F4** 64.55N 125.29W
Fort Peck Dam U.S.A. **86 E6** 47.55N 106.15W
Fort Peck Resr. U.S.A. **86 E6** 47.55N 107.00W
Fort Randall U.S.A. **90 B3** 55.10N 162.47W
Fort Reliance Canada **90 H4** 62.45N 109.08W
Fort Resolution Canada **90 G4** 61.10N 113.39W
Fortrose Scotland **24 D4** 57.34N 4.07W
Fort Rupert Canada **91 K3** 51.30N 79.45W
Fort Scott U.S.A. **87 H4** 37.52N 94.43W
Fort Severn Canada **91 J3** 56.00N 87.40W
Fort Shevchenko Kazakhstan **60 E2** 44.31N 50.15E
Fort Sibut C.A.R. **104 D2** 5.46N 19.06E
Fort Simpson Canada **90 F4** 61.46N 121.15W
Fort Smith Canada **90 G4** 60.00N 111.51W
Fort Smith *d.* Canada **90 G4** 63.30N 118.00W
Fort Smith U.S.A. **87 H4** 35.22N 94.27W
Fort St. John Canada **90 F3** 56.14N 120.55W
Fortuneswell England **13 E2** 50.33N 2.27W
Fort Vermilion Canada **90 G3** 58.22N 115.59W
Fort Wayne U.S.A. **87 I5** 41.05N 85.08W
Fort William Scotland **24 C3** 56.49N 5.07W
Fort Worth U.S.A. **87 G3** 32.45N 97.20W
Fort Yukon U.S.A. **90 D4** 66.35N 145.20W
Foshan China **75 H2** 23.03N 113.08E
Fougères France **48 C5** 48.21N 1.12W
Foula *i.* Scotland **24 F7** 60.08N 2.05W
Foulness I. England **15 C2** 51.35N 0.55E
Foulness Pt. England **15 C2** 51.37N 1.00E
Fowey England **12 C2** 50.20N 4.39W
Foxe Basin *b.* Canada **91 K4** 67.30N 79.00W
Foxe Channel Canada **91 J4** 65.00N 80.00W
Foyle *r.* N. Ireland **23 B1** 55.00N 7.20W
Foyle, Lough Rep. of Ire./N. Ireland **23 B2** 55.07N 7.06W
Framlingham England **15 D3** 52.14N 1.20E
France Europe **48 C4** 47.00N 2.00E
Francistown Botswana **106 C2** 21.11S 27.32E
Frankfort U.S.A. **87 J4** 38.11N 84.53W
Frankfurt Brandenburg Germany **52 G5** 52.20N 14.32E
Frankfurt Hessen Germany **52 D4** 50.06N 8.41E
Franklin D. Roosevelt L. U.S.A. **86 C6** 47.55N 118.20W
Franz Josef Land *is.* Russian Fed. **60 E5** 81.00N 54.00E
Fraser *r.* Canada **90 F2** 49.05N 123.00W
Fraserburgh Scotland **24 G4** 57.42N 2.00W
Fredericia Denmark **46 C3** 55.34N 9.47E
Fredericksburg U.S.A. **87 K4** 38.18N 77.30W
Fredericton Canada **91 L2** 45.57N 66.40W
Frederiksborg *d.* Denmark **46 F3** 55.50N 12.10E
Frederikshåb Greenland **91 N4** 62.05N 49.30W
Frederikshavn Denmark **46 D5** 57.28N 10.33E
Frederikssund Denmark **46 F3** 55.51N 12.04E
Fredrikstad Norway **58 B2** 59.15N 10.55E
Freeport Bahamas **93 I5** 26.40N 78.30W
Freetown Sierra Leone **104 A2** 8.30N 13.17W
Freiberg Germany **52 F4** 50.54N 13.20E
Freiburg Germany **52 C2** 48.00N 7.52E
Freilingen Germany **47 F2** 50.33N 7.50E
Freising Germany **52 E3** 48.24N 11.45E
Fréjus France **48 G2** 43.26N 6.44E
Freshford Rep. of Ire. **28 D2** 52.43N 7.25W
Fresno U.S.A. **86 C4** 36.41N 119.57W
Fribourg Switz. **52 C2** 46.50N 7.10E
Friedrichshafen Germany **52 D2** 47.39N 9.29E
Friedrichstadt Germany **46 C2** 54.23N 9.07E
Friesland *d.* Neth. **47 D5** 53.05N 5.45E
Friesoythe Germany **47 F5** 53.02N 7.52E
Frinton England **15 D2** 51.50N 1.16E
Frio, Cabo *c.* Brazil **97 E5** 22.50S 42.10W
Frisa, Loch Scotland **26 B3** 56.33N 6.05W
Frisian Is. Europe **40 G5** 53.30N 6.00E
Frobisher B. Canada **91 L4** 63.00N 66.45W
Frobisher Bay *town* Canada **91 L4** 63.45N 68.30W
Frodsham England **20 C2** 53.17N 2.45W
Frohavet *est.* Norway **58 B3** 63.55N 9.05E
Frome England **13 E3** 51.16N 2.17W
Frome, L. Australia **80 C2** 30.45S 139.45E
Frosinone Italy **54 D4** 41.36N 13.21E
Fröya *i.* Norway **58 B3** 63.45N 8.30E
Frýdek-Místek Czech Rep. **57 F4** 49.41N 18.22E
Fuerte *r.* Mexico **92 C5** 25.42N 109.20W
Fuerteventura *i.* Canary Is. **104 A4** 28.20N 14.10W
Fujairah U.A.E. **69 J2** 25.10N 56.20E
Fujian *d.* China **75 I3** 26.30N 118.00E
Fujin China **75 K6** 47.15N 131.59E
Fujiyama *mtn.* Japan **76 D4** 35.23N 138.42E
Fukui Japan **76 C5** 36.04N 136.12E
Fukuoka Japan **76 A3** 33.39N 130.21E
Fukushima Japan **76 D5** 37.44N 140.28E
Fukuyama Japan **76 B4** 34.29N 133.21E
Fulda Germany **52 D4** 50.35N 9.45E
Fumay France **47 C1** 49.59N 4.42E
Funabashi Japan **76 D4** 35.42N 139.59E
Funafuti Tuvalu **82 H7** 8.31S 179.13E
Funchal Madeira Is. **104 A5** 32.38N 16.54W
Fundy, B. of N. America **87 M5** 44.30N 66.30W
Fünen *i.* Denmark **46 D3** 55.15N 10.30E
Furakawa Japan **76 D6** 38.30N 140.50E
Furg Iran **69 I3** 28.19N 55.10E
Furnas Dam Brazil **97 E5** 20.40S 46.22W
Furneaux Group *is.* Australia **82 E3** 40.10S 148.05E
Furnes Belgium **47 A3** 51.04N 2.40E
Fürstenau Germany **47 F4** 52.32N 7.41E
Fürstenwalde Germany **52 F5** 52.22N 14.04E
Fürth Germany **52 E3** 49.28N 11.00E
Fusagasugá Colombia **94 E1** 4.22N 74.21W
Fushun China **75 J5** 41.51N 123.53E
Futa Jalon *f.* Guinea **104 A3** 11.30N 12.30W
Fuxin China **75 J5** 42.08N 121.39E
Fuyu China **75 J6** 45.12N 124.49E
Fuzhou Fujian China **75 I3** 26.01N 119.20E
Fuzhou Jiangxi China **75 I3** 28.03N 116.15E
Fyne, Loch Scotland **26 C2** 55.55N 5.23W
Fyns *d.* Denmark **46 D3** 55.10N 10.30E

G

Gabès Tunisia **104 D5** 33.52N 10.06E
Gabès, G. of Tunisia **104 D5** 34.00N 11.00E
Gabon Africa **106 B4** 0.00 12.00E
Gaborone Botswana **106 C2** 24.45S 25.55E
Gach Saran Iran **69 H3** 30.13N 50.49E
Gadsden U.S.A. **87 I3** 34.00N 86.00W
Gaeta Italy **54 D4** 41.13N 13.35E
Gaeta, G. of Med. Sea **54 D4** 41.05N 13.30E
Gaferut *i.* Caroline Is. **79 L5** 9.14N 145.23E
Gagnon Canada **91 L3** 51.56N 68.16W
Gaillac France **48 D2** 43.54N 1.53E
Gainesville U.S.A. **87 J2** 29.37N 82.31W
Gainford England **22 C1** 54.34N 1.44W
Gainsborough England **16 D3** 53.23N 0.46W
Gairdner, L. Australia **80 C2** 31.30S 136.00E
Gairloch *town* Scotland **24 C4** 57.43N 5.41W
Galapagos Is. Pacific Oc. **83 Q7** 0.30S 90.30W
Galashiels Scotland **27 F2** 55.37N 2.49W
Galati Romania **59 B3** 45.27N 27.59E
Galena U.S.A. **90 C4** 64.43N 157.00W
Galicia *d.* Spain **50 A5** 43.00N 8.00W
Galle Sri Lanka **71 E1** 6.01N 80.13E
Gállego *r.* Spain **50 E4** 41.40N 0.55W
Galley Head Rep. of Ire. **28 C1** 51.31N 8.57W
Gallinas, C. Colombia **94 E3** 12.20N 71.30W
Gallipoli Italy **54 G4** 40.02N 18.01E
Gallipoli Turkey **68 B6** 40.25N 26.31E
Gällivare Sweden **58 E4** 67.10N 20.40E
Galloway *f.* Scotland **26 D2** 55.00N 4.28W
Gallup U.S.A. **86 E4** 35.32N 108.46W
Galston Scotland **26 D2** 55.36N 4.23W
Galtby Finland **58 E3** 60.08N 21.33E
Galty Mts. Rep. of Ire. **28 C2** 52.20N 8.10W
Galveston U.S.A. **87 H2** 29.17N 94.48W
Galveston B. U.S.A. **87 H2** 29.40N 94.40W
Galway Rep. of Ire. **28 B3** 53.17N 9.04W
Galway *d.* Rep. of Ire. **28 B3** 53.25N 9.00W
Galway B. Rep. of Ire. **28 B3** 53.12N 9.07W
Gambia Africa **104 A3** 13.30N 15.00W
Gambia *r.* Gambia **104 A3** 13.28N 15.55W
Gambier, Îles *is.* Pacific Oc. **83 M5** 23.10S 135.00W
Gander Canada **91 M2** 48.58N 54.34W
Gandía Spain **50 E3** 38.59N 0.11W
Ganges *r.* India **71 G4** 23.30N 90.25E
Ganges, Mouths of the India/Bangla. **71 F4** 22.00N 89.35E
Gangtok India **71 F5** 27.20N 88.39E
Gannat France **48 E4** 46.06N 3.11E
Gannett Peak *mtn.* U.S.A. **86 E5** 43.10N 109.38W
Gansu *d.* China **74 G4** 36.00N 103.00E
Ganzhou China **75 I2** 25.52N 114.51E
Gao Mali **104 C3** 16.19N 0.09W
Gaoxiong Taiwan **75 J2** 22.36N 120.17E
Gap France **48 G3** 44.33N 6.05E
Gara, Lough Rep. of Ire. **28 C3** 53.56N 8.28W
Gard *r.* France **48 F2** 43.52N 4.40E
Garda, L. Italy **54 C6** 45.40N 10.40E
Garelochhead Scotland **26 D3** 56.05N 4.49W
Garforth England **21 D2** 53.48N 1.22W
Garissa Kenya **106 D4** 0.27S 39.39E
Garlieston Scotland **26 D1** 54.46N 4.22W
Garmisch Partenkirchen Germany **52 E2** 47.30N 11.05E
Garonne *r.* France **48 C3** 45.00N 0.37W
Garoua Cameroon **104 D2** 9.17N 13.22E
Garrison Resr. U.S.A. **86 F6** 47.30N 102.20W
Garroch Head Scotland **26 C2** 55.43N 5.02W
Garron Pt. N. Ireland **23 D2** 55.03N 5.58W
Garry L. Canada **91 I4** 66.00N 100.00W
Garstang England **20 C2** 53.53N 2.47W
Garth Wales **18 C2** 52.08N 3.32W
Garthorpe England **21 E2** 53.40N 0.42W
Garut Indonesia **78 D2** 7.15S 107.55E
Garvagh N. Ireland **23 C1** 54.59N 6.42W
Garvão Portugal **50 A2** 37.42N 8.21W
Garve Scotland **24 D4** 57.37N 4.41W

Langeoog *i.* Germany 47 F5 53.46N 7.30E
Langeskov Denmark 46 D3 55.21N 10.32E
Langholm Scotland 27 E2 55.09N 3.00W
Langkawi *i.* Malaysia 78 B5 6.20N 99.30E
Langness *c.* I.o.M. 20 A3 54.03N 4.37W
Langon France 48 C3 44.33N 0.14W
Langöy *i.* Norway 58 C5 68.50N 15.00E
Langport England 13 E3 51.02N 2.51W
Langres France 48 F4 47.53N 5.20E
Langsa Indonesia 78 B4 4.28N 97.59E
Långseleån *r.* Sweden 58 D3 63.30N 16.53E
Lang Son Vietnam 78 D8 21.50N 106.55E
Langstrothdale Chase *hills* England 20 C3 54.13N 2.15W
Lannion France 48 B5 48.44N 3.27W
Lansing U.S.A. 87 J5 42.44N 84.34W
Lanzarote *i.* Canary Is. 104 A4 29.00N 13.55W
Lanzhou China 74 G4 36.01N 103.45E
Laoag Phil. 79 G7 18.14N 120.36E
Laois *d.* Rep. of Ire. 28 D2 53.00N 7.20W
Laokay Vietnam 78 C8 22.30N 104.00E
Laon France 47 B1 49.34N 3.37E
La Oroya Peru 96 B6 11.36S 75.54W
Laos Asia 78 C7 19.00N 104.00E
La Palma *i.* Canary Is. 104 A4 28.50N 18.00W
La Palma Spain 50 B2 37.23N 6.33W
La Paragua Venezuela 95 G2 6.53N 63.22W
La Paz Bolivia 96 C6 16.30S 68.10W
La Paz Mexico 92 B4 24.10N 110.17W
La Peña, Sierra de *mts.* Spain 50 E5 42.30N 0.50W
La Perouse Str. Russian Fed. 61 L2 45.50N 142.30E
Lapford England 13 D2 50.52N 3.49W
Lapland *f.* Sweden/Finland 58 E5 68.10N 24.00E
La Plata Argentina 97 D4 34.52S 57.55W
La Plata, Río de *est.* S. America 97 D4 35.15S 56.45W
Lappajärvi *l.* Finland 58 E3 63.05N 23.30E
Lappeenranta Finland 58 G3 61.04N 28.05E
Laptev Sea Russian Fed. 61 K4 74.30N 125.00E
L'Aquila Italy 54 D5 42.22N 13.25E
Lar Iran 69 I2 27.37N 54.16E
Laramie U.S.A. 86 E5 41.20N 105.38W
Laramie Mts. U.S.A. 86 E5 42.00N 105.40W
Larbert Scotland 27 E3 56.02N 3.51W
Larch *r.* Canada 91 L3 57.40N 69.30W
Laredo U.S.A. 86 G2 27.32N 99.22W
Largo Ward Scotland 27 F3 56.15N 2.52W
Largs Scotland 26 D2 55.48N 4.52W
La Rioja Argentina 97 C5 29.26S 66.50W
La Rioja *d.* Spain 50 D5 42.15N 2.30W
Lárisa Greece 56 F3 39.36N 22.24E
Lark *r.* England 15 C3 52.26N 0.20E
Larkana Pakistan 70 C5 27.32N 68.18E
Larkhall Scotland 27 E2 55.45N 3.59W
Larnaca Cyprus 68 D4 34.54N 33.39E
Larne N. Ireland 23 D1 54.51N 5.50W
Larne Lough N. Ireland 23 D1 54.50N 5.47W
La Roche Belgium 47 D2 50.11N 5.35E
La Rochelle France 48 C4 46.10N 1.10W
La Roche-sur-Yon France 48 C4 46.40N 1.25W
La Roda Spain 50 D3 39.13N 2.10W
La Romana Dom. Rep. 93 K3 18.27N 68.57W
La Ronge Canada 90 H3 55.07N 105.18W
Larvik Norway 58 B2 59.04N 10.02E
La Sagra *mtn.* Spain 50 D2 37.58N 2.35W
Las Cruces U.S.A. 86 E3 32.18N 106.47W
La Seine, Baie de France 48 C5 49.40N 0.30W
Lashio Myanma 71 H4 22.58N 97.48E
Las Palmas Canary Is. 104 A4 28.08N 15.27W
Las Perlas, Archipelago de Panama 93 I1 8.45N 79.30W
La Spezia Italy 54 B6 44.07N 9.49E
Lastovo *i.* Croatia 56 C5 42.45N 16.52E
Las Vegas U.S.A. 86 C4 36.10N 115.10W
Latakia Syria 68 D4 35.31N 35.47E
Latvia Europe 58 C3 57.00N 25.00E
Lauchhammer Germany 52 F4 51.30N 13.48E
Lauder Scotland 27 F2 55.43N 2.45W
Lauderdale *f.* Scotland 27 F2 55.43N 2.42W
Laugharne Wales 18 B1 51.45N 4.28W
Lau Group *is.* Fiji 82 I6 19.00S 178.30W
Launceston Australia 80 D1 41.25S 147.07E
Launceston England 12 C2 50.38N 4.21W
Laurencekirk Scotland 24 F3 56.50N 2.30W
Lauritsala Finland 58 G3 61.05N 28.20E
Lausanne Switz. 52 C2 46.32N 6.39E
Laut *i.* Indonesia 78 F3 3.45S 116.20E
Lauterecken Germany 47 F1 49.39N 7.36E
Lavagh More *mtn.* Rep. of Ire. 28 C4 54.45N 8.07W
Laval France 48 C5 48.04N 0.45W
La Vega Dom. Rep. 93 J3 19.15N 70.33W
Lavernock Pt. Wales 18 C1 51.25N 3.10W
Lawra Ghana 108 A3 10.40N 2.49W
Laxey I.o.M. 20 A3 54.14N 4.24W
Laysan *i.* Hawaiian Is. 82 I10 25.46N 171.44W
Leadburn Scotland 27 E2 55.47N 3.14W
Leadhills Scotland 27 E2 55.25N 3.46W
Leaf *r.* Canada 91 K3 58.47N 70.06W
Leatherhead England 15 B2 51.18N 0.20W
Lebanon Asia 68 D4 34.00N 36.00E
Łebork Poland 57 E7 54.33N 17.44E
Lebrija Spain 50 B2 36.55N 6.10W
Le Cateau France 47 B2 50.07N 3.33E
Lecce Italy 54 G4 40.21N 18.11E
Lech *r.* Germany 52 E3 48.45N 10.51E
Le Chesne France 47 C1 49.31N 4.46E
Lechlade England 13 F3 51.42N 1.40W
Le Creusot France 48 F4 46.48N 4.27E
Lectoure France 48 D2 43.56N 0.38E
Ledbury England 16 B2 52.03N 2.25W
Ledesma Spain 50 C4 41.05N 6.00W
Lee *r.* Rep. of Ire. 28 C1 51.53N 8.25W
Leech L. U.S.A. 87 H6 47.10N 94.30W
Leeds England 21 D2 53.48N 1.34W
Leek England 16 B3 53.07N 2.02W
Leer Germany 47 F5 53.14N 7.27E
Leeuwarden Neth. 47 D5 53.12N 5.48E
Leeuwin, C. Australia 80 A2 34.00S 115.00E
Leeward Is. C. America 93 L3 18.00N 61.00W
Legazpi Phil. 79 G6 13.10N 123.45E
Leghorn Italy 54 C5 43.33N 10.18E
Legionowo Poland 57 G6 52.25N 20.56E
Legnica Poland 57 E5 51.12N 16.10E
Leh Jammu & Kashmir 71 D6 34.09N 77.35E
Le Havre France 48 D5 49.30N 0.06E
Leicester England 16 C2 52.39N 1.09W
Leicestershire *d.* England 16 C2 52.29N 1.10W
Leiden Neth. 47 C4 52.10N 4.30E
Leie *r.* Belgium 47 B3 51.03N 3.44E
Leigh G.M. England 20 C2 53.30N 2.33W
Leighton Buzzard England 15 B2 51.55N 0.39W
Leipzig Germany 52 F4 51.20N 12.20E
Leiston England 15 D3 52.13N 1.35E
Leith Scotland 27 E2 55.59N 2.09W
Leith Hill England 15 B2 51.11N 0.21W
Leitrim *d.* Rep. of Ire. 28 D4 54.08N 8.00W
Leizhou Pen. China 75 H2 20.40N 109.30E
Lek *r.* Neth. 47 C3 51.55N 4.29E
Lelystad Neth. 47 D4 52.32N 5.29E
Le Mans France 48 D5 48.01N 0.10E
Lemmer Neth. 47 D4 52.50N 5.43E
Lemmon U.S.A. 86 F6 45.56N 102.00W
Lemvig Denmark 46 B4 56.33N 8.19E
Lena *r.* Russian Fed. 61 K4 72.00N 127.10E
Lena Mts. Russian Fed. 64 N9 61.00N 115.00E
Lengerich Germany 47 F4 52.12N 7.52E
Lenina Canal Russian Fed. 59 F2 43.46N 45.00E
Lenina, Peak *mtn.* Tajikistan 74 B5 39.20N 72.55E
Leninogorsk Kazakhstan 60 G2 50.23N 83.32E
Leninsk Kuznetskiy Russian Fed. 60 H3 54.44N 86.13E
Lenkoran Azerbaijan 69 H5 38.45N 48.50E
Lenne *r.* Germany 47 F3 51.24N 7.30E
Lennoxtown Scotland 26 D2 55.59N 4.12W
Lens France 47 A2 50.26N 2.50E
Leominster England 16 B2 52.15N 2.43W
León Mexico 92 D4 21.10N 101.42W
León Nicaragua 93 G2 12.24N 86.52W
Léon Spain 50 C5 42.35N 5.34W
Le Puy France 48 E3 45.03N 3.54E
Le Quesnoy France 47 B2 50.15N 3.39E
Lerma Spain 50 D5 42.02N 3.46W
Lerwick Scotland 24 G7 60.09N 1.09W
Les Cayes Haiti 93 J3 18.15N 73.46W
Les Ecrins *mtn.* France 48 G3 44.50N 6.20E
Leshan China 74 G3 29.34N 103.42E
Leskovac Yugo. 56 E5 43.00N 21.56E
Leslie Scotland 27 E3 56.13N 3.13W
Lesmahagow Scotland 27 E2 55.38N 3.54W
Lesotho Africa 106 C2 29.30S 28.00E
Les Sables d'Olonne France 48 C4 46.30N 1.47W
Lesser Antilles *is.* C. America 93 K2 13.00N 65.00W
Lesser Slave L. Canada 90 G3 55.30N 115.00W
Lesser Sunda Is. Indonesia 78 F2 8.30S 118.00E
Lessines Belgium 47 B2 50.43N 3.50E
Lésvos *i.* Greece 68 B5 39.10N 26.16E
Leszno Poland 57 E5 51.51N 16.35E
Letchworth England 15 B2 51.58N 0.13W
Lethbridge Canada 90 G2 49.43N 112.48W
Lethem Guyana 95 H1 3.23N 59.48W
Letícia Colombia 96 C7 4.09S 69.57W
Leti Is. Indonesia 79 H2 8.20S 128.00E
Le Tréport France 48 D6 50.04N 1.22E
Letterkenny Rep. of Ire. 28 D4 54.56N 7.45W
Leuser *mtn.* Indonesia 78 B4 3.50N 97.10E
Leuze Hainaut Belgium 47 B2 50.36N 3.37E
Leven England 21 E2 53.54N 0.18W
Leven Scotland 27 F3 56.12N 3.00W
Leven, Loch Scotland 27 E3 56.13N 3.23W
Le Verdon France 48 C3 45.33N 1.04W
Leverkusen Germany 47 E3 51.02N 6.59E
Levis Canada 91 K2 46.47N 71.12W
Levkás *i.* Greece 56 E3 38.44N 20.37E
Lewes England 15 C1 50.53N 0.02E
Lewis *i.* Scotland 24 B5 58.10N 6.40W
Lexington U.S.A. 87 J4 38.02N 84.30W
Leyburn England 20 D3 54.19N 1.50W
Leyland England 20 C2 53.41N 2.42W
Leysdown-on-Sea England 15 C2 51.23N 0.57E
Leyte *i.* Phil. 79 G6 10.40N 124.50E
Lezignan France 48 E2 43.12N 2.46E
Lhasa China 74 E3 29.41N 91.10E
Lhokseumawe Indonesia 78 B5 5.09N 97.09E
Lianyungang China 75 I4 34.37N 119.10E
Liaocheng China 75 I4 36.29N 115.55E
Liaodong B. China 75 J5 40.20N 121.00E
Liaodong Pen. China 75 J5 40.00N 122.50E
Liaoning *d.* China 75 J5 41.30N 123.00E
Liaoyang China 75 J5 41.16N 123.12E
Liaoyuan China 75 J5 42.53N 125.10E
Liard *r.* Canada 90 F4 61.56N 120.35W
Libenge Zaïre 106 B5 3.39N 18.39E
Liberal U.S.A. 86 F4 37.03N 100.56W
Liberec Czech Rep. 57 D5 50.48N 15.05E
Liberia Africa 104 B2 6.30N 9.30W
Liberia Costa Rica 93 G2 10.39N 85.28W
Libourne France 48 C3 44.55N 0.14W
Libreville Gabon 106 A5 0.30N 9.25E
Libya Africa 104 D4 26.30N 17.00E
Libyan Desert Africa 105 E4 25.00N 26.10E
Libyan Plateau *f.* Africa 68 B3 30.45N 26.00E
Licata Italy 54 D2 37.07N 13.58E
Lichfield England 16 C2 52.40N 1.50W
Lichinga Mozambique 106 D3 13.19S 35.13E
Liddesdale *f.* Scotland 27 F2 55.10N 2.50W
Lidköping Sweden 58 C2 58.30N 13.10E
Liechtenstein Europe 52 D2 47.08N 9.35E
Liège Belgium 47 D2 50.38N 5.35E
Liège *d.* Belgium 47 D2 50.32N 5.35E
Lieksa Finland 58 G3 63.13N 30.01E
Lienz Austria 57 C3 46.50N 12.47E
Liepāja Latvia 58 E2 56.30N 21.00E
Lier Belgium 47 C3 51.08N 4.35E
Liévin France 47 A2 50.27N 2.49E
Liffey *r.* Rep. of Ire. 28 E3 53.21N 6.14W
Ligurian Sea Med. Sea 54 B5 43.30N 9.00E
Lihue Hawaii U.S.A. 86 O9 21.59N 159.23W
Likasi Zaïre 106 C3 10.58S 26.47E
Lille France 47 B2 50.39N 3.05E
Lille Baelt *str.* Denmark 46 C3 55.10N 9.50E
Lillehammer Norway 58 B3 61.06N 10.27E
Lillers France 47 A2 50.34N 2.29E
Lilleström Norway 58 B2 59.58N 11.05E
Lilongwe Malaŵi 106 D3 13.58S 33.49E
Lim *r.* Yugo. 56 D5 43.45N 19.13E
Lima Peru 96 B6 12.06S 77.03W
Lima *r.* Portugal 50 A4 41.40N 8.50W
Limassol Cyprus 68 D4 34.40N 33.03E
Limavady N. Ireland 23 C2 55.03N 6.57W
Limbang Malaysia 78 F4 4.50N 115.00E
Limbourg Belgium 47 D2 50.36N 5.57E
Limbourg *d.* Belgium 47 D3 51.00N 5.30E
Limburg *d.* Neth. 47 D3 51.15N 5.45E
Limerick Rep. of Ire. 28 C2 52.40N 8.37W
Limerick *d.* Rep. of Ire. 28 C2 52.40N 8.37W
Limfjorden *str.* Denmark 46 C4 56.55N 9.10E
Límnos *i.* Greece 56 G3 39.55N 25.14E
Limoges France 48 D3 45.50N 1.15E
Límon Costa Rica 93 H2 10.00N 83.01W
Limpopo *r.* Mozambique 106 D2 25.14S 33.33E
Lina Saudi Arabia 69 F3 28.48N 43.45E
Linares Mexico 92 E4 24.54N 99.38W
Linares Spain 50 D3 38.05N 3.38W
Lincang China 74 F2 24.00N 100.10E
Lincoln England 17 D3 53.14N 0.32W
Lincoln Nebr. U.S.A. 87 G5 40.49N 96.41W
Lincoln Edge *hills* England 17 D3 53.13N 0.31W
Lincolnshire *d.* England 17 D3 53.14N 0.32W
Lincoln Wolds *hills* England 17 D3 53.22N 0.08W
Lindesnes *c.* Norway 58 A2 58.00N 7.05E
Line Is. Pacific Oc. 83 K7 3.00S 155.00W
Lingayen Phil. 79 G7 16.02N 120.14E
Lingen Germany 47 F4 52.32N 7.19E
Lingfield England 15 B2 51.11N 0.01W
Lingga *i.* Indonesia 78 C3 0.20S 104.30E
Linköping Sweden 58 C2 58.25N 15.35E
Linlithgow Scotland 27 E2 55.58N 3.36W
Linney Head Wales 18 A1 51.37N 5.05W
Linnhe, Loch Scotland 26 C3 56.35N 5.25W
Linosa *i.* Italy 54 D1 35.52N 12.50E
Linslade England 15 B2 51.55N 0.40W
Lintan China 74 G4 34.39N 103.40E
Linton England 15 C3 52.06N 0.19E
Linxe France 48 C2 43.56N 1.10W
Linxia China 74 G4 35.31N 103.08E
Linz Austria 57 D4 48.19N 14.18E
Lions, G. of France 48 F2 43.12N 4.15E
Lipari Is. Italy 54 E3 38.35N 14.45E
Lipetsk Russian Fed. 59 D4 52.37N 39.36E
Liphook England 15 B2 51.05N 0.49W
Lippe *r.* Germany 47 E3 51.38N 6.37E
Lippstadt Germany 52 D4 51.41N 8.20E
Lisala Zaïre 106 C5 2.08N 21.37E
Lisboa *see* Lisbon Portugal 50
Lisbon Portugal 50 A3 38.44N 9.08W
Lisburn N. Ireland 23 C1 54.31N 6.03W
Lisburne, C. U.S.A. 90 B4 69.00N 165.50W
Liscannor B. Rep. of Ire. 28 B2 52.55N 9.25W
Lishui China 75 I3 28.30N 119.59E
Lisianski *i.* Hawaiian Is. 82 I10 26.04N 173.58W
Lisichansk Ukraine 60 D2 48.53N 38.25E
Liskeard England 12 C2 50.27N 4.29W
Liski Russian Fed. 59 D4 51.00N 39.30E
Lismore Australia 80 E3 28.48S 153.17E
Lismore Rep. of Ire. 28 D2 52.08N 7.59W
Lismore *i.* Scotland 26 C3 56.31N 5.30W
Lisnaskea N. Ireland 23 B1 54.15N 7.28W
Liss England 15 B2 51.03N 0.53W
Listowel Rep. of Ire. 28 B2 52.27N 9.30W
Lithuania Europe 58 E1 55.00N 24.00E
Little Andaman *i.* India 71 G2 10.50N 92.38E
Little Cayman *i.* Cayman Is. 93 H3 19.40N 80.00W
Little Coco *i.* Myanma 78 A6 13.50N 93.10E
Little Fen *f.* England 15 C3 52.18N 0.30E
Littlehampton England 15 B1 50.48N 0.32W
Little Inagua *i.* Bahamas 93 J4 21.30N 73.00W
Little Ouse *r.* England 15 C3 52.34N 0.20E
Littleport England 15 C3 52.27N 0.18E
Little Rock *town* U.S.A. 87 H3 34.42N 92.17W
Little St. Bernard Pass France/Italy 54 A6 45.40N 6.53E
Little Zab *r.* Iraq 69 F4 35.15N 43.27E
Liuzhou China 75 H2 24.17N 109.15E
Livermore, Mt. U.S.A. 86 F3 30.39N 104.11W
Liverpool Canada 91 L2 44.03N 64.43W
Liverpool England 20 C2 53.25N 3.00W
Liverpool B. England 20 B2 53.30N 3.10W
Livingston Scotland 27 E2 55.54N 3.31W
Livingstone *see* Maramba Zambia 106
Lizard England 12 B1 49.58N 5.12W
Lizard Pt. England 12 B1 49.57N 5.15W
Ljubljana Slovenia 56 B7 46.04N 14.28E
Ljungan *r.* Sweden 58 D3 62.20N 17.19E
Ljungby Sweden 58 C2 56.49N 13.55E
Ljusdal Sweden 58 D3 61.49N 16.09E
Ljusnan *r.* Sweden 58 D3 61.15N 17.08E
Ljusnarsberg Sweden 58 C2 59.48N 14.57E
Llanbedr Wales 18 B2 52.40N 4.07W
Llanberis Wales 18 B3 53.07N 4.07W
Llanbister Wales 18 C2 52.22N 3.19W
Llandeilo Wales 18 B1 51.54N 4.00W
Llandovery Wales 18 C1 51.59N 3.49W
Llandrillo Wales 18 C2 52.55N 3.25W
Llandrindod Wells Wales 18 C2 52.15N 3.23W
Llandudno Wales 18 C3 53.19N 3.49W
Llandyssul Wales 18 B2 52.03N 4.20W
Llanelli Wales 18 B1 51.41N 4.11W
Llanerchymedd Wales 18 B3 53.20N 4.22W
Llanes Spain 50 C5 43.25N 4.45W
Llanfair-ar-y-bryn Wales 18 C2 52.04N 3.43W
Llanfair Caereinion Wales 18 C2 52.39N 3.20W
Llanfairfechan Wales 18 C3 53.15N 3.58W
Llanfihangel-Ystrad Wales 18 B2 52.11N 4.11W
Llanfyllin Wales 18 C2 52.47N 3.17W
Llangadfan Wales 18 C2 52.41N 3.28W
Llangadog Wales 18 C1 51.56N 3.53W
Llangefni Wales 18 B3 53.15N 4.20W
Llangollen Wales 18 C2 52.58N 3.10W
Llangynog Wales 18 C2 52.50N 3.24W
Llanidloes Wales 18 C2 52.28N 3.31W
Llanos *f.* Colombia/Venezuela 96 B8 5.30N 72.00W
Llanrhystyd Wales 18 B2 52.19N 4.09W
Llanrwst Wales 18 C3 53.08N 3.48W
Llantrisant Wales 18 C1 51.33N 3.23W
Llantwit Major Wales 18 C1 51.24N 3.29W
Llanuwchllyn Wales 18 C2 52.52N 3.41W
Llanwrtyd Wells Wales 18 C2 52.06N 3.39W
Llanybyther Wales 18 B2 52.04N 4.10W
Lleida Spain 50 F4 41.37N 0.38E
Llerena Spain 50 B3 38.14N 6.00W
Lleyn Pen. Wales 18 B2 52.50N 4.35W
Lloydminster Canada 90 H3 53.18N 110.00W
Loanhead Scotland 27 E2 55.53N 3.09W
Lobito Angola 106 B3 12.20S 13.34E
Locarno Switz. 52 D2 46.10N 8.48E
Lochboisdale *town* Scotland 24 A4 57.09N 7.19W
Lochbuie Scotland 26 C3 56.22N 5.52W
Lochdonhead Scotland 26 C3 56.26N 5.41W
Lochearnhead Scotland 26 D3 56.23N 4.17W
Lochem Neth. 47 E4 52.10N 6.25E
Loches France 48 D4 47.08N 1.00E
Lochgelly Scotland 27 E3 56.08N 3.19W
Lochgilphead Scotland 26 C3 56.02N 5.26W
Lochgoilhead Scotland 26 D3 56.10N 4.54W
Lochinver Scotland 24 C5 58.09N 5.13W
Lochmaben Scotland 27 E2 55.08N 3.27W
Lochmaddy *town* Scotland 24 A4 57.36N 7.10W
Lochnagar *mtn.* Scotland 24 E3 56.57N 3.15W
Lochranza Scotland 26 C2 55.42N 5.18W
Lochwinnoch Scotland 26 D2 55.48N 4.38W
Lochy, L. Scotland 24 D3 56.58N 4.57W
Lockerbie Scotland 27 E2 55.07N 3.21W
Loc Ninh Vietnam 78 D6 11.55N 106.35E
Lodeynoye Pole Russian Fed. 59 C6 60.43N 33.30E
Łódź Poland 57 F5 51.49N 19.28E
Lofoten *is.* Norway 58 C5 68.15N 13.50E
Loftus England 22 D1 54.33N 0.52W
Logan, Mt. Canada 90 D4 60.45N 140.00W
Logone *r.* Cameroon/Chad 104 D3 12.10N 15.00E
Logroño Spain 50 D5 42.28N 2.26W
Lögstör Denmark 46 C4 56.58N 9.16E
Lögumkloster Denmark 46 B3 55.04N 8.50E
Loimaa Finland 58 E3 60.50N 23.05E
Loir *r.* France 48 C4 47.29N 0.32W
Loire *r.* France 48 C4 47.18N 2.00W
Loja Ecuador 96 B7 3.59S 79.16W
Loja Spain 50 C2 37.10N 4.09W
Lokeren Belgium 47 B3 51.06N 3.59E
Lökken Denmark 46 C5 57.22N 9.43E
Lokoja Nigeria 108 C2 7.49N 6.44E
Lolland *i.* Denmark 46 E2 54.50N 11.30E
Lom Bulgaria 56 F5 43.49N 23.13E
Lombok *i.* Indonesia 78 F2 8.30S 116.20E
Lomé Togo 108 B2 6.10N 1.21E
Lomond, Loch Scotland 26 D3 56.07N 4.36W
Łomża Poland 57 H6 53.11N 22.04E
London Canada 91 J2 42.58N 81.15W
London England 15 B2 51.32N 0.06W
Londonderry N. Ireland 23 B1 55.00N 7.20W
Londonderry *d.* N. Ireland 23 B1 55.00N 7.00W
Londrina Brazil 97 D5 23.30S 51.13W
Long Beach *town* U.S.A. 86 C3 33.57N 118.15W
Long Bennington England 16 D3 52.59N 0.45W
Longbenton England 22 C2 55.02N 1.33W
Long Cay *i.* Bahamas 94 E5 22.30N 74.15W
Long Eaton England 16 C2 52.54N 1.16W
Longford Rep. of Ire. 28 D3 53.44N 7.48W
Longford *d.* Rep. of Ire. 28 D3 53.42N 7.45W
Longhorsley England 22 C2 55.15N 1.46W
Longhoughton England 22 C2 55.26N 1.36W
Long I. Bahamas 93 J4 23.00N 75.00W
Long I. U.S.A. 87 L5 40.50N 73.00W
Longlac *town* Canada 91 J2 49.47N 86.34W
Long, Loch Scotland 26 D3 56.05N 4.52W
Long Mtn. Wales 18 C2 52.40N 3.05W
Longniddry Scotland 27 F2 55.58N 2.53W
Longridge England 20 C2 53.50N 2.37W
Longs Peak U.S.A. 86 E5 40.16N 105.37W
Long Sutton England 17 E2 52.47N 0.09E
Longtown England 22 B2 55.01N 2.58W
Longwy France 47 D1 49.32N 5.46E
Longxi China 74 G4 35.00N 105.00E
Long Xuyen Vietnam 78 D6 10.23N 105.25E
Löningen Germany 47 F4 52.44N 7.46E
Looe England 12 C2 50.21N 4.26W
Lookout, C. U.S.A. 87 K3 34.34N 76.34W
Loop Head Rep. of Ire. 28 B2 52.33N 9.56W
Lop Buri Thailand 78 C6 14.49N 100.37E
Lopez, C. Gabon 106 A4 0.36S 8.45E
Lop Nur *l.* China 74 E5 40.30N 90.30E
Lopphavet *est.* Norway 58 E5 70.30N 21.00E
Loralai Pakistan 71 C5 30.20N 68.41E
Lorca Spain 50 E2 37.40N 1.41W
Lord Howe I. Pacific Oc. 80 E2 31.33S 159.06E
Lordsburg U.S.A. 86 E3 32.22N 108.43W
Lorengau P.N.G. 79 L3 2.01S 147.15E
Lorient France 48 B4 47.45N 3.21W
Los Angeles U.S.A. 86 C3 34.00N 118.17W
Los Blancos Spain 50 E2 37.37N 0.48W
Los Canarreos, Archipiélago de Cuba 93 H4 21.40N 82.30W

Massa Italy **54 C6** 44.02N 10.09E
Massachusetts *d.* U.S.A. **87 L5** 42.20N 72.00W
Massawa Eritrea **105 F3** 15.36N 39.29E
Massif Central *mts.* France **48 E3** 45.00N 3.30E
Masurian Lakes Poland **57 G6** 53.50N 21.40E
Matabele Upland *f.* Zimbabwe **102 F3** 19.00S 30.00E
Matadi Zaïre **106 B4** 5.50S 13.32E
Matagorda B. U.S.A. **87 G2** 28.30N 96.20W
Matamoros Coahuila Mexico **92 D5** 25.33N 103.15W
Matamoros Tamaulipas Mexico **92 E5** 25.50N 97.31W
Matanzas Cuba **93 H4** 23.04N 81.35W
Matapan, C. Greece **56 F2** 36.22N 22.28E
Mataram Indonesia **78 F2** 8.36S 116.07E
Mataró Spain **50 G4** 41.32N 2.27E
Matehuala Mexico **92 D4** 23.40N 100.40W
Matera Italy **54 F4** 40.41N 16.36E
Mathura India **71 D5** 27.30N 77.30E
Matlock England **16 C3** 53.08N 1.32W
Mato Grosso *town* Brazil **96 D6** 15.05S 59.57W
Mato Grosso, Planalto do *f.* Brazil **96 D6** 15.00S 55.00W
Matrah Oman **69 J1** 23.37N 58.33E
Matruh Egypt **68 B3** 31.21N 27.15E
Matsue Japan **76 B4** 35.29N 133.00E
Matsu Is. Taiwan **75 J3** 26.12N 120.00E
Matsumoto Japan **76 C5** 36.18N 137.58E
Matsusaka Japan **76 C4** 34.34N 136.32E
Matsuyama Japan **76 B3** 33.50N 132.47E
Matterhorn *mtn.* Switz. **52 C2** 45.58N 7.38E
Matthews Ridge *town* Guyana **95 G2** 7.30N 60.05W
Maturín Venezuela **95 G2** 9.45N 63.16W
Maubeuge France **47 B2** 50.17N 3.58E
Mauchline Scotland **26 D2** 55.31N 4.23W
Maughold Head I.o.M. **20 A3** 54.18N 4.19W
Maui *i.* Hawaii U.S.A. **86 O9** 20.45N 156.15W
Maumere Indonesia **79 G2** 8.35S 122.13E
Mauritania Africa **104 A3** 20.00N 10.00W
Mauritius Indian Oc. **115 L3** 20.10S 58.00E
Mawlaik Myanma **71 G4** 23.40N 94.26E
Maya *i.* Indonesia **78 D3** 1.05S 109.25E
Maya Spain **50 E5** 43.12N 1.29W
Mayaguana I. Bahamas **93 J4** 22.30N 73.00W
Mayaguez Puerto Rico **93 K3** 18.13N 67.09W
Maya Mts. Belize **93 G3** 16.30N 89.00W
Maybole Scotland **26 D2** 55.21N 4.41W
May, C. U.S.A. **87 L4** 38.55N 74.55W
Mayen Germany **47 F2** 50.19N 7.14E
Mayenne France **48 C5** 48.18N 0.37W
Mayenne *r.* France **48 C4** 47.30N 0.37W
Mayfield E. Sussex England **15 C2** 51.01N 0.17E
May, Isle of Scotland **27 F3** 56.12N 2.32W
Maykop Russian Fed. **59 E2** 44.37N 40.48E
Maymyo Myanma **71 H4** 22.05N 96.33E
Maynooth Rep. of Ire. **28 E3** 53.23N 6.40W
Mayo *d.* Rep. of Ire. **28 B3** 53.47N 9.07W
Mayo Daga Nigeria **108 D2** 6.59N 11.25E
Mayo Landing Canada **90 E4** 63.45N 135.45W
Mayo, Plains of *f.* Rep. of Ire. **28 B3** 53.46N 9.00W
Mazatenango Guatemala **92 F2** 14.31N 91.30W
Mazatlán Mexico **92 C4** 23.11N 106.25W
Mažeikiai Lithuania **58 E2** 56.06N 23.06E
Mbabane Swaziland **106 D2** 26.20S 31.08E
Mbandaka Zaïre **106 B5** 0.03N 18.28E
Mbarara Uganda **106 D4** 0.36S 30.40E
Mbuji Mayi Zaïre **106 C4** 6.10S 23.39E
McClintock Channel Canada **91 H5** 71.20N 102.00W
McClure Str. Canada **90 G5** 74.30N 116.00W
McConaughy, L. U.S.A. **86 F5** 41.20N 102.00W
McCook U.S.A **86 F5** 40.15N 100.45W
McGrath U.S.A. **90 C4** 62.58N 155.40W
McKinley, Mt. U.S.A. **90 C4** 63.00N 151.00W
Mead, L. U.S.A. **86 D4** 36.10N 114.25W
Meath *d.* Rep. of Ire. **28 E3** 53.30N 6.30W
Meaux France **48 E5** 48.58N 2.54E
Mecca Saudi Arabia **105 F4** 21.26N 39.49E
Mecklenburg Bay Germany **46 E2** 54.20N 11.30E
Mecklenburg-Vorpommern *d.* Germany **52 F5** 53.30N 13.15E
Medan Indonesia **78 B4** 3.35N 98.39E
Mededsiz *mtn.* Turkey **68 D5** 37.33N 34.38E
Medellín Colombia **94 D2** 6.15N 75.36W
Medenine Tunisia **104 D5** 33.24N 10.25E
Medicine Hat Canada **90 G3** 50.03N 110.41W
Medina Saudi Arabia **68 E2** 24.30N 39.35E
Medina del Campo Spain **50 C4** 41.20N 4.55W
Medina de Ríoseco Spain **50 C4** 41.53N 5.03W
Mediterranean Sea 40 H2 37.00N 15.00E
Medveditsa *r.* Russian Fed. **59 E3** 49.35N 42.45E
Medway *r.* England **15 C2** 51.24N 0.31E
Meerut India **71 D5** 29.00N 77.42E
Mégara Greece **56 F3** 38.00N 23.21E
Meghalaya *d.* India **71 G4** 25.30N 91.00E
Meiktila Myanma **71 G4** 20.53N 95.54E
Meiningen Germany **52 E4** 50.34N 10.25E
Meissen Germany **52 F4** 51.10N 13.28E
Mei Xian China **75 I2** 24.19N 116.13E
Meknes Morocco **104 B5** 33.53N 5.37W
Mekong *r.* Asia **78 D6** 10.00N 106.20E
Mekong Delta Vietnam **78 D6** 10.00N 106.20E
Mekongga *mtn.* Indonesia **79 G3** 3.39S 121.15E
Mékrou *r.* Benin **108 B3** 12.20N 2.47E
Melaka Malaysia **78 C4** 2.11N 102.16E
Melanesia *is.* Pacific Oc. **82 G7** 5.00N 165.00E
Melbourn England **15 C3** 52.05N 0.01E
Melbourne Australia **80 D2** 37.45S 144.58E
Melbourne England **16 C2** 52.50N 1.25W
Meldorf Germany **46 C2** 54.07N 9.07E
Melfi Italy **54 E4** 40.59N 15.39E
Melilla Spain **104 B5** 35.17N 2.57W
Melitopol Ukraine **59 D3** 46.51N 35.22E
Melksham England **13 E3** 51.22N 2.09W
Mellerud Sweden **58 C2** 58.42N 12.27E
Melmore Pt. Rep. of Ire. **28 D5** 55.15N 7.50W
Melrose Scotland **27 F2** 55.36N 2.43W
Meltham England **20 D2** 53.36N 1.52W
Melton Mowbray England **16 D2** 52.46N 0.53W
Melun France **48 E5** 48.32N 2.40E
Melvich Scotland **24 E5** 58.32N 3.55W
Melville I. Australia **80 C4** 11.30S 131.00E
Melville I. Canada **90 G5** 75.30N 110.00W
Melville Pen. Canada **91 J4** 68.00N 84.00W
Melvin, Lough Rep. of Ire./N. Ireland **23 A1** 54.25N 8.10W
Memmingen Germany **52 E2** 47.59N 10.11E
Memphis *ruins* Egypt **68 C3** 29.52N 31.12E
Memphis U.S.A. **87 I4** 35.05N 90.00W
Menai Bridge *town* Wales **18 B3** 53.14N 4.11W
Menai Str. Wales **18 B3** 53.17N 4.20W
Mendawai *r.* Indonesia **78 E3** 3.17S 113.20E
Mende France **48 E3** 44.32N 3.30E
Menderes *r.* Turkey **68 B5** 37.30N 27.05E
Mendi P.N.G. **79 K2** 6.13S 143.39E
Mendip Hills England **13 E3** 51.15N 2.40W
Mendocino, C. U.S.A. **86 B5** 40.26N 124.24W
Mendoza Argentina **97 C4** 33.00S 68.52W
Mengzi China **74 G2** 23.20N 103.21E
Menin Belgium **47 B2** 50.48N 3.07E
Menongue Angola **106 B3** 14.40S 17.41E
Menorca *i. see* Minorca *i.* Spain **51**
Menstrup Denmark **46 E3** 55.11N 11.32E
Mentawai Is. Indonesia **78 B3** 2.50S 99.00E
Menteith, L. of Scotland **26 D3** 56.10N 4.18W
Mentok Indonesia **78 D3** 2.04S 105.12E
Menton France **48 G2** 43.47N 7.30E
Menyapa, Gunung *mtn.* Indonesia **78 F4** 1.00N 116.20E
Meppel Neth. **47 E4** 52.42N 6.12E
Meppen Germany **47 F4** 52.42N 7.17E
Merano Italy **54 C7** 46.41N 11.10E
Merauke Indonesia **79 K2** 8.30S 140.22E
Merced U.S.A. **86 B4** 37.17N 120.29W
Mercedes San Luis Argentina **97 C4** 34.00S 65.00W
Mere England **13 E3** 51.05N 2.16W
Mergenevo Kazakhstan **59 G3** 49.59N 51.19E
Mergui Myanma **78 B6** 12.26N 98.34E
Mergui Archipelago *is.* Myanma **78 B6** 11.30N 98.30E
Mérida Mexico **93 G4** 20.59N 89.39W
Mérida Spain **50 B3** 38.55N 6.20W
Mérida Venezuela **94 E2** 8.24N 71.08W
Mérida, Cordillera de *mts.* Venezuela **94 E2** 8.00N 71.30W
Meridian U.S.A. **87 I3** 32.21N 88.42W
Merir *i.* Caroline Is. **79 I4** 4.19N 132.18E
Merksem Belgium **47 C3** 51.14N 4.25E
Merowe Sudan **105 F3** 18.30N 31.49E
Merrick *mtn.* Scotland **26 D2** 55.08N 4.29W
Merse *f.* Scotland **27 F2** 55.45N 2.15W
Mersea I. England **15 C2** 51.47N 0.58E
Merseburg Germany **52 E4** 51.22N 12.00E
Mersey *r.* England **20 C2** 53.22N 2.37W
Merseyside *d.* England **20 B2** 53.28N 3.00W
Mersin Turkey **68 D5** 36.47N 34.37E
Mersing Malaysia **78 C4** 2.25N 103.50E
Merthyr Tydfil Wales **18 C1** 51.45N 3.23W
Mértola Portugal **50 B2** 37.38N 7.40W
Merzifon Turkey **68 D6** 40.52N 35.28E
Merzig Germany **47 E1** 49.26N 6.39E
Mesolóngion Greece **56 E3** 38.23N 21.23E
Mesopotamia *f.* Iraq **69 G4** 33.30N 44.30E
Messina Italy **54 E3** 38.13N 15.34E
Messina, G. of Med. Sea **56 F2** 36.50N 22.05E
Messina, Str. of Med. Sea **54 E2** 38.10N 15.35E
Mesta *r.* Greece **56 G4** 40.51N 24.48E
Meta *r.* Venezuela **95 F2** 6.10N 67.30W
Metheringham England **17 D3** 53.09N 0.22W
Methven Scotland **27 E3** 56.25N 3.37W
Methwold England **15 C3** 52.30N 0.33E
Metković Croatia **56 C5** 43.03N 17.38E
Metz France **48 G5** 49.07N 6.11E
Meulaboh Indonesia **78 B4** 4.10N 96.09E
Meuse *r. see* Maas *r.* Belgium **47**
Mevagissey England **12 C2** 50.16N 4.48W
Mexborough England **21 D2** 53.29N 1.18W
Mexicali Mexico **92 A6** 32.26N 115.30W
Mexico C. America **92 D4** 20.00N 100.00W
México *d.* Mexico **92 E3** 19.45N 99.30W
Mexico City Mexico **92 E3** 19.25N 99.10W
Mexico, G. of N. America **92 F4** 25.00N 90.00W
Meyadin Syria **68 F4** 35.01N 40.28E
Mezen Russian Fed. **60 D4** 65.50N 44.20E
Mézenc, Mont *mtn.* France **48 F3** 44.54N 4.11E
Mezőkövesd Hungary **57 G3** 47.50N 20.34E
Miami U.S.A. **87 J2** 25.45N 80.10W
Mianduab Iran **69 G5** 36.57N 46.06E
Mianeh Iran **69 G5** 37.23N 47.45E
Mianwali Pakistan **71 C6** 32.32N 71.33E
Miass Russian Fed. **60 F3** 55.00N 60.00E
Michigan *d.* U.S.A. **87 I5** 45.00N 85.00W
Michigan City U.S.A. **87 I5** 41.43N 86.44W
Michigan, L. U.S.A. **87 I5** 44.00N 87.00W
Michipicoten Canada **91 J2** 47.57N 84.55W
Michoacán *d.* Mexico **92 D3** 19.20N 101.00W
Michurinsk Russian Fed. **59 E4** 52.54N 40.30E
Micronesia *is.* Pacific Oc. **82 E9** 8.00N 160.00E
Mid Atlantic Ridge Atlantic Oc. **112 G6** 25.00N 45.00W
Middelburg Neth. **47 B3** 51.30N 3.36E
Middelfart Denmark **46 C3** 55.30N 9.44E
Middlesbrough England **22 C1** 54.34N 1.13W
Middleton England **20 C2** 53.33N 2.12W
Middleton in Teesdale England **22 B1** 54.38N 2.05W
Middleton on the Wolds England **21 E2** 53.56N 0.35W
Middleton Reef Pacific Oc. **82 F5** 29.28S 159.06E
Middlewich England **20 C2** 53.12N 2.28W
Mid Glamorgan *d.* Wales **18 C1** 51.38N 3.25W
Midhurst England **15 B1** 50.59N 0.44W
Mid Indian Basin *f.* Indian Oc. **113 N4** 15.00S 80.00E
Mid Indian Ridge *f.* Indian Oc. **113 M3** 25.00S 70.00E
Midleton Rep. of Ire. **28 C1** 51.55N 8.12W
Midsomer Norton England **13 E3** 51.17N 2.29W
Midway Is. Hawaiian Is. **82 I10** 28.15N 177.25W
Mielec Poland **57 G5** 50.18N 21.25E
Mieres Spain **50 C5** 43.15N 5.46W
Mijares *r.* Spain **50 E3** 39.58N 0.01W
Mikhaylovka Russian Fed. **59 E4** 50.05N 43.15E
Mikkeli Finland **58 F3** 61.44N 27.15E
Mikuni sammyaku *mts.* Japan **76 D5** 37.00N 139.20E
Milan Italy **54 B6** 45.28N 9.16E
Milâs Turkey **68 B5** 37.18N 27.48E
Milborne Port England **13 E2** 50.58N 2.28W
Mildenhall England **15 C3** 52.20N 0.30E
Miles City U.S.A. **86 E6** 46.24N 105.48W
Milford England **15 B2** 51.10N 0.40W
Milford Haven *b.* Wales **18 A1** 51.42N 5.05W
Milford Haven *town* Wales **18 A1** 51.43N 5.02W
Milford on Sea England **14 A1** 50.44N 1.36W
Milk *r.* U.S.A. **86 E6** 47.55N 106.15W
Millau France **48 E3** 44.06N 3.05E
Mille Lacs L. U.S.A. **87 H6** 46.15N 93.40W
Millerovo Russian Fed. **59 E3** 48.55N 40.25E
Milleur Pt. Scotland **26 C2** 55.01N 5.07W
Millom England **22 A1** 54.13N 3.16W
Millport Scotland **26 D2** 55.45N 4.56W
Milnathort Scotland **27 E3** 56.14N 3.26W
Milngavie Scotland **26 D2** 55.57N 4.19W
Milnthorpe England **22 B1** 54.14N 2.47W
Mílos *i.* Greece **56 G2** 36.40N 24.26E
Milton Abbot England **12 C2** 50.35N 4.16W
Milton Keynes England **15 B3** 52.03N 0.42W
Milverton England **13 D3** 51.02N 3.15W
Milwaukee U.S.A. **87 I5** 43.03N 87.56W
Minab Iran **69 J2** 27.07N 57.05E
Minamata Japan **76 A3** 32.13N 130.24E
Mina Saud Kuwait **69 H3** 28.48N 48.24E
Minatitlán Mexico **92 F3** 17.59N 94.32W
Mindanao *i.* Phil. **79 H5** 7.30N 125.00E
Minden Germany **52 D5** 52.18N 8.54E
Mindoro *i.* Phil. **79 G6** 13.00N 121.00E
Mindoro Str. Pacific Oc. **79 G6** 12.30N 120.10E
Mindra, Mt. Romania **56 F6** 45.20N 23.32E
Minehead England **13 D3** 51.12N 3.29W
Minna Nigeria **108 C2** 9.39N 6.32E
Minneapolis U.S.A. **87 H5** 45.00N 93.15W
Minnesota *d.* U.S.A. **87 H5** 46.00N 95.00W
Mino Japan **76 C4** 35.32N 136.55E
Miño *r.* Spain **50 A4** 41.50N 8.52W
Minorca *i.* Spain **51 H3** 40.00N 4.00E
Minot U.S.A. **86 F6** 48.16N 101.19W
Minsk Belorussia **59 B4** 53.51N 27.30E
Minster England **15 C2** 51.25N 0.50E
Minsterley England **16 B2** 52.38N 2.56W
Miraj India **71 D3** 16.51N 74.42E
Miranda de Ebro Spain **50 D5** 42.41N 2.57W
Miranda do Douro Portugal **50 B4** 41.30N 6.16W
Mirande France **48 D2** 43.31N 0.25E
Mirandela Portugal **50 B4** 41.28N 7.10W
Mirecourt France **48 G5** 48.18N 6.08E
Miri Malaysia **78 E4** 4.28N 114.00E
Mirim, L. Brazil **97 D4** 33.10S 53.30W
Mirpur Khas Pakistan **71 C4** 25.33N 69.05E
Mirzapur India **71 E4** 25.09N 82.34E
Mi saki *c.* Japan **76 E7** 40.09N 141.52E
Misawa Japan **76 E7** 40.41N 141.24E
Miskolc Hungary **57 G4** 48.07N 20.47E
Misoöl *i.* Indonesia **79 I3** 1.50S 130.10E
Mississippi *d.* U.S.A. **87 I3** 33.00N 90.00W
Mississippi *r.* U.S.A. **87 I2** 28.55N 89.05W
Mississippi Delta U.S.A. **87 I2** 29.00N 89.10W
Missoula U.S.A. **86 D6** 46.52N 114.00W
Missouri *d.* U.S.A. **87 H4** 39.00N 93.00W
Missouri *r.* U.S.A. **87 H4** 38.40N 90.20W
Mistassini, L. Canada **91 K3** 50.45N 73.40W
Misurata Libya **104 D5** 32.24N 15.04E
Mitchell *r.* Australia **80 D4** 15.12S 141.40E
Mitchell U.S.A. **86 G5** 43.40N 98.01W
Mitchell, Mt. U.S.A. **87 J4** 35.57N 82.16W
Mitchelstown Rep. of Ire. **28 C2** 52.16N 8.19W
Mitilíni Greece **68 B5** 39.06N 26.34E
Mito Japan **76 D5** 36.30N 140.29E
Mittelland Canal Germany **47 F4** 52.24N 7.52E
Mitú Colombia **94 F1** 1.08N 69.58W
Mitumba Mts. Zaïre **102 E4** 3.00S 28.00E
Miyako Japan **76 E6** 39.40N 141.59E
Miyako *i.* Japan **75 J2** 24.45N 125.25E
Miyazaki Japan **76 A1** 31.58N 131.50E
Miyokonajo Japan **76 A1** 31.43N 131.02E
Mizen Head Rep. of Ire. **28 B1** 51.27N 9.50W
Mizoram *d.* India **71 G4** 23.40N 92.40E
Mjölby Sweden **58 C2** 58.19N 15.10E
Mjösa *l.* Norway **58 B3** 60.50N 10.50E
Mladá Boleslav Czech Rep. **57 D5** 50.26N 14.55E
Mljet *i.* Croatia **56 C5** 42.45N 17.30E
Mobile U.S.A. **87 I3** 30.40N 88.05W
Mobile B. U.S.A. **87 I3** 30.30N 87.50W
Mobridge U.S.A. **86 F6** 45.31N 100.25W
Moçambique *town* Mozambique **106 E3** 15.00S 40.55E
Modane France **48 G3** 45.12N 6.40E
Modbury England **13 D2** 50.21N 3.53W
Modena Italy **54 C6** 44.39N 10.55E
Modica Italy **54 E2** 36.51N 14.51E
Moffat Scotland **27 E2** 55.20N 3.27W
Mogadishu Somali Rep. **105 G2** 2.02N 45.21E
Mogaung Myanma **71 H4** 25.20N 97.00E
Moghan Steppe *f.* Azerbaijan **69 H5** 39.40N 48.30E
Mogilev Belorussia **59 C4** 53.54N 30.20E
Mogilev Podolskiy Ukraine **59 B3** 48.29N 27.49E
Mogok Myanma **71 H4** 23.00N 96.40E
Mo-i-Rana Norway **58 C4** 66.20N 14.12E
Moisie *r.* Canada **91 L3** 50.15N 66.00W
Moissac France **48 D3** 44.07N 1.05E
Mokmer Indonesia **79 J3** 1.13S 136.13E
Mokpo S. Korea **75 K4** 34.50N 126.25E
Mold Wales **18 C3** 53.10N 3.08W
Moldavia Europe **59 B3** 47.30N 28.30E
Molde Norway **58 A3** 62.44N 7.08E
Molfetta Italy **54 F4** 41.12N 16.36E
Molina de Aragón Spain **50 E4** 40.50N 1.54W
Mollendo Peru **96 B6** 17.20S 72.10W
Mollösund Sweden **46 E6** 58.04N 11.24E
Molodechno Belorussia **59 B4** 54.16N 26.50E
Molokai *i.* Hawaii U.S.A. **86 O9** 21.20N 157.00W
Molopo *r.* R.S.A. **106 C2** 28.30S 20.07E
Moluccas *is.* Indonesia **79 H3** 4.00S 128.00E
Molucca Sea Pacific Oc. **79 H4** 2.00N 126.30E
Mombasa Kenya **106 D4** 4.04S 39.40E
Mompós Colombia **94 E2** 9.15N 74.29W
Mön *i.* Denmark **46 F2** 54.58N 12.20E
Mona *i.* Puerto Rico **93 K3** 18.06N 67.54W
Monaco Europe **48 G2** 43.40N 7.25E
Monadhliath Mts. Scotland **24 D4** 57.09N 4.08W
Monaghan Rep. of Ire. **28 E4** 54.15N 6.58W
Monaghan *d.* Rep. of Ire. **23 D4** 54.15N 7.00W
Mon Cai Vietnam **78 D8** 21.31N 108.00E
Monchegorsk Russian Fed. **58 H4** 67.55N 33.01E
Mönchen-Gladbach Germany **47 E3** 51.12N 6.25E
Monclova Mexico **92 D5** 26.55N 101.20W
Moncton Canada **91 L2** 46.06N 64.50W
Mondovì Italy **54 A6** 44.24N 7.50E
Moneymore N. Ireland **23 C1** 54.42N 6.41W
Monforte Spain **50 B5** 42.32N 7.30W
Monga Zaïre **105 E2** 4.05N 22.56E
Monghyr India **71 F4** 25.24N 86.29E
Mongolia Asia **74 G6** 46.30N 104.00E
Moniaive Scotland **27 E2** 55.12N 3.55W
Monifieth Scotland **27 F3** 56.29N 2.50W
Monmouth Wales **18 D1** 51.48N 2.43W
Monnow *r.* England/Wales **18 D1** 51.49N 2.42W
Monopoli Italy **54 F4** 40.56N 17.19E
Monroe La. U.S.A. **87 H3** 32.31N 92.06W
Monrovia Liberia **104 A2** 6.20N 10.46W
Mons Belgium **47 B2** 50.27N 3.57E
Montalbán Spain **50 E4** 40.50N 0.48W
Montana *d.* U.S.A. **86 D6** 47.00N 110.00W
Montargis France **48 E4** 48.00N 2.44E
Montauban France **48 D3** 44.01N 1.20E
Montbéliard France **48 G4** 47.31N 6.48E
Montbrison France **48 F3** 45.37N 4.04E
Mont Cenis Pass France **48 G3** 45.15N 6.55E
Montcornet France **47 C1** 49.41N 4.01E
Mont de Marsan *town* France **48 C2** 43.54N 0.30W
Monte Carlo Monaco **48 G2** 43.44N 7.25E
Montecristo *i.* Italy **54 C5** 42.20N 10.19E
Montego Bay *town* Jamaica **93 I3** 18.27N 77.56W
Montélimar France **48 F3** 44.33N 4.45E
Monterey U.S.A. **86 B4** 36.35N 121.55W
Monterey B. U.S.A. **86 B4** 36.45N 122.00W
Montería Colombia **94 D2** 8.45N 75.54W
Monterrey Mexico **92 D5** 25.40N 100.20W
Monte Santu, C. Italy **54 B4** 40.05N 9.44E
Montes Claros Brazil **96 E6** 16.45S 43.52W
Montevideo Uruguay **97 D4** 34.55S 56.10W
Montfort-sur-Meu France **48 C5** 48.08N 1.57W
Montgomery Ala. U.S.A. **87 I3** 32.22N 86.20W
Montgomery Wales **18 C2** 52.34N 3.09W
Montijo Portugal **50 A3** 38.42N 8.59W
Montijo Dam Spain **50 B3** 38.52N 6.20W
Montluçon France **48 E4** 46.20N 2.36E
Montmédy France **47 D1** 49.31N 5.21E
Montmorillon France **48 D4** 46.26N 0.52E
Montoro Spain **50 C2** 38.02N 4.23W
Montpelier U.S.A. **87 L5** 44.16N 72.34W
Montpellier France **48 E2** 43.36N 3.53E
Montreal Canada **91 K2** 45.30N 73.36W
Montrejeau France **48 D2** 43.05N 0.33E
Montreuil France **48 D6** 50.28N 1.46E
Montrose Scotland **27 F3** 56.43N 2.29W
Montrose U.S.A. **86 E4** 38.29N 107.53W
Montserrat *i.* Leeward Is. **93 L3** 16.45N 62.14W
Montserrat, Sierra de *mts.* Spain **50 F4** 41.20N 1.00E
Monywa Myanma **71 G4** 22.07N 95.11E
Monza Italy **54 B6** 45.35N 9.16E
Monzón Spain **50 F4** 41.52N 0.10E
Moorfoot Hills Scotland **27 E2** 55.43N 3.03W
Moorhead U.S.A. **87 G6** 46.51N 96.44W
Moose Jaw Canada **90 H3** 50.23N 105.35W
Moosonee Canada **91 J3** 51.18N 80.40W
Mopti Mali **104 B3** 14.29N 4.10W
Mora Sweden **58 C3** 61.00N 14.30E
Moradabad India **71 E5** 28.50N 78.45E
Morar, Loch Scotland **24 C3** 56.56N 4.00W
Morava *r.* Czech Rep. **57 E4** 48.10N 16.59E
Morava *r.* Yugo. **56 E6** 44.43N 21.02E
Moray Firth *est.* Scotland **24 E4** 57.35N 3.50W
Morcenx France **48 C3** 44.02N 0.55W
Morden Canada **91 I2** 49.15N 98.10W
Morecambe England **20 C3** 54.03N 2.52W
Morecambe B. England **20 C3** 54.05N 3.00W
Morelia Mexico **92 D3** 19.40N 101.11W
Morella Spain **50 E4** 40.37N 0.06W
Morelos *d.* Mexico **92 E3** 18.40N 99.00W
Morena, Sierra *mts.* Spain **50 C3** 38.10N 5.00W
Moretonhampstead England **13 D2** 50.39N 3.45W
Morez France **48 G4** 46.31N 6.02E
Morgan City U.S.A. **87 H2** 29.41N 91.13W
Morioka Japan **76 E6** 39.43N 141.10E
Morlaix France **48 B5** 48.35N 3.50W
Morley England **21 D2** 53.45N 1.36W
Morocco Africa **104 B5** 31.00N 5.00W
Moro G. Phil. **79 G5** 6.30N 123.20E
Morogoro Tanzania **106 D4** 6.49S 37.40E

Morón Cuba **93 I4** 22.08N 78.39W
Mörön Mongolia **74 F6** 49.36N 100.08E
Morotai *i.* Indonesia **79 H4** 2.10N 128.30E
Morpeth England **22 C2** 55.10N 1.40W
Mors *i.* Denmark **46 B4** 56.50N 8.45E
Morsbach Germany **47 F2** 50.52N 7.44E
Mortagne France **48 D5** 48.32N 0.33E
Morte Pt. England **12 C3** 51.12N 4.13W
Mortimer Common England **14 A2** 51.22N 1.05W
Morvern *f.* Scotland **24 C3** 56.37N 5.45W
Morwell Australia **80 D2** 38.14S 146.25E
Moscow Russian Fed. **59 D5** 55.45N 37.42E
Mosel *r.* Germany **47 F2** 50.23N 7.37E
Moselle *r. see* Mosel *r.* France/Lux. **47**
Moshi Tanzania **106 D4** 3.20S 37.21E
Mosjöen Norway **58 C4** 65.50N 13.10E
Moskog Norway **58 A3** 61.30N 5.59E
Moskva *r.* Russian Fed. **59 D5** 55.08N 38.50E
Mosquitia Plain Honduras **93 H3** 15.00N 84.00W
Mosquito Coast *f.* Nicaragua **93 H2** 13.00N 84.00W
Mosquitos, G. of Panama **93 H1** 9.00N 81.00W
Moss Norway **58 B2** 59.26N 10.41E
Mosso *l.* Denmark **46 C4** 56.02N 9.47E
Mossoró Brazil **96 F7** 5.10S 37.20W
Most Czech Rep. **57 C5** 50.31N 13.39E
Mostar Bosnia. **56 C5** 43.20N 17.50E
Mosul Iraq **68 F5** 36.21N 43.08E
Motagua *r.* Guatemala **93 G3** 15.56N 87.45W
Motala Sweden **58 C2** 58.34N 15.05E
Motherwell Scotland **27 E2** 55.48N 4.00W
Moulins France **48 E4** 46.34N 3.20E
Moulmein Myanma **78 B7** 16.20N 97.50E
Mountain Ash Wales **18 C1** 51.42N 3.22W
Mount Bellew *town* Rep. of Ire. **28 C3** 53.29N 8.30W
Mount Gambier *town* Australia **80 D2** 37.51S 140.50E
Mount Hagen *town* P.N.G. **79 K2** 5.54S 144.13E
Mount Isa *town* Australia **80 C3** 20.50S 139.29E
Mount Magnet *town* Australia **80 A3** 28.06S 117.50E
Mountmellick Rep. of Ire. **28 D3** 53.08N 7.21W
Mount Newman *town* Australia **80 A3** 23.20S 119.39E
Mount's B. England **12 B2** 50.05N 5.25W
Mourne *r.* N. Ireland **23 B1** 54.50N 7.29W
Mourne Mts. N. Ireland **23 C1** 54.10N 6.02W
Moy N. Ireland **23 C1** 54.27N 6.43W
Moy *r.* Rep. of Ire. **28 B4** 54.10N 9.09W
Mozambique Africa **106 D3** 18.00S 35.00E
Mozambique Channel Indian Oc. **106 E3** 16.00S 42.30E
Mozdok Russian Fed. **59 E2** 43.45N 44.43E
Mozyr Belorussia **59 B4** 52.02N 29.10E
Msta *r.* Russian Fed. **59 C5** 58.28N 31.20E
Mtsensk Russian Fed. **59 D4** 53.18N 36.35E
Mtwara Tanzania **106 E3** 10.17S 40.11E
Muang Chiang Rai Thailand **78 B7** 19.56N 99.51E
Muang Khon Kaen Thailand **78 C7** 16.25N 102.50E
Muang Lampang Thailand **78 B7** 18.16N 99.30E
Muang Nakhon Phanom Thailand **78 C7** 17.22N 104.45E
Muang Nakhon Sawan Thailand **78 C7** 15.35N 100.10E
Muang Nan Thailand **78 C7** 18.45N 100.42E
Muang Phitsanulok Thailand **78 C7** 16.50N 100.15E
Muang Phrae Thailand **78 C7** 18.07N 100.09E
Muar Malaysia **78 C4** 2.01N 102.35E
Muara Brunei **78 F5** 5.01N 115.01E
Muara Indonesia **78 C3** 0.32S 101.20E
Mubi Nigeria **108 D3** 10.16N 13.17E
Muchinga Mts. Zambia **102 F3** 12.00S 31.00E
Much Wenlock England **16 B2** 52.36N 2.34W
Muck *i.* Scotland **24 B3** 56.50N 6.14W
Muckamore N. Ireland **23 C1** 54.42N 6.11W
Mudanjiang China **75 K6** 44.36N 129.42E
Mudhnib Saudi Arabia **69 G2** 25.52N 44.15E
Mugía Spain **50 A5** 43.06N 9.14W
Muğla Turkey **68 C5** 37.12N 28.22E
Muharraq Bahrain **69 H2** 26.16N 50.38E
Mühlhausen Germany **52 E4** 51.12N 10.27E
Muine Bheag Rep. of Ire. **28 E2** 52.41N 6.59W
Muirkirk Scotland **27 D2** 55.31N 4.04W
Mukachevo Ukraine **57 H4** 48.26N 22.45E
Mukah Malaysia **78 E4** 2.56N 112.02E
Mukalla Yemen **105 G3** 14.34N 49.09E
Mukawa *r.* Japan **76 E8** 42.30N 142.20E
Mulgrave I. Australia **79 K1** 10.05S 142.00E
Mulhacén *mtn.* Spain **50 D2** 37.04N 3.22W
Mülheim N.-Westfalen Germany **47 F2** 50.58N 7.00E
Mülheim N.-Westfalen Germany **47 E3** 51.25N 6.50E
Mulhouse France **48 G4** 47.45N 7.21E
Mull *i.* Scotland **26 C3** 56.28N 5.56W
Mullaghanattin *mtn.* Rep. of Ire. **28 B1** 51.55N 9.52W
Mullaghareirk Mts. Rep. of Ire. **28 B2** 52.20N 9.10W
Mullaghcarn *mtn.* N. Ireland **23 B1** 54.40N 7.14W
Mullaghmore *mtn.* N. Ireland **23 C1** 54.51N 6.51W
Mullet Pen. Rep. of Ire. **28 A4** 54.10N 10.05W
Mullingar Rep. of Ire. **28 D3** 53.31N 7.21W
Mullion England **12 B2** 50.01N 5.15W
Mull of Galloway *c.* Scotland **26 D1** 54.39N 4.52W
Mull of Kintyre *c.* Scotland **26 C2** 55.17N 5.45W
Mull of Oa *c.* Scotland **26 B2** 55.36N 6.20W
Mull, Sd. of *str.* Scotland **26 C3** 56.32N 5.55W
Multan Pakistan **71 C5** 30.10N 71.36E
Multyfarnham Rep. of Ire. **28 D3** 53.37N 7.24W
Muna *i.* Indonesia **79 G2** 5.00S 122.30E
Mundesley England **15 D3** 52.53N 1.24E
Mundo *r.* Spain **50 E3** 38.20N 1.50W
Munich Germany **52 E3** 48.08N 11.35E
Münster Germany **47 F3** 51.58N 7.37E
Muonio Finland **58 E4** 67.52N 23.45E
Muonio *r.* Sweden/Finland **58 E4** 67.13N 23.30E
Murallón *mtn.* Argentina/Chile **97 B3** 49.48S 73.26W
Murashi Russian Fed. **59 F5** 59.20N 48.59E
Murat *r.* Turkey **41 M2** 38.40N 39.30E
Murchison *r.* Australia **80 A3** 27.30S 114.10E
Murcia Spain **50 E2** 37.59N 1.08W
Murcia *d.* Spain **50 E3** 38.00N 1.30W
Mureş *r.* Romania **57 G3** 46.16N 20.10E
Muret France **48 D2** 43.28N 1.19E
Murghab *r.* Afghan. **70 B6** 36.50N 63.00E
Müritz, L. Germany **52 F5** 53.25N 12.45E
Murmansk Russian Fed. **58 H5** 68.59N 33.08E
Murom Russian Fed. **59 E5** 55.04N 42.04E
Muroran Japan **76 D8** 42.21N 140.59E
Murray *r.* S.A. Australia **80 C2** 35.23S 139.20E
Murrumbidgee *r.* Australia **80 D2** 34.38S 143.10E
Murud *mtn.* Malaysia **78 F4** 3.45N 115.30E
Murwara India **71 E4** 23.49N 80.28E
Muryo *mtn.* Indonesia **78 E2** 6.30S 110.55E
Murzuq Libya **104 D4** 25.56N 13.57E
Muş Turkey **68 F5** 38.45N 41.30E
Musala *mtn.* Bulgaria **56 F5** 42.11N 23.35E
Muscat Oman **69 J1** 23.36N 58.37E
Musgrave Ranges *mts.* Australia **80 C3** 26.30S 131.10E
Musi *r.* Indonesia **78 C3** 2.20S 104.57E
Muskegon U.S.A. **87 I5** 43.13N 86.10W
Muskogee U.S.A. **87 G4** 35.45N 95.21W
Musselburgh Scotland **27 E2** 55.57N 3.04W
Mustang Nepal **71 E5** 29.10N 83.55E
Mustjala Estonia **58 E2** 58.30N 22.10E
Mut Turkey **68 D5** 36.38N 33.27E
Mutare Zimbabwe **106 D3** 18.58S 32.38E
Mutsu wan *b.* Japan **76 E7** 41.10N 141.05E
Muwai Hakran Saudi Arabia **68 F1** 22.41N 41.37E
Muzaffarnagar India **71 D5** 29.28N 77.42E
Muzaffarpur India **71 F5** 26.07N 85.23E
Mwanza Tanzania **106 D4** 2.30S 32.54E
Mwene Ditu Zaïre **106 C4** 7.01S 23.27E
Mweru, L. Zambia/Zaïre **106 C4** 9.00S 28.40E
Myanaung Myanma **71 G3** 18.25N 95.10E
Myanma Asia **71 G4** 21.00N 95.00E
Myingyan Myanma **71 G4** 21.25N 95.20E
Myitkyina Myanma **71 H4** 25.24N 97.25E
Mymensingh Bangla. **71 G4** 24.45N 90.23E
Mynydd Bach *mts.* Wales **18 B2** 52.18N 4.03W
Mynydd Eppynt *mts.* Wales **18 C2** 52.06N 3.30W
Mynydd Prescelly *mts.* Wales **18 B1** 51.58N 4.47W
Myrdal Norway **58 A3** 60.44N 7.08E
Mysore India **71 D2** 12.18N 76.37E
My Tho Vietnam **78 D6** 10.21N 106.21E
Mytishchi Russian Fed. **59 D5** 55.54N 37.47E

N

Naas Rep. of Ire. **28 E3** 53.13N 6.41W
Naberezhnye Chelny Russian Fed. **59 G5** 55.42N 52.20E
Nacala Mozambique **106 E3** 14.30S 40.37E
Nadiad India **71 D4** 22.42N 72.55E
Naestved Denmark **46 E3** 55.14N 11.47E
Naft Safid Iran **69 H3** 31.38N 49.20E
Naga Phil. **79 G6** 13.36N 123.12E
Nagaland *d.* India **71 G5** 26.10N 94.30E
Nagano Japan **76 D5** 36.39N 138.10E
Nagaoka Japan **76 D5** 37.30N 138.50E
Nagappattinam India **71 E2** 10.45N 79.50E
Nagasaki Japan **76 A3** 32.45N 129.52E
Nagercoil India **71 D2** 8.11N 77.30E
Nag' Hammadi Egypt **68 D2** 26.04N 32.13E
Nagles Mts. Rep. of Ire. **28 C2** 52.05N 8.31W
Nagoya Japan **76 C4** 35.08N 136.53E
Nagpur India **71 E4** 21.10N 79.12E
Nagykanizsa Hungary **57 E3** 46.27N 17.01E
Naha Japan **75 K3** 26.10N 127.40E
Nahavand Iran **69 H4** 34.13N 48.23E
Nahe *r.* Germany **47 F1** 49.58N 7.54E
Nailsworth England **13 E3** 51.41N 2.12W
Nain Canada **91 L3** 56.30N 61.45W
Nairn Scotland **24 E4** 57.35N 3.52W
Nairobi Kenya **106 D4** 1.17S 36.50E
Nakaminato Japan **76 D5** 36.21N 140.36E
Nakatsu Japan **76 A3** 33.37N 131.11E
Nakhichevan Azerbaijan **69 G5** 39.12N 45.24E
Nakhodka Russian Fed. **75 L5** 42.53N 132.54E
Nakhon Pathom Thailand **78 C6** 13.50N 100.01E
Nakhon Ratchasima Thailand **78 C7** 15.02N 102.12E
Nakhon Si Thammarat Thailand **78 B5** 8.29N 99.55E
Naknek U.S.A. **90 C3** 58.45N 157.00W
Nakskov Denmark **46 E2** 54.50N 11.10E
Nakuru Kenya **106 D4** 0.16S 36.04E
Nalchik Russian Fed. **59 E2** 43.31N 43.38E
Nalón *r.* Spain **50 B5** 43.35N 6.06W
Nalut Libya **104 D5** 31.53N 10.59E
Namangan Uzbekistan **74 A5** 40.59N 71.41E
Nam Co *l.* China **74 E3** 30.40N 90.30E
Nam Dinh Vietnam **78 D8** 20.25N 106.12E
Namib Desert Namibia **106 B2** 22.50S 14.40E
Namibe Angola **106 B3** 15.10S 12.10E
Namibia Africa **106 B2** 22.00S 17.00E
Namlea Indonesia **79 H3** 3.15S 127.07E
Namonuito *i.* Pacific Oc. **82 F8** 8.46N 150.02E
Nampo N. Korea **75 J5** 38.40N 125.30E
Nampula Mozambique **106 D3** 15.09S 39.14E
Namsos Norway **58 B4** 64.28N 11.30E
Namur Belgium **47 C2** 50.28N 4.52E
Namur *d.* Belgium **47 C2** 50.20N 4.45E
Nanaimo Canada **90 F2** 49.08N 123.58W
Nanao Japan **76 C5** 37.03N 136.58E
Nanchang China **75 I3** 28.38N 115.56E
Nanchong China **74 G3** 30.54N 106.06E
Nancy France **48 G5** 48.42N 6.12E
Nanda Devi *mtn.* India **71 E5** 30.21N 79.50E
Nander India **71 D3** 19.11N 77.21E
Nanga Parbat *mtn.* Jammu & Kashmir **71 D6** 35.10N 74.35E
Nanjing China **75 I4** 32.00N 118.40E
Nan Ling *mts.* China **75 H2** 25.20N 110.30E
Nanning China **75 H2** 22.50N 108.19E
Nanping Fujian China **75 I3** 26.40N 118.07E
Nanshan Is. S. China Sea **78 F6** 10.30N 116.00E
Nantaise *r.* France **48 C4** 47.12N 1.35W
Nantes France **48 C4** 47.14N 1.35W
Nantong China **75 J4** 32.05N 120.59E
Nantucket I. U.S.A. **87 M5** 41.16N 70.00W
Nantwich England **20 C2** 53.05N 2.31W
Nanumea *i.* Tuvalu **82 H7** 5.40S 176.10E
Nanyang China **75 H4** 33.06N 112.31E
Napier New Zealand **80 G2** 39.30S 176.54E
Naples Italy **54 E4** 40.50N 14.14E
Naples, G. of Med. Sea **54 E4** 40.42N 14.15E
Narayanganj Bangla. **71 G4** 23.36N 90.28E
Narbada *r. see* Narmada *r.* India **71**
Narberth Wales **18 B1** 51.48N 4.45W
Narbonne France **48 E2** 43.11N 3.00E
Nare Head England **12 C2** 50.12N 4.55W
Nares Str. Canada **91 K5** 78.30N 75.00W
Narmada *r.* India **71 D4** 21.40N 73.00E
Narodnaya *mtn.* Russian Fed. **60 F4** 65.00N 61.00E
Narsimhapur India **71 E4** 22.58N 79.15E
Narva Estonia **58 G2** 59.22N 28.17E
Narva *r.* Estonia **58 F2** 59.30N 28.00E
Narvik Norway **58 D5** 68.26N 17.25E
Naryan Mar Russian Fed. **60 E4** 67.37N 53.02E
Nasarawa Nigeria **108 C2** 8.35N 7.44E
Nash Pt. Wales **18 C1** 51.25N 3.35W
Nashville U.S.A. **87 I4** 36.10N 86.50W
Näsijärvi *l.* Finland **58 E3** 61.30N 23.50E
Nasik India **71 D4** 20.00N 73.52E
Nasratabad Iran **69 J3** 29.54N 59.58E
Nassau Bahamas **94 D6** 25.03N 77.20W
Nassau I. Cook Is. **82 J6** 11.33S 165.25W
Nasser, L. Egypt **68 D1** 22.40N 32.00E
Nässjö Sweden **58 C2** 57.39N 14.40E
Natal Brazil **96 F7** 5.46S 35.15W
Natal Indonesia **78 B4** 0.35N 99.07E
Natchez U.S.A. **87 H3** 31.22N 91.24W
Natitingou Benin **108 B3** 10.17N 1.19E
Natron, L. Tanzania **106 D4** 2.18S 36.05E
Naumburg Germany **52 E4** 51.09N 11.48E
Nauru Pacific Oc. **82 G7** 0.32S 166.55E
Navalmoral de la Mata Spain **50 C3** 39.54N 5.33W
Navan Rep. of Ire. **28 E3** 53.39N 6.42W
Navarra *d.* Spain **50 E5** 42.40N 1.40W
Nave *i.* Scotland **26 B2** 55.55N 6.20W
Navenby England **17 D3** 53.07N 0.32W
Naver *r.* Scotland **24 D5** 58.29N 4.12W
Navojoa Mexico **92 C5** 27.06N 109.26W
Návpaktos Greece **56 E3** 38.24N 21.49E
Návplion Greece **56 F2** 37.33N 22.47E
Navrongo Ghana **108 A2** 10.51N 1.03W
Nawabshah Pakistan **70 C5** 26.15N 68.26E
Náxos *i.* Greece **56 G2** 37.03N 25.30E
Nayarit *d.* Mexico **92 D4** 21.30N 104.00W
Nayland England **15 C2** 51.59N 0.52E
Nazareth Israel **68 F4** 32.41N 35.16E
Nazas *r.* Mexico **92 D5** 25.34N 103.25W
Nazilli Turkey **68 C5** 37.55N 28.20E
N'Djamena Chad **104 D3** 12.10N 14.59E
Ndola Zambia **106 C3** 13.00S 28.39E
Neagh, Lough N. Ireland **23 C1** 54.36N 6.26W
Neath Wales **18 C1** 51.39N 3.49W
Neath *r.* Wales **18 C1** 51.39N 3.50W
Nebraska *d.* U.S.A. **86 F5** 41.30N 100.00W
Nebrodi Mts. Italy **54 E2** 37.53N 14.32E
Neches *r.* U.S.A. **87 H2** 29.55N 93.50W
Neckar *r.* Germany **52 D3** 49.32N 8.26E
Needham Market England **15 D3** 52.09N 1.02E
Needles U.S.A. **86 D3** 34.51N 114.36W
Neerpelt Belgium **47 D3** 51.13N 5.28E
Nefyn Wales **18 B2** 52.55N 4.31W
Negev *des.* Israel **68 D3** 30.42N 34.55E
Negoiu *mtn.* Romania **56 G6** 45.36N 24.32E
Negotin Yugo. **56 F6** 44.14N 22.33E
Negra, C. Peru **96 A7** 6.06S 81.09W
Negrais, C. Myanma **71 G3** 16.00N 94.30E
Negro *r.* Argentina **97 C3** 41.00S 62.48W
Negro *r.* Brazil **96 C7** 3.30S 60.00W
Negros *i.* Phil. **79 G5** 10.00N 123.00E
Neijiang China **74 G3** 29.32N 105.03E
Nei Monggol *d. see* Inner Mongolia *d.* China **75**
Neisse *r.* Poland/Germany **52 G5** 52.05N 14.42E
Neiva Colombia **94 D1** 2.58N 75.15W
Nejd *d.* Saudi Arabia **68 F2** 25.00N 43.00E
Neksö Denmark **58 C1** 55.04N 15.09E
Nellore India **71 E3** 14.29N 80.00E
Nelson Canada **90 G2** 49.29N 117.17W
Nelson *r.* Canada **91 I3** 57.00N 93.20W
Nelson England **20 C2** 53.50N 2.14W
Nelson New Zealand **80 G1** 41.16S 173.15E
Nelson U.S.A. **86 D4** 35.30N 113.16W
Neman *r.* Lithuania **58 E1** 55.23N 21.15E
Nemours France **48 E5** 48.16N 2.41E
Nemuro Japan **76 F8** 43.22N 145.36E
Nemuro kaikyo *str.* Japan **76 F8** 44.00N 145.50E
Nenagh Rep. of Ire. **28 C2** 52.52N 8.13W
Nenana U.S.A. **90 D4** 64.35N 149.20W
Nene *r.* England **15 C3** 52.49N 0.12E
Nenjiang China **75 J6** 49.10N 125.15E
Nepal Asia **71 E5** 28.00N 84.00E
Nephin Beg Range *mts.* Rep. of Ire. **28 B4** 54.00N 9.40W
Nera *r.* Italy **54 D5** 42.33N 12.43E
Neretva *r.* Croatia **56 C5** 43.02N 17.28E
Nero Deep Pacific Oc. **79 L6** 12.40N 145.50E
Nes Neth. **47 D5** 53.27N 5.46E
Ness, Loch Scotland **24 D4** 57.16N 4.30W
Nesterov Ukraine **59 A4** 50.04N 24.00E
Neston England **20 B2** 53.17N 3.03W
Netherlands Europe **47 D4** 52.00N 5.30E
Netherlands Antilles S. America **93 K2** 12.30N 69.00W
Nether Stowey England **13 D3** 51.10N 3.10W
Neto *r.* Italy **54 F3** 39.12N 17.08E
Neubrandenburg Germany **52 F5** 53.33N 13.16E
Neuchâtel Switz. **52 C2** 47.00N 6.56E
Neuchâtel, Lac de *l.* Switz. **52 C2** 46.55N 6.55E
Neuenhaus Germany **47 E4** 52.30N 6.58E
Neufchâteau Belgium **47 D1** 49.51N 5.26E
Neufchâtel France **48 D5** 49.44N 1.26E
Neukalen Germany **46 F1** 53.50N 12.47E
Neumünster Germany **52 D6** 54.05N 10.01E
Neuquén Argentina **97 C4** 38.55S 68.55W
Neuse *r.* U.S.A. **87 K4** 35.04N 77.04W
Neusiedler, L. Austria **57 E3** 47.52N 16.45E
Neuss Germany **47 E3** 51.12N 6.42E
Neustadt Germany **46 D2** 54.07N 10.49E
Neustrelitz Germany **52 F5** 53.22N 13.05E
Neuwied Germany **47 F2** 50.26N 7.28E
Nevada *d.* U.S.A. **86 C4** 39.00N 117.00W
Nevada de Santa Marta, Sierra *mts.* Colombia **94 E3** 11.00N 73.30W
Nevada, Sierra *mts.* Spain **50 D2** 37.04N 3.20W
Nevada, Sierra *mts.* U.S.A. **86 C4** 37.30N 119.00W
Nevel Russian Fed. **59 B5** 56.00N 29.59E
Nevers France **48 E4** 47.00N 3.09E
Nevinnomyssk Russian Fed. **59 E2** 44.38N 41.59E
Nevşehir Turkey **68 D5** 38.38N 34.43E
New Alresford England **14 A2** 51.06N 1.10W
New Amsterdam Guyana **95 H2** 6.14N 57.30W
Newark N.J. U.S.A. **87 L5** 40.44N 74.11W
Newark-on-Trent England **16 D3** 53.06N 0.48W
New Bedford U.S.A. **87 L5** 41.38N 70.55W
New Bern U.S.A. **87 K4** 35.05N 77.04W
Newbiggin-by-the-Sea England **22 C2** 55.11N 1.30W
Newbridge on Wye Wales **18 C2** 52.13N 3.27W
New Britain *i.* P.N.G. **80 D5** 6.00S 143.00E
New Brunswick *d.* Canada **91 L2** 47.00N 66.00W
Newburgh Fife Scotland **27 E3** 56.21N 3.15W
Newbury England **14 A2** 51.24N 1.19W
New Caledonia *i.* Pacific Oc. **80 F3** 22.00S 165.00E
Newcastle Australia **80 E2** 32.55S 151.46E
Newcastle N. Ireland **23 D1** 54.13N 5.54W
Newcastle Wyo. U.S.A. **86 F5** 43.52N 104.14W
Newcastle Emlyn Wales **18 B2** 52.02N 4.29W
Newcastleton Scotland **27 F2** 55.21N 2.49W
Newcastle-under-Lyme England **16 B3** 53.02N 2.15W
Newcastle upon Tyne England **22 C1** 54.58N 1.36W
Newcastle West Rep. of Ire. **28 B2** 52.27N 9.04W
New Cumnock Scotland **26 D2** 55.24N 4.11W
New Delhi India **71 D5** 28.37N 77.13E
Newent England **13 E3** 51.56N 2.24W
New Forest *f.* England **14 A1** 50.50N 1.35W
Newfoundland *d.* Canada **91 L3** 55.00N 60.00W
Newfoundland *i.* Canada **91 M2** 48.30N 56.00W
New Galloway Scotland **26 D2** 55.05N 4.09W
New Guinea *i.* Austa. **79 K2** 5.00S 140.00E
New Hampshire *d.* U.S.A. **87 L5** 44.00N 71.30W
Newhaven England **15 C1** 50.47N 0.04E
New Haven U.S.A. **87 L5** 41.14N 72.50W
New Holland England **21 E2** 53.42N 0.22W
New Ireland *i.* P.N.G. **80 E5** 2.30S 151.30E
New Jersey *d.* U.S.A. **87 L5** 40.00N 74.30W
Newmarket England **15 C3** 52.15N 0.23E
Newmarket Rep. of Ire. **28 B2** 52.13N 9.01W
Newmarket on Fergus Rep. of Ire. **28 C2** 52.46N 8.55W
New Mexico *d.* U.S.A **86 E3** 34.00N 106.00W
New Mills England **16 C3** 53.23N 2.00W
Newmilns Scotland **26 D2** 55.37N 4.20W
Newnham England **13 E3** 51.48N 2.27W
New Orleans U.S.A. **87 H2** 30.00N 90.03W
New Plymouth New Zealand **80 G2** 39.04S 174.04E
Newport Essex England **15 C2** 51.58N 0.13E
Newport Hants. England **14 A1** 50.43N 1.18W
Newport Shrops. England **16 B2** 52.47N 2.22W
Newport Mayo Rep. of Ire. **28 B3** 53.53N 9.35W
Newport Tipperary Rep. of Ire. **28 C2** 52.42N 8.26W
Newport Dyfed Wales **18 B2** 52.01N 4.51W
Newport Gwent Wales **18 D1** 51.34N 2.59W
Newport News U.S.A. **87 K4** 36.59N 76.26W
Newport-on-Tay Scotland **27 F3** 56.27N 2.56W
Newport Pagnell England **15 B3** 52.05N 0.42W
New Providence *i.* Bahamas **93 I5** 25.03N 77.25W
Newquay England **12 B2** 50.24N 5.06W
New Quay Wales **18 B2** 52.13N 4.22W
New Radnor Wales **18 C2** 52.15N 3.10W
New Romney England **15 C1** 50.59N 0.58E
New Ross Rep. of Ire. **28 E2** 52.23N 6.59W
Newry N. Ireland **23 C1** 54.11N 6.20W
New Scone Scotland **27 E3** 56.25N 3.25W
New Siberian Is. Russian Fed. **61 L4** 76.00N 144.00E
New South Wales *d.* Australia **80 D2** 33.45S 147.00E
Newton Abbot England **13 D2** 50.32N 3.37W
Newton Aycliffe England **22 C1** 54.36N 1.34W
Newton-le-Willows England **20 C2** 53.28N 2.38W
Newton Mearns Scotland **26 D2** 55.46N 4.18W
Newtonmore Scotland **24 D4** 57.03N 4.10W
Newton Stewart Scotland **26 D1** 54.57N 4.29W
Newtown Wales **18 C2** 52.31N 3.19W
Newtownabbey N. Ireland **23 D1** 54.40N 5.57W
Newtownards N. Ireland **23 D1** 54.35N 5.42W
Newtown Butler N. Ireland **23 B1** 54.11N 7.22W

Newtown Hamilton N. Ireland **23 C1** 54.11N 6.35W
Newtown St. Boswells Scotland **27 F2** 55.35N 2.40W
Newtownstewart N. Ireland **23 B1** 54.43N 7.25W
New York U.S.A. **87 L5** 40.40N 73.50W
New York *d.* U.S.A. **87 K5** 43.00N 75.00W
New Zealand Austa. **80 G1** 41.00S 175.00E
Neyland Wales **18 B1** 51.43N 4.58W
Nezhin Ukraine **59 C4** 51.03N 31.54E
Ngaoundéré Cameroon **104 D2** 7.20N 13.35E
Nguigmi Niger **104 D3** 14.00N 13.11E
Nguru Nigeria **108 D3** 12.53N 10.30E
Nha Trang Vietnam **78 D6** 12.15N 109.10E
Niagara Falls *town* U.S.A. **87 K5** 43.06N 79.04W
Niamey Niger **104 C3** 13.32N 2.05E
Niangara Zaïre **105 E2** 3.45N 27.54E
Niapa, Gunung *mtn.* Indonesia **78 F4** 1.45N 117.30E
Nias *i.* Indonesia **78 B4** 1.05N 97.30E
Nibe Denmark **46 C4** 56.59N 9.39E
Nicaragua C. America **94 B3** 13.00N 85.00W
Nicaragua, L. Nicaragua **94 B3** 11.30N 85.30W
Nicastro Italy **54 F3** 38.58N 16.16E
Nice France **48 G2** 43.42N 7.16E
Nicobar Is. India **71 G2** 8.00N 94.00E
Nicosia Cyprus **68 D4** 35.11N 33.23E
Nicoya, G. of Costa Rica **94 C2** 9.30N 85.00W
Nicoya Pen. Costa Rica **94 B3** 10.30N 85.30W
Nid *r.* Norway **58 B2** 58.26N 8.44E
Nidd *r.* England **21 D3** 54.01N 1.12W
Nidderdale *f.* England **20 D3** 54.07N 1.50W
Nidzica Poland **57 G6** 53.22N 20.26E
Niebüll Germany **46 B2** 54.47N 8.51E
Niederösterreich *d.* Austria **57 D4** 48.20N 15.50E
Niedersachsen *d.* Germany **52 D5** 53.00N 10.00E
Niers *r.* Neth. **47 D3** 51.43N 5.56E
Nieuw Nickerie Surinam **95 H2** 5.57N 56.59W
Nieuwpoort Belgium **47 A3** 51.08N 2.45E
Niğde Turkey **68 D5** 37.58N 34.42E
Niger Africa **104 C3** 17.00N 10.00E
Niger *r.* Nigeria **108 C1** 4.15N 6.05E
Niger Delta Nigeria **108 C1** 4.00N 6.10E
Nigeria Africa **108 C2** 9.00N 9.00E
Nihoa *i.* Hawaiian Is. **82 J10** 23.03N 161.55W
Niigata Japan **76 D5** 37.58N 139.02E
Niihama Japan **76 B3** 33.57N 133.15E
Niiza Japan **76 D4** 35.48N 139.34E
Nijmegen Neth. **47 D3** 51.50N 5.52E
Nikel Russian Fed. **58 G5** 69.20N 29.44E
Nikiniki Indonesia **79 G2** 9.49S 124.29E
Nikki Benin **108 B2** 9.55N 3.18E
Nikolayev Ukraine **59 C3** 46.57N 32.00E
Nikolayevsk-na-Amur Russian Fed. **61 L3** 53.20N 140.44E
Nikopol Ukraine **59 C3** 47.34N 34.25E
Niksar Turkey **68 E6** 40.35N 36.59E
Nikšić Yugo. **56 D5** 42.48N 18.56E
Nikumaroro *i.* Kiribati **82 I7** 4.40S 174.32W
Nila *i.* Indonesia **79 H2** 6.45S 129.30E
Nile *r.* Egypt **68 C3** 31.30N 30.25E
Nile Delta Egypt **68 C3** 31.00N 31.00E
Nilgiri Hills India **71 D2** 11.30N 77.30E
Nimba, Mt. Guinea **102 B5** 7.35N 8.28W
Nîmes France **48 F2** 43.50N 4.21E
Nineveh *ruins* Iraq **68 F5** 36.24N 43.08E
Ningbo China **75 J3** 29.54N 121.33E
Ningwu China **75 H5** 39.00N 112.19E
Ningxia-Huizu *d.* China **74 G4** 37.00N 106.00E
Ninh Binh Vietnam **78 D8** 20.14N 106.00E
Ninove Belgium **47 C2** 50.50N 4.02E
Niobrara *r.* U.S.A. **86 G5** 42.45N 98.10W
Nioro Mali **104 B3** 15.12N 9.35W
Niort France **48 C4** 46.19N 0.27W
Nipigon Canada **91 J2** 49.02N 88.26W
Nipigon, L. Canada **91 J2** 49.50N 88.30W
Niriz Iran **69 I3** 29.12N 54.17E
Niš Yugo. **56 E5** 43.20N 21.54E
Nissum Bredning *b.* Denmark **46 B4** 56.40N 8.20E
Nissum Fjord *b.* Denmark **46 B4** 56.21N 8.11E
Niterói Brazil **97 E5** 22.45S 43.06W
Nith *r.* Scotland **27 E2** 55.00N 3.35W
Nithsdale *f.* Scotland **27 E2** 55.15N 3.48W
Nitra Slovakia **57 F4** 48.20N 18.05E
Niue *i.* Cook Is. **82 J6** 19.02S 169.52W
Niut, Gunung *mtn.* Indonesia **78 D4** 1.00N 110.00E
Nivelles Belgium **47 C2** 50.36N 4.20E
Nizamabad India **71 E3** 18.40N 78.05E
Nizhneudinsk Russian Fed. **61 I3** 54.55N 99.00E
Nizhnevartovsk Russian Fed. **60 G3** 60.57N 76.40E
Nizhniy Novgorod Russian Fed. **59 E5** 56.20N 44.00E
Nizhniy Tagil Russian Fed. **60 F3** 58.00N 60.00E
Nkongsamba Cameroon **104 D2** 4.59N 9.53E
Nobeoka Japan **76 A3** 32.36N 131.40E
Nogales Mexico **92 B6** 31.20N 111.00W
Nogent-le-Rotrou France **48 D5** 48.19N 0.50E
Noguera Ribagorzana *r.* Spain **50 F4** 41.27N 0.25E
Noirmoutier, Île de *i.* France **48 B4** 47.00N 2.15W
Nokia Finland **58 E3** 61.29N 23.31E
Nome U.S.A. **90 B4** 64.30N 165.30W
Nong Khai Thailand **78 C7** 17.50N 102.46E
Nonthaburi Thailand **78 C6** 13.48N 100.31E
Noord Brabant *d.* Neth. **47 D3** 51.37N 5.00E
Noorvik U.S.A. **90 B4** 66.50N 161.14W
Nordborg Denmark **46 C3** 55.04N 9.47E
Norddeich Germany **47 F5** 53.35N 7.10E
Norden Germany **47 F5** 53.34N 7.13E
Nordenham Germany **52 D5** 53.30N 8.29E
Norderney *i.* Germany **47 F5** 53.45N 7.15E
Nordfjord *est.* Norway **58 A3** 61.50N 6.00E
Nordhausen Germany **52 E4** 51.31N 10.48E
Nordhorn Germany **47 F4** 52.27N 7.05E
Nord-Jyllands *d.* Denmark **46 C5** 57.20N 10.00E
Nordrhein-Westfalen *d.* Germany **52 D4** 51.30N 8.00E
Nordstrand *i.* Germany **46 B2** 54.30N 8.52E
Nordvik Russian Fed. **61 J4** 73.40N 110.50E
Nore *r.* Rep. of Ire. **28 E2** 52.25N 6.58W
Norfolk *d.* England **15 D3** 52.39N 1.00E
Norfolk U.S.A. **87 K4** 36.54N 76.18W
Norfolk Broads *f.* England **15 D3** 52.43N 1.35E
Norfolk I. Pacific Oc. **80 F3** 28.58S 168.03E
Norham England **22 B2** 55.43N 2.10W
Norilsk Russian Fed. **61 H4** 69.21N 88.02E
Normandie, Collines de *hills* France **48 C5** 48.50N 0.40W
Normanton England **21 D2** 53.41N 1.26W
Norman Wells Canada **90 F4** 65.19N 126.46W
Nörresundby Denmark **46 C5** 57.05N 9.52E
Norris L. U.S.A. **87 J4** 36.20N 83.55W
Norrköping Sweden **58 D2** 58.35N 16.10E
Norrtälje Sweden **58 D2** 59.46N 18.43E
Northallerton England **21 D3** 54.20N 1.26W
Northam England **12 C3** 51.02N 4.13W
North America 112
Northampton England **16 D2** 52.14N 0.54W
Northamptonshire *d.* England **16 D2** 52.18N 0.55W
North Battleford Canada **90 H3** 52.47N 108.19W
North Bay *town* Canada **91 K2** 46.20N 79.28W
North Bend U.S.A. **86 B5** 43.26N 124.14W
North Berwick Scotland **27 F3** 56.04N 2.43W
North Beveland *f.* Neth. **47 B3** 51.35N 3.45E
North C. Norway **58 F5** 71.10N 25.45E
North Canadian *r.* U.S.A. **87 G4** 35.30N 95.45W
North Carolina *d.* U.S.A. **87 K4** 35.30N 79.00W
North Channel U.K. **26 C2** 55.15N 5.52W
North China Plain *f.* China **75 I4** 34.30N 117.00E
North Dakota *d.* U.S.A. **86 F6** 47.00N 100.00W
North Dorset Downs *hills* England **13 E2** 50.46N 2.25W
North Downs *hills* England **15 C2** 51.18N 0.40E
North Dvina *r.* Russian Fed. **60 D4** 64.40N 40.50E
Northeast China Plain *f.* China **75 J6** 46.00N 125.00E
North East Polder *f.* Neth. **47 D4** 52.45N 5.45E
Northern Ireland *d.* U.K. **23 C1** 54.40N 6.45W
Northern Territory *d.* Australia **80 C4** 20.00S 133.00E
North Esk *r.* Scotland **24 F3** 56.45N 2.25W
North European Plain *f.* Europe **40 K6** 56.00N 27.00E
North Fiji Basin Pacific Oc. **113 R4** 17.00S 173.00E
North Foreland *c.* England **15 D2** 51.23N 1.26E
North Frisian Is. Germany **52 C6** 54.30N 8.00E
North Holland *d.* Neth. **47 C4** 52.37N 4.50E
North I. New Zealand **80 G2** 39.00S 175.00E
Northiam England **15 C1** 50.59N 0.39E
North Korea Asia **75 K5** 40.00N 128.00E
North Kyme England **17 D3** 53.04N 0.17W
Northleach England **13 F3** 51.49N 1.50W
North Platte U.S.A. **86 F5** 41.09N 100.45W
North Platte *r.* U.S.A. **86 F5** 41.09N 100.55W
North Ronaldsay *i.* Scotland **24 F6** 59.23N 2.26W
North Sea Europe **40 F6** 56.00N 4.00E
North Somercotes England **17 E3** 53.28N 0.08E
North Sporades *is.* Greece **56 F3** 39.00N 24.00E
North Tawton England **13 D2** 50.48N 3.55W
North Tidworth England **13 F3** 51.14N 1.40W
North Truchas Peak *mtn.* U.S.A. **86 E4** 35.58N 105.48W
North Tyne *r.* England **22 B1** 54.59N 2.08W
North Uist *i.* Scotland **24 A4** 57.35N 7.20W
Northumberland *d.* England **22 B2** 55.12N 2.00W
North Walsham England **15 D3** 52.49N 1.22E
Northway U.S.A. **90 D4** 62.58N 142.00W
North Western Atlantic Basin Atlantic Oc. **112 G6** 33.00N 55.00W
North West Highlands Scotland **24 C4** 57.30N 5.15W
North West River *town* Canada **91 L3** 53.30N 60.10W
Northwest Territories *d.* Canada **91 I4** 66.00N 95.00W
Northwich England **20 C2** 53.16N 2.30W
North York Moors *hills* England **21 E3** 54.21N 0.50W
North Yorkshire *d.* England **21 D3** 54.14N 1.14W
Norton England **21 E3** 54.08N 0.47W
Norton Sound *b.* U.S.A. **90 B4** 63.50N 164.00W
Norway Europe **58 B3** 65.00N 13.00E
Norway House *town* Canada **91 I3** 53.59N 97.50W
Norwegian Sea Europe **40 F8** 66.00N 2.00E
Norwich England **15 D3** 52.38N 1.17E
Noss Head Scotland **24 E5** 58.29N 3.02W
Nossob *r.* R.S.A./Botswana **106 C2** 26.54S 20.39E
Noteć *r.* Poland **57 D6** 52.44N 15.26E
Nottingham England **16 C2** 52.57N 1.10W
Nottinghamshire *d.* England **16 D3** 53.10N 1.00W
Nouadhibou Mauritania **104 A4** 20.54N 17.01W
Nouakchott Mauritania **104 A3** 18.09N 15.58W
Nouméa New Caledonia **82 G5** 22.16S 166.27E
Nouvelle Calédonie *is.* Pacific Oc. **82 G5** 21.30S 165.30E
Novara Italy **54 B6** 45.27N 8.37E
Nova Scotia *d.* Canada **91 L2** 45.00N 64.00W
Novaya Ladoga Russian Fed. **59 C6** 60.09N 32.15E
Novaya Siberia *i.* Russian Fed. **61 M4** 75.20N 148.00E
Novaya Zemlya *i.* Russian Fed. **60 E4** 74.00N 56.00E
Novelda Spain **50 E3** 38.24N 0.45W
Nové Zámky Slovakia **57 F3** 47.59N 18.11E
Novgorod Russian Fed. **59 C5** 58.30N 31.20E
Novi Pazar Yugo. **56 E5** 43.08N 20.28E
Novi Sad Yugo. **56 D6** 45.16N 19.52E
Novocherkassk Russian Fed. **59 E3** 47.25N 40.05E
Novograd Volynskiy Ukraine **59 B4** 50.34N 27.32E
Novogrudok Belorussia **59 B4** 53.35N 25.50E
Novokazalinsk Kazakhstan **60 F2** 45.48N 62.06E
Novokuybyshevsk Russian Fed. **60 E3** 53.05N 49.59E
Novokuznetsk Russian Fed. **60 H3** 53.45N 87.12E
Novomoskovsk Russian Fed. **59 D4** 54.06N 38.15E
Novomoskovsk Ukraine **59 D3** 48.38N 35.15E
Novorossiysk Russian Fed. **59 D2** 44.44N 37.46E
Novoshakhtinsk Russian Fed. **59 D3** 47.46N 39.55E
Novosibirsk Russian Fed. **60 G3** 55.04N 82.55E
Novouzensk Russian Fed. **59 F4** 50.29N 48.08E
Novy Port Russian Fed. **60 G4** 67.38N 72.33E
Nowa Sól Poland **57 D5** 51.49N 15.41E
Nowgong India **71 G5** 26.20N 92.41E
Nowy Korczyn Poland **57 G5** 50.19N 20.48E
Nowy Sącz Poland **57 G4** 49.39N 20.40E
Noyon France **47 A1** 49.35N 3.00E
Nsukka Nigeria **108 C2** 6.51N 7.29E
Nubian Desert Sudan **105 F4** 21.00N 34.00E
Nueces *r.* U.S.A. **87 G2** 27.55N 97.30W
Nueva Gerona Cuba **94 C5** 21.53N 82.49W
Nuevitas Cuba **94 D5** 21.34N 77.18W
Nuevo Laredo Mexico **92 E5** 27.30N 99.30W
Nuevo León *d.* Mexico **92 E5** 26.00N 99.00W
Nui *i.* Tuvalu **82 H7** 7.12S 177.10E
Nu Jiang *r. see* Salween *r.* China **74**
Nukha Azerbaijan **69 G6** 41.12N 47.10E
Nuku'alofa Tonga **82 I5** 21.07S 175.12W
Nuku Hiva *i.* Marquesas Is. **83 L7** 8.56S 140.00W
Nukunono Pacific Oc. **82 I7** 9.10S 171.55W
Nukus Uzbekistan **60 E2** 42.28N 59.07E
Nullarbor Plain *f.* Australia **80 B2** 31.30S 128.00E
Numazu Japan **76 D4** 35.08N 138.50E
Nuneaton England **16 C2** 52.32N 1.29W
Nunivak I. U.S.A. **90 B3** 60.00N 166.30W
Nuqra Saudi Arabia **68 F2** 25.35N 41.28E
Nurmes Finland **58 G3** 63.32N 29.10E
Nürnberg Germany **52 E3** 49.27N 11.05E
Nusaybin Turkey **68 F5** 37.05N 41.11E
Nuuk *see* Godthåb Greenland **91**
Nyala Sudan **105 E3** 12.01N 24.50E
Nyasa, L. Africa **106 D3** 12.00S 34.30E
Nyborg Denmark **46 D3** 55.19N 10.49E
Nybro Sweden **58 C2** 56.44N 15.55E
Nyíregyháza Hungary **57 G3** 47.59N 21.43E
Nykøbing Falstar Denmark **46 E2** 54.47N 11.53E
Nykøbing Thisted Denmark **46 B4** 56.49N 8.50E
Nykøbing Zealand Denmark **46 E3** 55.55N 11.40E
Nyköping Sweden **58 D2** 58.45N 17.03E
Nynäshamn Sweden **58 D2** 58.54N 17.55E
Nyons France **48 F3** 44.22N 5.08E
Nysa Poland **57 E5** 50.29N 17.20E

O

Oadby England **16 C2** 52.37N 1.07W
Oahe Resr. U.S.A. **86 F6** 45.45N 100.20W
Oahu *i.* Hawaiian Is. **83 K10** 21.30N 158.00W
Oakengates England **16 B2** 52.42N 2.29W
Oakham England **16 D2** 52.40N 0.43W
Oakland U.S.A. **86 B4** 37.50N 122.15W
Oaxaca Mexico **92 E3** 17.05N 96.41W
Oaxaca *d.* Mexico **92 E3** 17.30N 97.00W
Ob *r.* Russian Fed. **60 F4** 66.50N 69.00E
Oban Scotland **26 C3** 56.26N 5.28W
Obbia Somali Rep. **105 G2** 5.20N 48.30E
Oberhausen Germany **47 E3** 51.28N 6.51E
Oberösterreich *d.* Austria **57 C4** 48.15N 14.00E
Ob, G. of Russian Fed. **60 G4** 68.30N 74.00E
Obi *i.* Indonesia **79 H3** 1.45S 127.30E
Obihiro Japan **76 E8** 42.55N 143.00E
Obuasi Ghana **108 A2** 6.15N 1.36W
Ocaña Colombia **94 E2** 8.16N 73.21W
Ocaña Spain **50 D3** 39.57N 3.30W
Occidental, Cordillera Colombia **94 D1** 5.00N 76.15W
Ocean I. *see* Banaba *i.* Kiribati **82**
Ochil Hills Scotland **27 E3** 56.16N 3.25W
Ocotlán Mexico **92 D4** 20.21N 102.42W
October Revolution *i.* Russian Fed. **61 I5** 79.30N 96.00E
Oda Ghana **108 A2** 5.55N 0.56W
Odádhahraun *mts.* Iceland **58 J7** 65.00N 17.30W
Odate Japan **76 D7** 40.16N 140.34E
Odawara Japan **76 D4** 35.20N 139.08E
Odda Norway **58 A3** 60.03N 6.45E
Odder Denmark **46 D3** 55.59N 10.11E
Ödemiş Turkey **59 B1** 38.12N 28.00E
Odense Denmark **46 D3** 55.24N 10.25E
Oder *r.* Poland/Germany **57 D6** 53.30N 14.36E
Odessa Ukraine **59 C3** 46.30N 30.46E
Odessa U.S.A. **86 F3** 31.50N 102.23W
Odorhei Romania **56 G7** 46.18N 25.18E
Oeno I. Pacific Oc. **83 M5** 23.55S 130.45W
Ofanto *r.* Italy **54 F4** 41.22N 16.12E
Offaly *d.* Rep. of Ire. **28 D3** 53.15N 7.30W
Offenbach Germany **52 D4** 50.06N 8.46E
Offenburg Germany **52 C3** 48.29N 7.57E
Ogaki Japan **76 C4** 35.25N 136.36E
Ogbomosho Nigeria **108 B2** 8.05N 4.11E
Ogden U.S.A. **86 D5** 41.14N 111.59W
Ogeechee *r.* U.S.A. **87 J3** 32.54N 81.05W
Ognon *r.* France **48 F4** 47.20N 5.37E
Ogoja Nigeria **108 C2** 6.40N 8.45E
Ogooué *r.* Gabon **106 A4** 1.00S 9.05E
Ogosta *r.* Bulgaria **56 F5** 43.44N 23.51E
Ogulin Croatia **56 B6** 45.17N 15.14E
Ohio U.S.A. **87 J5** 40.00N 83.00W
Ohio *r.* U.S.A. **87 I4** 37.07N 89.10W
Ohře *r.* Czech Rep. **57 D5** 50.32N 14.08E
Ohrid Macedonia **56 E4** 41.06N 20.48E
Ohridsko, L. Albania/Macedonia **56 E4** 41.00N 20.43E
Oil City U.S.A. **87 K5** 41.26N 79.30W
Oise *r.* France **48 E5** 49.00N 2.10E
Oita Japan **76 A3** 33.15N 131.40E
Ojocaliente Mexico **92 D4** 22.35N 102.18W
Oka *r.* Russian Fed. **59 E5** 56.09N 43.00E
Okaba Indonesia **79 J2** 8.06S 139.46E
Okanogan *r.* U.S.A. **86 B6** 47.45N 120.05W
Okavango *r.* Botswana **106 C3** 18.30S 22.04E
Okavango Basin *f.* Botswana **106 C3** 19.30S 23.00E
Okayama Japan **76 B4** 34.40N 133.54E
Okazaki Japan **76 C4** 34.58N 137.10E
Okeechobee, L. U.S.A. **87 J2** 27.00N 80.45W
Okefenokee Swamp *f.* U.S.A. **87 J3** 30.40N 82.40W
Okehampton England **13 C2** 50.44N 4.01W
Okement *r.* England **13 C2** 50.50N 4.04W
Okha India **70 C4** 22.25N 69.00E
Okha Russian Fed. **61 L3** 53.35N 142.50E
Okhotsk Russian Fed. **61 L3** 59.20N 143.15E
Okhotsk, Sea of Russian Fed. **61 M3** 55.00N 150.00E
Oki gunto *is.* Japan **76 B5** 36.10N 133.10E
Okinawa *i.* Japan **75 K3** 26.30N 128.00E
Okino Torishima *i.* Pacific Oc. **79 J8** 20.24N 136.02E
Okitipupa Nigeria **108 B2** 6.31N 4.50E
Oklahoma *d.* U.S.A. **87 G4** 35.00N 97.00W
Oklahoma City U.S.A. **87 G4** 35.28N 97.33W
Oksby Denmark **46 B3** 55.33N 8.11E
Okushiri shima *i.* Japan **76 D7** 42.00N 139.50E
Öland *i.* Sweden **58 D2** 56.50N 16.50E
Olbia Italy **54 B4** 40.55N 9.29E
Old Crow Canada **90 E4** 67.34N 139.43W
Oldenburg Nschn. Germany **47 G5** 53.08N 8.13E
Oldenburg Sch.-Hol. Germany **52 E6** 54.17N 10.52E
Oldenzaal Neth. **47 E4** 52.19N 6.55E
Old Fletton England **15 B3** 52.34N 0.14W
Oldham England **20 C2** 53.33N 2.08W
Old Head of Kinsale *c.* Rep. of Ire. **28 C1** 51.37N 8.33W
Old Rhine *r.* Neth. **47 C4** 52.14N 4.26E
Olean U.S.A. **87 K5** 42.05N 78.26W
Olekma *r.* Russian Fed. **61 K3** 60.20N 120.30E
Olekminsk Russian Fed. **61 K3** 60.25N 120.00E
Olenëk Russian Fed. **61 J4** 68.38N 112.15E
Olenëk *r.* Russian Fed. **61 K4** 73.00N 120.00E
Olenekskiy G. Russian Fed. **61 J4** 74.00N 120.00E
Oléron, Île d' *i.* France **48 C3** 45.55N 1.16W
Oleśnica Poland **57 E5** 51.13N 17.23E
Olga Russian Fed. **75 L5** 43.46N 135.14E
Ölgod Denmark **46 B3** 55.49N 8.39E
Olhão Portugal **50 B2** 37.01N 7.50W
Olifants *r.* Namibia **106 B2** 25.28S 19.23E
Olivares Spain **50 D3** 39.45N 2.21W
Olney England **15 B3** 52.09N 0.42W
Ölögey Mongolia **74 E6** 48.54N 90.00E
Olomouc Czech Rep. **57 E4** 49.36N 17.16E
Olonets Russian Fed. **59 C6** 61.00N 32.59E
Oloron France **48 C2** 43.12N 0.35W
Olot Spain **50 G5** 42.11N 2.30E
Olpe Germany **47 F3** 51.02N 7.52E
Olsztyn Poland **57 G6** 53.48N 20.29E
Oltenița Romania **56 H6** 44.05N 26.31E
Olteț *r.* Romania **56 G6** 44.13N 24.28E
Olympus, Mt. Cyprus **68 D4** 34.55N 32.52E
Olympus, Mt. Greece **56 F4** 40.04N 22.20E
Omagh N. Ireland **23 B1** 54.35N 7.20W
Omaha U.S.A. **87 G5** 41.15N 96.00W
Oman Asia **105 H4** 22.30N 57.30E
Oman, G. of Asia **69 J2** 25.00N 58.00E
Ombrone *r.* Italy **54 C5** 42.40N 11.00E
Omdurman Sudan **105 F3** 15.37N 32.59E
Ommen Neth. **47 E4** 52.32N 6.25E
Omolon *r.* Russian Fed. **61 N4** 68.50N 158.30E
Omono *r.* Japan **76 D6** 39.44N 140.05E
Omsk Russian Fed. **60 G3** 55.00N 73.22E
Omulew *r.* Poland **57 G6** 53.05N 21.32E
Omuta Japan **76 A3** 33.02N 130.26E
Oña Spain **50 D5** 42.44N 3.25W
Onda Spain **50 E3** 39.58N 0.16W
Onega, L. Russian Fed. **60 D3** 62.00N 35.30E
Onitsha Nigeria **108 C2** 6.10N 6.47E
Onstwedde Neth. **47 F5** 53.04N 7.02E
Ontaki san *mtn.* Japan **76 C4** 35.55N 137.29E
Ontario *d.* Canada **91 J3** 52.00N 86.00W
Ontario, L. N. America **87 K5** 43.40N 78.00W
Oosterhout Neth. **47 C3** 51.38N 4.50E
Oosthuizen Neth. **47 C4** 52.33N 5.00E
Oostmalle Belgium **47 C3** 51.18N 4.45E
Opole Poland **57 E5** 50.40N 17.56E
Oporto Portugal **50 A4** 41.09N 8.37W
Oradea Romania **57 G3** 47.03N 21.55E
Oran Algeria **104 B5** 35.45N 0.38W
Orange Australia **80 D2** 33.19S 149.10E
Orange France **48 F3** 44.08N 4.48E
Orange *r.* R.S.A. **106 B2** 28.43S 16.30E
Orangeburg U.S.A. **87 J3** 33.28N 80.53W
Orange, C. Brazil **96 D8** 4.25N 51.32W
Orchies France **47 B2** 50.28N 3.15E
Orchila *i.* Venezuela **95 F3** 11.52N 66.10W
Ordu Turkey **68 E6** 41.00N 37.52E
Orduña Spain **50 D5** 43.00N 3.00W
Örebro Sweden **58 C2** 59.17N 15.13E
Oregon *d.* U.S.A. **86 B5** 44.00N 120.00W
Öregrund Sweden **58 D3** 60.20N 18.30E
Orekhovo-Zuyevo Russian Fed. **59 D5** 55.47N 39.00E
Orel Russian Fed. **59 D4** 52.58N 36.04E
Ore Mts. Europe **40 H5** 50.30N 12.50E
Orenburg Russian Fed. **60 E2** 51.50N 55.00E
Orense Spain **50 B5** 42.20N 7.52W
Ore Sund *str.* Denmark **46 F3** 55.40N 12.40E
Orford England **15 D3** 52.06N 1.31E
Orford Ness *c.* England **15 D3** 52.05N 1.36E
Orgeyev Moldavia **59 B3** 47.24N 28.50E
Oriental, Cordillera *mts.* Colombia **94 E1** 5.00N 74.30W

Q

R

Rakvere Estonia **58 F2** 59.22N 26.28E
Raleigh U.S.A. **87 K4** 35.46N 78.39W
Ralik Chain *is.* Pacific Oc. **82 G8** 8.00N 168.00E
Rama Nicaragua **93 H2** 12.09N 84.15W
Ramah Saudi Arabia **69 G2** 25.33N 47.08E
Ramat Gan Israel **68 D4** 32.05N 34.48E
Rame Head England **12 C2** 50.18N 4.13W
Ramelton Rep. of Ire. **28 D5** 55.02N 7.40W
Ramhormoz Iran **69 H3** 31.14N 49.37E
Ramillies Belgium **47 C2** 50.39N 4.56E
Ramingstein Austria **57 C3** 47.04N 13.50E
Ramishk Iran **69 J2** 26.52N 58.46E
Ramos Arizpe Mexico **92 D5** 25.35N 100.59W
Rampur India **71 E5** 28.48N 79.03E
Ramree I. Myanma **71 G3** 19.10N 93.40E
Ramsar Iran **69 H5** 36.54N 50.41E
Ramsbottom England **20 C2** 53.38N 2.20W
Ramsey England **15 B3** 52.27N 0.06W
Ramsey I.o.M. **20 A3** 54.19N 4.23W
Ramsey *i.* Wales **18 A1** 51.53N 5.21W
Ramsey B. I.o.M. **20 A3** 54.20N 4.20W
Ramsgate England **15 D2** 51.20N 1.25E
Rancagua Chile **97 B4** 34.10S 70.45W
Ranchi India **71 F4** 23.22N 85.20E
Randalstown N. Ireland **23 C1** 54.45N 6.20W
Randers Denmark **46 D4** 56.28N 10.03E
Rangiroa *i.* Pacific Oc. **83 L6** 15.00S 147.40W
Rannoch, Loch Scotland **24 D3** 56.41N 4.20W
Rann of Kutch *f.* India **71 C4** 23.50N 69.50E
Rantauparapat Indonesia **78 B4** 2.05N 99.46E
Rantekombola *mtn.* Indonesia **78 F3** 3.30S 119.58E
Raoul *i.* Pacific Oc. **82 I5** 29.15S 177.55W
Rapa *i.* Pacific Oc. **83 L5** 27.35S 144.20W
Rapallo Italy **54 B6** 44.20N 9.14E
Rapid City U.S.A. **86 F5** 44.06N 103.14W
Raqqa Syria **68 E4** 35.57N 39.03E
Rarotonga *i.* Cook Is. **83 K5** 21.14S 159.46W
Ras al Hadd *c.* Oman **69 J1** 22.32N 59.49E
Ras al Khaimah U.A.E. **69 I2** 25.48N 55.56E
Ras Banas *c.* Egypt **68 D1** 23.54N 35.48E
Ras Dashan *mtn.* Ethiopia **105 F3** 13.20N 38.10E
Rashîd Egypt **68 C3** 31.25N 30.25E
Rasht Iran **69 H5** 37.18N 49.38E
Râs Muhammad *c.* Egypt **68 D2** 27.42N 34.13E
Rass Saudi Arabia **68 F2** 25.54N 43.30E
Ras Tanura *c.* Saudi Arabia **69 H2** 26.40N 50.10E
Ratak Chain *is.* Pacific Oc. **82 H8** 8.00N 172.00E
Rat Buri Thailand **78 B6** 13.30N 99.50E
Rathcormack Rep. of Ire. **28 C2** 52.03N 8.19W
Rathdrum Rep. of Ire. **28 E2** 52.55N 6.14W
Rathenow Germany **52 F5** 52.37N 12.21E
Rathfriland N. Ireland **23 C1** 54.14N 6.10W
Rathlin *i.* N. Ireland **23 C2** 55.18N 6.12W
Rathlin Sd. N. Ireland **23 C2** 55.15N 6.15W
Rath Luirc Rep. of Ire. **28 C2** 52.20N 8.40W
Rathmullen Rep. of Ire. **28 D5** 55.06N 7.34W
Ratlam India **71 D4** 23.18N 75.06E
Raton U.S.A. **86 F4** 36.54N 104.27W
Rattray Head Scotland **24 G4** 57.37N 1.50W
Rättvik Sweden **58 C3** 60.56N 15.10E
Rauma Finland **58 E3** 61.09N 21.30E
Raunds England **17 D2** 52.21N 0.33W
Ravenna Italy **54 D6** 44.25N 12.12E
Ravensburg Germany **52 D2** 47.47N 9.37E
Ravi *r.* Pakistan **71 D5** 30.30N 72.13E
Rawaki *i.* Kiribati **82 I7** 3.43S 170.43W
Rawalpindi Pakistan **71 D6** 33.40N 73.08E
Rawicz Poland **57 E5** 51.37N 16.52E
Rawlins U.S.A. **86 E5** 41.46N 107.16W
Rawmarsh England **21 D2** 53.27N 1.20W
Rawtenstall England **20 C2** 53.42N 2.18W
Rayen Iran **69 J3** 29.34N 57.26E
Rayleigh England **15 C2** 51.36N 0.36E
Razan Iran **69 H4** 35.22N 49.02E
Razgrad Bulgaria **56 H5** 43.32N 26.30E
Reading England **15 B2** 51.27N 0.57W
Reay Forest *f.* Scotland **24 D5** 58.20N 4.55W
Rebun jima *i.* Japan **76 E9** 45.25N 141.04E
Recife Brazil **96 F7** 8.06S 34.53W
Recklinghausen Germany **47 F3** 51.36N 7.11E
Recknitz *r.* Germany **46 F2** 54.09N 12.41E
Red *r.* Canada **91 I3** 50.30N 96.50W
Red *r.* U.S.A. **87 H3** 31.10N 92.00W
Red *r.* Vietnam **78 D8** 20.15N 106.32E
Red B. N. Ireland **23 C2** 55.05N 6.02W
Red Basin *f.* China **74 G3** 30.30N 105.00E
Red Bluff U.S.A. **86 B5** 40.11N 122.16W
Redbridge England **15 C2** 51.35N 0.06E
Redcar England **22 C1** 54.37N 1.04W
Red Deer Canada **90 G3** 52.15N 113.48W
Redding U.S.A. **86 B5** 40.35N 122.24W
Redditch England **16 C2** 52.18N 1.57W
Redhill England **15 B2** 51.14N 0.11W
Red L. U.S.A. **87 H6** 48.00N 95.00W
Red Lake *town* Canada **91 I3** 50.59N 93.40W
Redruth England **12 B2** 50.14N 5.14W
Red Sea Africa/Asia **105 F4** 20.00N 39.00E
Red Tower Pass Romania **56 G6** 45.37N 24.17E
Red Volta *r.* Ghana **108 A3** 10.32N 0.31W
Red Wharf B. Wales **18 B3** 53.20N 4.10W
Reedham England **15 D3** 52.34N 1.33E
Ree, Lough Rep. of Ire. **28 D3** 53.31N 7.58W
Rega *r.* Poland **57 D7** 54.10N 15.18E
Regensburg Germany **52 F3** 49.01N 12.07E
Reggane Algeria **104 C4** 26.30N 0.30E
Reggio Calabria Italy **54 E3** 38.07N 15.38E
Reggio Emilia-Romagna Italy **54 C6** 44.40N 10.37E
Regina Canada **90 H3** 50.30N 104.38W
Reigate England **15 B2** 51.14N 0.13W
Ré, Île de *i.* France **48 C4** 46.10N 1.26W
Reims France **48 F5** 49.15N 4.02E
Reinberg Germany **46 G2** 54.12N 13.14E
Reindeer L. Canada **90 H3** 57.00N 102.20W
Reinosa Mexico **92 E5** 26.09N 97.10W
Reinosa Spain **50 C5** 43.01N 4.09W
Rembang Indonesia **78 E2** 6.45S 111.22E
Remich Lux. **47 E1** 49.34N 6.23E
Remscheid Germany **47 F3** 51.10N 7.11E
Renaix Belgium **47 B2** 50.45N 3.36E
Rendsburg Germany **52 D6** 54.19N 9.39E
Renfrew Scotland **26 D2** 55.52N 4.23W
Rengat Indonesia **78 C3** 0.26S 102.35E
Renkum Neth. **47 D3** 51.59N 5.46E
Rennes France **48 C5** 48.06N 1.40W
Reno *r.* Italy **54 D6** 44.36N 12.17E
Reno U.S.A. **86 C4** 39.32N 119.49W
Republican *r.* U.S.A. **87 H4** 39.05N 94.50W
Republic of Ireland Europe **28 D3** 53.00N 8.00W
Republic of South Africa Africa **106 C2** 30.00S 27.00E
Requena Spain **50 E3** 39.29N 1.08W
Resistencia Argentina **97 D5** 27.28S 59.00W
Reşiţa Romania **57 G2** 45.17N 21.53E
Resolute Canada **91 I5** 74.40N 95.00W
Rethel France **47 C1** 49.31N 4.22E
Réthimnon Greece **56 G1** 35.22N 24.29E
Réunion *i.* Indian Oc. **113 L3** 22.00S 55.00E
Reus Spain **50 F4** 41.10N 1.06E
Reutlingen Germany **52 D3** 48.30N 9.13E
Revelstoke Canada **90 G3** 51.02N 118.12W
Revilla Gigedo Is. Mexico **92 B3** 19.00N 111.00W
Rey Iran **69 H4** 35.35N 51.27E
Reykjavík Iceland **58 I7** 64.09N 21.58W
Rezaiyeh Iran **69 G5** 37.32N 45.02E
Rēzekne Latvia **58 F2** 56.30N 27.22E
Rhayader Wales **18 C2** 52.19N 3.30W
Rheden Neth. **47 E4** 52.01N 6.02E
Rheine Germany **47 F4** 52.17N 7.26E
Rheinland-Pfalz *d.* Germany **52 C4** 50.00N 7.00E
Rhenen Neth. **47 D3** 51.58N 5.34E
Rheydt Germany **47 E3** 51.10N 6.25E
Rhine *r.* Europe **47 E3** 51.53N 6.03E
Rhinelander U.S.A. **87 I5** 45.39N 89.23W
Rhinns of Kells *hills* Scotland **26 D2** 55.08N 4.21W
Rhinns Pt. Scotland **26 B2** 55.40N 6.29W
Rhode Island *d.* U.S.A. **87 L5** 41.30N 71.30W
Rhodes *i.* Greece **68 C5** 36.12N 28.00E
Rhodes *town* Greece **68 C5** 36.24N 28.15E
Rhodope Mts. Bulgaria **56 F4** 41.35N 24.35E
Rhondda Wales **18 C1** 51.39N 3.30W
Rhondda Valley *f.* Wales **18 C1** 51.38N 3.29W
Rhône *r.* France **48 F2** 43.25N 4.45E
Rhosllanerchrugog Wales **18 C3** 53.03N 3.04W
Rhosneigr Wales **18 B3** 53.14N 4.31W
Rhum *i.* Scotland **24 B3** 57.00N 6.20W
Rhyddhywel *mtn.* Wales **18 C2** 52.25N 3.27W
Rhyl Wales **18 C3** 53.19N 3.29W
Riau Is. Indonesia **78 C4** 0.50N 104.00E
Ribadeo Spain **50 B5** 43.32N 7.04W
Ribble *r.* England **20 C2** 53.45N 2.44W
Ribblesdale *f.* England **20 C3** 54.03N 2.17W
Ribe Denmark **46 B3** 55.19N 8.47E
Ribe *d.* Denmark **46 B3** 55.40N 8.30E
Ribeirão Prêto Brazil **97 E5** 21.09S 47.48W
Ribérac France **48 D3** 45.14N 0.22E
Ribnitz-Damgarten Germany **46 F2** 54.14N 12.28E
Riccall England **21 D2** 53.50N 1.04W
Richland U.S.A. **86 C6** 46.20N 119.17W
Richmond England **20 D3** 54.24N 1.43W
Richmond Va. U.S.A. **87 K4** 37.34N 77.27W
Rickmansworth England **15 B2** 51.39N 0.29W
Ridderkerk Neth. **47 C3** 51.53N 4.39E
Riesa Germany **52 F4** 51.18N 13.18E
Rieti Italy **54 D5** 42.24N 12.53E
Riga Latvia **58 F2** 56.53N 24.08E
Riga, G. of Latvia **58 E2** 57.30N 23.50E
Rigan Iran **69 J3** 28.40N 58.58E
Rigmati Iran **69 J2** 27.40N 58.11E
Riihimäki Finland **58 F3** 60.45N 24.45E
Rijeka Croatia **56 B6** 45.20N 14.25E
Rijswijk Neth. **47 C4** 52.03N 4.22E
Rima, Wadi *r.* Saudi Arabia **68 F2** 26.10N 44.00E
Rimini Italy **54 D6** 44.01N 12.34E
Rimouski Canada **91 L2** 48.27N 68.32W
Ringe Denmark **46 D3** 55.14N 10.30E
Ringköbing Denmark **46 B4** 56.06N 8.15E
Ringköbing *d.* Denmark **46 B4** 56.10N 8.40E
Ringköbing Fjord *l.* Denmark **46 B4** 56.00N 8.15E
Ringsjön *l.* Sweden **46 G3** 55.52N 13.30E
Ringsted Denmark **46 E3** 55.28N 11.49E
Ringvassöy *i.* Norway **58 D5** 70.00N 19.00E
Ringwood England **13 F2** 50.50N 1.48W
Riobamba Ecuador **96 B7** 1.44S 78.40W
Rio Branco Brazil **96 C7** 10.00S 67.49W
Rio de Janeiro Brazil **97 E5** 22.50S 43.17W
Rio Gallegos Argentina **97 C2** 51.35S 69.15W
Rio Grande *town* Brazil **97 D4** 32.03S 52.18W
Rio Grande *r.* N. America **84 K4** 25.55N 97.08W
Rio Grande *r.* Nicaragua **93 H2** 12.48N 83.30W
Ríohacha Colombia **94 E3** 11.34N 72.58W
Riosucio Colombia **94 D2** 7.25N 77.05W
Ripley Derbys. England **16 C3** 53.03N 1.24W
Ripon England **21 D3** 54.08N 1.31W
Risca Wales **18 C1** 51.36N 3.06W
Risha, Wadi *r.* Saudi Arabia **69 F2** 26.00N 43.40E
Rishiri jima *i.* Japan **76 E9** 45.11N 141.15E
Risör Norway **58 B2** 58.44N 9.15E
Ristikent Russian Fed. **58 G5** 68.40N 31.47E
Rivas Nicaragua **93 G2** 11.26N 85.50W
Rivers *d.* Nigeria **108 C1** 4.45N 6.35E
Riyadh Saudi Arabia **69 G2** 24.39N 46.44E
Rize Turkey **68 F6** 41.03N 40.31E
Rizzuto, C. Italy **54 F3** 38.53N 17.06E
Rjukan Norway **58 B2** 59.54N 8.33E
Roag, L. Scotland **24 B5** 58.17N 6.52W
Roanne France **48 F4** 46.02N 4.05E
Roanoke *r.* U.S.A. **87 K4** 36.00N 76.35W
Roberval Canada **91 K2** 48.31N 72.16W
Robin Hood's Bay *town* England **21 E3** 54.26N 0.31W
Robson, Mt. Canada **90 G3** 53.00N 119.09W
Roca, Cabo de *c.* Portugal **50 A3** 38.40N 9.31W
Roccella Italy **54 F3** 38.19N 16.24E
Rocha Uruguay **97 D4** 34.30S 54.22W
Rochdale England **20 C2** 53.36N 2.10W
Rochechouart France **48 D3** 45.49N 0.50E
Rochefort Belgium **47 D2** 50.10N 5.13E
Rochefort France **48 C3** 45.57N 0.58W
Rochester Kent England **15 C2** 51.22N 0.30E
Rochester Northum. England **22 B2** 55.16N 2.16W
Rochester N.Y. U.S.A. **87 K5** 43.12N 77.37W
Rochfort Bridge Rep. of Ire. **28 D3** 53.25N 7.19W
Rockford U.S.A. **87 I5** 42.16N 89.06W
Rockhampton Australia **80 E3** 23.22S 150.32E
Rockingham Forest *f.* England **17 D2** 52.30N 0.35W
Rock Springs U.S.A. **86 E5** 41.35N 109.13W
Rocky Mts. N. America **86 E5** 42.30N 109.30W
Rocroi France **47 C1** 49.56N 4.31E
Rödby Denmark **46 E2** 54.42N 11.24E
Rodel Scotland **24 B4** 57.47N 6.58W
Roden *r.* England **16 B2** 52.42N 2.36W
Rodez France **48 E3** 44.21N 2.34E
Rodonit, C. Albania **56 D4** 41.34N 19.25E
Rödvig Denmark **46 F3** 55.13N 12.20E
Roe *r.* N. Ireland **23 C2** 55.06N 7.00W
Roermond Neth. **47 D3** 51.12N 6.00E
Rogan's Seat *mtn.* England **20 C3** 54.25N 2.05W
Rohtak India **71 D5** 28.54N 76.35E
Rokan *r.* Indonesia **78 C4** 2.00N 101.00E
Rolla U.S.A. **87 H4** 37.56N 91.55W
Roma *i.* Indonesia **79 H2** 7.45S 127.20E
Romain, C. U.S.A. **87 K3** 33.01N 79.23W
Romaine *r.* Canada **91 L3** 50.20N 63.45W
Romania Europe **57 H3** 46.30N 24.00E
Romano, C. U.S.A. **87 J2** 25.50N 81.42W
Romans France **48 F3** 45.03N 5.03E
Rome Italy **54 D4** 41.54N 12.29E
Romilly France **48 E5** 48.31N 3.44E
Romney Marsh *f.* England **15 C2** 51.03N 0.55E
Römö *i.* Denmark **46 B3** 55.10N 8.30E
Romorantin France **48 D4** 47.22N 1.44E
Romsey England **14 A1** 51.00N 1.29W
Rona *i.* Scotland **24 C4** 57.33N 5.59W
Ronda Spain **50 C2** 36.45N 5.10W
Rönde Denmark **46 D4** 56.18N 10.30E
Rönne Denmark **58 C1** 55.07N 14.43E
Roof Butte *mtn.* U.S.A. **86 E4** 36.29N 109.05W
Roosendaal Neth. **47 C3** 51.32N 4.28E
Roosevelt *r.* Brazil **96 C7** 5.00S 60.30W
Roraima, Mt. Guyana **95 G2** 5.11N 60.44W
Röros Norway **58 B3** 62.35N 11.23E
Rosa, Monte *mtn.* Italy/Switz. **52 C2** 45.56N 7.51E
Rosario Argentina **97 C4** 33.00S 60.40W
Roscommon Rep. of Ire. **28 C3** 53.38N 8.13W
Roscommon *d.* Rep. of Ire. **28 C3** 53.38N 8.11W
Roscrea Rep. of Ire. **28 D2** 52.57N 7.49W
Roseau Dominica **93 L3** 15.18N 61.23W
Roseburg U.S.A. **86 B5** 43.13N 123.21W
Rosenheim Germany **52 F2** 47.51N 12.09E
Rosetown Canada **90 H3** 51.34N 107.59W
Roshage *c.* Denmark **46 B5** 57.10N 8.30E
Rosières France **47 A1** 49.49N 2.43E
Roskilde Denmark **46 F3** 55.39N 12.07E
Roskilde *d.* Denmark **46 F3** 55.30N 12.05E
Roslavl Russian Fed. **59 C4** 53.55N 32.53E
Rossall Pt. England **20 B2** 53.55N 3.03W
Rossington England **21 D2** 53.29N 1.01W
Rosslare Rep. of Ire. **28 E2** 52.17N 6.23W
Rosslea N. Ireland **23 B1** 54.15N 7.11W
Ross of Mull *pen.* Scotland **26 B3** 56.19N 6.10W
Ross-on-Wye England **16 B1** 51.55N 2.36W
Rossosh Russian Fed. **59 D4** 50.12N 39.35E
Ross Sea Antarctica **113 R1** 73.00S 179.00E
Rössvatnet *l.* Norway **58 C4** 65.50N 14.00E
Rostock Germany **52 F6** 54.06N 12.09E
Rostov Russian Fed. **59 D5** 57.11N 39.23E
Rostov Russian Fed. **59 D3** 47.15N 39.45E
Rosyth Scotland **27 E3** 56.03N 3.26W
Rota *i.* Mariana Is. **79 L6** 14.10N 145.15E
Rothbury England **22 C2** 55.19N 1.54W
Rothbury Forest *f.* England **22 C2** 55.18N 1.52W
Rother *r.* W. Sussex England **15 B1** 50.57N 0.32W
Rotherham England **21 D2** 53.26N 1.21W
Rothes Scotland **24 E4** 57.31N 3.14W
Rothesay Scotland **26 C2** 55.50N 5.03W
Rothwell Northants. England **16 D2** 52.25N 0.48W
Rothwell W. Yorks. England **21 D2** 53.46N 1.29W
Roti *i.* Indonesia **79 G1** 10.30S 123.10E
Rotterdam Neth. **47 C3** 51.55N 4.29E
Roubaix France **47 B2** 50.42N 3.10E
Rouen France **48 D5** 49.26N 1.05E
Roulers Belgium **47 B2** 50.57N 3.06E
Roundup U.S.A. **86 E6** 46.27N 108.34W
Rourkela India **71 F4** 22.16N 85.01E
Rousay *i.* Scotland **24 E6** 59.10N 3.02W
Rouyn Canada **91 K2** 48.15N 79.00W
Rovaniemi Finland **58 F4** 66.29N 25.40E
Rovinj Croatia **56 A6** 45.06N 13.39E
Rovno Ukraine **59 B4** 50.39N 26.10E
Roxburgh Scotland **27 F2** 55.34N 2.23W
Royale, I. U.S.A. **87 I6** 48.00N 88.45W
Royal Leamington Spa England **16 C2** 52.18N 1.32W
Royal Tunbridge Wells England **15 C2** 51.07N 0.16E
Roye France **47 A1** 49.42N 2.48E
Royston Herts. England **15 B3** 52.03N 0.01W
Royston S. Yorks. England **21 D2** 53.37N 1.27W
Rtishchevo Russian Fed. **59 E4** 52.16N 43.45E
Ruabon Wales **18 C2** 52.59N 3.03W
Rub al Khali *des.* Saudi Arabia **105 H4** 20.20N 52.30E
Rubha A'Mhàil *c.* Scotland **26 B2** 55.57N 6.08W
Rubio Colombia **94 E2** 7.42N 72.23W
Rubtsovsk Russian Fed. **60 G2** 51.29N 81.10E
Rudan *r.* Iran **69 J2** 27.02N 56.53E
Rud-i-Pusht *r.* Iran **69 J3** 29.09N 58.09E
Rudnichnyy Russian Fed. **59 G5** 59.10N 52.28E
Rudolstadt Germany **52 E4** 50.44N 11.20E
Ruffec France **48 D4** 46.02N 0.12E
Rufford England **20 C2** 53.38N 2.50W
Rufiji *r.* Tanzania **106 D4** 8.02S 39.17E
Rugao China **75 J4** 32.27N 120.35E
Rugby England **16 C2** 52.23N 1.16W
Rugby U.S.A. **86 G6** 48.24N 99.59W
Rugeley England **16 C2** 52.47N 1.56W
Rügen *i.* Germany **52 F6** 54.30N 13.30E
Ruhr *f.* Germany **47 F3** 51.22N 7.26E
Ruhr *r.* Germany **47 E3** 51.27N 6.41E
Rukwa, L. Tanzania **106 D4** 8.00S 32.20E
Ruma Yugo. **56 D6** 44.59N 19.51E
Rum Cay *i.* Bahamas **93 J4** 23.41N 74.53W
Rumney Wales **18 C1** 51.32N 3.07W
Rumoi Japan **76 E8** 43.56N 141.39E
Runabay Head N. Ireland **23 C2** 55.09N 6.02W
Runcorn England **20 C2** 53.20N 2.44W
Ruoqiang China **74 D5** 39.00N 88.00E
Ruo Shui *r.* China **74 F5** 42.15N 101.03E
Rupununi *r.* Guyana **95 H1** 3.53N 58.46W
Rur *r.* Neth. **47 D3** 51.12N 5.58E
Rurutu *i.* Pacific Oc. **83 K5** 22.25S 151.20W
Ruse Bulgaria **56 G5** 43.50N 25.59E
Rushden England **17 D2** 52.17N 0.37W
Russian Federation Europe/Asia **60 E3** 62.00N 80.00E
Rustavi Georgia **59 E2** 41.34N 45.03E
Rütenbrock Germany **47 F4** 52.51N 7.06E
Ruteng Indonesia **79 G2** 8.35S 120.28E
Rutherglen Scotland **26 D2** 55.49N 4.12W
Ruthin Wales **18 C3** 53.07N 3.18W
Rutland Water *resr.* England **16 D2** 52.39N 0.40W
Rutog China **74 C4** 33.30N 79.40E
Ruvuma *r.* Mozambique/Tanzania **106 E3** 10.30S 40.30E
Ruwandiz Iraq **69 G5** 36.38N 44.32E
Ruwenzori Range *mts.* Uganda/Zaïre **106 C5** 0.30N 30.00E
Ruzayevka Russian Fed. **59 E4** 54.04N 44.55E
Rwanda Africa **106 D4** 2.00S 30.00E
Ryan, Loch Scotland **26 C1** 54.56N 5.02W
Ryazan Russian Fed. **59 D4** 54.37N 39.43E
Ryazhsk Russian Fed. **59 E4** 53.40N 40.07E
Rybachi Pen. Russian Fed. **58 H5** 69.45N 32.30E
Rybinsk Resr. Russian Fed. **59 D5** 58.30N 38.25E
Rybnik Poland **57 F5** 50.06N 18.32E
Ryde England **14 A1** 50.44N 1.09W
Ryder's Hill England **13 D2** 50.31N 3.53W
Rye England **15 C1** 50.57N 0.46E
Rye *r.* England **21 E3** 54.10N 0.44W
Rye B. England **15 C1** 50.53N 0.48E
Ryki Poland **57 G5** 51.39N 21.56E
Ryton England **22 C1** 54.59N 1.47W
Ryukyu Is. Japan **75 J2** 26.00N 126.00E
Ryukyu Is. Trench Pacific Oc. **82 C10** 25.00N 129.00E
Rzeszów Poland **57 G5** 50.04N 22.00E
Rzhev Russian Fed. **59 C5** 56.15N 34.18E

S

Saale *r.* Germany **52 E4** 51.58N 11.53E
Saar *r.* Germany **47 E1** 49.43N 6.34E
Saarbrücken Germany **52 C3** 49.15N 6.58E
Saarburg Germany **47 E1** 49.36N 6.33E
Saaremaa *i.* Estonia **58 E2** 58.30N 22.30E
Saarijärvi Finland **58 F3** 62.44N 25.15E
Saarland *d.* Germany **52 C3** 49.20N 7.00E
Saba *i.* Leeward Is. **93 L3** 17.42N 63.26W
Šabac Yugo. **56 D6** 44.45N 19.41E
Sabadell Spain **50 G4** 41.33N 2.07E
Sabah *d.* Malaysia **78 F5** 5.00N 117.00E
Sabana, Archipiélago de Cuba **93 H4** 23.30N 80.00W
Sabanalarga Colombia **94 E3** 10.38N 75.00W
Sabinas Mexico **92 D5** 27.51N 101.10W
Sabinas Hidalgo Mexico **92 D5** 26.33N 100.10W
Sabine *r.* U.S.A. **87 H2** 29.40N 93.50W
Sable, C. Canada **91 L2** 43.30N 65.50W
Sable, C. U.S.A. **84 L4** 25.00N 81.20W
Sable I. Canada **91 M2** 44.00N 60.00W
Sacedón Spain **50 D4** 40.29N 2.44W
Sachsen *d.* Germany **52 F4** 50.45N 13.00E
Sachsen-Anhalt *d.* Germany **52 E4** 52.00N 11.30E
Sacramento U.S.A. **86 B4** 38.32N 121.30W
Sacramento *r.* U.S.A. **86 B4** 38.05N 122.00W
Sacramento Mts. U.S.A. **86 E3** 33.10N 105.50W
Sádaba Spain **50 E5** 42.19N 1.10W
Saddleworth Moor *hills* England **20 D2** 53.32N 1.55W
Sadiya India **71 G5** 27.49N 95.38E
Sado *i.* Japan **76 D6** 38.00N 138.20E
Saeby Denmark **46 D5** 57.20N 10.30E
Safaha *des.* Saudi Arabia **68 E2** 26.30N 39.30E
Safaniya Saudi Arabia **69 H3** 28.00N 48.48E
Säffle Sweden **58 C2** 59.08N 12.55E
Saffron Walden England **15 C3** 52.02N 0.15E
Safi Morocco **104 B5** 32.20N 9.17W
Safonovo Russian Fed. **59 C5** 55.08N 33.16E
Saga Japan **76 A3** 33.08N 130.30E
Sagaing Myanma **71 G4** 22.00N 95.56E
Sagamihara Japan **76 D4** 35.35N 139.30E
Sagar India **71 E4** 23.50N 78.44E
Saglouc Canada **91 K4** 62.10N 75.40W
Sagua la Grande Cuba **93 H4** 22.55N 80.05W
Sagunto Spain **50 E3** 39.40N 0.17W
Sahagún Spain **50 C5** 42.23N 5.02W
Sahara *des.* Africa **104 D3** 18.00N 12.00E
Saharan Atlas *mts.* Algeria **104 C5** 34.20N 2.00E
Saharanpur India **71 D5** 29.58N 77.33E